SMALL BUT FLOURISHING

Small but Flourishing

Towns of North-east Hertfordshire's Extra-urban Matrix

PETER BYSOUTH

EAH Press - Cambridge

EAH Press

7 Thornton Court, Thornton Road, Girton, Cambridge, CB3 0NS

First published in Great Britain in 2013

A catalogue record for this book is available from the British Library

ISBN 978-0-9560384 -5-6

The publication of this volume has been made possible by
a generous grant from the Scouloudi Foundation
in association with the Institute of Historical Research

Cover design
by
Blue Ocean Publishing, Cambridge

Printed in Great Britain
by
MPG Biddles Limited, King's Lynn

Nothing can give a greater prospect of thriving to a young tradesman, than his own diligence; it fills himself with hope, and gives him credit with all who know him … To delight in business is making business pleasant and agreeable, and such a tradesman cannot but be diligent in it, which, according to Solomon, makes him certainly rich, and in time raises him above the world and able to instruct and encourage those who come after him.

Daniel Defoe,
The Complete English Tradesman, 1726

Contents

Maps

Plates

ii

Figures

Tables

Acknowledgements

I am indebted to a great many people for making this publication possible. Firstly, Professor Steve Hindle and Doctor Sarah Richardson, my invaluable joint supervisors over several years at the University of Warwick, who provided many constructive comments and stimulating ideas on innumerable topics. Secondly, the knowledgeable staff of the Hertfordshire Archives and Local Studies centre who willingly engaged with my queries. Thirdly, to Phillip Judge who drew the excellent maps. In addition, my thanks go to Doctor David Dymond for his valuable comments and suggestions on the final text of this volume. Finally, I must acknowledge the enormous contribution of my late wife Molly for the length of time she spent patiently and painstakingly proof-reading and editing the many drafts of my original doctoral thesis.

My own photographs of advertisements are included by the kind permission of the current Editor of The Royston Crow, and the Legal Director of Reed Elsevier (UK) Limited in regard of those from Kelly's Directory.

Letchworth Garden City, January, 2013

Preface

For simplicity, this volume frequently utilises two acronyms, PTPS and ATPS, as umbrella descriptions of the two broad groups of individuals investigated. Their full meanings, detailed below, are very similar to that of Andrew Hann's definition of the service sector used in his study of Midland towns between 1700 and 1840. There, he included all 'listed "public service and professional" occupations [using a modified Booth-Armstrong classification], plus most of those classified as "dealing", and a significant part of "manufacturing", specifically craftsmen-retailers'.[1] Individual PTPSs and ATPSs in this study were similarly assigned to eight occupational sectors based on an adaptation of Booth's classification (see Appendix).[2]

PTPS (Principal Traders Professionals & Service providers)

In the context of this particular research the term 'trader' is taken to include all those engaged in the buying and selling of commodities for profit, i.e. it includes all the individuals that the present analysis identifies as being in the agricultural, manufacturing and dealing sectors. Traders in the agricultural sector include those farmers not living on isolated farms but in the study towns where they would have conducted business with many of their suppliers and customers. Included in the manufacturing sector are the blacksmiths, braziers, brewers, cabinet makers, coopers, harness makers, maltsters, saddlers, upholsterers and wheelwrights, and other master craftsmen who may also have operated their own retail outlets. Traders in the dealing sector include coal merchants, drapers, ironmongers, milliners, publicans, wine and spirit merchants, etc.

As used here the term 'trader' also covers that of 'tradesman', i.e. those engaged in the trade or sale of commodities, especially the shopkeeper.[3] Hence it covers the frequently occurring high street bakers, butchers, confectioners, fishmongers, greengrocers, grocer, etc. It further covers those skilled in and following a particular trade after a period of apprenticeship, especially those

---

[1] A. Hann, 'Industrialisation and the Service Economy', in J. Stobart and N. Raven (eds), *Towns, Regions and Industries: Urban and Industrial Change in the Midlands, c. 1700-1840* (Manchester, 2005), p. 43.

[2] The eight occupational sectors are Agriculture, Building, Manufacturing, Transport, Dealing, Industrial Services, Public and Professional, and Domestic Services.

[3] Like Nancy Cox, I too 'am very aware of the issue of gender in using the term "tradesman" but many sources do characteristically use the male pronoun and it can be tortuous, as she argued, 'to twist what they say into neutral frame'. I do recognize, as did Cox, that 'both men and women acted as retailing tradesmen, though men were more common in most parts of the retail sector'. N. Cox, *The Complete Tradesman: A Study of Retailing, 1550-1820* (Aldershot, 2000), p. 15.

operating in the building sector, such as bricklayers, carpenters, glaziers, painters, plumbers, stonemasons, etc.

The term 'professional' includes the individuals identified in the public and professional sector, e.g. chemists and druggists, librarians, police officers, postmasters/mistresses, school teachers, solicitors, surgeons and tax officials. Other trained 'professionals' that, for the purposes of this present study, are placed in other sectors include accountants (industrial services sector), architects (building sector), surveyors (building sector) and veterinary surgeons (agricultural sector).

The term 'service provider' includes those identified as providing a facility to meet the needs, or for the use, of a person or people, i.e. those in the domestic, industrial and transport services sectors. Here the domestic services sector includes chimney-sweepers, hairdressers, launderers and vermin destroyers. Included under the industrial services sector are bankers, company officials and insurance agents. The transport services sector covers independent carters or carriers, and railway station masters.

ATPS (Ancillary Traders Professionals & Service providers)

Many of those identified as PTPSs provided employment opportunities to a wide range of skilled and semi-skilled ATPSs, including both journeymen and apprentices. However, the ATPS group does not, in the context of this present volume, include either domestic servants or labourers, both of which are specifically excluded.

Here the traders include a variety of retailers' foremen, assistants, storekeepers and apprentices. Also included are miscellaneous hawkers and travelling salesmen. Ancillary professionals include chemist and druggists' assistants and apprentices, postmen and telegraphists. Within the industrial services sector are manufacturers' agents and a range of ancillary clerical staff, e.g. bankers' clerks, solicitors' clerks and surveyors' articled clerks. Ancillary workers in the transport services sector include drivers of road and railway engines, brewers' draymen, cab drivers and railway porters.

Part I of this book explores the challenges of utilizing two disparate but complementary sources, trade directories and census enumerators' books (CEBs in subsequent discussion), to analyse nineteenth-century provision of goods and services in the four towns. Furthermore, it examines the value of utilizing nominal record linkage between the two sources as a means of enhancing the amount of data on individual providers. Using trade directories (1811–1890) and CEBs (1851–1891), allows quantitative analyses of the changing range of business and professional activities of the four towns' *principal traders, professionals and service providers* (PTPSs in subsequent discussion). Included among the PTPSs are manufacturers, traders, members of the professions and public servants. Furthermore, the important role of women is assessed in the business activities of the four towns. Again utilizing only CEBs (1851–1891), the analysis looks at the employment opportunities generated in the towns for skilled and semi-skilled *ancillary traders, professionals and service providers* (ATPSs in subsequent discussion). It examines their roles, including those of women, especially in the manufacturing, dealing, building and transport sectors of the regional economy and explores the level and types of apprenticeship that were available.

The research aims to test Marshall's hypothesis that while the market towns of a region might in successive periods occupy changing hierarchical positions, they 'were in fact interrelated through complementarity of function, or through specialisation in the manufacture, sale or collection of given products'.[4] In other words, it asks whether there was a regional hierarchy and a pattern of trading between the selected towns and their environs. Utilizing the analysis of the provision of goods and services, chapter four examines the role of these four small north-east Hertfordshire towns and considers where they might fit into Walter Christaller's hierarchy of 'central places'.[5] To this end, an analysis of the services provided by rural craftsmen-retailers in the villages of their hinterlands is included. The chapter introduces the original notion of an *'extra-urban matrix'* within which such small towns play a key service role.

Using the CEBs birth-place data of family members, Part II explores facets of the migratory behaviour and stability of both the principal and ancillary trading and service provider communities in the towns. Any growth amongst these groups is examined to ascertain whether it was achieved organically or by inward migration. It assesses the degree of inward migration from the four towns' immediate hinterlands plus the appeal of north-east Hertfordshire to clearly identifiable migrant streams from East Anglia and the south-west of England. This analysis concludes by examining the stability and continuity of family businesses, and some examples of the migratory behaviour of PTPSs leaving the four towns. Finally, there is consideration of the part played by improved nineteenth-century communications on the trading activities of the region's business community. Using trade directories and some surviving business records, it evaluates the impact of changes in road and rail transport together with the business benefits of nineteenth-century improvements in postal services and the invention of the electric telegraph. Evidence is presented of how wider market integration by these small towns' local traders led to the beginnings

---

[4] Marshall, 'Cumbrian Market Town', p. 132.
[5] W. Christaller, 'Central Places in Southern Germany' ([Unpublished Doctoral Dissertation, Friedrich-Alexander University of Erlangen, Nuremberg, 1933] trans. C.W. Baskin, New Jersey, 1966).

of modern retailing in their high streets. Part II of this book concludes with a look at newspaper advertising in Royston from the point of view of business support and the possible insight it gives into conspicuous consumption of the folk of that town.

Overall, this study of north-east Hertfordshire seeks to ascertain whether the small towns of nineteenth-century England were the death-like entities described by Trollope or the regional nerve-knots characterized by Hardy. It concludes there is sufficient evidence to suggest that very small towns, as exemplified in this analysis, could take advantage of the nineteenth-century's changing balance between rural and industrial society to integrate successfully into the wider national economy and become modest centres of enterprise and prosperity.

Introduction

In his novel *Dr Thorne*, Anthony Trollope was rather dismissive of the traditional rural town of mid-nineteenth-century 'Barsetshire', believing that such towns 'add nothing to the importance of the county; they consist, with the exception of the assize-town, of dull, all but death-like, single streets. Each possesses two pumps, three hotels, ten shops, fifteen beer-houses, a beadle, and a market-place'.[1] Trollope's rather patronizing depiction, an epitome of the negative stereotype of the nature and significance of small towns, clearly minimizes their importance. Another nineteenth-century representation which offered a more positive view of small towns is exemplified by Casterbridge (Dorchester), described by Thomas Hardy as 'the pole, focus, or nerve-knot of the surrounding country life' which 'lived by agriculture at one remove further from the fountain-head than the adjoining villages – no more'. Casterbridge was a town where the populace 'understood every fluctuation in the rustic's condition, for it affected their receipts as much as the labourers'.[2] While these perspectives may have been used by Trollope and Hardy for literary effect they would have had some resonance with other social commentators of the period. Their opposing views encapsulate the divergence of contemporary opinion regarding nineteenth-century small town life.

The juxtaposition of the views of Trollope and Hardy poses the question of the fate of small towns over the course of the nineteenth century. Were their fortunes over the period generally rising or declining? As the balance shifted from a largely agricultural economy to an increasingly industrial one, were small towns a proliferating entity of the growing urban scene or a frequently declining remnant of a bygone age?

This book examines the regional economy of a cluster of four small nineteenth-century towns; Ashwell, Baldock, Buntingford and Royston, situated in the north-east corner of Hertfordshire. It analyses a large data set compiled from trade directories and census returns to determine the changes in the provision of goods and services in these towns and their integration into the wider national economy. An examination of the traders operating in the surrounding villages of their hinterlands allows the construction of a regional urban hierarchy based upon indices of centrality. It explores the migratory behaviour and stability of their business communities while assessing the impact of improved communications. This introduction looks at the problems of defining a small town, reviews the

---

[1] A. Trollope, *Dr Thorne* (Everyman's Library edn, London, 1993), p. 2.
[2] T. Hardy, *The Life and Death of the Mayor of Casterbridge: A Story of a Man of Character* (Wordsworth Classics edn, Ware, 1994), pp. 47, 48.

relevant approaches to researching these entities and details the scope of the case study.

The conundrum of the small town

Brian Robson argued in the early 1970s that ever since the town has been studied 'there has been agonized debate about its definition' which has led to a variety of interpretations based on legal, economic or sociological grounds.[3] That debate is further complicated by continuing attempts to distinguish the 'small town' within the urban hierarchy. The fundamental question with which urban historians have struggled is whether small towns should be defined demographically, functionally or both. Robson himself, drawing on Law's earlier work, argued that nineteenth-century towns were discrete entities where 'the minimum size is taken at 2,500'.[4]

Indeed, much conventional literature has concentrated on the changing demographic size of small towns. Pre-eminent here is urban historian Peter Clark's detailed analysis of what he described as that 'great mass' of towns which until the early Victorian era 'remained relatively small'. In Clark's definition a 'small town' had fewer than 5,000 inhabitants in 1811.[5] His discussion, covering almost 800 small English regional towns, considered demographic trends and economic performance together with social and cultural change. Furthermore, Clark suggested that by the early nineteenth century the status of some small towns 'was confirmed and consolidated ... through an accession of administrative activities'. Lutterworth, for example, 'became the venue for local petty sessions and the county court, and also acquired parish and union workhouses, a post office and, later on, the district police station'.[6]

Clark's study included calculations of the population distribution across these small urban centres for eight geographical regions in 1811 and 1851. He calculated that the three largely agricultural regions of East Anglia, the East Midlands and South-east England contained in total 366 of the 800 nineteenth-century 'small towns'. It is the nature and proximity of these three regions to the present study's four towns that makes them particularly relevant. From 1811

---

[3] B.T. Robson, *Urban Growth: An Approach* (London, 1973), p. 3.

[4] C.M. Law, 'The Growth of Urban Population in England and Wales, 1801-1911', *Transactions of the Institute of British Geographers*, 41 (1967), pp. 125-43, cited in Robson, *Urban Growth*, p. 47.

[5] P. Clark, 'Small Towns 1700–1840', in P. Clark (ed.), *The Cambridge Urban History of Britain, Vol. 2, 1540–1840* (Cambridge, 2000), p. 735.

[6] J. McCormack, 'Lutterworth: A Comparative Study of Economic and Social Structure in Leicestershire' (Certificate Dissertation, Centre for Urban History, University of Leicester, 1992), p. 2, cited in Clark, 'Small Towns 1700-1840', p. 754.

% Total inhabitants in towns of different sized populations within a region					
	Population Range, c. 1811				Number of Towns
Region	<1650	1651-3300	3301-5000	>5000	
E. Anglia	54.4	38.0	6.3	1.3	79
E.	39.1	32.2	11.5	17.2	87
SE England	33.0	40.0	17.0	10.0	200

Table 01: Population distribution in small towns of three English regions
Source: Extracted from Peter Clark's table in 'Small towns 1700–1840', p. 740.

(Table 01, above) to 1851 (Table 02, below) the proportion of the population living in Clark's smallest category of towns (populations less than 1,650) across the three regions declined by between 15.0 and 19.0 per cent. The reduction over the same period in the proportion living in the next group of towns (populations of between 1,651 and 3,300) was less noticeable at around 6.5 per cent. In contrast, the industrial North-west at that time had no towns with populations below 1,650 while 67.4 per cent of the region's populace lived in towns with populations above 5,000.[7] By 1851, the proportion of the population living in the larger towns with populations between 3,301 and 5,000 had increased across all

% Total inhabitants in towns of different sized populations within a region					
	Population Range, c. 1851				Number of Towns
Region	<1650	1651-3300	3301-5000	>5000	
E. Anglia	38.0	31.6	20.3	10.1	79
E.	24.1	25.3	16.1	34.5	87
SE England	14.0	33.5	22.5	30.0	200

Table 02: Population distribution in small towns of three English regions
Source: Extracted from Peter Clark's table in 'Small towns 1700–1840', p. 741.

three agricultural regions: by 4.6 per cent (East Midlands), 5.5 per cent (South-east England) and 14.0 per cent (East Anglia). This increase was even more pronounced in the final group of towns (populations larger than 5,000) where the proportion of each region's population living in them rose by 8.8 per cent (East Anglia), 17.3 per cent (East Midlands) and 20.0 per cent (South-east England). Again, in contrast, the proportion of people in three of Clark's industrial regions

---

[7] Clark, 'Small Towns', p. 740.

who were living in the largest towns (populations above 5,000) had increased to 42.3 per cent (West Midlands), 49.2 per cent (Yorkshire) and 75.0 per cent (North-west England).[8]

The above figures confirm a clear demographic shift over the first half of the nineteenth century with a loss across all three agricultural regions of approximately one quarter of the population from the smaller urban centres (populations < 3,300) being balanced by gains in the larger centres (populations > 3,300). Throughout the later decades of the nineteenth century, Clark suggests, small towns continued to experience change where many of the smallest died while others grew and survived.

Within the demographic approach to defining the 'small town' lies the added conundrum of agreeing the upper and lower limits of 'small'. A growing number of historians have recently supported the notion that the demographic definition of what constituted a 'small town' changed over the course of the eighteenth and nineteenth centuries. Charles Phythian-Adams has argued that in the shadow of overall population growth in general and of urbanization in particular, there was a proliferation of 'Toy-towns and Trumptons, traditionally-sized towns with which generations of British people had long been comfortable'. Phythian-Adams defined this 'traditional town' as one having a population of between 2,500 and 9,990. He estimated that their numbers had increased dramatically from 66 in c. 1700 to 260 in 1801, and to 548 by 1841 to form a greater proportion of total towns.[9] Thus, he implied, these 'small towns' are equally important, if not more so, in the nineteenth century.

Not everyone agrees with Phythian-Adams's lower threshold of 2,500 for defining the 'small town'. David Eastwood, for instance, argues that if one defines a town as having over 2,500 inhabitants, nineteenth-century urban growth would be very striking indeed, since that threshold puts '54% of the population in towns by 1851 and 78% by 1901'. Eastwood nonetheless noted that 'such figures distort as much as they describe' because, he believed, 'many settlements of 2,500

---

[8] Clark, 'Small Towns', p. 741.

[9] C. Phythian-Adams, ' "Small-scale Toy-towns and Trumptons"? Urbanization in Britain and the new Cambridge Urban History', *Urban History*, 28, 2 (2001), p. 267. Phythian-Adams was here using Patrick Collinson's idiom in P. Collinson, *The Birthpangs of Protestant England: Religious and Cultural Change in the Sixteenth and Seventeenth Centuries* (London, 1988), pp. 32, 33; '... just as those English towns [at the time of the English Reformation] were themselves small-scale Toytowns and Trumptons when compared with' various German towns. 'Out of 600 or 700 English towns, fully 500 were so small as to prompt the modern mind to question what it was about these little places ... which was distinctly *urban*. Only about a hundred would today rank as towns at all, most of them places of 2000 to 4000 inhabitants.'

were hardly towns at all' by the end of the nineteenth century.[10] Conversely, in Alan Dyer's view, 'the threshold above which "small" becomes an inappropriate term' for applying to a town has to be adjusted over time. While 'five thousand seems too large in 1600', for example, it appears a far more appropriate threshold in 1800.[11] In suggesting that, 'by 1840 some readjustments to the definition of urban status are needed', Rosemary Sweet had earlier arrived at a similar conclusion arguing that 'a population of 5,000, for example, would constitute a "small town" by nineteenth-century standards'.[12]

For the second half of the nineteenth century, Stephen Royle noted that while 'a population of 10,000' is often 'used as a [upper] *benchmark* [for the small town] in urban histories', defining a lower demographic threshold is not always deemed necessary.[13] Some, like Edwin Jaggard, have since, in conjunction with other parameters, raised the bar still higher. In his study of the 1841 general election he sampled '26 small towns – "small" being those with fewer than 10,000 inhabitants and 1,000 voters between 1832 and 1868, and fewer than 20,000 and 2,000 voters thereafter'.[14] However, according to Royle, 2.1 million people (7.8 per cent of England's population) in 1901 still lived in 641 small towns with fewer than 10,000 inhabitants.[15]

To add further complexity and confusion to this issue of where to draw the line between the large village and the small town, Lynn Hollen Lees observed that 'the census labelled settlements with more than 2,000 inhabitants as urban, although few such places had municipal governments or clear, unique geographic boundaries'.[16] Many of these supposed 'urban' settlements, she argued, lacked obvious nucleation and were neither clearly delineated by the boundary of a municipal borough, local board district nor even the operational range of a utility company.

From the foregoing discussion it is clear that no obvious consensus exists among historians on the demographic definition of a small town. Wherever the nineteenth-century threshold lies between 5,000 and 2,500, or even lower, 'small

---

[10] D. Eastwood, *Government and Community in the English Provinces, 1700-1870* (Basingstoke, 1997), p. 57.

[11] A. Dyer, 'Small Towns in England, 1600-1800', *Proceedings of the British Academy*, 108 (2002), p. 53.

[12] R. Sweet, *The English Town, 1680-1840: Government, Society and Culture* (Harlow, 1999), p. 9.

[13] S.A. Royle, 'The Development of Small Towns in Britain', in M. Daunton (ed.), *The Cambridge Urban History of Britain, Vol. 3, 1840–1950* (Cambridge, 2000), p. 152.

[14] E. Jaggard, 'Small Town Politics in Mid-Victorian Britain', *History*, 89, 1 (2004), p. 6.

[15] Royle, 'Development of Small Towns', p. 159.

[16] L. Hollen Lees, 'Urban Networks', in M. Daunton (ed.), *The Cambridge Urban History of Britain, Vol. 3, 1840-1950* (Cambridge, 2000), p. 67.

towns' of this period are arguably better defined by the range of goods and services they offer and therefore deserve explicit study from this functional perspective. The more successful small towns demonstrated an impressive ability 'to maintain a competitive edge despite their modest size' and should not, according to Dyer, 'be prematurely consigned to the sidelines of urban history' on the basis of their size alone.[17]

There is, therefore, a growing sense that the size of an urban centre's population is less important than whether the distinctive functions of a town are present, irrespective of population size. This idea that as long as the functions of a town are fulfilled then size does not matter is not, it should be emphasized, new. Almost thirty years ago, Susan Reynolds was arguing in her discussion of twelfth and thirteenth-century urban developments that the primary difference between villages and towns 'is that people living in the first were predominantly engaged in farming and other closely related occupations (or lived off the work of those who were), whereas a significant proportion (if not always a majority) of those in the second lived off a variety of quite different occupations, notably trade, manufacturing and administration of various sorts'. Reynolds argued that the 'second mark of a town derives from the first: both the inhabitants of a town and those who live in the countryside around recognize them as separate and different. Townsmen form a social unit which, however internally divided, they and their neighbours feel to be distinct'. Reynolds claimed her 'working definition' reflected 'social realities more accurately than do the traditional definitions based on constitutional forms, topography, or size of population'.[18] Reynolds's view of the distinct nature of a town is no less applicable in a nineteenth-century context, not least since the gulf in structure and function between towns and villages had by then widened considerably.

More recently, Reynolds's view has been echoed by Joyce Ellis who was equally clear that 'urban identity was not merely a matter of numbers'. Ellis argued that small towns, where the majority of inhabitants 'do not earn their living directly from working on the land', by definition relied on trade for their success. These settlements, she suggested, seem 'set apart from the surrounding villages by distinctive patterns of employment and activity; they were in the countryside but not part of it'.[19]

Responses to changing functions influenced the fortunes of small towns which, according to Jonathan Brown, 'were closely bound up with those of agriculture'

---

[17] Dyer, 'Small Towns in England', p. 66.

[18] S. Reynolds, *Kingdoms and Communities in Western Europe 900–1300* (Oxford, 1984), pp. 156, 157.

[19] J.M. Ellis, *The Georgian Town, 1680-1840* (Basingstoke, 2001), p. 12.

from 1750 to 1914. It was a period of great change when enclosure, new rotation schemes, new crops, improved farm implements and the use of more fertilizers increased the volume of produce sold through the market towns. A pivotal view of the role of small towns in the early Victorian period was provided by Peter Clark who argued that by 'bridging the urban and rural worlds' they provided their surrounding countryside with channels for the sale of farm produce and served both the domestic and social needs of the villagers. As a result, until the arable depression of the last quarter of the nineteenth century, business for the corn dealers, millers, fertilizer dealers, implement makers and other tradesmen increased as did 'the demands on the town's shopkeepers'. However, parts of the traditional small town economy were, Clark contended, undermined when fashionable factory-made goods from the North and the Midlands displaced those of local craftsmen.[20]

Regarding their fortunes, Clark argued that 'by the Victorian era the position of British small towns, particularly the lesser ones, was coming under pressure, and considerable numbers were experiencing retardation or even eclipse', especially in the more agrarian regions (Table 02, above).[21] It is generally accepted that, despite the increased proliferation of towns with populations between 3,301 and 5,000, many of their economies declined rather than expanded during the Victorian period. This was due to the combined effects of the general population growth of the period being coupled with the failure of rural crafts and 'an influx of country poor into town'. All these factors led to mounting poverty and 'the stagnation of local [consumer] demand'.[22] After about 1850, as both Raven and Lawton similarly noted, many small towns suffered a decay in local crafts and industries that resulted in depopulation. This phenomenon was due to an increased level of outward migration that was further encouraged by the greater mobility offered by the growing railway infrastructure.[23]

Yet, Clark argued, other small towns continued to thrive as a result of their multi-functional nature, especially those having roles beyond simple marketing.[24] These specialities might have been in manufacturing, for example, or in the trading of specific commodities, the servicing of the growing volume of inland

---

[20] J. Brown, *The English Market Town: A Social and Economic History, 1750–1914* (Marlborough, 1986), p. 8; Clark, 'Small Towns 1700–1840', p. 733.

[21] Clark, 'Small Towns 1700-1840', p. 742.

[22] Clark, 'Small Towns 1700-1840', p. 758.

[23] N. Raven, 'Occupational Structures of Three North Essex Towns: Halstead, Braintree and Great Coggeshall, c. 1780–1880. Research in Progress', *Urban History Newsletter*, 12 (1992), p. 2 and R. Lawton, 'Population Changes in England and Wales in the Later Nineteenth Century: An Analysis of Trends by Registration Districts', *Transactions of the Institute of British Geographers*, 44 (1968), 55-74, both cited in Royle, 'Development of Small Towns', p. 166.

[24] Clark, 'Small Towns 1700-1840', p. 748.

trade or the provision of an improved transport infrastructure. Clark emphasized in particular that 'the service sector of small town economies continued to thrive' not least because they provided 'social activities to attract the local gentry', including clusters of attorneys, booksellers, physicians and schoolteachers. The decline of traditional fairs and open markets was, therefore, offset by the emergence of a class of modestly affluent shopkeepers.[25] One example of a small multi-functional town is Lutterworth which had a population in 1851 of only 2,446. Census enumerators' books show that while only 16 per cent of its workforce remained on the land, as many as 46 per cent were in services. Royle, who like Reynolds, followed Robert Dickinson's ruling that 'the definition of an urban settlement is fundamentally a question of function, not of population', argued that this distribution placed Lutterworth 'within the parameters for the recognition of a mid-nineteenth-century rural town, rather than just a village'.[26]

The significant historiographical shift from simple demographic to increasingly sophisticated functional analyses of the fortunes of small towns has in turn promoted more complex discussion of the experience of smaller urban settlements. These debates regarding economic performance, demographic effects of inward migration, and aspects of cultural change, are all crucial to the analysis of the hierarchy of small towns explored in this book.

Approaches to the study of small towns

Historians have long recognized the need to analyse the trauma brought to rural regional economies by the nineteenth-century experience of social upheaval, demographic change and industrial growth. They have sought to understand how the business communities of the rural economy evolved as the horse gave way to mechanized transport and the manufacturing revolution, with its mass produced merchandise, changed their patterns of distribution and retailing. While the historiography on nineteenth-century towns is extensive, it has tended to concentrate on the larger regional urban centres and towns with specialized functions. Therefore, it is crucial to appreciate how the pressures associated with the Victorian era operated at the level of the small town. How did nineteenth-century economic developments transform the role of small towns and the composition of the populations who lived there? Many smaller urban communities possessed specialist business enterprises that changed their composition and functioning, creating opportunities for entrepreneurial providers of goods and services that in turn led to inward economic migration.

[25] Clark, 'Small Towns 1700-1840', p. 753.
[26] R.E. Dickinson, 'The Distribution and Functions of the Smaller Urban Settlements of East Anglia', *Geography*, 17 (1932), p. 20, cited in Royle, 'Development of Small Towns', p. 152; Royle, 'Development of Small Towns', p. 160.

These are critical issues since there were so many small towns in nineteenth-century England and because a substantial proportion of Britain's population lived in them. Many of these smaller urban communities became embedded in the nation's road and rail transport infrastructure thus becoming ideally placed to act as stepping-stones along major internal migratory pathways. They were in a position to benefit from the improved communications of the Victorian age. Nonetheless, some small urban settlements failed to seize these opportunities and melded back into the countryside of their rural hinterlands. The question of why others accepted the challenges and seized the opportunities to become more successfully integrated into the changing world of nineteenth-century Britain is one worthy of more detailed investigation.

It is also important to understand the interface between small towns and the village tradesmen operating in the countryside of the surrounding hinterlands. Examining trade directory entries for the small settlements of Lincolnshire's Lindsey region, for example, Holderness concluded that it was because of the vitality of their local tradesmen that 'the small towns or large villages situated at the focal point of an agricultural hinterland, reached the apogee of their influence and economic importance in the century before 1870'.[27] More recently, analysing eighteenth-century probate inventories and wills, Jon Stobart found rural craftsmen-retailers in Cheshire, such as shoemakers and tailors, to be 'widespread within and central to life in rural communities'. Furthermore, he felt these village tradesmen lay 'at the functional and geographical margins of retailing and are too easily overlooked in favour of fashionable urban shops, modern selling practices and novel goods'.[28] In an earlier study, Martin had argued that not all the village traders of south Warwickshire in the early nineteenth century 'were mere cottagers; some were men of more substance, employed in some form of dual enterprise coupled with farming' and he identified a range of thirty-one additional occupations outside farming.[29] These studies cumulatively suggest that the rural craftsman-trader was not totally eliminated by nineteenth-century advances in production and distribution but frequently survived by diversifying their business interests.

The pressures on village traders, situated at the bottom of their area's urban hierarchy, are clearly demonstrated by numerous case studies that have

---

[27] B.A. Holderness, 'Rural Tradesmen, 1660-1850: A Regional Study in Lindsey', *Lincolnshire History and Archaeology*, 7 (1972), p. 82.

[28] J. Stobart, 'The Economic and Social Worlds of Rural Craftsmen-retailers in Eighteenth-century Cheshire', *The Agricultural History Review*, 52, 2 (2004), p. 142.

[29] J.M. Martin, 'Village Traders and the Emergence of a Proletariat in South Warwickshire, 1750-1851', *The Agricultural History Review*, 32, 2 (1984), p. 181.

investigated the larger county towns and market centres such as Ashbourne, Banbury, Chelmsford, Grantham, Maidstone, Nottingham, Stamford and Wetherby.[30] Typical of these is Neil Raven's recent study of early nineteenth-century Chelmsford, county town of Essex, with a population of almost 7,000 by 1841. Using trade directories, Raven describes a dynamic town responding to the expansion of its role as 'an agricultural marketing and servicing centre, a leisure and administrative centre, and a thoroughfare' benefiting from its proximity to London.[31] However, despite the relevance of many of Raven's themes to the small nineteenth-century (market) town, relatively few researchers have focused on them and even fewer have attempted a comparative regional evaluation of a number of small towns. Raven's approach clearly provides a model for this kind of functional analysis, one that could be usefully applied to similar studies of towns smaller than Chelmsford.

The new historiographical agenda for the study of small towns was arguably crystallized in three key comparative regional studies of them that appeared during the 1980s. In the first, Unwin focused on the nineteen marketing communities in the Vale of York over the period 1660 to 1830 and identified 'patterns of social structure, religious allegiance and education'. Analysis of their 'mixed economies of trades, crafts, professions, commerce, and secondary manufactures' identified transport networks and town hierarchies which suggested that these market towns had more in common with one another than with larger industrial communities nearby.[32] The second study, John Marshall's work on Cumbrian market towns, covered aspects of population change, retailing, local politics, small-town entertainments, and a pioneering analysis of wagon traffic between towns. Marshall concluded that 'even the small centres which lost their markets had a great variety of shops and services, and, in that important sense, their profound usefulness to a rural population remained'.[33] In the third study, Margaret Noble looked at the demographic, economic and specialized dimensions of change between 1700 and 1850 in the small town hierarchy of eastern

---

[30] See amongst others; A. Henstock (ed.), *Early Victorian Country Town: A Portrait of Ashbourne in the Mid-Nineteenth Century* (Ashbourne, 1968); W. Potts, *A History of Banbury: The Study of the Development of a Country Town* (2nd edn, Banbury, 1978); N. Raven, 'Chelmsford during the Industrial Revolution, c. 1790–1840', *Urban History*, 30, 1 (2003), pp. 44–62; M. Honeybone, *The Book of Grantham: The History of a Market and Manufacturing Town* (Buckingham, 1980); P. Clark and L. Murfin, *The History of Maidstone: The Making of a Modern County Town* (Stroud, 1995); R.A. Church, *Economic and Social Change in a Midland Town: Victorian Nottingham, 1815–1900* (London, 1966); A. Rogers (ed.), *The Making of Stamford* (Leicester, 1965); R. Unwin, *Wetherby: The History of a Yorkshire Market Town* (Leeds, 1986).

[31] Raven, 'Chelmsford During the Industrial Revolution', p. 61.

[32] R.W. Unwin, 'Tradition and Transition: Market Towns of the Vale of York, 1660–1830', *Northern History*, 17 (1981), pp. 72, 73.

[33] J.D. Marshall, 'The Rise and Transformation of the Cumbrian Market Town, 1660–1900', *Northern History*, 19 (1983), p. 208.

Yorkshire. She characterized the differing growth experiences as those of 'dynamic centres' (e.g. Selby), 'expanding centres' (e.g. Beverley), 'stable centres' (e.g. Thirsk), or 'declining centres' such as Kilham. Noble discussed six main forces that determined these experiences, 'namely, location, nodality, externality, competition, economic structure and migration'.[34]

The foregoing agenda was developed by two other significant contributions to the comparative study of small towns by Stephen Royle and Catherine Smith. Royle's comparative investigation into small town society looked at the three Leicestershire towns of Coalville, Hinckley and Melton Mowbray. Coalville was principally engaged in mining, Hinckley in textile manufacturing and Melton Mowbray was a prosperous marketing and agricultural service centre. Royle looked at employment patterns, social interaction through marriage, and migration patterns. He concluded that it was 'the degree of prosperity and the buoyancy of the economy locally associated with the towns' predominant functions that were of greatest significance in the structuring and operation of their societies'.[35] Social interaction in Melton Mowbray was greatly aided by the fact that the town was a leisure centre for well-to-do visitors who came for the neighbourhood's hunting and stayed in its many lodges and inns; the Quorn Hunt was a particularly important attraction.

Importantly, Catherine Smith has questioned the nemesis of many small market towns allegedly caused by improvements in transport and communications which extended the 'range of facilities and services offered by the larger towns'.[36] She argued that until the work by Unwin, Marshall and Noble, the lack of research into the development of small towns had left the traditional view of their decline unchallenged. Smith's study of Newark and Mansfield in Nottinghamshire between 1770 and 1840 utilized archival material including probate inventories and wills. She concluded that 'the image of the eighteenth [and nineteenth]-century market town as a traditional, somnolent community is in need of qualification'.[37] Smith later extended her work on urban improvement by the inclusion of Worksop and East Retford, and on population growth and economic change in market towns by a further extension that included Ollerton and

---

[34] M. Noble, 'Growth and Development in a Regional Urban System: The Country Towns of Eastern Yorkshire, 1700–1850', *Urban History Yearbook* (1987), pp. 16, 18.

[35] S.A. Royle, 'Aspects of Nineteenth-century Small Town Society: A Comparative Study from Leicestershire', *Midland History*, 5 (1979 – 80), p. 60.

[36] C. Smith, 'Image and Reality: Two Nottinghamshire Market Towns in Late Georgian England', *Midland History*, 17 (1992), p. 59.

[37] Smith, 'Image and Reality', p. 72.

Bingham.[38]   She argued that the resilience of these communities as seen in the 'diversification' of their occupational structure and 'growing sophistication of trades and crafts within them' was the 'rejuvenation of the traditional role of these towns as trading and service centres'.[39]

Until comparatively recently, many historians had (by largely ignoring small towns and focusing on aspects of large towns and cities) *ipso facto* endorsed the Trollopian view. Admittedly, urban historians interested in retailing examine the effects of industrialization on small towns between 1750 and 1851 but there have been comparatively few studies of the wider business activities of very small towns (populations below 3,000) during the latter half of the nineteenth century. However, there is now interest in reassessing the significance of small Victorian towns which is beginning to offer a more optimistic statement of their significance and function. A number of key issues, which are arguably central to such an appraisal, were highlighted by the pivotal studies discussed earlier. These issues are setting a new agenda for the study of small towns that tries to assess their demographic and economic fortunes in the light of internal migration, of improved transport and communication, and of developments in marketing and retailing. The following discussion examines the importance of each of these three themes.

Internal migration

The population of England and Wales quadrupled from 9.2 million in 1801 to 36.1 million by 1911 and against this background of demographic growth the period witnessed increased internal migration. It is over a century since Ernst Georg Ravenstein first enunciated his laws of migration but in that time there has been little fundamental revision of his theories by historians.[40] In general, as re-stated by David Grigg, Ravenstein's theories covered the ideas that migrants, motivated by economic forces, usually only go short distances proceeding in a step by step manner, most frequently from agricultural areas to those of developing industry and commerce.[41] Later research has accordingly often focused on the basic questions of who migrated and why? What were their

---

[38] C. Smith, 'Urban Improvement in the Nottinghamshire Market Town, 1770–1840', *Midland History*, 25 (2000), pp. 98–114; C. Smith, 'Population Growth and Economic Change in some Nottinghamshire Market Towns, 1680–1840', *Local Population Studies*, 65 (2000), pp. 29-46.

[39] Smith, 'Population Growth and Economic Change', p. 40.

[40] E.G. Ravenstein, 'The Laws of Migration', *Journal of the Statistical Society*, 48 (1885), pp. 167-227;E.G. Ravenstein, 'The Laws of Migration', *Journal of the Statistical Society*, 52 (1889), pp. 214-301; E.G. Ravenstein, 'Census of the British Isles, 1871: Birthplaces and Migration', *Geographical Magazine*, 3 (1876), pp. 173-77, 201-06, 229-33.

[41] D.B. Grigg, 'E.G. Ravenstein and Laws of Migration', in M. Drake (ed.), *Time, Family and Community: Perspectives on Family and Community History* (Oxford, 1994), pp. 147-64.

origins, destinations and patterns of flow between them and what, asked Paul White and Robert Woods, were the effects on the donor and recipient communities? [42]

These questions have prompted historians to identify the main reasons for people migrating. For example, John Marshall elucidated the 'propulsive' motives, such as wage reductions, the side-effects of enclosure and poor housing; and the 'attractive' inducements, including higher wages, the chance of earlier marriage and the opportunities for regular child employment. Additionally, he recognized 'stabilising' or 'neutralising' factors which included housing, family ties in a locality and the normally conservative character of rural inhabitants.[43] Furthermore, Everett Lee developed the 'push and pull' argument around the identification of an 'origin and destination [and] a set of intervening obstacles'. The number and difficulty of these obstacles might prevent or discourage migration in a particular direction and may be crucial in the decision to go, to stay, or indeed return.[44] A related approach by Peter Clark, stressed that rural-urban migration was a 'powerful adhesive' which 'integrated towns with the villages of their hinterlands, linking together the communities of a sub-regional *pays*'.[45] This idea supported the earlier notion of 'place utility', that is, the individual's degree of satisfaction or dissatisfaction with respect to a particular place, developed by Wolpert and identified as fundamental to the decision to stay or go.[46]

There is a consensus that two separate but related nineteenth-century processes, industrialization and urbanization, created a 'spatially differentiated economy and society' that encouraged migrants to believe, rightly or wrongly, that greater satisfaction would be achieved by moving to a new place. White and Woods argued that evaluation by a migrant of another place as a potential destination was influenced by visits or letters from earlier migrants, by information in newspapers and books, or by having visited the destination themselves. Nineteenth-century urban growth and industrial development, in Dudley Baines's view, created an increasingly regionally concentrated specialized manufacturing economy. This

---

[42] P. White and R. Woods (eds), *The Geographical Impact of Migration* (London, 1980), p. 1.

[43] J.D. Marshall, 'The Lancashire Rural Labourer in the Early Nineteenth Century', *Transactions of the Lancashire and Cheshire Antiquarian Society*, 71 (1961), p. 95.

[44] E.S. Lee, 'A Theory of Migration', in J.A. Jackson (ed.), *Migration* (Sociological Studies, Vol. 2, Cambridge, 1969), p. 288.

[45] P. Clark, 'Migration in England during the Late Seventeenth and Early Eighteenth Centuries', in P. Clark and D. Souden (eds), *Migration and Society in Early Modern England* (London, 1987), p. 214.

[46] J. Wolpert, 'Behavioural Aspects of the Decision to Migrate', *Papers and Proceedings, Regional Science Association*, 15 (1965), p. 162.

increased a potential migrant's employment options and, according to Richard Lawton, was responsible for a substantial increase in population mobility.[47]

It is possible, according to White and Woods, 'to recognize directional bias in migration streams' for example from rural areas to urban centres. Moreover, Arthur Getis and Barry Boots argued, these patterns were dependent on people being influenced by 'growth and relocation' factors including the 'diffusion of information' which increased as the nineteenth century progressed. Within this directional bias is the 'principle of least effort' which, according to Miller, means migrants will choose the destination, frequently only a short distance away, with which they are more familiar.[48] However, in contrast to Ravenstein's belief in short stepwise moves, the relative importance of long distance migration, Grigg suggested, 'would have risen in the nineteenth century as the rail net extended and urbanization proceeded'.[49] This longer distance movement, Colin Pooley and Jean Turnbull concluded, was mostly undertaken by those in higher socio-economic groups where 'marketable skills, knowledge of opportunities and access to transport' were enabling factors for such people.[50] Furthermore, although small towns are often starting points they may also attract long-stay migrants when their economies are sufficiently dynamic.

This study offers an appraisal of how nineteenth-century internal migration influenced the business and professional communities of small centres like Ashwell, Baldock, Buntingford and Royston situated in a largely agricultural region. It seeks to shed light on whether these communities remained isolated in the nineteenth century within their immediate regional hinterlands, were viewed by potential migrants as merely intermediate stopping-off points, or were recognised as offering sufficient inducements to be considered 'attractive' long-term centres of opportunity in the wider national context.

---

[47] White and Woods, *Geographical Impact of Migration*, pp. 7–8; D. Baines, *Migration in a Mature Economy: Emigration and Internal Migration in England and Wales, 1861–1900* (Cambridge, 1985), pp. 213–14; R. Lawton, 'Population and Society, 1730-1914', in R.A. Dodgshon and R.A. Butlin (eds), *An Historical Geography of England and Wales* (2nd edn, London, 1990), p. 285.

[48] White and Woods, *Geographical Impact of Migration*, p. 29; A. Getis and B. Boots, *Models of Spatial Processes: An Approach to the Study of Point, Line and Area Patterns* (Cambridge, 1978), p. 5; E. Miller, 'A Note on the Role of Distance in Migration: Costs of Mobility versus Intervening Opportunity', *Journal of Regional Science*, 12 (1972), p. 475.

[49] D.B. Grigg, 'E.G. Ravenstein and Laws of Migration', in M. Drake (ed.), *Time, Family and Community: Perspectives on Family and Community History* (Oxford, 1994), p. 150.

[50] C. Pooley and J. Turnbull, *Migration and Mobility in Britain since the 18th Century* (London, 1998), pp. 17, 13.

Improved transport and communication

Mobility was encouraged by two pivotal mid-nineteenth-century developments, the introduction of a uniform Penny Post and the rapid spread of the railway network, enabling wider circulation of information. Distribution of London newspapers and radical broad-sheets, together with growth of provincial newspapers, overcame what Derek Gregory has called the 'friction of distance'. The fact that even the most humble could use railway services, Donald Gordon suggested, impacted enormously on mobility and opportunity; 'thousands of excursionists', for example, visited the 1851 Great Exhibition in London.[51]

Unfortunately, much of the literature on improvements to the transport infrastructure concentrates on the wider economic issues and on larger centres of population. One exception is that provided by Theo Barker and Dorian Savage's review of road services provided by 'carriers' which they described as regular, numerous and systematic, but still slow by the 1760s. Along the main trunk routes, 'carriers' left at advertised times, delivering and collecting at specified inns, often located in small town centres, which were encouraged to cater for this trade. Another exception is Alan Everitt's observation that by the use of their storerooms these inns 'became covered or private market places, often of a rather specialised kind', a role that would have benefited the local economies of these small towns.[52] These observations indicate that the servicing of carrier traffic, whether locally-based or passing through, would have greatly benefited the economies of small towns strategically situated on the country's road network.

Several studies have demonstrated that the expansion of the waterway network during the late eighteenth and early nineteenth centuries had a considerable impact upon the development of road transport. By the late 1830s, 'over 20,000 miles of main road had been turnpiked' and this coupled with the introduction of lighter faster vans, Barker and Savage argued, encouraged carriers to win back much of the packet and parcel freight traffic from the waterways. Roads retained 'their advantage over waterways for all short-distance traffic', i.e. up to five or six miles, by door-to-door delivery, and it was 'along roads that cattle and other animals continued to be driven to market'.[53] It was speed which gave road transport the advantage over longer distances with the advent of such technical

---

[51] D. Gregory, 'The Friction of Distance? Information Circulation and the Mails in Early Nineteenth-century England', *Journal of Historical Geography*, 13, 2 (1987), pp. 130–54; Gordon, *Regional History of the Railways*, p. 129.

[52] T.C. Barker and C.I. Savage, *An Economic History of Transport in Britain* (3rd edn, London, 1974), p. 45; A. Everitt, 'The English Urban Inn, 1560–1760', in A. Everitt, (ed.), *Perspectives in English Urban History* (London, 1973), pp. 97, 120-23.

[53] Barker and Savage, *Economic History of Transport*, p. 47.

developments as the 'flying coaches' mounted on steel springs. Local economies too benefited, according to Barker and Savage, as 'innkeepers along each road horsed particular coaches over their stages at an agreed rate in return for a share of that coach's profits'.[54]

The idea that a 'transport revolution' accompanied the Industrial Revolution was dismissed by Michael Freeman who argued that few turnpikes 'consisted of entirely new roads; by far the majority covered roads already in existence'. Furthermore, while the canal was significant in civil engineering terms 'the fact remains that the horse continued to be the means of traction and that one of the natural elements remained its fundamental basis'. Freeman contended that the 'revolution' only came later 'because of the progressive application of steam power' from the 1820s. This major technological advance, no longer dependent on the elements and the horse, led to 'a transformation in the pace, scale and conduct of trade'.[55] A true 'transport revolution', Freeman believed, had to await the steam engine that undeniably ushered in the age of the railway. By the mid-1890s the network, according to Gourvish, covered 18,000 route miles employing, as detailed by Barker and Savage, vast numbers of workers in what was an industrial giant of the Victorian economy.[56]

There is a general consensus that from the middle of the nineteenth century demand fell dramatically for both road passenger coaches and those carrying mail, the latter having transferred to rail by 1830. In contrast, the railways 'generated more short-distance traffic to and from railway stations' by commercial carriers who were either taking local produce to the station or collecting goods brought from distant manufacturing centres by rail. Barker and Savage referred to the contemporary estimate of Dionysius Lardner that overall by 1848 'the daily passenger traffic by rail throughout the kingdom would have required over 140,000 horses to convey it if it had been carried by road'.[57] Transport networks were often crucial to the fortunes of small towns in largely rural areas. Their survival or decline could be heavily dependent on decisions relating to the routing of roads, railways and canals. Unfortunately, historians have tended to focus on

---

[54] Barker and Savage, *Economic History of Transport*, pp. 48, 50.

[55] M.J. Freeman, 'Introduction', in D.H. Aldcroft and M.J. Freeman (eds), *Transport in the Industrial Revolution* (Manchester, 1983), p. 2.

[56] M.J. Freeman, 'Introduction', in M.J. Freeman and D.H. Aldcroft (eds), *Transport in Victorian Britain* (Manchester, 1988), p. 1; Barker and Savage, *Economic History of Transport*, pp. 63, 70, 80, 98. In addition to the 50% of operatives who were labourers and craftsmen, there were 8000 porters, 4500 platelayers, 4000 engine drivers and stokers and 1000 administrators. Total numbers employed rose to 250,000 by the mid-1870s and nearly 350,000 by 1890. T.R. Gourvish, 'Railways 1830-70: The Formative Years', in Freeman and Aldcroft, *Transport in Victorian Britain*, p. 57.

[57] Barker and Savage, *Economic History of Transport*, pp. 63, 64.

the impact that developing transport networks had on larger industrial centres and major cities.

By mid-century, thanks to the train, farm produce grown far from cities was able to compete with that produced on their outskirts. This must have profoundly affected, either beneficially or detrimentally, the economic prosperity of many small towns but has not been subject to much detailed analysis. Newspapers 'enjoyed much larger circulations with the spread of railways' and because of their weight and volume constituted the bulk of mail traffic carried by the network in the late 1830s. Within ten years of the introduction of the pre-paid, flat-rate penny post in 1840, the number of letters grew fivefold and Barker and Savage argued that 'such an increase, coming so soon after the growth of newspaper traffic, would have been unthinkable without railways to handle it all'. They saw this growth in mass communication as 'one of the railways' main contributions not just to the commercial efficiency of the country but to the whole of its social life'.[58] Furthermore, it greatly enhanced the decision-making process of potential migrants.

As long-distance traffic quickly transferred to rail, according to Barker and Savage, the number of turnpike trusts fell with only two surviving to 1890. This change would have initially impacted negatively on small trust-side settlements by reducing the passing trade that their publicans and shopkeepers relied on. However, the doubling of Britain's population from 1841 to 1901 'swelled the numbers of road users' and the amount of freight carried short distances, to and from railway stations, and thus caused the number of wheeled vehicles to grow considerably.[59] This further change would have benefited greatly the economic prosperity of many small towns linked to the rail network, a subject worthy of more attention. Pioneer research on the village carrier by Alan Everitt, determined that in 1884 there were direct carrier services into the county town of Leicester from 220 of its surrounding villages and that ninety-four of those were also linked by carrier to smaller market centres in the county. A more recent study by Raven similarly analysed weekly carrier and coach services to and from Chelmsford in 1839.[60] The use of a similar approach in this present study provides part of a more holistic view of transport. By combining stagecoach services, road carriers and the advent of railways it balances the provision of short-distance traffic to and from villages and towns of the region with that of long-distance traffic linking north-east Hertfordshire to major business centres. The analysis thus provides for

[58] Barker and Savage, *Economic History of Transport*, p. 82.
[59] Barker and Savage, *Economic History of Transport*, pp. 122, 124.
[60] A. Everitt, 'Town and Country in Victorian Leicestershire: The Role of the Village Carrier', in A. Everitt (ed.), *Perspectives in English Urban History* (London, 1973), pp. 213–40; Raven, 'Chelmsford During the Industrial Revolution', pp. 53-59.

a better understanding as to how these transport networks helped some small towns survive and thrive.

Developments in buying and selling of goods

Developments in retailing were a consequence of improvements in the nineteenth-century's transport infrastructure, which helped bring an increased range of foodstuffs and mass-produced goods from the nation's industrial centres to even the smallest towns. This encouraged the establishment of specialist retailers who took advantage of the middle class echoing the rich in their demand for 'novelties' and the latest fashions. Specialist purveyors with larger stocks began to outnumber traditional producer-retailers; the start of Neil McKendrick's 'consumer revolution'.[61]

These new features of distribution, in John Clapham's view, emerged in the first half of that century when 'everywhere, down to the smallest country towns and some of the villages, the shop, specialised or general, was supplanting the pedlar, the itinerant tradesman of the fairs, and the ancient custom of making clothes at home'.[62] Initially, consumers viewed the emergence of middlemen with suspicion, but this lessened, suggested Clapham, as the role of 'intermediaries between producer and consumer, or even between producer and retailer' reflected the 'growing variety of both production and consumption'.[63]

By mid-century the railways, Alexander argued, provided the means of fast, frequent and reliable distribution of goods 'into the wholesale markets of the great cities, and from there some of the produce flowed back to the country towns'. Unlike the periodic fairs which often declined in the face of this increased competition, regular markets continued through the nineteenth century despite local growers' inability to supply all the needs of a town's inhabitants. These weekly retail markets, Brown argued, proved more 'resilient and adaptable' to the increased competition from shops and survived by offering cheap food and manufactured goods to the poorer sections of the townsfolk.[64] Furthermore, their continued resilience in the face of change was demonstrated by Deborah Hodson's study of industrial Lancashire, where the supposed diminishing value of

---

[61] N. McKendrick, J. Brewer and J.H. Plumb, *The Birth of a Consumer Society: The Commercialisation of Eighteenth-century England* (London, 1982), pp. 1–11.

[62] J.H. Clapham, *An Economic History of Modern Britain, Vol. 1, The Early Railway Age, 1820–1850* (2nd Edn, Cambridge, 1930), p. 224.

[63] J.H. Clapham, *An Economic History of Modern Britain, Vol. 2, Free Trade and Steel, 1850-1886* (Cambridge, 1932), p. 308.

[64] D. Alexander, *Retailing in England During the Industrial Revolution* (London, 1970), p. 232; Brown, *English Market Town*, p. 42.

the market place from 1850 was countered by local authority-owned covered markets, opening daily and thriving in the late nineteenth century.[65]

Although shops proliferated between the 1820s and 1850s Alexander found them to be 'dominated by the small general shop which tended to be operated by men and women of a similar social background to the urban poor'. Although credit allowed people to buy things they would not otherwise obtain, Hamish Fraser argued, these local shopkeepers appreciated that 'with the poorer section of the population ... credit was largely for necessities'. The downside, he acknowledged, was that the provision of credit probably encouraged some to buy things they might well have done without. In spite of this reservation, Fraser saw the small general store 'providing almost all the regular needs of the populace in the necessary small quantities and with reasonable credit' as continuing to be the key shop in villages and working-class areas of towns up to 1914.[66]

Alexander has described the aggressive and competitive 'entrepreneurial concepts' such as refashioned shop fronts, promotional displays and the special attention towards pricing that arose in the cities but spread across the whole country. He was convinced that by 1850 'the difference between city and country retailing was one lying along a continuum rather than across an unpassable chasm'.[67] A massive 'disentangling of production and distribution' of many commodities, Alexander argued, was reflected in the decline of the number of craftsmen selling their own products. For example, by mid-century 'the bespoke tailoring trade was being challenged by the new "clothier and outfitter" who retailed the ready-made goods produced in city sweatshops'. Fraser concurred with this view, observing that from the 1870s onwards, as incomes and tastes changed, some shopkeepers 'began to perceive that there was a place for cheapness *and* reasonable quality'.[68]

It is obvious from the foregoing discussion, as Nancy Cox argued, that many historians have wrongly concluded that the retailing sector was 'slow to adapt to a changing world and remained much as it had always been until after 1850' when it changed rapidly and dramatically.[69] As for a possible 'consumer revolution' she believes there to be 'no agreement on precisely what the term means'. Furthermore, Jon Stobart has since observed that 'broadening of consumption is

---

[65] D. Hodson, ' "The Municipal Store": Adaptation and Development in the Retail Markets of Nineteenth-century Urban Lancashire', in Alexander and Akehurst, *Modern Retailing*, pp. 94–114.

[66] Alexander, *Retailing in England*, p. 234; W.H. Fraser, *The Coming of the Mass Market, 1850–1914* (London, 1981), pp. 90, 101.

[67] Alexander, *Retailing in England*, p. 235.

[68] Alexander, *Retailing in England*, p. 235; Fraser, *Mass Market*, p. 110.

[69] N. Cox, *The Complete Tradesman: A Study of Retailing, 1550-1820* (Aldershot, 2000), p. 223.

traditionally linked to industrialisation' and the mass production of consumer goods that 'were affordable to the working as well as the middle classes'. However this commonly assumed link, he argued, is too simplistic and not proof of a 'revolution' as many aspects of consumerism can be traced back well into the eighteenth century.[70] Proof of many innovative practices, such as fixed-pricing, branding and promotional tools, being in use in the eighteenth century was demonstrated by Christina Fowler's examination of provincial retailing in southern England. She thus provided a further indication that many modern approaches to retailing were adopted long before the traditionally stated retail development boundary of 1850.[71]

Mass advertising as a promotional tool for wholesalers and retailers still lacked respectability in the mid-nineteenth century and was dismissed as 'puffery' by its critics. However, with improved printing processes, the wall poster rapidly became a significant nationwide phenomenon. Soon, as Fraser described, 'Every gable and naked wall … every surface exposed to the passing public gaze was hastily covered with posters extolling the virtues of some product or some service'.[72] In comparison, more refined and targeted blandishments had long been utilized to appeal to the tastes of the fashion conscious. Again, mirroring the arguments of Cox and Fowler, Laura Ugolini, in an investigation of menswear retailers' press advertisements, similarly concluded that advertising was not 'a new phenomenon at the end of the nineteenth century'. Tailors and many other retailers already 'enjoyed a long tradition of printed advertisements dating back to the eighteenth century and earlier'.[73] As well as pandering to people's acquisitive impulses and the need to improve their lifestyles, advertisers exploited their personal fears about health. Nancy Cox and Claire Walsh, for example, argued that selling goods, especially patent medicines, at fixed prices advertised in national and provincial newspapers was commonplace. Their study, although usually focused on larger urban centres, provides further confirmation that innovation in retailing had started 'well before the period of so-called "modern retailing" after 1850'.[74]

---

[70] Cox, *Complete Tradesman*, p. 2; J. Stobart, *Spend, Spend, Spend! A History of Shopping* (Stroud, 2008), p.129.

[71] N. Alexander and G. Akehurst (eds), *The Emergence of Modern Retailing, 1750–1950* (London, 1999), p. 1; C. Fowler, 'Changes in Provincial Retail Practice During the Eighteenth Century, with Particular Reference to Central-Southern England', in Alexander and Akehurst, *Modern Retailing*, pp. 37–54.

[72] Fraser, *Mass Market*, p. 135; C. Sheldon, *A History of Poster Advertising* (London, 1937), pp. 3–20.

[73] L. Ugolini, 'Men, Masculinities, and Menswear Advertising, c. 1890-1914', in J. Benson and L. Ugolini (eds), *A Nation of Shopkeepers: Five Centuries of British Retailing* (London, 2003), p. 83.

[74] N. Cox and C Walsh, ' "Their Shops are Dens, the Buyer is their Prey": Shop Design and Sale Techniques', in N. Cox, *The Complete Tradesman: A Study of Retailing, 1550-1820* (Aldershot, 2000), p. 102.

Regarding social and economic relations within the business community, Phillip Waller argued that one should not denounce the Victorian town merely as a 'relentless manufacturing slum' creating bleak human suffering. He reasoned that 'Towns display the economic standing, the social relations, the cultural appreciation and the governmental dynamic, of the people who inhabit them. Towns summarize civilisation.'[75] If that is the case, then the many small towns, despite being frequently ignored by urban historians, are a large part of that civilisation.

These major historical themes provide the most appropriate backdrop, as this present analysis demonstrates, to an analysis of the provision of goods and services in small nineteenth-century towns. In the light of our knowledge about the effects of migration, improved communications and developments in retailing and marketing, the significance of small towns becomes clearer, especially when viewed as part of a developing regional economy.

Small towns of north-east Hertfordshire

The traditional concept of market towns in a region being 'mutually competitive entities' and part of a changing hierarchy that over time became increasingly centralized was, John Marshall argued, 'over-simple or misleading'. Furthermore, he suggested that the field of analytical and comparative studies of market towns was 'a desperately neglected one' and called for some informed explorations to tackle this omission.[76] Although Marshall expressed the above views almost thirty years ago, the evidence of the secondary literature suggests there is still a paucity of such comparative studies of small (market) towns that investigate the effect of the changing economic climate of the nineteenth century. Urban and social historians have studied large cities, major industrial centres, county towns, the larger regional market towns, cotton towns, garrison towns, ports and even Victorian seaside towns but little attention has been paid to the myriad small towns that would surely have felt the ripples of change.[77]

Until the work of Catherine Smith, it seems that economic, social and urban historians, with few exceptions, largely ignored the small nineteenth-century

---

[75] P.J. Waller, *Town, City, and Nation: England, 1850 –1914* (Oxford, 1983), pp. 317, 318.

[76] Marshall, 'Cumbrian Market Town', p. 132.

[77] See amongst others; T.C. Barker and J.R. Harris, *A Merseyside Town in the Industrial Revolution: St Helens, 1750-1900* (London, 1959); W.A. Armstrong, *Stability and Change in an English County Town: A Social Study of York, 1801-51* (London, 1974); D.J. Olsen, *The Growth of Victorian London* (London, 1976); R.S. Neale, *Bath: A Social History, 1680-1850* (London, 1981); J.K. Walton, *The English Seaside Resort: A Social History, 1750-1914* (Leicester, 1983); E. Hopkins, *The Rise of the Manufacturing Town: Birmingham and the Industrial Revolution* (Stroud, 1998).

market town and the publication of comparative regional studies was rare.[78] Smith argued that by adaptation and specialization these resilient trade and service centres flourished by the mid-nineteenth century.[79]

In view of the limited number of such regional studies, this volume contributes to the literature by focusing on some of the small towns of north-east Hertfordshire. However, in dealing with these particular towns one is faced with what Alan Everitt observed to be the difficult question of exactly what historians mean by a 'region'. As he suggested, it may simply be 'a perception of historians and geographers, and which probably had no conscious significance for contemporaries'.[80] Since Everitt's observation, there has been a great deal of speculation regarding the historical roots of regionalism, and in particular the significance of industrialization in regional development. During the 1980s, John Langton challenged the 'widespread belief shared by geographers and historians, that industrialization destroyed regional distinctiveness in England' and was supported by Pat Hudson who was convinced by the argument that the latter did grow 'during the industrial revolution period and in the mid-nineteenth century'.[81]

Many authorities concur that the seventeenth-century origins of regionalism were in the 'county' which Everitt described as an artificial region, as opposed to a natural one, being 'an essentially human creation, often with no significant natural boundaries'. By the eighteenth century county towns, Langton argued, had 'assumed a functional dominance over other central places for the provision of high goods and services' which provided a coherent 'urban economic structure of the shire'.[82] However, unlike most other counties, Hertfordshire 'failed to develop a single urban community of true regional significance'. The reason, according to Nigel Goose, was that 'the proximity of the capital city is no doubt paramount here'. He believed the range of goods and services offered by London and its 'array of social and cultural functions' would have 'represented a competitive presence that simply could not be rivalled'; Hertfordshire was destined to remain through the nineteenth century 'a county of small towns'.[83]

---

[78] Smith, 'Image and Reality', pp. 59–74; Smith, 'Urban Improvement', pp. 98–114; Smith, 'Population Growth and Economic Change', pp. 29-46.

[79] See pp. 11-12 above.

[80] A. Everitt, 'Country, County and Town: Patterns of Regional Evolution in England', *Transactions of the Royal Historical Society*, 5th Series, 29 (1979), p. 80.

[81] J. Langton, 'The Industrial Revolution and the Regional Geography of England', *Transactions of the Institute of British Geographers*, 9, 2 (1984), p. 145; P. Hudson, 'The Regional Perspective', in P. Hudson (ed.), *Regions and Industries: A Perspective on the Industrial Revolution in Britain* (Cambridge, 1989), p. 18.

[82] Everitt, 'Country, County and Town', p. 88; Langton, 'Industrial Revolution', p. 148.

[83] N. Goose, 'Urban Growth and Economic Development in Early Modern Hertfordshire', in T. Slater and N. Goose, *A County of Small Towns: The Development of Hertfordshire's Urban Landscape to 1800* (Hatfield, 2008), p. 119.

Nevertheless, small towns, according to Hudson, contributed to the creation of local and regional identities, 'especially where towns and their hinterlands came to specialise in the production of particular craft goods for distant markets'. Her view echoed that expressed by Everitt, a decade earlier, that 'entrepreneurial' towns played a crucial role in the development of 'distinct craft-regions'.[84]

Charles Phythian-Adams placed Hertfordshire in the north-east corner of his large Thames 'cultural province', a concept based upon major river-drainage basins.[85] However, apart from being a constituent of the twentieth-century notion of the Home Counties, the relatively small and largely rural county of Hertfordshire never seems to have acquired its own characteristic regional appellation. Perhaps this is a consequence of its geographical sandwiching between London to the south (whose hinterland has gradually subsumed much of the county), the Chiltern ridge to the west, the Fens to the north, and the blending into Essex to the east. In spite of the 'coalescing forces unleashed by the industrial revolution', it was Jon Stobart's opinion that spatial units such as regions have no 'preordained size'. He also argued, from the results of his early nineteenth-century study of industrialization in the East Midlands, that it was 'common for localities and local identities to be nested within broader regions'.[86]

Having no significant textile industry, Hertfordshire was never a proto-industrial region in the ordinary sense yet, if one considers traditional activities such as malting and brewing as producing craft goods, a case can be made for an Everitt-like 'craft region' within Hertfordshire. By the mid-eighteenth century, Hertfordshire was among 'a handful of counties [that] already dominated malt production, emphasising their early pre-eminence as barley lands'. By the early nineteenth century, a comparison of excise collection centres by Christine Clark revealed 'the growing emphasis upon the eastern counties' with Bedford, Cambridge and Hertford being among the top five towns. For centuries London had relied on obtaining its malt supplies from the surrounding arable counties and Clark believed that 'Hertfordshire, particularly renowned for the quality of its brown malt, was the acknowledged capital of the malt trade'.[87]

In view of the limited number of regional studies to have concentrated on very small nineteenth-century towns, and given Goose's opinion that Hertfordshire

---

[84] Hudson, 'The Regional Perspective', p. 18; Everitt, 'Country, County and Town', pp. 93-4.

[85] C. Phythian-Adams, 'Introduction: an Agenda for English Local History', in C. Phythian-Adams (ed.), *Societies, Cultures and Kinship, 1580-1850: Cultural Provinces and English Local History* (Leicester, 1993), pp. 9-18.

[86] J. Stobart, 'Regions, Localities, and Industrialisation: Evidence from the East Midlands circa 1780-1840', *Environment and Planning A*, 33 (2001), p. 1322.

[87] C. Clark, *The British Malting Industry since 1830* (London, 1998), pp. 13, 14.

never developed an urban centre of regional significance, this present evaluation contributes to the literature by focusing on the roles played by some of the smaller urban centres in the north-east of the county. By investigating the activities of their changing business populations, it addresses the calls of Hey and of Levine for more demographic studies to be set in the context of particular local communities and also the more recent observation of Neil Raven and Tristram Hooley that what is largely absent regarding 'the role of towns [in the process of industrialization] is evidence from systemic regional investigations'.[88] The evidence presented here aims to explore how such a community reacted to changes in the agricultural practices of its hinterland, the effects of migration, the impact of improved communications, and how the services it offered to the surrounding rural population changed and developed. In addition to the question of whether, as Clark suggested, small towns act as a 'bridge' between the countryside and nearby growing urban centres, it is clear that 'towns were not isolated points of activity' but were, as Stobart and Raven argued, 'linked together by flows of goods, capital, information and people'. This monograph will present evidence that the small towns and villages of nineteenth-century north-east Hertfordshire co-existed in a hierarchical network.[89]

The evidence gathered here focuses on four small nineteenth-century towns, Ashwell, Baldock, Buntingford and Royston (Plates 01 – 04 below), situated in the north-east corner of Hertfordshire. Despite their modest size they have been viewed as towns as far back as the late-seventeenth century when Richard Blome described Baldock as 'a considerable large *Town* ... of chief note for the many *Maultsters* here residing', Buntingford as 'a good thorough-fare *Town*, and Royston as 'a famous *Market-town* ... well inhabited, frequented, and full of *Inns*'.[90] All four entities were ancient market towns especially Baldock founded by the Templars where, according to Evelyn Lord, an inquest of 1185 showed it 'to be a fully developed borough with holdings set out as burgage tenures for freeman'.[91] They lie between thirty and forty miles north of London close to the county boundaries of Cambridgeshire to the north, Essex to the east, Bedfordshire to the west (Map 01 below). Three of the towns were situated at that time on the two major roads from London to the north-east of England, Baldock on the Great North Road, Buntingford and Royston on the Old North Road. It is interesting to

---

[88] N. Raven and T. Hooley, 'Industrial and Urban Change in the Midlands: A Regional Survey', in J. Stobart and N. Raven (eds), *Towns, Regions and Industries: Urban and Industrial Change in the Midlands, c. 1700-1840* (Manchester, 2005), p. 23.

[89] Clark, 'Small Towns 1700-1840', p. 733; J. Stobart and N. Raven, 'Introduction: Industrialisation and Urbanisation in a Regional Context', in Stobart and Raven, *Towns, Regions and Industries*, p. 4.

[90] R. Blome, *Britannia, or, A Geographical Description of the Kingdoms of England, Scotland, and Ireland, with the Isles and Territories Thereto Belonging* (London, 1673), p. 115.

[91] E. Lord, *The Knights Templar in Britain* (Pbk edn, Harlow, 2004), p. 78.

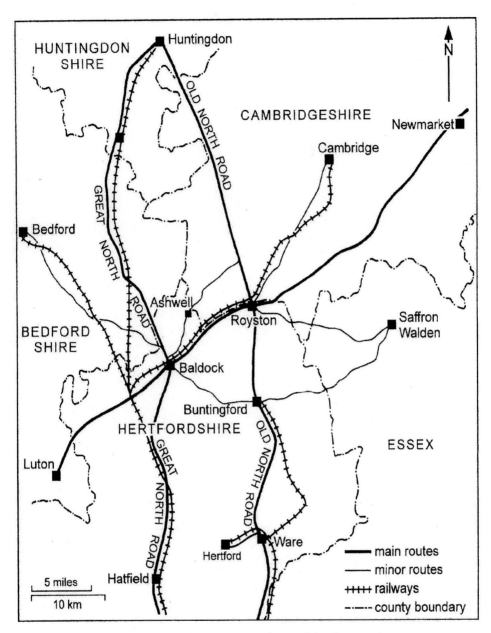

Map 01: Road and railway connections of the four study towns
Source: Phillip Judge

note that even in the fourteenth century the importance of Buntingford's location on a major north-south road was noted by the king 'wishing to show special grace to the lords and tenants of Buntingford, where there is common passage of the magnates and people of the realm from north to south'.[92] Ashwell, the fourth town, lies on a minor road a little over four miles to the north-east of Baldock. Importantly, Baldock and Royston are both sited at crossroads where the east-west route from Oxford, around the chalk escarpment of the Chilterns, crosses the two north roads following the line of the ancient Icknield Way, heading for East Anglia. In addition, Baldock was just eight miles east of Shefford and the navigable waterway of the River Ivel, while Buntingford lay eleven miles north of Ware from where the River Lea provided access to London's breweries for the region's barley and malt.

Plate 01: Mill Street, Ashwell

In north-east Hertfordshire the road between Baldock and Royston runs through the Vale of Baldock along a belt of light chalky marl producing fertile arable land.[93] Here, sheep grazing gave way to the plough during the Napoleonic Wars

---

[92] *Calendar of Charter Rolls, Vol. V, 1341–1417* (London, 1916), *41 Edward III, 1367*, p. 209.
[93] L.G. Cameron, 'Hertfordshire', in L.D. Stamp (ed.), *The Land of Britain: The Report of the Land Utilisation Survey of Britain. Part 80* (London, 1941), p. 311.

Plate 02: High Street, Baldock

Plate 03: High Street, Buntingford

Plate 04: Upper King Street, Royston

encouraged by the proximity of London as both a market and supplier of manure.[94] In the opinion of Lionel Munby this area had 'some of the best barley land in the country' during the nineteenth century.[95] Both Arthur Young and Gordon Mingay described how local farmers, encouraged by the increased

---

[94] *VCH Hertfordshire, Vol. II*, pp. 129–39.

[95] L.M. Munby, *The Hertfordshire Landscape* (The Making of the English Landscape Series, London, 1977), p. 26.

demand from maltsters, developed six-course rotation schemes which allowed for a second barley crop.[96] Royston, an important malting centre from the sixteenth century, sent its produce south to Ware and 'thence presumably to London' along the River Lea.[97] During the early nineteenth century, hay and straw were carried

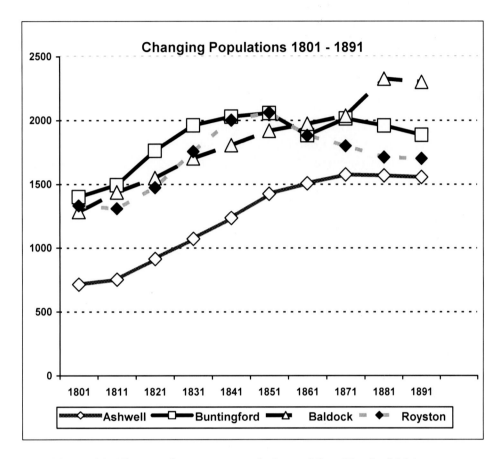

Figure 01: Nineteenth-century populations of four Hertfordshire towns

Source: 1801–1891 Censuses (Ashwell, Baldock, Buntingford, Royston)

the forty miles from Baldock to London, and 'ashes, soot and sheep's trotters brought back as a substitute for dung'.[98] According to Cameron and Mingay it was the use until mid-century of 'milky' straw from milling wheat that led to the expansion of the straw-plaiting industry in this area, especially to the south-west

---

[96] A. Young, *General View of the Agriculture of Hertfordshire* (First published 1804, Facsimile Edn, Newton Abbot, 1971), pp. 73–75; G.E. Mingay (ed.), The *Agrarian History of England and Wales, Vol. 6, 1750–1850* (Cambridge, 1989), p. 281.

[97] Mingay, *Agrarian History*, pp. 512, 516.

[98] Mingay, *Agrarian History*, p. 834.

of Baldock and around Luton.[99]

In 1801, the population of Ashwell, the smallest of the four towns, was only 715 compared with the three larger towns which had very similar populations ranging from 1283 in Baldock to 1402 in Buntingford (Figure 01 above). Tony Wrigley has estimated that Hertfordshire's total population was stable at around 96,000 between 1761 and 1791, rising modestly to 102,000 by 1801.[100] Nineteenth-century census figures suggest that there was very little growth in the population of any of the four towns from 1801 to 1811. However, by 1851, Ashwell's population had doubled to 1425 while that of the three other towns had increased by approximately 50 per cent to range from 1920 in the case of Baldock to 2060 in both Buntingford and Royston. Forty years later, in 1891, the populations of Ashwell and Baldock had continued to rise more slowly to 1556 and 2301 respectively. In contrast, that of Buntingford (down 8.3 per cent) and Royston (down 17.5 per cent) had fallen to levels between that of the other two towns. Thus, despite their modest size and location in a largely agricultural region, these figures clearly do not support either Raven's or Lawton's idea of nineteenth-century 'decay'.[101]

After 1834 Buntingford (Plate 05 below) and Royston were centres of two Poor Law Unions and Rural Sanitary Authorities. Ashwell was part of the Royston Union and while Baldock came under the Hitchin Union it was itself an Urban Sanitary District until 1894.[102] Malting and brewing played an important part in the business communities of Ashwell, Baldock and Royston throughout the nineteenth century, greatly aided by changes in road transport and the dramatic arrival of the railways between 1850 and 1863.[103] As well as transporting fuel and raw materials to the nation's industrial centres they enabled these small towns' manufacturing enterprises to reach more easily a far wider market than previously possible. The railways were also the means by which mass-produced goods were distributed across Britain, leading to dramatic changes in retailing. These changes in the four towns' high streets, coupled with

---

[99] Cameron, 'Hertfordshire', p. 336; Mingay, *Agrarian History*, p. 858.

[100] E.A. Wrigley, 'English County Populations in the Later Eighteenth Century', *Economic History Review*, 60, 1 (2007), p. 54.

[101] See p. 7 above.

[102] *Post Office Directory Six Home Counties, 1851*, p. 183; *Post Office Directory Six Home Counties, 1862*, pp. 318, 319, 376; Place: Baldock Hertfordshire, Dept Geography, University of Portsmouth, www.visionofbritain.org.uk/place (17 April 2008).

[103] The Great Northern Railway's extension from Hitchin to Royston opened in October 1850. The line was extended to Shepreth in August 1851, coinciding with the completion by Eastern Counties Railway of the Shelford to Shepreth line, thus linking Hitchin to Cambridge; D.I. Gordon, *A Regional History of the Railways of Great Britain*. Vol. 5. *The Eastern Counties* (2nd edn, Newton Abbot, 1977), pp. 145-48.

Plate 05: Former Buntingford Union Workhouse

their specialist manufacturers' new ability to integrate into the wider national market, turned them into wealth-creating centres and extended the quartet's regional sphere of influence. Such success made them attractive to potential migrants who, because of the century's improved communications, were aware of the opportunities and able to reach them in order to offer their specialist skills and services. Analysis of the data presented here allows an examination of the changing nature of business and the rise of Walker's 'commercial and service occupations' in what had been a predominantly rural region of Hertfordshire.[104]

---

[104] J. Walker, *British Economic and Social History, 1700-1967* (London, 1968).

Part I

The provision of goods and services in nineteenth-century Hertfordshire

1

Analysing provision of goods and services

This chapter evaluates the potential use of commercial trade directories published from 1811 to 1890 and the decennial census enumerations from 1851 to 1891 as the two main sources of evidence for the nature and scale of the provision of goods and services in the four towns under consideration. It looks at the varied challenges arising from the combined utilization of these sources which, although originally designed for two very distinct purposes and possessing different strengths and weaknesses, do provide complementary information. It explores the benefits of maximising the amount of relevant data available for each individual by employing nominal record linkage techniques between directory and census data for the period 1851 to 1891 when both sources were available.

Value and potential limitations of the trade directory

From the latter part of the seventeenth century the motivation behind the development of trade directories, according to Gareth Shaw and Allison Tipper, was 'the driving force of commerce'. By the eighteenth century, the increased number and specialization of traders, together with wider geographical business links, 'created a new demand for informative literature on aspects of commerce and industry'.[1] Subsequently by the nineteenth-century, printed trade directories were essential reading for anyone engaged in business or commerce. For many historians, the directories provide an extremely valuable source of data relating to the occupations and activities of individually identified men, women, companies and public servants. While these publications are not totally comprehensive they do provide much information that is not available elsewhere in such a readily accessible form. Nevertheless, in order to establish a comprehensive picture of a town's business population, the contents of its directory listings must be analysed in conjunction with the evidence retrieved from other sources such as census data and any surviving original business records.

---

[1] G. Shaw and A. Tipper, *British Directories: A Bibliography and Guide to Directories Published in England and Wales (1850–1950) and Scotland (1773–1950)* (Leicester, 1989), p. 5.

A number of potentially problematic features of trade directories must be recognised. Methods employed to collect data varied according to the resources available but usually involved agents visiting houses and premises, or the sending or leaving of circulars to be filled in and collected later. Results, according to Shaw and Tipper, 'depended very much on the response and co-operation of the public and their willingness to provide information'. Charging traders for inclusion in a directory was never a great incentive, as Jane Norton's early example of Charles Pye's Birmingham directory clearly demonstrated. In 1800, his required payment of 6d for an entry resulted in only sixteen pages while a rival directory, compiled by house-to-house visits and with no charge for insertion, produced a ninety-six page listing.[2] Many canvassed, especially the uneducated, were suspicious of directory agents who they suspected were government employees. In 1880 a Plymouth publisher was forced to admit that the inhabitants were 'short in their replies to our agents' enquiries, having been pestered beyond enduring in the matter of directories'.[3] Publishers were constantly faced with the appearance of new trades and the problem of traders, especially grocers, pursuing more than one line of business at the same location. A trader could change from being listed as a grocer to tea dealer, provision dealer or just shopkeeper while frequently being a draper too. James Pigot tried the one category of 'Shopkeepers and Dealers in Groceries and Sundries' but others adopted multiple categories. Indeed Frederick Kelly, never one to miss an opportunity, offered 'to list the names of traders under more than one heading on payment of a fee'! [4]

Baldock provides a good example of this kind of confusion. In 1834 the town, according to Pigot, boasted nine 'grocers & dealers in sundries' but by 1851 Kelly listed eight plain 'grocers'. In 1882, Baldock had three unspecified 'shopkeepers' in addition to the five 'grocers' of whom one was also a 'provision dealer'. Kelly's directory of 1890 shows that of the seven 'grocers' four were 'drapers' of which two were also 'wine & spirit merchants'. A fifth 'grocer' was also listed as a 'baker', there was still one 'shopkeeper' and Baldock's first 'greengrocer' had opened for business.

In addition to listing traders in the towns under consideration, most directories also included important details of services offered by goods carriers and coach proprietors. Other individuals listed only by name under such headings as 'Gentry and Clergy' (before 1851) or 'Private residents' (1862 onwards) are

---

[2] J.E. Norton, *Guide to the National and Provincial Directories of England and Wales, Excluding London, Published Before 1856* (RHS Guides and Handbooks, No. 5, 1950), pp. 17–18.

[3] Eyre Brothers, *Post Office Plymouth Directory* (1880), cited in Shaw and Tipper, *British Directories*, p. 23.

[4] Shaw and Tipper, *British Directories*, p. 23.

excluded from this Hertfordshire study. However, entries associated with the officials of local public institutions contribute significantly to the understanding of the 'public and professional' sector. Buntingford and Royston were both centres of Poor Law Unions and from 1851 onwards their directory entries included increasing numbers of Union officials. In addition, Royston listings included officers of the County Court, the Association for the Prosecution of Felons and, from 1882, those of the Rural Sanitary Authority.[5]

These town or county directories, more usually known as trade or commercial directories were, Pryce argued, prime sources of data relating to local business people, professionals, holders of public office, and 'for tracing developments over time'.[6] This view was echoed by Edward Duggan who described Birmingham's business directories as 'perhaps the most fruitful source' for measuring change in the 'structure and composition' of the early nineteenth-century urban business community.[7]

On the other hand, the comprehensiveness of directories has frequently been questioned in relation to who was, or was not, included. Some traders, as Pryce observed, 'refused to allow their names to be included for fear of being recruited, unwittingly, into the county militia, or because it would give a competitor knowledge of their business activities!'. Others, they suggested, 'seem to have been concerned lest their tax liabilities were increased when their names had been published!'.[8] Many small firms might be excluded, argued Duggan, because they were part of larger enterprises, felt 'their business was strictly local', or 'they simply could not afford it'.[9]

Significant changes in content and format were most evident in general trade listings but it was not until 1814 that Pigot had finally achieved a national classified trade directory. Shortly afterwards, in 1817, Andrew Johnstone published a London directory that included trades arranged alphabetically with the names of persons engaged in each trade and a miscellaneous section covering details of postal, coach and waggon services. By 1841, Kelly's *Post Office Directory of London* had adopted Johnstone's format and, from 1845, in addition

[5] Certain traders' detailed advertisements were also included in specific sections of some directories but unfortunately the majority of such pages are lost from the bound copies held by HALS.

[6] Shaw and Tipper, *British Directories*, p. 33; W.T.R. Pryce, 'Using Written Sources: Some Key Examples, 1, Directories', in M. Drake and R. Finnegan (eds), *Studying Family and Community History: 19th and 20th Centuries, Vol. 4, Sources and Methods for Family and Community Historians: A Handbook* (2nd edn, Cambridge, 1999), p. 58.

[7] E.P. Duggan, 'Industrialization and the Development of Urban Business Communities: Research Problems, Sources and Techniques', *Local Historian*, 11, 8 (1975), p. 457.

[8] Pryce, 'Written Sources', p. 60.

[9] Duggan, 'Industrialization and Urban Business Communities', p. 458.

to names and addresses of 'chief/private' residents and traders, Kelly's provincial directories also contained 'sections on transport, local histories, maps and town plans, and a wide variety of advertisements'.[10] His first directory of Hertfordshire published in 1851 included entries for all four towns under consideration.[11] New editions of major directories, according to Dennis Mills, were 'published at the rate of about two or three a decade from c.1840 to c.1940'.[12]

The fact that directories were frequently re-published without careful correction and updating allowed errors to be perpetuated to the extent, as Stephen Porter warned, that 'the names of residents could still be listed some time after they had moved or died'.[13] This is a potential problem in record linkage between directories and Census Enumerators' Books (CEBs in subsequent discussion) and undoubtedly contributes to the number of directory entrants apparently missing from the corresponding census return. While acknowledging occasional misprints and misspellings in Wiltshire directories, Rogers had rarely found them 'so far from the correct form as to mislead'. For instance, in the town of Trowbridge, he found three traders listed as Coxdell, Dood and Rowling whom he recognised as being Cogswell, Dodd and Rawlings.[14] Some simple examples from the Hertfordshire directories included George Atkins (shopkeeper, Ashwell, 1870) who became Adkins (1882), William Lilley (baker, Royston, 1851) who became Lilly (1861), John Gaylor (watch and clockmaker, Buntingford, 1882) who became Gayler (1890) and James Newberry (insurance agent, Baldock, 1862) who became Newbury (1870).

Compilers of directories concentrated on the significant members of the local economy and important public servants. Directories 'were intended to appeal to those in commerce who needed to send goods and circulars out to persons of particular occupation and standing' and thus, according to Mills, excluded the 'ordinary working man' together with the majority of householders in any given community.[15] By concentrating on those people who ran their own businesses,

---

[10] Shaw and Tipper, *British Directories*, pp. 18, 20; James Pigot commenced a series of national directories in 1820. These were based upon regional surveys and published every six or seven years until 1853. By that time, Frederick Kelly's county and/or provincial *Post Office Directories*, first launched in 1836, were the clear market-leader. Kelly's dominant position was further enhanced by his acquisition of Pigot's entire publishing enterprise in 1853. Kelly's directories continued to be published well into the second half of the twentieth century.

[11] *Post Office Directory of the Six Home Counties: Essex, Herts, Middlesex, Kent, Surrey & Sussex, 1851* (London, 1851).

[12] D.R. Mills, *Rural Community History from Trade Directories: A Local Population Studies Supplement* (Aldenham, 2001), p. 11.

[13] S. Porter, *Exploring Urban History: Sources for Local Historians* (London, 1990), p. 70.

[14] K.H. Rogers (ed.), *Early Trade Directories of Wiltshire* (Wiltshire Record Society, Vol. 47, Trowbridge, 1992), p. xii.

[15] Mills, *Community History from Trade Directories*, pp. 13, 14.

directories published from 1851 onwards complement related data from census enumerators' books where the detail of whether a person was a master-craftsman, journeyman or apprentice was often omitted. Yet, 'the directories are silent', Mills observed, on the numbers employed by various businesses whereas between 1851 and 1881, census enumerators were instructed to record the numbers employed by masters.[16] Studying mid-nineteenth-century Ashby-de-la-Zouch, David Page illustrated some of Mills's general concerns and suggested that directories could be biased towards the higher-status trades. The two directories used covered the main streets but largely ignored the working-class districts and only included 'one third of the town's householders'. Using an 1861 Church Rate Book, Page showed that the majority 'were ratepayers and the higher the value of the land and houses they occupied, the more likely they were to be included' irrespective of their importance to potential directory users.[17] Determining entries on rateable value would exclude many shopkeepers in working-class areas, a problem noted by Gareth Shaw, because their shops 'were not rated as retail establishments since business was conducted from the front room of a house and consequently these were assessed as purely residential property'.[18]

Differences in terminology that various directories used to describe businesses, trades and occupations can present a particular problem in comparative studies. For instance, in his work on the silk manufacturing industry of some small towns in the south-west Pennines, Peter Wilde warned of the problems of terminology that 'varied quite considerably among the towns, despite their close proximity and broadly similar activities' and recommended, wherever possible, the use of the same publisher's directory for different places at a given time.[19] In his later study of three north Essex 'silk' towns, Neil Raven challenged this view that problems of terminology made it impossible to estimate the size of businesses in towns and villages during the nineteenth-century period of economic upheaval.[20]

A number of potential limitations to the accuracy of directories clearly exist: their coverage of a given community, the replication of errors, their focus on

---

[16] Mills, *Community History from Trade Directories*, p. 27.

[17] D. Page, 'Commercial Directories and Market Towns', *Local Historian*, 11, 2 (1974), pp. 87, 88. The two directories used were E.S. Drake and Co., *Commercial Directory of Leicestershire, 1861*, pp. 250 sqq. and William White, *History, Gazeteer and Directory of the Counties of Leicester and Rutland*, 1862, pp. 477 sqq.

[18] G. Shaw, 'The Content and Reliability of Nineteenth-century Trade Directories', *Local Historian*, 13, 4 (1978), pp. 206.

[19] P. Wilde, 'The Use of Business Directories in Comparing the Industrial Structure of Towns: An Example from the South-West Pennines', *Local Historian*, 12 (1976), p. 154. The term 'manufacturer' had quite different connotations for silk establishments in Leek compared to those of Macclesfield and Congleton.

[20] N. Raven, 'Trade Directories and Business Size: Evidence from the Small Towns of North Essex, 1851', *Local Historian*, 31, 2 (2001), pp. 83–94.

'important' people and problems of the occupational terminology employed. In fact, 'exclusive reliance on directories as a means of charting change in the pattern of economic activity' is, according to John Walton, 'always hazardous'. As a source, 'their use should be supplemented by whatever else happens to be available'; in his Oxfordshire study it was newspapers; in this particular case it is linkage to census data.[21]

Linkage between trade directories and other sources

It is important to note that occupational categories utilized by a directory publisher (often multiple for a given trader or service provider) differed considerably, for example, from those of a census enumerator's entries (usually just a single occupation) which were far more concerned with the status of a person's occupation as a means to classify the population by social class. Two of the limited number of systematic studies of late nineteenth-century rural craftsmen and tradesmen by Catherine Crompton ably demonstrate the value of linkage between sources. In the first of these, she claimed that 'very little conscious evaluation' of directories relative to census enumerators' books had been undertaken 'for the study of late nineteenth-century occupations in a rural context'.[22] Her study of thirty-one parishes in two contiguous areas around Stevenage and Buntingford in Hertfordshire included attempted nominal record linkage between the corresponding sources for 1850/51 and 1890/91 on the basis of matching parish names, individuals' names and occupations. Record linkage, she observed, provides important additional and sometimes completely different details of occupational information and 'exposes some of the duality' of occupation of individuals that would be missed by relying solely on one source. Crompton concluded that although directories should be 'treated with caution as sources for the detailed study of occupational structure at the level of the parish', they do nonetheless indicate 'employment status much more consistently' than census enumerators' books.[23] In her second study, Crompton explored the craft and trade structure of two Hertfordshire villages, Much Hadham and St Paul's Walden. Again using directories and census data between 1851 and 1891, she analysed the numbers of self-employed and master craftsmen, the numbers of

---

[21] J.R. Walton, 'Trades and Professions in Late 18th-Century England: Assessing the Evidence of Directories', *Local Historian*, 17, 6 (1987), pp. 343, 344.

[22] C.A. Crompton, 'Changes in Rural Service Occupations During the Nineteenth Century: An Evaluation of Two Sources for Hertfordshire, England', *Rural History*, 6, 2 (1995), p. 193.

[23] Crompton, 'Rural Service Occupations', pp. 201, 202.

traders, the size of enterprises, and continuity of occupation, ie whether or not substantial numbers of children continued in their family businesses.[24]

This larger regional study utilizes a technique, similar to that used by Crompton, of nominal record linkage between the PTPSs identified from directories and their corresponding census entries, but observes change over time by applying linkage to all five censuses between 1851 and 1891.[25]

Directories have enormous advantages as they are published far more frequently than the taking of the decennial census but the coverage of a particular town can vary from publisher to publisher in terms of comprehensiveness and descriptive vocabulary. Record linkage to the appropriate census helps overcome some errors and omissions that undoubtedly exist in directories but conversely, and very importantly for this Hertfordshire study, directories frequently provide additional occupational data and illuminating terminology that is totally ignored by the enumerator. For example, the enumerator described Daniel Smith of Ashwell in 1891 as simply a 'General Dealer & Shopkeeper' whereas his directory entry of 1890 had described him more specifically as a 'Beer retailer & Fruiterer'.[26] One other significant way that these two sources complement each other stems from the fact that while directories list the self-employed, master craftsmen and public servants, the census provides additional access to the 'ancillary traders, professionals and service providers', the 'ordinary' employed workers and apprentices.

The National Census

The first national census was taken in 1801. Others followed at ten year intervals in 1811, 1821 and 1831 but almost the only evidence that survives is the official population statistics published as Parliamentary Papers. Limited questions were asked in these early censuses and that, plus the lack of any centrally surviving detailed returns, means that gathering evidence for the early decades of the nineteenth century is reliant on trade directory entries alone for creating a picture of the four business communities. From 1841 onwards the census became the responsibility of the Registrar-General's office. Registration districts were set up to be co-extensive with the Poor Law unions of 1834. These were further sub-

---

[24] C.A. Crompton, 'An Exploration of the Craft and Trade Structure of Two Hertfordshire Villages, 1851–1891: An Application of Nominal Record Linkage to Directories and Census Enumerators' Books', *Local Historian*, 28, 3 (1998), pp. 145–58.
[25] Links were established between successive trade directories and CEBs as well as between the selected directories and the nearest chronologically matching census.
[26] 1891 Census (Ashwell); *Kelly's Directory of the Six Home Counties, Part 1: Essex, Herts & Middlesex* (London, 1890), p. 700.

divided into enumerator districts of an approximately standard size containing no more than about 200 inhabited houses.[27] This scheme remained largely unaltered until 1891 thus allowing for ease of comparison over the fifty-year period. The enumerators collected the previously distributed census forms, completed by each householder, the day after census night and then transcribed population numbers and associated socio-demographic information into standard Census Enumerators' Books which survive to this day.

The 1841 census was the first to gather information on each individual's occupation however its scope was limited in comparison to those from 1851 onwards. It ignored the occurrence of multiple occupations and details of birthplace, beyond whether it was in the same county as the person's current residence, and is thus of little use to this particular analysis. From 1851 onwards, answers to the standard questions provide the historian with the name of every individual, their marital status, sex, age, their relationship within the household (e.g. wife, lodger, apprentice or visitor), their rank, status or occupation, and parish of birth. Such a wealth of 'uniform and extensive detail' is, as Kate Tiller observed, ideal for the various sampling techniques, computer storage and data analysis exploited extensively within this particular survey.[28] Enumerators' books supplement the use of trade directories by enabling the identification of those individuals engaged in business or the professions but not listed in a directory. Furthermore, they provide additional occupational data plus details of age, status and geographical origin that directories do not cover but which are crucial to this project. One important difference between the two sources which needs to be taken into consideration if seeking to apply record linkage between them lies in their treatment of addresses. Both identify street names, the directory providing the business address of the individual and the census providing the individual's home address which, for some, is the same in both sources.

Although frequently analysed, census occupational data from the CEB column headed 'Rank, Profession, or Occupation', in the view of Dennis Mills and Kevin Schurer, 'contains the most conceptually complex entries'. There are differences between the frequent 'minimum response' and the occasional multi-occupational details, provided by conscientious householders and enumerators, in addition to the 'relative lack of information about part-time workers, notably married women and young people residing with their parents'.[29] Inconsistencies between

---

[27] E. Higgs, *Making Sense of the Census Revisited: Census Records for England and Wales, 1801–1901: A Handbook for Historical Researchers* (London, 2005), p. 15.

[28] K. Tiller, *English Local History: An Introduction* (Stroud, 1992), p. 229.

[29] D.R. Mills and K. Schurer, 'Communities in the Victorian Censuses: An Introduction', in D.R. Mills and K. Schurer (eds), *Local Communities in the Victorian Census Enumerators' Books* (Oxford, 1996), p. 8.

occupational data from different sources led Mills and Schurer to speculate that 'directory entries will be fuller than census entries' because of the need for directory entrants to advertise the whole range of their services.[30] The case of William Dear in 1851 clearly supports their speculation. According to the census Dear, of Middle Row, Baldock, was just a 'victualler' but his directory entry of the same year lists him as ' *"Plume of Feathers"*, ironmonger, hairdresser & insurance agent (Farmers' Fire & Life & General Hail Storm Company) and Assessor & Collector of Taxes'.[31]

Attempting to define an occupation and work is, Edward Higgs suggested, confused by what constitutes 'domestic' and 'business' activities in the homes of retailers and small businesses where 'the help of the servant, wife, or children was indispensable'.[32] Between 1851 and 1871 a wife who assisted her husband would appear, for example, as a butcher's wife or shoemaker's wife but, noted Joyce Bellamy, 'no account was taken in the nineteenth century of differences between place of work and place of residence'.[33] Between 1851 and 1881, the census schedules' question relating to occupation changed little. However, the three extremely useful occupational status columns of 'employer', 'employed' and 'neither employer nor employed' were used first in the census of 1891. It was not until 1901 that individuals were asked whether they worked at home or elsewhere.

The massive volume of data compiled by the nineteenth-century enumerators ensures, as Mills claimed, that 'the census is undoubtedly the most important source' for community historians of the nineteenth century.[34] While it is true that the overwhelming majority of the population will appear somewhere in a given census, for a variety of reasons they will not necessarily all be at their normal place of residence. Because of those absent from home on each census night, for business or various personal reasons, it is not possible from the evidence gathered here to gain a complete picture of the towns' business communities from CEBs alone. Hence the importance of utilising other suitable sources such as trade directories.

---

[30] D.R. Mills and K. Schurer, 'Employment and Occupations', in Mills and Schurer, *Local Communities*, p. 137.

[31] 1851 Census (Baldock); *Post Office Directory Six Home Counties, 1851*, pp. 172-73.

[32] E. Higgs, 'The Tabulation of Occupations in the Nineteenth-century Census, with Special Reference to Domestic Servants', in Mills and Schurer, *Local Communities*, p. 35.

[33] J.M. Bellamy, 'Occupation Statistics in the Nineteenth Century Censuses', in R. Lawton (ed.), *The Census and Social Structure: An Interpretative Guide to Nineteenth-century Censuses for England and Wales* (London, 1978), pp. 169, 173.

[34] D. Mills, 'Using Sources: The Census, 1801–1991', in Drake and Finnegan, *Family and Community History, Vol. 4, Sources and Methods*, p. 25.

Data for small towns of north-east Hertfordshire

For the purposes of analysing the business communities of the towns under consideration, data regarding manufacturers, dealers, retailers, members of the professional classes and public officials have been extracted from trade directories available at the Hertfordshire Archives and Local Studies (HALS) centre and used to create a series of searchable databases.[35] For the period between 1811 and 1890 directories were selected, depending on their actual date of publication, at approximately ten-year intervals with the additional aim, from 1851 onwards, of providing the nearest chronological match to the decennial census returns (Figure 1.1 below). In practice, between 1851 and 1891, the trade directories utilised were published either in the same year as the census or just one year earlier or later.

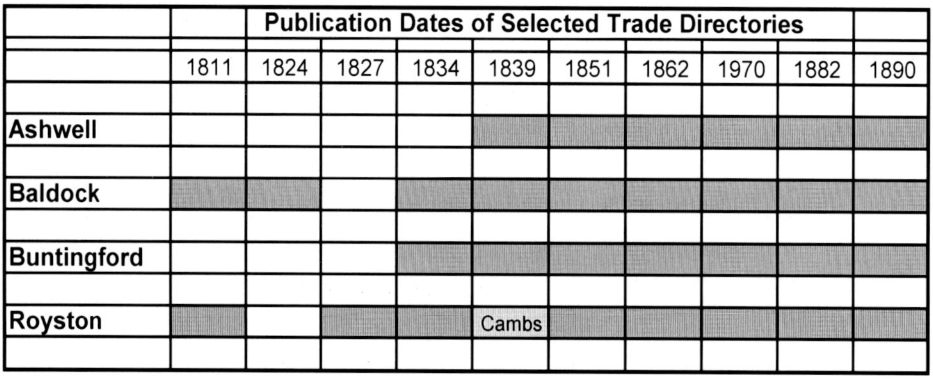

		Publication Dates of Selected Trade Directories									
		1811	1824	1827	1834	1839	1851	1862	1970	1882	1890
Ashwell						▓	▓	▓	▓	▓	▓
Baldock		▓	▓		▓	▓	▓	▓	▓	▓	▓
Buntingford					▓	▓	▓	▓	▓	▓	▓
Royston		▓		▓	▓	Cambs	▓	▓	▓	▓	▓

Figure 1.1: Coverage of selected Hertfordshire trade directories

The patchy coverage relating to the four towns during the first half of the nineteenth century was obviously a problem in the selected sample of directories. Only Baldock and Royston featured in Holden's directory of 1811.[36] Baldock alone was covered in Pigot's initial directory of 1824; Royston appeared in his second edition of 1827.[37] By 1834, Baldock, Buntingford and Royston all had

---

[35] These EXCEL databases have four searchable data fields: Surname, Other Names, Directory Occupational Heading(s) and Address.

[36] *Holden's Annual London and County Directory of the United Kingdom and Wales in Three Volumes for the Year 1811, Vol. 3* (London, 1811), un-paginated.

[37] *Pigot and Co.'s Commercial Directory for 1823–24, Hertfordshire* (London, 1824), pp. 349-50; *Pigot and Co.'s Commercial Directory for 1826–27, Hertfordshire* (London, 1827), pp. 575-77.

entries in Pigot's Hertfordshire directory.[38] Ashwell, probably because its population was considerably smaller than the other three towns between 1801 and 1851, did not feature in any of these early directories. It first appeared in Pigot's 1839 publication but then only under the heading of Baldock. This 1839 edition, covering Essex, Hertfordshire and Middlesex, omitted Royston whose data Pigot chose to locate in the Cambridgeshire directory for that year.[39] From 1851, the selected directories all had separate listings for Ashwell, Baldock, Buntingford and Royston.[40]

Year	Ashwell	Baldock	Buntingford	Royston
1811	-	68	-	63
1823/4	-	97	-	-
1826/7	-	-	-	134
1833/4	-	118	87	149
1839	35	125	87	140
1851	59	103	97	160
1862	70	136	103	201
1870	72	142	107	189
1882	82	149	87	204
1890	88	140	95	218
Total	406	1078	663	1458

Table 1.1: Numbers of PTPSs identified from trade directories
Source: Holden's Directory, 1811; Pigot's Directories, 1823–4, 1826–7, 1833–4, 1839; Post Office Directories, 1851, 1862, 1870; Kelly's Directories, 1882, 1890.

A total of 3605 identified individuals (Table 1.1 above), frequently employers of others, are considered to be PTPSs of the local economy. Examination of the

---

[38] *Pigot and Co.'s Commercial Directory & Topography of Hertfordshire, 1833–34* (London, 1834), pp. 726–27, 730–31, 752-54.

[39] *Pigot and Co.'s Royal National and Commercial Directory and Topography of the Counties of Essex, Hertfordshire, Middlesex* (London, 1839), pp. 94–96, 100-101; *Pigot & Co.'s Directory for 1839, Cambridgeshire* (London, 1839), pp. 65-68. At this time, the town of Royston was administratively, partly in Cambridgeshire and partly in Hertfordshire, being 'situated partly in Armingford hundred in Cambridgeshire, and the chief portion in the hundred of Odsey, Hertfordshire', as Pigot & Co.'s 1830 National Commercial Directory of Bedfordshire, Huntingdonshire, Cambridgeshire, Lincolnshire, Northamptonshire had explained.

[40] *Post Office Directory of the Six Home Counties: Essex, Herts, Middlesex, Kent, Surrey & Sussex, 1851* (London, 1851), pp. 170–73, 184–85, 215-17; *Post Office Directory of the Six Home Counties: Essex, Herts, Middlesex, Kent, Surrey & Sussex, 1862* (London, 1862), pp. 318–21, 334–35, 376-79; E.R. Kelly (ed.), *Post Office Directory of the Six Home Counties, Part I: Essex, Herts, Middlesex, Kent* (London, 1870), pp. 408–12, 428–29, 476-79; E.R. Kelly (ed.), *Kelly's Directory of the Six Home Counties, Part I: Essex, Herts & Middlesex* (London, 1882), pp. 560–64, 585–86, 646-50; *Kelly's Directory of the Six Home Counties, Part I: Essex, Herts & Middlesex* (London, 1890), pp. 699–704, 731–32, 806-10.

census returns between 1851 and 1891, provided additional and sometimes different occupational data on the PTPSs and also identified 550 other such individuals, relevant to this data-set, but not listed in the directories (Table 1.2 below). These included, for example, farmers, publicans, schoolteachers, those identified as 'master' or 'mistress' craftsmen and women, and those listed as employing others. A second series of searchable databases was created merging the initial directory data with that extracted from the CEBs.[41]

Year	Ashwell	Baldock	Buntingford	Royston
1851	16	21	28	57
1861	30	18	18	38
1871	19	39	11	34
1881	15	27	28	40
1891	16	25	25	45
Total	96	130	110	214

Table 1.2: Additional PTPSs identified from CEBs
Source: Census enumerations, 1851–1891.

Additionally, the inclusion in a further series of databases of other self-employed skilled and semi-skilled workers identified from the CEBs provides an aggregated picture of 2937 individuals, the ATPSs, largely representing the non-labouring employees of the study towns' workforces (Table 1.3 below).

Year	Ashwell	Baldock	Buntingford	Royston
1851	60	158	116	230
1861	54	147	113	228
1871	73	141	119	232
1881	74	162	138	214
1891	98	173	168	239
Total	359	781	654	1143

Table 1.3: ATPSs and others identified from CEBs
Source: Census enumerations, 1851–1891.

---

[41] This second set of EXCEL databases has six searchable data fields: Surname, Other Names, Directory Occupational Heading(s), Census Occupation(s), Address, Census Age/Geographical Origin. In addition, comments were attached to the Age/Origin field giving marital and familial details. This latter information, providing evidence of possible migratory pathways as suggested by an individual's geographical origin and a number of different birthplaces for their children, is discussed in Chapter 4.

An additional investigation of the geographical origins and migratory pathways of 'incomers' to the four towns was carried out by determining the details of their birthplace, together with that of their husband or wife and those of their children, listed by the census enumerators.

Analytical methodology

Names and details of occupations for around 7000 traders, retailers, skilled and semi-skilled workers, apprentices, and members of the professional classes were identified from nineteenth-century commercial trade directories and CEBs. As far as possible nominal record linkage was established between the two sources utilising data from the five censuses held between 1851 and 1891. It should be noted that because of their large numbers, for the purposes of this analysis, the labouring and domestic service sectors of the towns' workforces were excluded.

The thrust of the evidence presented made it necessary to devise an appropriate scheme for the classification of occupations, as identified from both CEBs and trade directories, which reflected nineteenth-century changes in the type of service and/or product being provided, irrespective of the social background of the provider. Most schemes have utilized or elaborated upon classifications devised by successive Registrars General since T.H.C. Stevenson's initial attempt of 1911.[42] However, all such breakdowns are heavily orientated towards a classification based on a hierarchical class and social structure, as exemplified by the work of both Banks and Bellamy.[43] The classification chosen here was largely based on the scheme devised by Charles Booth and provides a non-hierarchical framework for determining the anatomy of a town's business community (details provided in Appendix 1).[44]

From its inception, meaningful [economic] analysis of census data was, Alan Armstrong argued, dependent on distinguishing between individuals' occupations, as entered by the enumerators, and their employment in particular manufacturing or service industries. An individual's occupation was seen by many in Victorian

---

[42] T.H.C. Stevenson, 'Review of the Vital Statistics of the Year, 1911', *Seventy-fourth Annual Report of the Registrar General of Births, Deaths and Marriages in England and Wales, 1911* (HMSO, London, 1913).

[43] Bellamy, 'Occupation Statistics', pp. 165 - 77; J.A. Banks, 'The Social Structure of Nineteenth Century England as Seen Through the Census', in Lawton, *Census and Social Structure*, pp. 179–223.

[44] C. Booth, 'Occupations of the People of the United Kingdom, 1801–81', from a paper delivered in London to The Statistical Society on 18 May 1886, reproduced in G. Routh, *Occupations of the People of Great Britain, 1801–1981, with a Compendium of a Paper 'Occupations of the People of the United Kingdom, 1801–81' by Charles Booth* (London, 1987), pp. 1–17.

society as an indicator of that person's proper place in the social hierarchy. To others however, identification of the particular industry was the more useful economic variable. From 1841 the census office produced occupational abstracts which attempted to group occupations according to a set of defined rules. After the 1851 census the abstracts provided a system of seventeen classes, or orders, and ninety-one sub-classes that were meant to accommodate the 'many thousands of occupations originally stated in the census enumerators' books'.[45]

Though these nineteenth-century census occupational categories were roughly aligned to the prevailing industrial groups, they were, according to Armstrong, 'not without social-class overtones (in that the average level of prestige of some occupational orders was clearly higher than that of others)'. After 1911, highly specific distinctions were made to fit occupations to the Registrar-General's five-class scheme of social classification: I, Professional; II, Intermediate; III, Skilled; IV, Partly skilled; V, Unskilled. This present analysis, by opting for a scheme based on that of Charles Booth, reflects Armstrong's view that, in the absence of systematic enquiries 'into the individual's field of employment', historians cannot use a modern industrial classification to make sense of nineteenth-century data.[46]

It was Booth's seminal paper published in 1886 that in Armstrong's opinion 'set out to restate the census information in "a more uniform and accessible shape", having regard "less to occupation as such than to the industries within which people worked", so far as the nature of the information allowed'.[47] To achieve this, he summarised the working population under nine major industrial divisions with fifty-one sub-divisions. This project's trade directory data for the period between 1839 and 1890 was accordingly analysed using eight of Booth's major categories (see Appendix 1). Booth added two other categories that are outside the scope of this project, 'property-owning/independent' and 'indefinite', the latter of which he called 'a meaningless remainder'. The scheme of classification adopted here incorporates two additional relevant modifications derived from the scheme of classification used by Carr-Saunders, Jones and Moser in their work on the census of 1931 and 1941. It adds 'communications' to 'transport' and 'distributive trades' to 'dealing'.[48] It is, as Armstrong observed, much more difficult in the nineteenth century to distinguish accurately between manufacturer

---

[45] W.A. Armstrong, 'The Use of Information about Occupations', in E.A. Wrigley (ed.), *Nineteenth-century Society: Essays in the Use of Quantitative Methods for the Study of Social Data* (Cambridge, 1972), p. 194.

[46] Armstrong, 'Information about Occupations', p. 195, 227.

[47] C. Booth, 'Occupations of the People of the United Kingdom, 1801-81', *Journal of the Statistical Society*, XLIX (1886), pp. 314–444, cited in Armstrong, 'Information about Occupations', p. 229.

[48] A.M. Carr-Saunders, D.C. Jones and C.A. Moser, *Survey of Social Conditions in England and Wales* (Oxford, 1958), p. 92, cited in Armstrong, 'Information about Occupations', p. 227.

and retailer when many people were clearly both.[49] While Booth's 'dealing' sector listed drapers, hosiers, haberdashers and hatters, he placed boot and shoemakers, tailors, milliners and dressmakers under manufacture. Similarly, while butchers, grocers and fruiterers were listed under 'dealing', bakers and confectioners were placed under manufacture. For the purposes of this study, all such relatively small-scale, small-town, manufacturing retailers are placed under 'dealing and distributive trades'.

One major complication of any analysis of nineteenth-century trade directory or census enumerators' data is that of apparent dual or multiple occupations. Mills attributed this phenomenon to a lack of specialisation by many craftsmen who, unable to live by the fruits of a single craft, 'combined this with small-scale farming, or with another often related craft, or with a retail trade'.[50] Mills to this extent agreed with Collins who, in exploring business diversity outside urban areas, had analysed data from Sun Insurance records between 1821 and 1822 and found that sixty-five (59.1%) out of 110 millers had second occupations.[51]

CEBs, argued Matthew Woollard, are 'the only source of representative individual-level [multi-occupational] data', as the [1881] enumerators 'asked respondents explicitly to list more than one occupation if they followed more than one distinct occupation'. Woollard cautioned that directories by contrast might be 'biased' towards exaggeration of dual occupations as entrants listed 'as many as possible to gain maximum custom' a perfectly proper ploy, one would think, since to advertise a product or service that you could not actually provide would rapidly destroy your credibility.[52]

Any analysis, including that presented in this volume, requires an 'operational definition of a multiple occupation' and in the case of Woollard's survey he identified five different categories.[53] His first category, exemplified here by William Gordon, a 'Wine & Spirit Merchant' in Royston (1862), John Gayler, a Buntingford 'Watch & Clockmaker' (1870) and John Skelton of Ashwell, 'Chemist & Druggist' (1882), are in fact single occupations.[54] Woollard's second category of related occupations includes the likes of Arundel Hoye, a 'Plumber &

---

[49] Armstrong, 'Information about Occupations', p.231.

[50] Mills, *Community History from Trade Directories*, p. 22.

[51] E.J.T. Collins, 'Introduction to Chapter 5, The Agricultural Servicing and Processing Industries', in G.E. Mingay (ed.), *The Agrarian History of England and Wales, Vol. 6, 1750–1850* (Cambridge, 1989), p. 393.

[52] M. Woollard, 'The Classification of Multiple Occupational Titles in the 1881 Census of England and Wales', *Local Population Studies*, 72 (2004), pp. 36, 34.

[53] Woollard, 'Multiple Occupational Titles', p. 37.

[54] *Post Office Directory Six Home Counties, 1862*, p. 377; *Post Office Directory Six Home Counties, Pt 1* (1870), p. 429; *Kelly's Directory Six Home Counties, Pt 1* (1882), p. 561.

Glazier' in Baldock (1871) and Alfred Patterson also of Baldock, 'Saddler & Harness Maker' (1891). In the former case both services require working with lead while in the latter both products utilise leather and would have been produced on the same premises. Here such examples are treated as a single occupation.[55] The third category of people like Charles Andrews, an 'Ironmonger & Upholsterer' from Royston (1851), George Christy, an Ashwell 'Grocer & Draper' (1871) and Charles Miles, 'Hair Dresser & Beer Retailer' in Buntingford (1890) clearly have distinct dual occupations within the same broad class.[56] Woollard's fourth and fifth categories cover more disparate combinations such as 'stone mason and grocer' and ambiguous entries such as 'retired grocer and baker' or 'grocer and farmer's wife'.

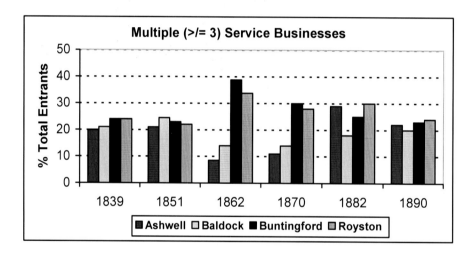

Figure 1.2: Proportion (%) entrants offering dual or multiple services
Source: Pigot's Directory, 1839; Post Office Directories, 1851, 1862, 1870; Kelly's Directories, 1882, 1890.

Overall, the data from the Hertfordshire directories (Figure 1.2 above) shows that the general level of dual or multiple occupations was running at between 15 and 30 per cent of the listed craftsmen between 1839 and 1890. Unusually low levels occurred in Ashwell in 1862 and 1870 (8.5 and 11.0 per cent respectively) and unusually high levels in Buntingford (38.8 per cent) and Royston (33.8 per cent) in 1862. Data for PTPSs listed with three or more occupations (Figure 1.3 below) show that Baldock and Royston generally had levels significantly higher than

---

[55] 1871 Census (Baldock); 1891 Census (Baldock).

[56] *Post Office Directory Six Home Counties, 1851,* p. 215; 1871 Census (Ashwell); *Kelly's Directory Six Home Counties, Pt 1* (1890), p. 65.

those found in Ashwell with the exception of 1839 when the latter's figure was 8.6 per cent. Buntingford's figures, while more in line with those of Baldock and Royston, were more volatile, with figures of 0.9 per cent in 1851 and 16.5 per cent in 1862. A limited number of people offered an amazing multiplicity of services. In 1870, for example, Henry Routledge of Baldock was listed as a draper, grocer, insurance agent for the 'Liverpool & London & Globe Fire & Life' company, a sub-distributor of stamps and a wine merchant.[57] In 1882, similarly, Joseph Clayton of Buntingford was a draper, fruiterer, furniture

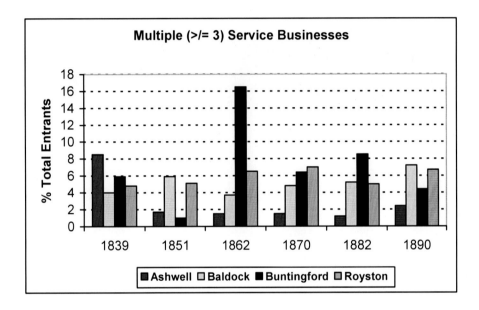

Figure 1.3: Proportion (%) directory entrants offering multiple services
Source: Pigot's Directory, 1839; Post Office Directories, 1851, 1862, 1870; Kelly's Directories, 1882, 1890.

dealer, ironmonger, glass and china dealer, and stationer.[58] In 1890, in Royston, the Warren brothers were bookbinders and engravers, booksellers and stationers, circulating librarians, music sellers, newsagents, printers and publishers, and stamp distributors.[59]

Davies, Giggs and Herbert cited further problems of double-entry listings where, for example, the same retailer has branches at different addresses, or people in

---

[57] *Post Office Directory Six Home Counties, Pt I* (1870), pp. 411–12.
[58] *Kelly's Directory of Six Home Counties, Pt I* (1882), p. 586.
[59] *Kelly's Directory of Six Home Counties, Pt I* (1890), p. 810.

partnerships are listed together and as individuals, or public houses are listed under both their names and that of the licensee.[60] These problems, warned Pryce, 'can result in more services being attributed to a particular town than, in reality, it discharged'.[61] Such entries, however, were not a feature of the Hertfordshire directories examined here. In contrast to directory entrants, only thirty-nine (7.2 per cent) of the 545 additional PTPSs identified from CEBs, had dual roles indicated by the enumerator; twelve of these were in Baldock, eleven each in Ashwell and Royston, and only five in Buntingford. Unlike several of the directory entrants, there were no cases identified from the CEBs of individual PTPSs with multiple roles.

Problem of trade directory entrants missing in CEBs

Record linkage failed to locate in the corresponding census returns a surprisingly high proportion of PTPSs listed in the trade directories. The average proportion of PTPSs missing from the CEBs between 1851 and 1891 was 15.6 per cent in Ashwell, 24.8 per cent in Baldock, 28.0 per cent in Buntingford and 31.5 per cent

Combined Figures for Ashwell, Baldock, Buntingford and Royston			
Directory Year	Census Year (Difference)	Missing Entrants	% Directory Entrants
1851	1851 (0)	66	15.8
1862	1861 (-1)	118	23.1
1870	1871 (+1)	115	22.5
1882	1881 (-1)	123	23.6
1890	1891 (+1)	151	27.9
	Total = 573		

Table 1.4: Directory PTPS entrants absent from CEBs, 1851-1891
Source: Census enumerations, 1851–1891.

in Royston. There are several possible reasons for this observation. The total of 667 missing PTPSs included ninety-four women (14.0 per cent), most of whom were listed in the directories as schoolmistresses, dressmakers and milliners. Given that the majority of these women were probably quite young, they have been excluded from Table 1.4 above as, in addition to other possible explanations

---

[60] W.K.D. Davies, J.A. Giggs and D.T. Herbert, 'Directories, Rate Books and the Commercial Structure of Towns', *Geography*, 53 (1968), p. 42.
[61] Pryce, 'Written Sources', p. 61.

for their absence from the CEBs, they may have recently married and changed their surname.

There is no particular pattern of differentiation between the missing PTPSs of the four towns (See Figure 1.4 below). Apart from the 5.1 per cent for Ashwell in 1851, these levels of exclusion from the census are surprisingly high when

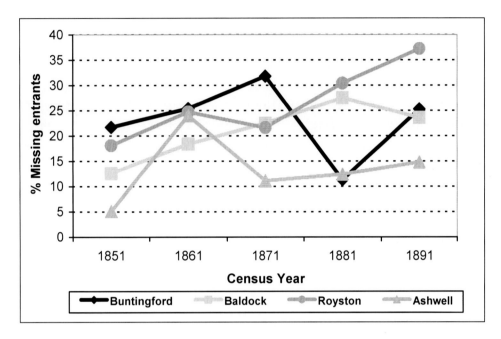

Figure 1.4: Proportion of directory PTPSs (male) missing from CEBs
Source: Census enumerations, 1851-1891.

compared with other dual source studies. For example, in a comparison between electoral registers and the census, Sarah Richardson allowed only 2.0 per cent of the total for deaths per annum and 4.0 per cent for removals.[62]

For the purposes of the census a 'household' was defined as only those persons, including visitors, who were actually present in a house on the night of the census. Thus the simplest explanation for not finding a directory entrant is that on census night they were away on business or perhaps visiting a friend or relative. Another explanation is that some individuals and households were simply missed. Such omissions, according to Edward Higgs, 'might reflect clerical error' or 'it might have been difficult for hard-pressed enumerators to ensure that they had

---

[62] S. Richardson, 'Independence and Deference: A Study of the West Riding Electorate, 1832–1841' (PhD thesis, University of Leeds, 1995), pp. 88-89.

handed a household schedule to every family'. There is little quantitative data for Victorian Britain although Higgs notes that 'preliminary studies in the USA suggest that approximately 15 per cent of [eligible] adults were omitted' in their mid-nineteenth-century censuses.[63]

One must assume that entrants listed in a specific town's trade directory actually had a commercial, professional or public service interest in that town. However, a reason for not appearing in that town's census return might have been that, despite that interest, they lived somewhere else.

A further complicating factor of the evidence presented here is that the selected directories were sometimes published either one year before or one year after the nearest census. Taking the case of Ashwell for example (See Table 1.5 below), it is possible that those 'missing' directory entrants who made their first or only

Characteristic	Number	% Missing Entrants
Single Directory entry	26	44.1
In previous Census	13	22.0
In later Census	7	11.9
Previous Census & later Directory	1	1.7
In previous Directory	4	6.8
In later Directory	6	10.2
In previous & later Directory	2	3.4
Total	**59**	

Table 1.5: Features of Ashwell's missing directory entrants, 1851–1891
Source: Trade directories, 1851–1890 and census enumerations, 1851-1891.

appearance in the editions of 1862 (15 individuals) and 1882 (8 individuals) may not have arrived in Ashwell before the 1861 and 1881 enumerations. Similarly, those 'missing' directory entrants found in the editions of 1870 (5 individuals) and 1890 (12 individuals) may have left Ashwell or died by 1871 and 1891.

While Kelly's Directory does indicate that Thomas Shell, Clerk to the Ashwell School Board, lived in Royston, an electronically searchable version of the 1881 census was utilized in an attempt to elicit some of the other reasons for the apparent non-appearance of Ashwell directory entrants in that census.[64] Three

---

[63] E. Higgs, *Making Sense of the Census Revisited*, pp. 117, 118.
[64] CJCLDS, *Family History Resources Files, V. 2.0, 1881 British Census* (Salt Lake City, 1999).

others were absent from the census for Ashwell because they actually lived in another enumeration area. The 'Station House' lived in by Charles Moss, Ashwell's Station Master, was by the station situated in the nearby parish of Steeple Morden. Herbert George Fordham, an accountant and manager at Fordham's Brewery in Ashwell, lived at Odsey in the adjoining parish of Guilden Morden. Charles Nash, a directory listed farmer of 1200 acres, lived in Melbourn Street, Royston. A further three had not been retrieved in the census because their occupations differed from those given in the trade directory. William Bonfield, Benjamin Covington and William Evans all listed as beer retailers in the directory, appeared as an agricultural labourer, a farm labourer and a coal merchant's labourer respectively in the census. These census occupations were outside the scope of this study. Finally, three other 'missing' entrants, Jane Don and Annie Turner, two schoolmistresses, and Chester Webb, a beer retailer, were not located in the electronic version of the census.

Conclusion

The foregoing dual approach of utilizing nineteenth-century trade directories and census returns as complementary sources for the analysis of business communities is one that should commend itself to other historians. The methodology is not without its problems. In the case of directories, these include the question of their comprehensiveness, the problem of re-publishing data without careful editing and updating, the emphasis only on people running their own businesses, and the total lack of data regarding numbers of employees. In the case of the census, the enumerators frequently provide only minimal employment details, largely ignore working women, provide variable details of the numbers employed by businesses, and frequently misspell or phonetically corrupt an individual's birthplace. This present approach provides considerable evidence regarding the roles of working women in addition to highlighting the problems associated with such an analysis. Above all, this Hertfordshire data-set contained a significant number of business people listed in trade directories that were missing from the census.

In spite of these limitations, this methodology offers an effective means of comparing a number of parameters relating to the provision of goods and services in urban centres. Use of nominal record linkage between trade directories and CEBs effectively manages the limitations of both sources to fully identify those individuals with multiple occupations. It allows the present analysis to distinguish clearly between 'principal' and 'ancillary' provision of goods and services, and to assess the four study towns' potential role as central places (chapter four) within the regional economy of north-east Hertfordshire.

2

The changing face of business

Subsequent to the identification of almost 4200 PTPSs the following in-depth analysis of their occupations facilitates the exploration of the changing nature of business and service provision between 1811 and 1891 in the four towns under consideration. In so doing, it allows for a reappraisal of the widespread assumption among many urban historians that by the second half of the nineteenth century successful seventeenth and eighteenth-century small market towns in rural areas had either experienced a reduced level of demand for goods and services by a declining population and 'failed', reverting to the status of villages, or had grown substantially due to industrialization.

Each of the four centres had a population below 2000 for most of the nineteenth century, well below many urban historians' threshold for small towns. However, this analysis supports an appraisal of Robert Dickinson's argument that the status of 'small town' is fundamentally a question of the nature and range of functions within it rather than the size of its population.[1] In particular, it focuses on the men and women of the 'tertiary service sector', including traders, retailers, members of the professions and public servants, as distinct from primary agricultural and secondary manufacturing and construction activities. Evidence of local change and innovation in transportation, communications, finance and distribution, as Mark Thomas suggested, might indicate the integration of such small towns as Ashwell, Baldock, Buntingford and Royston into the developing national market.[2]

Early C19th provision of goods and services

It is difficult to reconstruct the economy of the chosen towns before 1851 in as much detail as is possible for the second half of the nineteenth century. In terms of their geographical coverage and depth of content trade directories were still expanding during these early decades while only aggregated tabular reports,

---

[1] R.E. Dickinson, 'The Distribution and Functions of the Smaller Urban Settlements of East Anglia', *Geography*, 17 (1932), p. 20.
[2] M. Thomas, 'The Service Sector', in R. Floud and P. Johnson (eds), *The Cambridge Economic History of Modern Britain, Vol. II: Economic Maturity, 1860–1939* (Cambridge, 2004), pp. 100, 132.

which contained no individual occupational details, exist for the four decennial censuses conducted between 1801 and 1831. Here the 1841 census, 'a rather *ad hoc* affair' according to Edward Higgs, has been excluded as 'very much a transitional stage' to the 'mature Victorian censuses from 1851 onwards'.[3]

Due to the lack of any available directory data for Ashwell before 1839 and for Buntingford before 1833/34 a direct comparison of the provision of goods and services in the four towns at the beginning of the nineteenth century is only possible between Baldock and Royston.[4] The early directories indicate a dramatic increase in the number of listed entrants between 1811 and 1833/34, up from 61 to 144 (136 per cent growth) in the case of Royston and from 68 to118 (73.5 per cent growth) in the case of Baldock (Figure 2.1 below). It could be argued that these changes reflect different approaches by the two publishers: William Holden

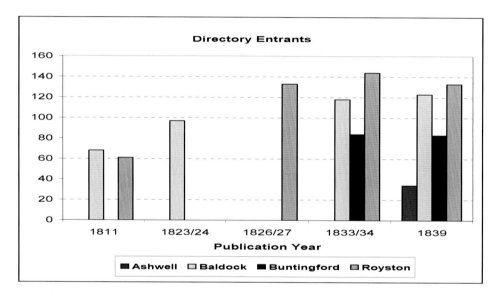

Figure 2.1: Number of directory entrants, 1811–1839
Source: Holden's Directory, 1811; Pigot's Directories,
1823–24, 1826–27, 1833–34, 1839.

---

[3] E.Higgs, *Making Sense of the Census Revisited: Census Records for England and Wales, 1801-1901: A Handbook for Historical Researchers* (London, 2005), p. 11.

[4] *Holden's Annual London and County Directory of the United Kingdom and Wales in Three Volumes for the Year 1811, Vol. 3* (London, 1811), un-paginated (Baldock & Royston); *Pigot's Commercial Directory for 1823-24, Hertfordshire* (London, 1824), pp. 349-50 (Baldock); *Pigot's Commercial Directory for 1826-27, Hertfordshire* (London, 1827), pp. 575-77 (Royston); *Pigot's Commercial Directory & Topography of Hertfordshire, 1833-34* (London, 1834), pp. 726-27, 752-54 (Baldock & Royston).

in 1811; James Pigot in 1826/27 and 1833/34. Additionally, one could reason that an increase is to be expected, given that these huge increases in the number of entrants occurred over a similar period of time in which Baldock's population grew to 1704 (up 18.5 per cent) and Royston's to 1757 (up 34.2 per cent) by the time of the 1831 census. Such increases in the population of small towns at this time have been noted by many other historians including Marshall, who expressed little doubt that 'Cumbria's main market centres grew considerably ... between about 1740 and 1830' owing to large-scale inward migration from their surrounding rural hinterlands.[5] Expressed as a percentage of total population (using figures from the 1811 and 1831 census) the listed PTPSs grew from 4.7 per cent in both towns to 6.9 per cent in Baldock and 8.2 per cent in Royston. Thus it seems likely that during this time either the size of these two towns' economies expanded or PTPSs came to recognise the opportunities afforded them by having entries published in trade directories, or both effects played a part.

Pigot featured Buntingford for the first time in his 1833/34 directory with a total of 84 entrants; at only 4.3 per cent of the total population (1962 in the 1831 census) this represents a level similar to those found in Baldock and Royston back in 1811. An initial reluctance on the part of Buntingford's PTPSs seems an unlikely explanation as the proportion based on the 1841 census figure remained virtually unchanged at 4.1 per cent in the 1839 edition of Pigot's directory. Entries finally appear for 'the village of Ashwell and neighbourhoods' with 34 people, just 2.8 per cent of the population, featured in Pigot's Baldock listing of 1839.[6]

Among directory publishers there were possibly different criteria for an individual's inclusion, probably different methods of data gathering and even different attitudes towards them by the individual PTPSs themselves. This can be demonstrated, for example, by comparing the content of Robson's 1838 directory with that of Pigot's for the following year (Figure 2.2 below).[7]

In the case of Baldock and Royston, a substantial majority of their directory entrants (69.2 per cent and 72.4 per cent respectively) appeared in both publications in contrast to Buntingford where the total was less than half (46.2 per cent). The proportion of entries unique to Robson was fairly consistent, ranging

---

[5] J.D. Marshall, 'The Rise and Transformation of the Cumbrian Market Town, 1660–1900', *Northern History*, XIX (1983), p.153.

[6] *Pigot's Commercial Directory, 1833–34*, pp. 730–31 (Buntingford); *Pigot's Royal National and Commercial Directory and Topography of the Counties of Essex, Hertfordshire, Middlesex* (London, 1839), pp. 94-96 (Ashwell included under Baldock).

[7] *Robson's Directory of London & the Six Home Counties [Essex, Herts, Kent, Mdsx, Surrey, Sussex with parts of Berks & Bucks], Vol. II* (London, 1838), pp. 4–5, 14–16, 46–49; *Pigot's Commercial Directory, Essex, Hertfordshire, Middlesex* (1839), pp. 94–96.

between 10.8 per cent for Baldock to 13.1 per cent for Royston. There was no particular pattern to these unique entries across the three towns. They included the usual bakers, butchers, fishmongers, milliners, tailors and bricklayers plus

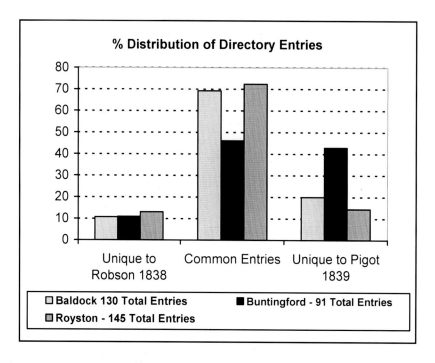

Figure 2.2: Comparison of two directories: Robson's 1838 and Pigot's 1839
Source: Robson's Directory, 1838; Pigot's Directory, 1839.

Cockett & Nash the Royston auctioneers, John Hooper a surgeon and Robert Freeman a veterinary surgeon from Buntingford, and James Newby an actuary at a Savings Bank in Baldock.[8] Again, for the majority of the eighty-six entries unique to Pigot in 1839, there was no particular discernible pattern apart from the inclusion of a significant number of women, twenty-three in total. There were three dressmakers in Royston and one in Buntingford, six milliners and straw hat makers in Baldock and seven schoolmistresses, three in Baldock and four in Buntingford. Others listed were Kezia Castle a pork butcher in Baldock and, in Buntingford, Sarah Farrington a boot and shoemaker, Sophia Geldard a grocer and dealer in sundries, Martha Bowman a coal and corn dealer, Elizabeth Munns a straw hat maker and Louisa Dalton the Mistress of the Workhouse.[9] Some of

---

[8] *Robson's Directory London & the Six Home Counties, Vol. II* (1838), pp. 5, 9, 15, 47.
[9] *Pigot's Commercial Directory, Essex, Hertfordshire, Middlesex* (1839), pp. 95, 100–101.

these women's trades, in particular those of butcher, grocer and coal dealer, would have been considered unusual, even undesirable, at the time.

Because publishers were still developing their products and potential contributors appeared to remain cautious, the earlier trade directories provide an incomplete picture of a town's business community. As the foregoing comparison of Robson (1838) and Pigot (1839) illustrates, no one publication provides a complete listing for a given location. By 1839 however, it is obvious that a combination of improved sampling by publishers and an increased willingness by individuals to be listed, resulted in substantial growth of directories' content. Their inclusion is proof that women realised the business benefits of directories too but curiously the Robson/Pigot analysis shows that for Baldock, Buntingford and Royston three times as many women were listed by Pigot (42 entries) compared to Robson (15 entries): this suggests a statistically significant bias whether on the part of the publishers or the attitude of the women themselves towards them.

In the apparent doubling of the business community, i.e. the dramatic increase in directory entrants for Baldock and Royston between 1811 and 1833/34, publicans, inn keepers and beer retailers led the way with their entries increasing from thirteen to twenty-two in Baldock and from four to twenty-nine in Royston. Similar was the case of maltsters, rising from two to seven and from three to eleven in Baldock and Royston respectively. This high level of provision of inns and taverns in Baldock and Royston is, surprisingly, much greater than the twenty-five inns that Marshall identified trading in Ulverston (pop. ca 4000) in 1829. He calculated the ratio of such establishments to be one to every 150 persons in the town. Here that ratio in 1833/34 is 1:77 in Baldock and 1:61 in Royston (population in both ca 1700). As Marshall suggested 'the rhythmic nature of custom or movement, and also the nature of travel' must be examined. Baldock and Royston being situated at major crossroads on well-used routes, like Ulverston, 'provided some excuses for visitors to assemble there'.[10]

However, in comparison to Marshall's estimates for 1829, by 1833/34 the increased number of premises selling alcohol in Baldock and Royston would have been greatly influenced by the 1830 Parliamentary 'Act to permit the general Sale of Beer and Cyder by Retail in England' which took away local magistrates' control of the licensing of brewers and publicans and passed it to Excise authorities. As Nicholas Mason explained, it allowed any rate-paying householder to open a 'beer shop' or 'beer house' and 'for the modest annual licensing fee of two guineas … brew and vend from their own residence', though few chose to actually brew themselves. According to Gourvish and Wilson over

---

[10] Marshall, 'Cumbrian Market Town', pp. 174, 175.

24,000 beer houses opened within six months of the Act.[11] Although this 'created a big demand for wholesale beer from [common] brewers' such as the Pryor brothers of Baldock, whose production according to Alan Whitaker doubled between 1829 and 1840, not everyone was happy. Their father, John Izzard Pryor who leased them the brewery, wrote in his diary that this 'unjust and sweeping measure would ruin the publicans, victuallers and many small brewers, and seriously injure all of them'. Gerald Curtis suggested he was particularly concerned that the beer houses would lead to the depreciation in the value of the brewery's 'tied houses'.[12] Responsibility for licensing was to be returned to local magistrates by an Act of 1869.

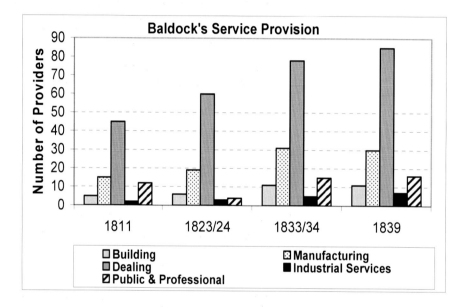

Figure 2.3: Baldock's changing major service sectors, 1811–1839
Source: Holden's Directory, 1811; Pigot's Directories, 1823–24, 1833–34, 1839.

Millers did not feature in Baldock until 1833/34 by which time eight were listed. A similar example in Royston was the emergence in 1826/27 of eight insurance agents. The changing pattern in the provision of goods and services, as indicated

---

[11] N. Mason, ' "The Sovereign People are in a Beastly State": The Beer Act of 1830 and Victorian Discourse on Working-class Drunkenness', *Victorian Literature and Culture*, 29, 1 (2001), p. 109; T.R. Gourvish and R.G. Wilson, *The British Brewing Industry, 1830-1980* (Cambridge, 1994), p. 16.
[12] A. Whitaker, *Brewers in Hertfordshire: A Historical Gazetteer* (Hatfield, 2006), p. 56; G. Curtis, *A Chronicle of Small Beer: The Early Victorian Diaries of a Hertfordshire Brewer* (Chichester, 1970), pp. 180, 181. From the eighteenth century the term 'common brewer' was used to distinguish the larger producers from the domestic and publican brewers.

by directory entries for the two towns, is shown in Figures 2.3 (above) and 2.4 (below).

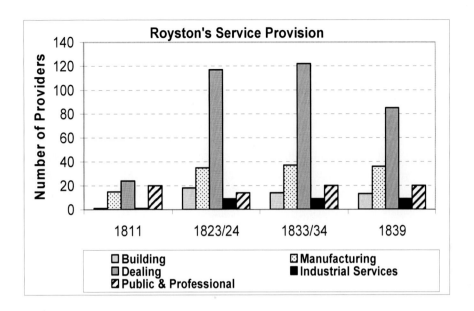

Figure 2.4: Royston's changing major service sectors, 1811–1839
Source: Holden's Directory, 1811; Pigot's Directories, 1826–27, 1833–34, 1839.

Both Baldock and Royston exhibit major growth in the dealing activities listed. For example in Royston the number of retailers increases substantially between 1811 and 1826/27: butchers (from 1 to 4); bakers (from 2 to 5); tailors (from 2 to 7); drapers (from 3 to 9); grocers (from 3 to 10). Furthermore by 1833/34 the two towns showed an increase in the range of retailing outlets available to the local populace. By now there were two booksellers (Royston) and a stationer (Baldock), four chemists and druggists (3 in Baldock and 1 in Royston), four watch and clock makers (3 in Royston, 1 in Baldock), a china and glass dealer in Royston and two wine and spirit merchants in Baldock.

The fragmentary nature of the availability and content of directory entries before 1839 coupled with lack of individual detail from early censuses means that these sources can only provide an impressionistic sketch of the developing regional economy. Hence the above breakdown by sector of Baldock and Royston's business activities is only indicative and this approach is explored at far greater depth in the following section covering the second half of the century.

Provision of goods and services from 1851 to 1891

From 1851 onwards detailed directory entries were regularly published for all four towns. Combining this data with the considerably greater individual detail now available from CEBs and utilizing record linkage techniques allows a far more rigorous analysis to produce a more complete picture of the regional economy.

Combining the two groups of individuals extracted from either trade directories or CEBs for the period between 1851 and 1891 gives a total of 3052 PTPSs, 467 in Ashwell, 599 in Buntingford, 800 in Baldock and 1186 in Royston. In three of the towns this group of individuals represented between 5.3 and 8.9 per cent of the total population (Figure 2.5 below) during the period 1851 to 1891 but in the case of the fourth town, Royston, the group represented a significantly larger proportion, growing from 10.5 per cent in 1851 to 15.5 per cent by 1891. Actual numbers of craftsmen and those involved in trade are, according to Crompton, of 'less importance than the total number of craft and trade outlets, the number of

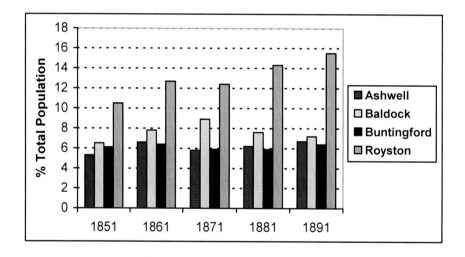

Figure 2.5: PTPSs as proportion of total population
Source: Post Office Directories, 1851, 1862, 1870; Kelly's Directories, 1882, 1890; Census enumerations, 1851-1891.

different services, and the presence or absence of specific services, for each settlement, relative to population size'.[13] Among the 3052 individual PTPSs, only 217 (7.1 per cent) were involved in a relatively small number of business partnerships, 102 in total (including 7 listed as companies). Ashwell and Baldock

---

[13] Crompton, 'Rural Service Occupations', p. 198.

had fewest, with averages across the period of 2.3 and 2.7 per cent respectively. Buntingford had more, averaging 3.6 per cent, while Royston with an average of 5.0 per cent, had most partnerships.

Almost two-thirds of these partnerships involved members of the same family. There were thirty instances of brothers working together, such as the carpenters George and Thomas Atkins (Ashwell, 1862) and the brewers Joseph and Thomas Simpson (Baldock, 1882), plus thirty examples of father and son(s) in partnership, including Thomas Hine and Son, drapers, grocers and insurance agents (Baldock, 1870) and William Nicholls Sanders and Sons, coach-makers (Buntingford, 1882). Within the other third, twenty-seven partnerships, such as Christy and Sale, farmers and brewers (Ashwell, 1851) and Feasey and Ironmonger, grocers and wine and spirit merchants (Buntingford, 1890), involved two people while just two others involved three people: Pyne, Balding and Archer, surgeons (Royston, 1870/71) and Burlingham, Innes and Paternoster, Ironmongers (Royston, 1890/91). The Misses Hide and Harrison, baby linen warehouse proprietors (Royston, 1870) were the sole example of two women in business together. The seven businesses listed as companies included Pryor, Reid & Co., maltsters (Baldock, 1890), Fordham, Gibson & Co., bankers (Buntingford, 1890) and Bray, Young & Co., auctioneers and valuers (Royston, 1890). The findings suggests that at this time either most businesses were of a size that could be managed by one individual or that most owners did not wish to dilute their opportunity for creating personal wealth.

Except for those engaged in the 'public and professional' sector, and because of the multiple services offered by many PTPSs, the following detailed analysis is based on the total number of services provided by each business rather than

Year	Ashwell	Baldock	Buntingford	Royston
1851	86	156	149	253
1861/62	112	176	181	326
1870/71	102	211	158	295
1881/82	123	214	146	309
1890/91	123	195	143	321

Table 2.1: Number of services from 'principal' business providers
Source: Post Office Directories, 1851, 1862, 1870; Kelly's Directories, 1882, 1890; Census enumerations, 1851–1891.

simply the number of individual business owners. Comparative figures (Table 2.1 above) for each of the four towns show the number of services available from the total of 2938 'principal' business enterprises identified over the period.

Sectoral distribution of businesses

Using an adapted Booth-based scheme of occupational classification (see Appendix 1) the following discussion examines eight business sectors: 'agriculture', 'building', 'dealing', 'domestic services', 'industrial services', 'manufacturing', 'public and professional' and 'transport'. A breakdown of the four towns' businesses, trades and occupations into these sectors (Figure 2.6 below) indicates that between 1851 and 1891 most of the activities identified from the directories and CEBs were in the three categories of 'dealing', 'manufacturing' and 'public and professional'.

Over the forty years almost half of the total business activities for the four towns (46.6 per cent) were consistently within the dealing sector. Apart from Buntingford in 1851 (41.6 per cent), the proportion of 'dealing' activities was regularly between 44.0 and 51.0 per cent in the three larger towns of Baldock, Buntingford and Royston. Ashwell, the smallest of the four towns, was the exception where the proportion of services in the dealing sector was lower at between 41.5 and 45.4 per cent for the latter half of the century.

Generally, the proportion of manufacturing businesses in each of the four towns was between 9.0 and 15.5 per cent of the total listed. Nevertheless, between 1851 and 1891, Buntingford and Royston clearly experienced a decline from 14.8 per cent to 9.1 per cent and from 13.0 per cent to 10.0 per cent respectively. A similar decline in Baldock, from 13.5 per cent to 9.3 per cent by 1881, was reversed by an increase to 12.5 per cent by 1891.

Numbers in the public and professional sector grew considerably across the period in all four towns, rising from an initial range of 8.1 per cent (Ashwell) to 22.1 per cent (Royston) in 1851 to a range of 16.3 per cent (Ashwell) to 26.2 per cent (Royston) by 1890. Consistently high figures for this particular sector in Buntingford and Royston reflected their roles as the administrative centres of two Poor Law Unions. Remaining PTPSs were grouped in five smaller sectors comprising 'agriculture'; 'building'; 'domestic services'; 'industrial services' and 'transport'.

Combining all the data from trade directories and CEBs allows for a detailed analysis of each of the eight business sectors and their constituent sub-categories in the following order: 'dealing & distributive', 'manufacturing', 'public & professional', 'agriculture', 'building', 'industrial services', 'domestic services' and 'transport'. In order to show more clearly the many differences in provision between the four towns, or to illustrate certain changes that occurred over time, some of the sub-categories are further fragmented into particular trades or services.

The most frequently occurring sub-categories of the dealing and distributive sector (Figure 2.7 below) were 'dress' (414 entries), 'wine, spirits and hotels' (536 entries) and 'food' (366 entries), which together accounted for 74.5 per cent of the total entries. In the case of the four towns under consideration, Booth's sub-category of 'wine, spirits and hotels' is rather misleading since it also covers the 490 entries for the many publicans, innkeepers and beer retailers (91.4 per cent of the total sub-category). While Royston usually had between two and four 'wine and spirit merchants' across the period, the first such dealers to appear elsewhere were Mrs Elizabeth Chamberlain, confectioner and dealer in British wines (Buntingford, 1862), Henry Routledge, grocer, draper and wine merchant (Baldock, 1870), and Thomas Westrope, grocer, draper, wine and spirit merchant, and agent for W & A Gilbey of London (Ashwell, 1882).

Baldock and Royston, reflecting the importance of their strategic locations at major road junctions, had the most listed hotels and commercial inns. Baldock had three commercial inns, the *George* (1851), the *White Lion* (1851), the *Rose & Crown* (1851 – 1891) and the *White Horse Hotel* (1860 and 1880 - 1890). Similarly, Royston had two commercial inns, the *Bull* (1851 – 1871) and the *Crown* (1861), later the *Old Crown* (1881 - 1891). The former became the *Bull Hotel* (1881) and finally *The Bull Family & Commercial Hotel* (1891). Despite its situation on the Old North Road, just seven miles south of Royston, only a single commercial inn, the *George & Dragon*, was listed for Buntingford (1861 – 1871) but by 1891 it had *The George Hotel*, 'Family, Private & Commercial'. The emergence of two 'family hotels' might have reflected the needs of migrating families or the beginning of recreational travel. In comparison to the other three towns, Ashwell had no hotel listed over the latter half of the nineteenth century; a reflection of its more isolated location away from the region's major roads. Sale of alcohol, especially beer, was an important part of the four towns' local economy. On average, between 1851 and 1891, the numbers of public houses listed were 7 in Ashwell, 10 in Buntingford, 14 in Baldock and 22 in Royston while the corresponding numbers for individual 'beer retailers' were 11, 7, 14 and 12 respectively. Again, as well as providing for the local populace, this level of provision for the 'stopping' trade can be seen as a reflection of the volume of traffic passing through Baldock and Royston strategically astride important crossroads.

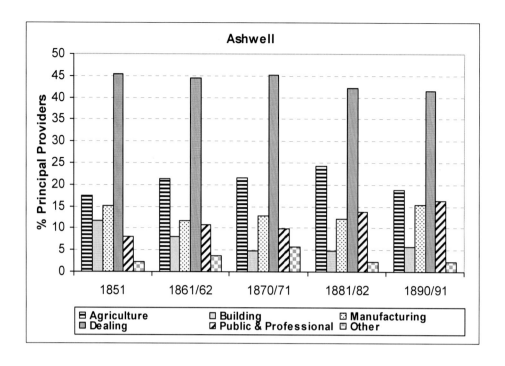

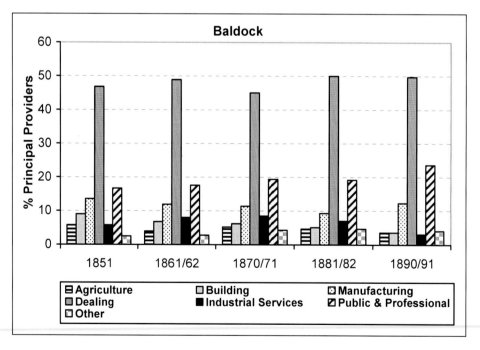

Figure 2.6: Changing business sector proportions in four towns
Source: Post Office Directories, 1851, 1862, 1870; Kelly's Directories,
1882, 1890; Census enumerations, 1851–1891.

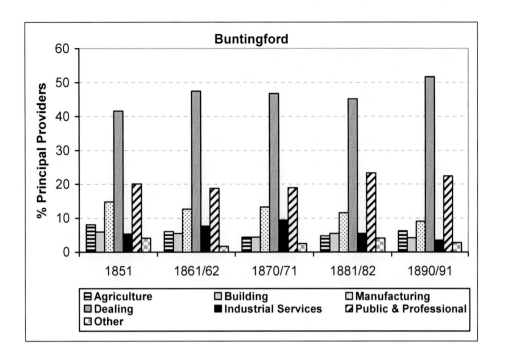

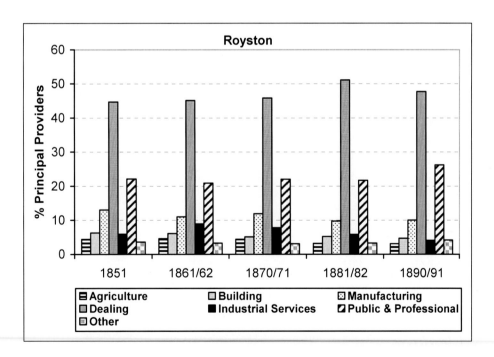

As noted, amendments to the 1830 Beer Act saw responsibility for licensing returned to local magistrates in 1869. Whitaker argued that these new restrictions forced many beer shop keepers into bankruptcy, a situation that allowed local breweries to buy 'many of the commercially viable beer houses to increase the size of their tied estates'.[14] Because of confusing terminology used by directories and CEBs, there is no clear evidence to support this view from the present analysis.[15] Overall in the four towns, the total number of beer retailers peaked in 1861/62 (n = 55), declined by over a quarter by 1870/71 (n = 40) and then rose again slightly over the next twenty years. During the same period the number of inns and public houses rose by only 11.3 per cent from 1861/62 (n = 53) to 1890/91 (n = 59).

Within the food sub-category of the dealing and distributive sector, the most commonly listed retailers (77.8 per cent total) were the grocers (105 entries), butchers (93 entries) and bakers (87 entries). Confectioners (29 entries), the fourth largest group of food purveyors and frequently involved in other retailing activities, were present only in the three larger towns. While Baldock and Buntingford had only one or two at any one time, in Royston the number of confectioners trebled from just two in 1851 to six between 1882 and 1890.[16] Half of the eighteen individually identified confectioners were also bakers and eight were women. Among the other confectioners, George Crout Davies (Baldock, 1862) for instance was also the town's Postmaster, Elizabeth Chamberlain (Buntingford, 1862) was also a dealer in boots, shoes and British wines, and Mrs Martha Miller (Royston, 1890/91) was a toy dealer.[17]

Examining the ratio of each town's population to its grocery outlets reveals surprisingly high densities of these particular retailers in contrast to Alexander's calculations for those found in some much larger urban centres in East Anglia

---

[14] Whitaker, *Brewers in Hertfordshire*, p. 6. A tied house was one owned by a brewery that only allowed its own beers to be sold by the publican.

[15] Directories never appear to have used the terms 'beer shop' or 'beer house' but referred to traders running a named inn or tavern (1851 – 1882), and later a named inn or public house (1890), with the term 'beer retailer' used throughout but never linked to a named establishment. However, the CEBs frequently associated a 'beer retailer' with a named premises, e.g. Joseph Harvey, 'Beer retailer, *Brewery Tap*' (Baldock, 1861) and John Farr, 'Beer retailer, *The Globe Inn*' (Buntingford, 1891). Very occasionally an enumerator would refer to a directory's 'Beer retailer' as a 'beer shop' or 'beer house' operator, e.g. Edward Kitchener, 'Beer house keeper' at the *White Hart Inn* (Baldock, 1881) and Thomas Barker, 'Agricultural labourer, Beer shop keeper' (Buntingford, 1862). An enumerator would sometimes identify a directory 'Beer retailer' as a 'Licensed victualler', e.g. James Hyde at the *Saracen's Head Inn* (Baldock, 1881), or a 'Publican', e.g. James Prior at the *Windmill* (Buntingford, 1871).

[16] Confectioners at this time made cakes, pastries, possibly chocolates, and 'confections', the latter being a sweet preparation of fruit, spices, sugar and chocolate.

[17] *Post Office Directory Six Home Counties, 1862*, pp. 320, 334; *Kelly's Directory Six Home Counties, Pt 1* (1890), p. 810; 1891 Census (Royston).

and the East Midlands. Figures for the head of population per grocery shop in 1851 were only 240 in Baldock, 294 in Buntingford, 412 in Royston and 475 in Ashwell compared with Alexander's significantly higher figures of 765 in Nottingham, 790 in Leicester and 800 in Norwich in the same year.[18] In contrast, twenty years later Martin Phillips argued that, from the mid-nineteenth century, CEBs 'indicate a substantial expansion in the grocery trade' as it moved away from principally dealing in foreign produce for just the better-off to become 'increasingly involved in selling a wider range of commodities to the working class'.[19] He calculated there were 4.9 grocers per 1000 of the population in 1851, rising to 5.8 and 5.9 in 1871 and 1911 respectively. In comparison to Phillips's figures , the density of grocers in the four towns was in fact considerably less than the national average ranging from 2.1 (Ashwell) to 4.2 (Baldock) per 1000 in 1851 and decreasing to between 1.9 (Ashwell) to 2.8 (Royston) per 1000 by 1871.[20] This trend probably reflects the growth in the listed number of non-specific 'shopkeepers'.

In addition to grocers, butchers, bakers and confectioners, a small number of other specialist food retailers were identified, almost exclusively in Baldock and Royston. Although the overall numbers are small they clearly show, especially in the case of Royston, an increasing variety of food retailers from the 1860s onwards. For example, the presence in both towns of fruiterers and greengrocers from 1862, and fishmongers in Royston and Baldock from 1851 and 1870 respectively, undoubtedly reflects the opportunities afforded by developments in wholesaling and the coming of the railway to the two towns. In comparison, and perhaps rather surprisingly, three other fishmongers, Samuel Bonnett (Ashwell), Edward Clambert (Buntingford) and William Hankin (Buntingford), all trading in 1851, are the last such dealers in these two towns. However, the appearance of these fishmongers, although short-lived in some instances, exemplifies how the retail market was, according to Gareth Shaw, 'rapidly extended by new transportation systems, which throughout the nineteenth century transformed the geography of market areas'. This particular case reflects that, from the 1840s onwards, rail companies began 'to organise the carriage of fish' from the coastal ports to the consumers of inland Britain.[21] In the above instances, the fish might have been brought by rail from Grimsby on the Lincolnshire coast, Great

---

[18] D. Alexander, *Retailing in England during the Industrial Revolution* (London, 1970), pp. 260-63.

[19] M. Phillips, 'The Evolution of Markets and Shops in Britain', in J. Benson and G. Shaw (eds), *The Evolution of Retail Systems, c. 1800-1914, Part 2, Fairs, Markets, Pedlars and Small-scale Shops* (Leicester, 1992), p. 64.

[20] Phillips, 'Evolution of Markets', p. 66.

[21] G. Shaw, 'The European Scene: Britain and Germany', in J. Benson and G. Shaw (eds), *The Evolution of Retail Systems, c. 1800-1914, Part 1, The Economic and Social Context of Retail Evolution* (Leicester, 1992), pp. 19, 20.

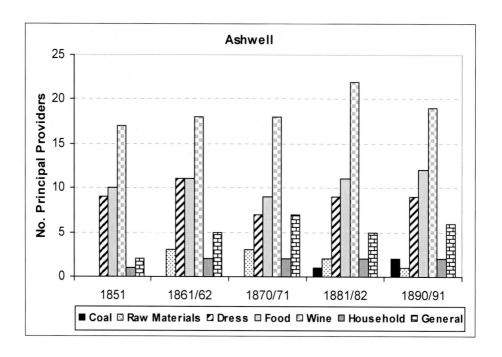

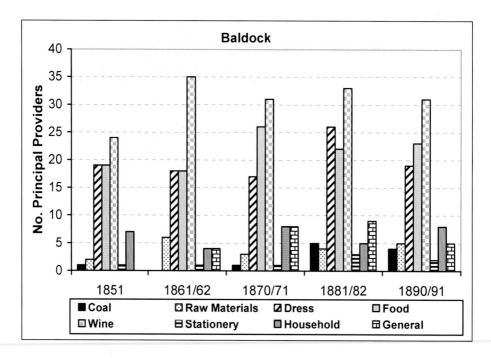

Figure 2.7: Details of dealing sector in four towns
Source: Post Office Directories, 1851, 1862, 1870; Kelly's
Directories, 1882, 1890; Census enumerations, 1851–1891.

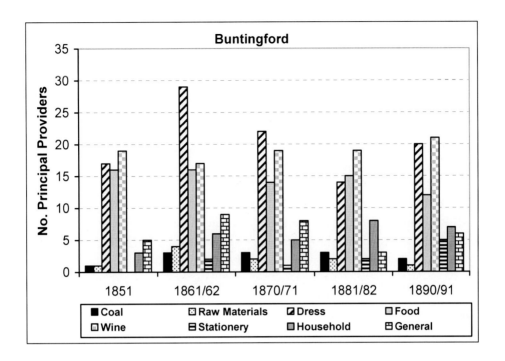

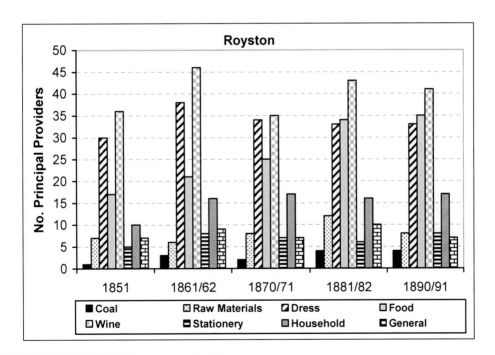

Yarmouth on Norfolk's coast or from London's Billingsgate Market. Another specialist retailer, John Edward Spinks, a grocer and tea dealer (Buntingford, 1862), was also listed as having an 'Italian Warehouse', i.e. a shop supplying Italian groceries, fruits, olive oil, etc., clear evidence that imported foodstuffs were able to reach quite small towns like Buntingford by the mid-nineteenth century.[22]

Over the latter half of the nineteenth century Baldock and Royston supported a small number of other specialist food retailers. Both had cheesemongers, Robert Edwards (Baldock, 1871) and Edward Titchmarsh (Royston, 1861 – 71). There were two poulterers trading in 1851, Charles Cook in Royston and George Reed in Baldock; the latter also happened to be the Town Crier. Other specialists included Margaret Pak, a widow, who ran a sweetshop in Baldock (1871) and, in Royston, John Lea (1881) and Joseph Miller (1891) who were both dairymen.[23]

The appearance of specialist food retailers like tea dealers might suggest that the supposed 'consumer revolution' often associated with the mass production and mass marketing of the Industrial Revolution was penetrating even very small towns by the latter part of the nineteenth century. However, another school of thought, Nancy Cox argued, has shown that the 'seeds of change were sown in the eighteenth century if not even earlier'. She suggested that 'evidence for the change is most easily observed' in the middling sort's 'symbol of consumption … the new pleasure of tea drinking' which by 1800 had become not only 'an adjunct of polite conversation but also a popular drink providing comfort to the poor'.[24] As a result many craftsmen had to produce the 'new or modified utensils for its consumption' that increasing numbers of retailers now had to stock to satisfy demand.[25] Evidence of the availability of tea in the four Hertfordshire towns is difficult to gauge from the contemporary directory entries. In 1823/4 Pigot's directory listed seven Baldock retailers under the one heading 'GROCERS & TEA DEALERS'. Ten years later, the town had nine retailers under the heading 'GROCERS AND DEALERS IN SUNDRIES'. Meanwhile Pigot still used the earlier heading for four and five retailers in Royston and Buntingford respectively although three of the latter bore the annotation '(& dealer in sundries)'. By 1839, the only directory heading was 'GROCERS AND DEALERS IN SUNDRIES' and thereafter, apart from the few instances mentioned previously, references to

---

[22] 1851 Census (Ashwell, Buntingford); *Shorter O.E.D.*; *Post Office Directory Six Home Counties (1862)*, p. 335.

[23] A cheesemonger sold butter and cheese, a poulterer dealt in poultry and usually game while a dairyman sold cheese and milk. Unlike many confectioners, a specialist sweet shop would not have been associated with a bakery and the selling of cakes and pastries.

[24] N. Cox, *The Complete Tradesman: A Study of Retailing, 1550-1820* (Aldershot, 2000), pp. 2, 3.

[25] Cox, *Complete Tradesman*. p. 3. The author lists tea kettles, tea tables and trays, crockery like teapots, teacups and saucers, and cutlery like teaspoons and sugar tongs among the required utensils.

tea dealers disappeared leaving one to assume that its availability had become commonplace from 'grocers' or 'shopkeepers', and no longer worthy of specific mention.[26]

Boot and/or shoemakers, with 116 entries, were the most frequently occurring retailers within the dress sub-category of the dealing and distributive sector in all four towns, along with drapers and/or haberdashers (104 entries), tailors and/or outfitters (96 entries) and dressmakers (29 entries). This group of clothing outlets accounted for 83.5 per cent of the total. Whilst there were regular entries for milliners or hatters (37) and several clothiers (12), in Baldock, Buntingford and Royston, none of these existed in Ashwell between 1851 and 1890. The few hosiers listed (4 entries) only appeared in Baldock and Buntingford.[27] Other specialist retailers were, for instance, Miss Ann Kitchener (Baldock, 1862) and Mrs Jane Dodd (Buntingford, 1882–90), 'Berlin wool' dealers, and Mrs Hope Ellis (Baldock, 1882) 'stay and corset maker'.[28] By the end of the nineteenth century, Royston possessed a baby linen warehouse, in Melbourne Street, run initially by Misses Hide and Harrison (1870) and later by Mrs Emma Woollard (1882–90).[29]

Again, examining the 1851 ratio of population to drapery outlets, substantially high densities are found compared to Alexander's calculations for much larger urban centres. Figures for the population per drapery shop were only 412 in Buntingford and Royston, 480 in Baldock and 713 in Ashwell compared to the 1345 in Nottingham, 1745 in Norwich and 1770 in Leicester calculated by Alexander for the same year.[30] This level of specialist textile retailing in these small towns suggests high levels of disposable income by people for whom clothing was fashionable, not just a functional necessity.

Among the smaller sub-categories of dealers (Table 2.2 below) were those supplying 'household utensils'. These included, for example, watch and clockmakers (44 entries), ironmongers (32 entries) and assorted combinations of china, glass and earthenware dealers (21 entries). Over half such businesses were

---

[26] *Pigot's Commercial Directory, 1823-24*, p. 350; *Pigot's Commercial Directory, 1833-34*, pp. 726, 753, 730.

[27] A draper sold woollen and/or linen cloth while a haberdasher additionally sold small articles related to dress such as tape, thread and ribbon. A clothier and outfitter both sold 'off the peg' men's clothes while a tailor produced and sold 'made to measure' outer clothes. A hosier sold knitted or woven underware and stockings.

[28] Berlin wool was a fine dyed merino wool used for knitting or embroidery; *Post Office Directory Six Home Counties, 1862*, p. 320; *Kelly's Directory Six Home Counties, Pt I* (1882), p. 564, 586; *Kelly's Directory Six Home Counties, Pt I* (1890), p. 732.

[29] *Post Office Directory Six Home Counties, Pt I* (1870), p. 478; *Kelly's Directory Six Home Counties, Pt I* (1882), p. 650; *Kelly's Directory Six Home Counties, Pt I* (1890), p. 810.

[30] Alexander, *Retailing during the Industrial Revolution*, pp. 260–63.

located in Royston but, apart from a watch/clockmaker, Ashwell had none, not even a hardware-dealing ironmonger. This suggests that Ashwell's inhabitants

Sub-Category of Dealing Sector	No. of Census &/or Directory Entries	% Total Entries (n = 1759)
Household Utensils	138	7.8
General Dealing	104	5.9
Raw Materials	80	4.5
Stationery	52	3.0
Coal	40	2.3
Unspecified Dealing	18	1.0
Furniture	8	0.5
Lodgings	8	0.5

Table 2.2: Smaller sub-categories of dealing and distributive sector
Source: Post Office Directories, 1851, 1862, 1870; Kelly's Directories, 1882, 1890; Census enumerations, 1851–1891.

were reliant on nearby Baldock's tradesmen for their household utensils. Within the 'general dealing' sub-category in all of the towns were a large number of non-specific 'shopkeepers' (70 entries), a few 'general dealers' (15 entries) and, apart from Ashwell, several 'marine store dealers' (17 entries).[31]

The term 'shopkeeper' originally referred to 'wealthy traders who sold goods to the public from fixed premises' but according to Phillips, as the nineteenth century progressed, the word was increasingly 'reserved in trade circles, in the pages of commercial directories and in imaginative literature' to describe small non-specialised traders 'who lacked capital or social standing'. Numbers of these small general retailers increased rapidly since it was, as Jon Stobart argued, 'a time of retail growth and differentiation as attempts were made to cater for the growing working classes'. Across the four towns, numbers rose from only 10 in 1851 to 17 by 1871 but fell back to 14 by the end of the century. They stocked a wide variety of goods that Stobart described as including 'foodstuffs, household sundries, cloth and clothing: a product range that led to them being labelled ... "shopkeepers" '.[32]

---

[31] A marine store keeper dealt in merchandise salvaged from old ships, e.g. rope, sailcloth, timber, etc.

[32] Phillips, 'Evolution of Markets', p. 63; J. Stobart, *Spend, Spend, Spend! A History of Shopping* (Stroud, 2008), pp. 102, 103.

In her study of two much larger Nottinghamshire towns, Mansfield (population 9,550 in 1841) and Newark (population 10,195 in 1841), Catherine Smith noted how new industries and expanding markets created an increase in the number of 'middle-class professionals'. As a result she found trade directories listed 'a growing number of leisure and luxury trades and services' such as booksellers, confectioners and watch makers.[33] Her findings were echoed by Stobart who believed that by the end of the eighteenth century the 'core of shops found in most towns [drapers, grocers, ironmongers, shoemakers and tailors] had expanded to include clockmakers and booksellers, and around half also contained china and glass sellers, wine merchants, confectioners and apothecaries'.[34] Between 1851 and 1890, Smiths's 'luxury trades' of booksellers, confectioners and watch makers regularly appeared in directory listings for the three larger study towns despite their more modest populations, indicating the presence of well-to-do professionals. Further evidence of a population with more disposable income available for non-essential goods is demonstrated by the fact that towards the end of the nineteenth century Baldock, Buntingford and Royston all possessed a number of other specialist retailers, which were not to be found in less affluent Ashwell. For instance, all three towns had tobacconists, toyshops and florists. Harry Izzard (Baldock, 1890) dealt in 'domestic machines', Harry Sewell (Buntingford, 1890), reflecting the local tanning industry, was a wallet maker and William Wale (Royston, 1870), James Lee (Royston, 1882) and his widow Mrs Mary Lee (Royston, 1890) were all umbrella makers. Presumably traditional portraits were the business of Harry Thurnall (Royston, 1890), an 'artist', listed in Kelly's directory, while Charles Shaw (Buntingford, 1880) exploited more recent developments in photographic techniques. In addition to being a photographer, William Norman (Royston, 1870 – 1890) was also a 'bird stuffer' (taxidermist), and Frank Hinkins (Royston, 1890) was an 'artist', photographer and 'lantern slide maker'.

Utilising Ulverston's parish registers to show increased numbers of traders within the food, drink and dress categories between 1755 and 1806, Marshall concluded 'that not only [changing] taste and fashion, but also the growth of rural wealth and spending power' were factors in the town's growth; an observation clearly applicable to the north-east corner of Hertfordshire in the later nineteenth century. Whilst there may have been changes in the area's agriculture, retail trade in the four towns measured in terms of overall totals of outlets at the end of the nineteenth century does not, as Marshall also noted for some towns in Cumbria, 'appear to have diminished in any serious fashion'.[35]

[33] C. Smith, 'Image and Reality: Two Nottinghamshire Market Towns in Late Georgian England', *Midland History*, 17 (1992), p. 66.

[34] Stobart, *Spend, Spend, Spend!*, p. 77.

[35] Marshall, 'Cumbrian Market Town', pp.173, 197.

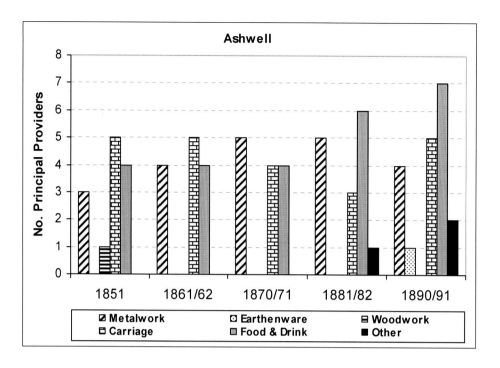

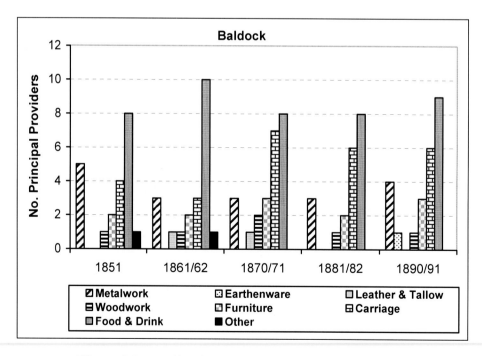

Figure 2.8: Details of manufacturing sector in four towns
Source: Post Office Directories, 1851, 1862, 1870; Kelly's
Directories, 1882, 1890; Census enumerations, 1851–1891.

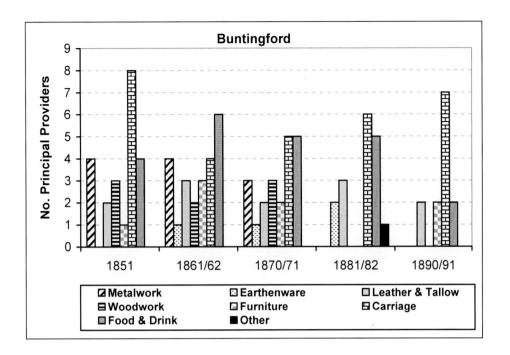

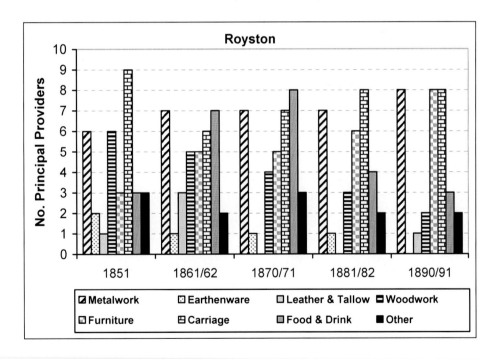

A breakdown of the manufacturing sector (Figure 2.8 above) reveals that the three most frequently occurring sub-categories in all four towns between 1851 and 1891 were 'iron and steel' (60 entries), 'drink preparation' (86 entries) and 'carriage and harness' (116 entries) which between them accounted for 58.9 per cent of the total entries. Iron manufacture in all these small towns was almost the exclusive province of the blacksmith, there being usually two to four in each period in each town excepting Buntingford where, inexplicably, none were listed in 1882 and 1890. Additionally there were a few 'iron founders' who, with the exception of Robert Bloom (Baldock, 1851), all traded in Royston.[36] They included John Bateson (Royston, 1851), iron and brass founder, George Innes (Royston, 1891), also listed as an engineer, and Nathan Varty, an iron founder and engineer (Royston, 1870 & 1882), who by 1890 in addition to being an hydraulic, mechanical and brewers' engineer was a manufacturer of seed mill machinery at the 'Royston Iron Works'.[37]

Plate 2.1: Phillips' malting, Kneesworth Street, Royston

---

[36] *Post Office Directory Six Home Counties, 1851*, p. 172; A founder is a caster of metal objects in brass or iron.
[37] *Post Office Directory Six Home Counties, 1851*, p. 216; 1891 Census (Royston); *Kelly's Directory Six Home Counties, Pt I* (1890), p. 810.

Plate 2.2: Former Phillips' brewery house, Baldock Street, Royston

Given that during the nineteenth century north-east Hertfordshire reputedly had 'some of the best barley land in the country', it is not surprising that the sub-category of 'drink preparation' included individual entries for 41 maltsters and 45 brewers.[38] Changing the occupational entries of a business over time, in directories and CEBs, suggest a degree of confusion as to whether an enterprise was solely engaged in malting or brewing or both. Buntingford appears not to have had a major brewery but a number of other businesses additionally operated small-scale brewing activities, e.g. Charles Nicholls, cooper and brewer (1851 – 71), John Biggs, Master cooper and brewer (1871), and William Rayment, maltster and brewer (1881 – 91). The large *Royston Brewery* and maltings was owned by the Phillips family between 1851 and 1891 (Plates 2.1 & 2.2 above). Over the same period in Ashwell, the major brewery and maltings in Mill Street and Green Lane were operated by the Fordham family (Plate 2.3 below), while

---

[38] L.M. Munby, *The Hertfordshire Landscape* (The Making of the English Landscape series, London, 1977), p. 26.

Plate 2.3: Fordham's Green Lane malting, Ashwell

Plate 2.4: Pryor and Simpson's malting, Clothall Road, Baldock

the smaller *Westbury Brewery* in the hands of farmers Benjamin Christy and John Sale between 1851 and 1871 was sold in 1879 to Joshua Richmond Page, a major Baldock maltster. The Oliver Family ran Baldock's small *White Horse Brewery* and maltings from 1851 to 1862 and the Steed family the *Pale Ale Brewery* from 1851 to 1881. John and Morris Pryor's larger *High Street Brewery* was acquired in 1853 by the brothers, Joseph and Thomas Simpson, nephews of John Phillips in Royston, though the Pryor family was still listed as Baldock maltsters in 1891 (Plates 2.4 above & 2.5 below). There was a high concentration of brewing and malting activities in north-east Hertfordshire across the second half of the nineteenth century but mergers and acquisitions saw the Fordham, Phillips and Simpson families dominating the region's brewing industry by 1891.[39]

Plate 2.5: Pryor and Simpson's malting, High Street, Baldock

The only exception to the production of beer in the four towns, was provided by James Dover a mineral water manufacturer (Ashwell, 1890), taking advantage of the pure water of the Ashwell Spring Head, source of the River Rhee (Plate 2.6 below). A profitable enterprise according to Albert Sheldrick, for until the

[39] Whitaker, *Brewers in Hertfordshire*, pp. 42–71, 178–88.

beginning of the twentieth century, 'people came from far and wide to take away large bottles of the water for some cure or other'.[40] This habit reflected the public's interest in hydropathy, which from the 1850s, had offered a controversial alternative to orthodox medical practice. Many hydropathists, according to James Bradley and Marguerite Dupree, claimed their regime could 'reproduce the effects of drugs, bleeding, and almost *all* other forms of allopathic practice'.[41]

Plate 2.6: Spring Head of River Rhee, below High Street, Ashwell [42]

In the manufacturing sub-category of 'carriage and harness' (Table 2.3 below) were entries for 51 saddlers and/or harness makers, 41 wheelwrights, 22 coach makers/builders and 2 specialist coach painters, 'master' John Johnson (Buntingford, 1851) and Walter Clayton (Buntingford, 1882).[43] In addition to making and repairing wheels, some wheelwrights also made carts and wagons. Thus they would have provided important services to the farming communities of the towns' rural hinterlands as well as to town-based commercial carriers. In

---

[40] *Kelly's Directory Six Home Counties, Pt I* (1890), p. 700; A. Sheldrick, *A Different World: Ashwell before 1939* (Baldock, 1992), p. 2.

[41] Hydropathy is the treatment of disorders by the application of water, either internally or externally. Allopathic practice is the treatment of disease by inducing an opposite condition. J. Bradley and M. Dupree, 'A Shadow of Orthodoxy? An Epistemology of British Hydropathy, 1840-1858', *Medical History*, 47 (2003), p. 177.

[42] Almost certainly the origin of the place-name Ashwell.

[43] 1851 Census (Buntingford); *Kelly's Directory Six Home Counties, Pt I* (1882), p. 586.

contrast coach/carriage builders and painters would have largely served the urban consumer. Despite the railway boom, thanks to the development of elliptical springs, coach and carriage building, according to A. N. Wilson, 'enjoy[ed] a magnificent flowering' in mid to late nineteenth century with the barouche, landau and phaeton in great demand by the middle classes.[44]

	Occupation	1851	1861/	1870/	1881/	1890/
Ashwell	Saddlers/Harness	1	1	1	1	1
	Wheelwrights	3	4	3	2	4
	Coach/Carriage Blds	1	-	-	-	-
Baldock	Saddlers/Harness	3	2	4	3	3
	Wheelwrights	1	-	1	1	1
	Coach/Carriage Blds	-	1	2	2	2
Buntingford	Saddlers/Harness	2	2	2	2	2
	Wheelwrights	4	1	2	2	3
	Coach/Carriage Blds	1	1	1	1	2
	Coach Painters	1	-	-	1	-
Royston	Saddlers/Harness	6	3	4	3	5
	Wheelwrights	2	2	2	2	1
	Coach/Carriage Blds	1	1	1	3	2
Total		26	18	23	23	26

Table 2.3: Manufacturing sub-category of 'carriage & harness'
Source: Post Office Directories, 1851, 1862, 1870; Kelly's Directories, 1882, 1890; Census enumerations, 1851–1891.

Among the smaller sub-categories those of 'furniture' and 'wood' together accounted for 18.4 per cent of the manufacturing sector (Table 2.4 below). Skilled furniture making was the province of the cabinet maker (23 entries) and upholsterer (15 entries) and occurred almost exclusively in Baldock and Royston, yet the role of undertaker (requiring carpentry if not cabinet making skills) rather surprisingly only appeared regularly in the directory listings for Buntingford (6 entries). Coopers (27 entries) formed the largest group in the 'wood' manufacturing sub-category, being regularly listed under Baldock, Buntingford and Royston, but there was only a single occurrence in Ashwell.

---

[44] A.N. Wilson, *The Victorians* (Pbk edn, London, 2003), p. 262.

Sub-Category of Manufacturing Sector	No. of Census &/or Directory Entries	% Total Entries (n = 445)
Furniture	47	10.5
Wood	35	7.9
Food Preparation	28	6.3
Copper & Tin	25	5.6
Leather & Tallow	19	4.3
Earthenware	11	2.5
Machinery	8	1.8
Flax & Hemp	7	1.6
Woollen	3	0.7

Table 2.4: Smaller sub-categories of manufacturing sector
Source: Post Office Directories, 1851, 1862, 1870; Kelly's Directories, 1882, 1890; Census enumerations, 1851–1891.

One third of the individuals identified in the public and professional sector were in the educational field (Table 2.5 below) with Baldock, Buntingford and Royston having 78, 49 and 94 entries respectively between 1851 and 1891. Even in the smallest town, Ashwell, teachers were by far the most numerous of the professionals listed with 31 entries across the same period. From 1851 onwards Baldock, Buntingford and Royston all had both 'National' and 'British' schools, the former run by the Church of England National Society and the latter by the non-denominational British and Foreign School Society. In contrast, Ashwell had the Merchant Taylors' Company's endowed school for boys, established in 1665 and educating 100 boys in 1882. Ashwell's girls' school was replaced in 1877 by one of the new, post 1870 Education Act, Board Schools which catered for 120 girls and 150 infants. All of these establishments were for the elementary education of working-class children and do not explain the total number of teachers and governesses identified.[45] There is no clear evidence from the two data sources of any dame schools or working-class 'private adventure schools'. The latter, although criticized by contemporary commentators as establishments that were 'shoddy by any standard', according to Grigg, did provide a basic curriculum that 'met the wishes of parents' at a price they could afford. Maybe many parents in the four small non-industrial study towns had higher ambitions for their children.[46]

---

[45] *Kelly's Directory Six Home Counties, Pt 1* (1882), pp. 560–61.
[46] G.R. Grigg, ' 'Nurseries of Ignorance'? Private Adventure and Dame Schools for the Working-classes in Nineteenth-century Wales', *History of Education*, 34, 3 (2005), pp. 257, 258.

	Educational Role	1851	1861/2	1870/1	1881/2	1890/1
Ashwell	Schoolteacher	3	6	3	9	9
	Private Tutor	-	-	1	-	-
Baldock	Schoolteacher	7	12	13	12	13
	Governess	-	-	9	3	6
	Music Teacher	-	-	1	1	1
Buntingford	Schoolteacher	11	8	4	7	9
	Governess	-	1	1	3	3
	Music Teacher	-	-	-	1	-
	School Matron		-	-	1	-
Royston	Schoolteacher	13	16	14	9	15
	Governess	8	1	-	2	3
	Music Teacher	-	2	3	1	2
	Drawing Teacher	-	-	-	-	1
	French Teacher	-	-	1	-	-
Royston District Educational Soc.		-	-	-	2	1
Total		42	46	50	51	63

Table 2.5: Members of the teaching profession, 1851–1891
Source: Post Office Directories, 1851, 1862, 1870; Kelly's Directories,
1882, 1890; Census enumerations, 1851–1891.

The answer, regarding the numbers of teachers, lies in the several private boarding schools and colleges that existed in all the towns, except Ashwell, in the second half of the nineteenth century, four in Baldock, three in Royston, two in Buntingford. Reader attributed this phenomenon to the middle-classes wanting to provide an education that would fit their children for trade, industry and the professions better than the 'rigidly classical curriculum' of the public schools and declining grammar schools of the period with their 'scornful dislike of money-making, technology and science'.[47]   He argued that these profit-making 'commercial academies' sprang-up to 'supply what the customers thought they wanted', that is vocational training and the acquisition of a desirable social background that was 'no lower than the parent's own and as much above it as they could afford'.[48]

---

[47] W.J. Reader, *Life in Victorian England* (London, 1964), p.117.
[48] Reader, *Victorian England*, p.120.

Brian Simon suggested it was the lower middle-classes who sent their children to lesser boarding schools established near to the larger towns. William Reader had observed that these schools were made 'increasingly accessible' by the spread of the railways. Simon suggested that these schools 'varied greatly in quality; but were by no means all as bad as the school rightly held up to obloquy by Charles Dickens', Mr Squeers's Dotheboys Hall in *Nicholas Nickleby*.[49] Two very noticeable features of the majority of these private schools in Baldock, Buntingford and Royston, were that they were educating 'ladies' of whom very few were from the towns themselves, exemplifying Reader's point on improved transport. For example, in 1861, Baldock-born Mrs Ann Balfour ran the Cambridge House Ladies School in Baldock High Street. The CEB lists twenty-one resident pupils (aged 9 to 17) including 8 from London, 6 from Sunderland and 2 from Newcastle but not a single local girl.[50] Between 1871 and 1891, Baldock's variously titled Grove House Ladies School, Ladies Boarding School and Grove House Academy (Plate 2.7 below) seemed to cater for pupils from the Home Counties with just two girls from Ashwell listed in 1881.[51] Its Principal, Mrs George Sibley, advertised moderate terms for preparing pupils for the 'Oxford, Cambridge and other Public Examinations'.[52] Among the five girls at the Misses Bore's (each identified in the CEB as 'governess') smaller Ladies Boarding School in Buntingford in 1861, was one from Barrowby in Lincolnshire, one from Edinburgh and one from Southampton.[53] This preponderance of private schools for girls has been noted elsewhere; for example in 1834 Manchester had seventy-eight for girls compared with thirty-six for boys.[54] It seems likely that these schools would have placed advertisements in various regional newspapers throughout the country in addition to their local publication, the *Royston Crow*, which also carried advertisements from more distant educational establishments. For example, on 1 February 1860, Mrs Trevethan Spicer of Helston House, Bayswater, offered to educate young ladies 'in all the requisites of a Gentlewoman'.[55]

A contrast to the above examples was provided by the Boarding and Day School run by Peter Ashton in Royston. In 1861 it had eight boy boarders (aged 9 to 13): three brothers from '[Stow-cum-] Quy' and a boy from Shingay, both in Cambridgeshire; one from Saffron Walden in Essex; three from nearby villages,

---

[49] B. Simon, *The Two Nations & the Educational Structure, 1780–1870* (Pbk edn, Southampton, 1976), p. 112; Reader, *Victorian England*, p.122.

[50] 1861 Census (Baldock).

[51] 1871 Census (Baldock); 1881 Census (Baldock); 1891 (Baldock).

[52] *Herts & Cambs Reporter and Royston Crow*, 26 September 1890, p. 1.

[53] 1861 Census (Buntingford).

[54] Simon, *Two Nations*, p. 113.

[55] *Herts & Cambs Reporter and Royston Crow*, 10 April 1891, p. 1.

two from Cottered and one from Therfield.[56] Terms here were again advertised as moderate and the establishment claimed to pursue a system of education that included 'Latin, Greek, and French Languages, Geometry, Algebra, Trigonometry, &c.'.[57]

Plate 2.7: Former Grove House Academy for girls, White Horse Street, Baldock

Further research is needed to understand how and why this type of educational establishment came to be located in these towns and what persuaded parents to send their children such long distances for the education offered. How common were these private schools in the small towns of England and were their proprietors more entrepreneurial than philanthropic?

A further third of the individuals in the public and professional sector were engaged in the medical and dispensing professions, the legal profession, the police force and fire service, and the Post Office, or were government tax

---

[56] 1861 Census (Royston).

[57] *The Royston Crow*, 1 October 1855, p. 62.

officials. Most numerous of these groups were various revenue officers (52 entries), policemen (41 entries), physicians and surgeons (48 entries), and solicitors (32 entries). Ashwell's decennial numbers for this sector were minimal, the Post Master, a police officer, a surgeon, a tax official, and from 1881 a chemist and Druggist. The only exceptions were in 1861 when there were two other tax officials present and in 1871 when an additional 'physician' was resident. Neither Ashwell nor Buntingford appear to have had a fire brigade during the latter part of the nineteenth century despite, in the case of Ashwell, the large scale devastation caused in the town by fire on the night of Saturday 2nd February 1850 when, according to Davey, help was summoned from Royston, Baldock and Hitchin.[58] Perhaps more surprisingly, Ashwell apparently did not have the services of a local solicitor over the fifty-year period.

It should be noted that most of the tax officials were based in either Baldock (17 entries) or Royston (24 entries). The focus of this activity was the local Tax Office in each case originally located in one of the town's inns. In the case of Baldock the Inland Revenue & Assessed Taxes Office, listed variously in the trade directories under Public/Official Establishments, was located in 1851 at the *George Commercial Inn* and later between 1862 and 1882 at the *Rose & Crown Inn*. This office regularly had a Supervisor, one or two Inland Revenue Officers and an Assessor & Collector of Taxes.[59] In 1851, Royston possessed an Excise Office situated at the *Green Man* but between 1861 and 1891 this establishment was listed as the Inland Revenue Office situated at the *Bull Inn, Hotel & Posting Office* in the High Street. In addition to the types of official found in Baldock, those in Royston included Surveyors of Taxes together with Clerks to Commissioners of Land, Assessed & Income Taxes. Throughout this period Ashwell and Buntingford never had more than a single Inland Revenue Officer at any one time.

While most of the tax officials appear to have been full-time operatives a town's Assessor & Collector of [Land, Assessed & Income] Taxes usually had other roles, for example, William Dear (Baldock, 1851) was also listed as a hairdresser, ironmonger, victualler of the *Plume of Feathers* and an insurance agent for the Farmers' Fire & Life & General Hail Storm Company. Similarly, Henry Smith (Royston, 1861 – 1871) was the town's Road Surveyor, Sanitary Inspector and Assistant Overseer. Supervisors appeared to be non-residents, for example,

---

[58] B.J. Davey, *Ashwell 1830–1914: The Decline of a Village Community. Dept English Local History, Occasional Papers, Third Series, No. 5* (Leicester, 1980), p. 34.

[59] Terminology of local tax offices occasionally changed over time and that of their officials sometimes differed between sources. The frequently occurring Inland Revenue Officer of the trade directories might appear in the corresponding censuses as an Exciseman, Inland Revenue Excise Officer, Division Officer Excise Branch and even Civil Servant Excise Officer 2nd Class.

Richard Humphry supervisor of both Baldock and Royston's Tax Office appeared not to reside in either town. One noticeable peculiarity was the prevalence of tax officials that according to the CEBs had migrated from Ireland; William Downes (Baldock, 1851), Matthew Thompson (Baldock, 1861), James MacDonald (Baldock, 1871 - 1881) and James Magowan (Royston, 1891).

It is not surprising, given the size of the 'wine, spirits and hotels' dealing sector and the prevalence of maltsters and brewers, that the agents of the Inland Revenue were so numerous in these centres. London brewers relied upon the surrounding arable counties for their malt supplies and according to Christine Clark the quality of Hertfordshire's brown malt made it the 'acknowledged capital of the malt trade'. In 1832 the county town Hertford was 'among the top ten excise collections in the country'.[60] It was suggested by William Ashworth that a 'powerful argument can be made that the foundation of the English/British fiscal state was built upon the public's addiction to alcohol' and that the 'duties on beer and malt were absolutely fundamental to the well-being of the public finances'.[61] This dependence on the malt tax, argued Clark, led to a 'complex web of legislation designed to prevent fraud and evasion' that gave excise officers the right of access to inspect premises at all times.[62] Brewers however, according to John Greenaway, often co-operated in voicing their opposition to 'greedy Chancellors of the Exchequer, erratic magistrates and, as the years went by, hostile temperance societies'.[63]

The County Police Act was passed by Parliament in 1839 and the Hertfordshire force created two years later comprising a chief constable, six inspectors and 60 constables. Hertfordshire's force until 1888 was administered, according to Tony Rook, by the quarter sessions and took from the parish constables their responsibility for law enforcement, vagrancy and weights and measures.[64] William Nathaniel Byrant, for example, was in 1851 Buntingford's 'Inspector of

---

[60] C. Clark, *The British Malting Industry Since 1830* (London, 1998), p. 14.

[61] W.J. Ashworth, *Customs and Excise: Trade, Production and Consumption in England, 1640 – 1845* (Oxford, 2003), pp. 210, 220. Malt tax first introduced in the late seventeenth century was followed by a tax on hops in 1711. Duty on beer was abolished by the 1830 Beer Act but re-introduced in 1880 on repeal of malt and sugar duties. Between 1830 and 1880 excise duty was levied upon bushels of malt (2s 8^{1}/2d per bushel from 1857 to 1880) used by a brewer rather than on the number of barrels of beer produced for sale. The 1830 Act allowed anyone to brew and sell beer on payment of an excise fee of two guineas (later increased according to rateable value of the premises) and Excise Officers collected data on numbers of brewers, victuallers and beer house keepers and the quantities brewed. The tax on hops was replaced in 1862 by an increase in the rate of brewers' licences. Beer duty in 1880 was re-imposed at 6s 3d per standard barrel of 36 gallons with an original gravity of 1057.

[62] Clark, *British Malting Industry*, p. 28.

[63] J. Greenaway, *Drink and British Politics Since 1830: A Study in Policy-Making* (Basingstoke, 2003), p. 23.

[64] T. Rook, *A History of Hertfordshire* (Chichester, 1984), pp. 91– 92.

Plate 2.8: Old Police Station, Kneesworth Street, Royston

Police & of Weights & Measures' while a decade later, Richard Edward Oliver was additionally responsible for the town's 'Lodging Houses'.[65] From 1851 to 1891 forty-one entries for law officers were identified across the four study centres, 15 in Buntingford, 14 in Royston, 7 in Baldock and 5 in Ashwell. Trade directories identified locations of Police Stations and the force's senior officers. Administratively, prior to 1897, Royston was split between Hertfordshire and Cambridgeshire with the latter's Constabulary being housed at Kneesworth Street (Plate 2.8 above) in the northern part of the town. Two-thirds of entries, largely identified from CEBs, related to constables with the occasional sergeant appearing from 1881 onwards. The one promotion identifiable by 1881 was that of Constable William Hurmmerston to Sergeant (aged 41) at the Police Station in Royston's High Street.[66]

The final third of the public and professional sector comprises those local individuals engaged in the administration of the poor, local health organisations and the courts (Table 2.6 below). For instance, public officials were numerous in Royston and Buntingford, the centres of two Poor Law Unions where, across the

---

[65] *Post Office Directory Six Home Counties, 1851*, p. 184; *Post Office Directory Six Home Counties, 1862*, p. 335.
[66] 1871 Census (Royston); 1881 Census (Royston).

directories examined, the number of union officials listed totalled fifty-eight and forty-four respectively.[67] The few individuals listed in Baldock, John Smith of Whitehorse Street, Registrar and Relieving Officer (1839 & 1851), James Hills of the High Street, Registrar for the Baldock District (1862), and Frederick Day, Overseer (1882), were all local officials of the Hitchin Union.[68] While Ashwell, the smallest town, had just two Justices of the Peace listed, Edward King Fordham (1870 and 1882) and Edward Snow Fordham (1890), the number of

Plate 2.9: Old County Court, between Fish Hill and Market Hill, Royston

such officials listed under Baldock and Buntingford over the same period was eighteen and fourteen respectively.[69] In contrast, over half (n = 48) of the total entries relating to Justices of the Peace and other local court officials were found

---

[67] The Buntingford Union consisted of sixteen parishes in Hertfordshire: Anstey, Ardeley, Aspenden, Broadfield, Buckland, Cottered, Great Hormead, Layston, Little Hormead, Meesden, Rushden, Sandon, Throcking, Wallington, Westmill and Wyddial. The Royston Union consisted of 28 parishes of which eight were in Hertfordshire: Ashwell, Barkway, Barley, Hinxworth, Kelshall, Nuthampstead, Reed and Therfield; sixteen in Cambridgeshire: Abington Piggotts, Barrington, Bassingbourn, Foulmire, Foxton, Guilden Morden, Kneesworth, Litlington, Melbourne, Meldreth, Shepreth, Shingay, Steeple Morden, Thriplow, Wendy and Whaddon; three in Essex: Great Chishall, Heydon and Little Chishall, and Royston itself, partly in Cambridgeshire and partly in Hertfordshire.

[68] *Pigot's Commercial Directory, Essex, Hertfordshire, Middlesex* (1839), p. 96; *Post Office Directory Six Home Counties, 1851*, p. 173; *Post Office Directory Six Home Counties, 1862*, p. 320; *Kelly's Directory Six Home Counties, Pt I* (1882), p. 564.

[69] *Kelly's Directory Six Home Counties, Pt I* (1890), p. 700.

under Royston. This variation in the number of judicial officials reflects the fact that while Baldock's miscreants had to appear before the petty sessions held at Stevenage or the county court at Hitchin, Royston had its own court whose jurisdiction covered forty-five parishes in north Hertfordshire and south Cambridgeshire including Ashwell and Buntingford. The Post Office Directory of 1851 described how 'the Petty sessions for the [Hertfordshire] Hundred of Odsey are holden here on the first and third Wednesdays in each month' and the area's county court (Plate 2.9 above) held monthly. By 1870 the same publication listed the 'special and petty sessions' at the *Bull Hotel* while the 'county court is held bi-monthly in the New Court House, Fish Hill'.[70]

In terms of local health officials, it was the cholera epidemic of 1832 that, according to Anthony Wohl, caused the government to issue a series of Sanitary Regulations calling for the establishment of local boards of health. These boards were to appoint District Inspectors to report on ' "the food, clothing and bedding of the poor, the ventilation of their dwellings, space, means of cleanliness [and] their habits of temperance" '.[71]

	Public Officials	**1851**	**1861/2**	**1870/1**	**1881/2**	**1890/1**
Baldock	Poor Law Union	1	1	-	1	1
	Health Authorities	-	-	-	3	4
	Court Officials	3	4	3	5	3
	Other	-	-	-	1	3
Buntingford	Poor Law Union	6	10	10	9	9
	Health Authorities	-	-	-	1	1
	Court Officials	2	5	4	1	2
	Other	-	-	2	-	-
Royston	Poor Law Union	8	10	8	13	19
	Health Authorities	-	2	3	5	4
	Court Officials	4	9	10	11	14
	Other	2	3	5	3	2
Total		26	44	45	53	62

Table 2.6: Local public officials
Source: Post Office Directories, 1851, 1862, 1870; Kelly's Directories, 1882, 1890; Census enumerations, 1851–1891.

---

[70] *Post Office Directory Six Home Counties, 1851*, p. 215; *Post Office Directory Six Home Counties, Pt 1* (1870), p. 476.
[71] A.S. Wohl, *Endangered Lives: Public Health in Victorian Britain* (London, 1983), p. 123.

By the 1880s, Baldock, Buntingford and Royston were all classed as local Sanitary Authorities each with a medical officer and a sanitary surveyor or inspector. These Inspectors of Nuisances carried out house-to-house visits in order 'to ferret out sanitary defects and nuisances' that included 'insanitary dwellings, stagnant and foul pools, gutters and water courses [and] broken and inadequate privies'. Not even the 1875 Public Health Act required these inspectors to possess any particular qualifications for the role and there were, as Wohl noted, complaints of too many 'grossly unqualified inspectors, among them watchmakers, grocers, dairymen, auctioneers, beershop-keepers and publicans'.[72] Such were the cases of tobacconist Charles Charter of Whitehorse Street (Baldock, 1890), who was also 'Surveyor and Sanitary Inspector to the Local Board of Health (Hitchin Rural District)'and Henry Maclin, Buntingford's 'Inspector of Nuisances' and 'Registrar of Births & Deaths' in 1882.[73]

In terms of healthcare provision Royston was fortunate in having had a cottage hospital erected in 1869 at the cost of £1000 raised by public subscription. It was a two-storey building with four wards that could normally hold six patients or eight in an emergency. Kelly described how the institution was 'supported by donations and annual subscriptions … aided by small weekly payments from those patients who can afford them'. Staff included Richard Pyne (consulting surgeon), D.B. Balding (surgeon) and H.R. Archer (assistant surgeon).[74]

There were two other significant professionals: Ernest Matthews (Royston, 1890) listed as a dentist in addition to being a chemist, wine and spirit merchant and the fire engine superintendent, and Louis Bate (Baldock, 1890) an optician acting as an 'Agent for Henry Laurance's spectacles (prompt attention given to all repairs)' in addition to being a clock and watchmaker, and jeweller.[75] These specialist professionals were more than one might expect in such modestly-sized settlements and were an indication that enough residents wished to avail themselves of their services and were able to afford them.

Apart from agriculture in Ashwell which averaged almost 21.0 per cent of the total number of services available across the period and the exception, in the same town, of building at 11.9 per cent in 1851, none of the five smaller business sectors in this study (agriculture, building, industrial services, transport and

---

[72] Wohl, *Endangered Lives*, p. 194.

[73] *Kelly's Directory Six Home Counties, Pt 1* (1882), p. 585; *Kelly's Directory Six Home Counties, Pt 1* (1890), p. 703.

[74] Kelly's Directory Six Home Counties, Pt 1 (1882), pp. 647 – 48. Deaths recorded in some contemporary parochial pedigrees compiled by Reverend John Hale of Therfield indicate that both male and female patients were admitted to the hospital.

[75] *Kelly's Directory Six Home Counties, Pt 1* (1890), pp. 809–10, 703.

domestic services) ever reached 10.0 per cent in any of the four towns. Given that all four towns were surrounded by prime farmland, the size of the agriculture sector in Ashwell appears somewhat anomalous. Analysis of actual acreages farmed between 1851 and 1891, when this detail was frequently noted by the enumerator, reveals that the overwhelming majority of Ashwell's farmers only had between 100 and 360 acres of land. In contrast, a substantial proportion of farmers in Buntingford and Royston (53.8 per cent and 35.7 per cent respectively) worked over 400 acres. For example, in Buntingford, Robert Clark farmed 500 acres in 1851 and widowed Isabella Porter held 1000 acres in 1881 while in Royston, Charles Nash's farm grew from 620 acres in 1861 to 1200 acres by 1881. Comparative figures for Baldock are difficult to assess, since in addition to acreages not being specified for four of the twenty-four farmers listed in directories between 1851 and 1890, a further nine farmers were totally absent from the corresponding CEBs. However, the limited data suggest similar large farms with William Farr holding 600 acres in 1871 and William Sale 655 acres in 1881. Thus the apparently larger agricultural sector in Ashwell is due its greater density of small acreage farms compared to the other three towns, not to an overall larger area of activity.[76]

Among those tradesmen active in the building sector, bricklayers (36), carpenters (36) and general builders (46) were some of the largest groups. There was however, a noticeable shift over time (Figure 2.9 below) away from specific bricklayers and carpenters to the more general category of 'builder' or 'builder & contractor'. This trend towards general contracting is in line with the view expressed by Richard Rodger that, from around 1790, the building industry moved away from independent master craftsmen to contractors with 'a permanent workforce in all crafts'.[77] This shift is demonstrated here by the fact that two-thirds of all bricklayers and carpenters listed in the three larger towns of Baldock, Buntingford and Royston were operating in 1851 and 1861/62 but their numbers thereafter declined while the number of builders in each town by 1890/91 had risen to three, four and six respectively. In contrast, and probably as a consequence of the disastrous fire of February 1850, the number of specialist bricklayers and carpenters listed in Ashwell was fairly constant, averaging three of each across the forty-year period, the latter including, for example, Thomas Picking, whose accounts (1855–1869) are discussed later. Ashwell's only 'Master builder' identified in the last three decades of the century was Frederick Bailey who in 1881 employed ten men and five boys.[78]

---

[76] 1851–1881 Census enumerations (Ashwell, Baldock, Buntingford, Royston).

[77] R. Rodger, *Housing in Urban Britain, 1780-1914* (Cambridge, 1995), p. 21.

[78] 1881 Census (Ashwell).

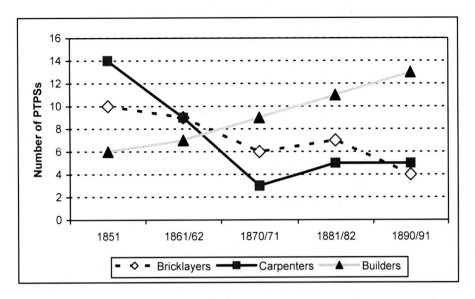

Figure 2.9: Growth in study towns' building contractors, 1851 to 1891
Source: Post Office Directories, 1851, 1862, 1870; Kelly's Directories, 1882, 1890; Census enumerations, 1851–1891.

The fourth prominent group of tradesmen in the building sector, and a constant presence in all four towns, were the 'plumbers, painters and glaziers' (37 entries in total), i.e. basically those working with lead. Plumbers from the 1860s onwards were, according to Rodger, increasingly in demand for the provision of the new housing 'amenities such as running water, gas [and] WCs'.[79] A smaller group were those identified as house decorators and painters (7 entries in total) that appeared from 1870/71 onwards in the larger of the four towns and who were probably indicative of the increased prosperity and fashion consciousness of their business communities.

Only one specialist stonemasonry business was identified across the region, that of the Whitehead family in Royston. It provides a good example of the continuity of a growing family business with Thomas Whitehead, 'Master stone & marble mason', employing five men in 1851, nine men and a boy by 1861, and thirteen men and five boys in 1871. In 1881, according to the CEB, the business is in the hands of Lydia Whitehead, 'Stonemason's widow', and ten years later the business of 'Whitehead & Son' had expanded to be that of 'stone, marble, granite & monumental masons & general contractors'.[80]

---

[79] Rodger, *Housing in Urban Britain,* p. 12.
[80] 1851–1891 Census enumerations (Royston); *Kelly's Directory Six Home Counties, Pt 1* (1890), p. 810.

Among the building sector PTPSs were a few surveyors including Edward Nash of Royston, 'architect & surveyor', between 1861 and 1881. Another surveyor, William Gibbons of Buntingford, provides an excellent example of the consistency and added detail of directory entries compared to that of CEBs. According to the 1861 CEB Gibbons was a 'Builder & surveyor' but ten years later simply a 'Builder'. However, the directories consistently identified him as a 'builder, surveyor & undertaker, brick, tile & drain pipe maker' and added 'lime burner' in 1882.[81]

As well as the obvious aftermath of Ashwell's fire, it is clear that the building sector was buoyant in the other three towns. Important contributory factors included the infrastructure associated with the arrival of the railway in each town, the modernizing of retail outlets, the building of gasworks and the installation of the new gas lighting services into domestic dwellings, commercial properties and the towns' streets.

In addition to such 'middle class professionals' as physicians, surgeons and solicitors, as we have seen earlier, Catherine Smith in her study of the industrial expansion of Mansfield and Newark, noted an increased number of bankers and 'insurers' by the middle of the nineteenth century.[82] The industrial services sector that includes banking, insurance and accountancy is well represented in the four towns.

Established in 1694, the Bank of England had an 'effective monopoly of the [bank] note circulation' to the end of the eighteenth century. However, its notes did not circulate much further than 60 miles from London and, beyond about 30 miles from the capital, private country banks 'could make a handsome profit' if their notes were widely accepted by the general public. According to Jack Parker, early small banks often developed from, and operated as part of, larger business enterprises among which, apart from the metals and textiles industries, 'brewing and malting was the only one to produce many bankers'.[83] An example of this is provided by the Royston Bank (Plate 2.10 below) that was established by the brewer Edward King Fordham in 1808 and operated successfully to the end of the century under various members of the Fordham dynasty.[84] Around 1862 the

---

[81] 1861–1881 Census enumerations (Royston); *Post Office Directory Six Home Counties, 1862*, p. 335; *Post Office Directory Six Home Counties, Pt 1* (1870), p. 429; *Post Office Directory Six Home Counties, Pt 1* (1882), p. 586.

[82] Smith, 'Image and Reality', p. 66.

[83] J. Parker, *'Nothing for Nothing for Nobody': A History of Hertfordshire Banks and Banking* (Stevenage, 1986), p. 11.

[84] Parker, *'Nothing for Nothing'*, pp. 19–20.

Plate 2.10: Former Fordham's Bank, High Street, Royston

Fordham's monopoly in Royston was challenged briefly by the opening of a branch of Foster & Co. from Cambridge; managed by Samuel Lambert, it was open on Wednesdays.[85] By 1891 the bank had established its own branch in

---

[85] *Post Office Directory Six Home Counties, 1862*, p. 378.

Buntingford, 'Fordham, Gibson & Co. bankers' which was only 'open fridays 11 a.m. to 2 p.m.'.[86] Similar to the case of the Fordhams, maltster John Williamson founded the Baldock Bank in 1807. After his death in 1830 it became 'Wells, Hogge & Lindsell', a branch of the Biggleswade & Baldock Bank whose partners were all brewers.[87] In 1851 the bank was managed by Benjamin Christian, a fire insurance agent in Baldock since 1823; his son William Christian took over the role from around 1862 until the turn of the century.[88]

These banks served the business community and the middle-classes but in the early decades of the nineteenth century there arose the concept of the savings bank designed to encourage saving among the less well off. For example, James Newberry was listed as Secretary of Baldock's Savings Bank in 1851 and 1862; the High Street bank which had opened in 1816 finally closed in 1864. Buntingford's Savings Bank had opened later in 1845 with Charles Nicholls as its actuary; it closed after twenty years in 1865.[89] The demise of these two banks, along with many others across the country, was a direct consequence of Gladstone's Post Office Savings Bank Act of 1861. This new institution, Parker observed, offered greater security and convenience to small savers 'since the Post Offices were open every weekday for long hours, not the short infrequent periods of the older savings banks', perhaps only limited hours one day a week.[90] In Baldock and Royston the new post office service prospered whilst at least some continuity was guaranteed to savers in Buntingford for when its Savings Bank closed, Charles Nicholls was already the town's Postmaster.

The main aim of friendly societies was to act as sources of financial benefit to their members in times of sickness and death. They also made significant contributions to nineteenth-century economic and social development since in addition to financial security, argued Simon Cordery, these voluntary organizations provided conviviality and the opportunity for working people to engage in respectable social and political activities.[91] Given that nearly 30,000 friendly societies existed by the late-nineteenth century it is surprising that their presence is totally absent from the data gathered for the four towns.

It would appear there were sufficient people, especially in Baldock, with either

---

[86] *Kelly's Directory Six Home Counties, Pt 1* (1890), p. 732.

[87] Parker, '*Nothing for Nothing*', pp. 16 – 17, 28.

[88] *Pigot's Commercial Directory, 1823–24*, p. 350; *Post Office Directory Six Home Counties, 1851*, pp. 172-73; *Post Office Directory Six Home Counties, 1862*, pp. 320-21.

[89] *Post Office Directory Six Home Counties, 1851*, pp. 173, 184; *Post Office Directory Six Home Counties, 1862*, pp. 321, 335.

[90] Parker, '*Nothing for Nothing*', p. 55.

[91] S. Cordery, *British Friendly Societies, 1750-1914* (Basingstoke, 2003).

very complex financial affairs or the desire to have their business accounts professionally handled, to require the services of professional accountants. These included John Scott situated in the High Street (1851), James Hills of Pembroke End (1870) and Henry Volhurn in Pembroke Road (1881).[92]

Along with the recognition of the value of savings came that of the need to protect one's assets. Eighteenth and nineteenth-century growth of industry, coupled with urban development, Barry Supple argued, was responsible for an increased 'awareness of the value of residential, social, industrial and commercial property' leading to 'a sustained boom in fire insurance'.[93] The large number of insurance agents plying their services in three of the four towns (Ashwell being the exception) clearly indicates that a substantial part of the local populace was very aware of the need to protect their assets. Twenty-four agents in Royston represents a ratio of 1:78 of the population in 1861/2, and fifteen agents, a ratio of 1:136 of the population in Baldock in 1870/1.[94] The fact that among the identified insurance agents three-quarters had at least one other occupation suggests that it was largely a part-time job. Clive Trebilcock found that in the early decades of the nineteenth century the Phoenix Assurance sales-force was concentrated among small traders 'whose high street shops served a rich and varied mix of property-holders'.[95] Later he observed an increased 'respectability' of agents as the company recruited from the banking and legal professions. Similarly, the present analysis found among 125 entries for agents with other occupations that 38.4 per cent were high street traders (21 grocer/draper/tailor combinations, 11 stationers, 9 chemist & druggists, 4 ironmongers and 3 bakers) and a further 17.6 per cent were involved in the building trades and manufacturing (9 builders, 5 saddlers, 3 plumbers, 3 upholsterers and 2 cabinet makers). Furthermore, the data reveals over a dozen members of the professional class prepared to act as insurance agents. For example, 'John Price, esq', Buntingford solicitor and 'Clerk to Deputy-Lieutenant of the County' was a Sun Fire & Life agent while William Christian, manager of the Baldock & Biggleswade Bank was an agent for

---

[92] 1851 Census (Baldock); *Post Office Directory Six Home Counties, Pt 1* (1870), p. 411; 1881 Census (Baldock).

[93] B. Supple, 'Insurance in British History', in O.M. Westall (ed.), *The Historian and the Business of Insurance* (Manchester, 1984), p. 4.

[94] In total, between 1851 and 1891, there were fifty-four insurance companies represented by a variety of agents. Agents from just seven of these companies were responsible for seventy-two entries (36.9 per cent total, n = 195): County Fire & Life (12 entries); Phoenix Fire & Life (12 entries); Norwich Union Fire & Life (11 entries); Royal & Exchange Fire & Life (10 entries); Sun Fire & Life (10 entries); Royal Farmers Fire, Life & Hailstorm (9 entries); Atlas Fire & Life (8 entries).

[95] C. Trebilcock, *Phoenix Assurance and the Development of British Insurance, Vol. 1, 1782–1870* (Cambridge, 1985), p. 86.

Rock Fire & Life.[96] This 'respectability' also rubbed off onto a few of the solicitors' clerks, for example William Daintry of Royston who also acted for Sun Fire Insurance.[97] Evidence from the current analysis also suggests that being an insurance agent appears to have provided respectable employment for a limited number of women (see detailed discussion in section 2.9 below). Baldock's Post Mistress in 1851, widowed Mrs Sarah Stocken, appeared in directories until 1870 as an agent for County Fire & Provident Life Insurance.[98] Another example is provided by Mrs Sarah Proctor who, in addition to running a 'ladies boot & shoe warehouse' in Royston with her husband George, was employed as 'agent to Suffolk & Bury fire office'.[99]

In spite of the apparent buoyancy of the regional economy across the latter half of the century, by 1890/1 there was a dramatic fall in numbers of insurance agents identified in Baldock, Buntingford and Royston from their peak between 1861 and 1871. As less than 5.0 per cent of these agents were identified in the CEBs, evidence that the role was not seen by the enumerators as a person's main occupation, does this collapse in their numbers indicate a change of policy on the part of the directory publishers or consolidation of the insurance industry leading to fewer agencies? Supple's research clearly suggests the latter explanation. He estimated that in 1806, three insurers, the Phoenix Fire Office, the Sun Fire Office, and the Royal Exchange Assurance, together had 60.0 per cent of the fire insurance business in England. By the middle of the nineteenth century there were almost 200 life insurance companies in existence (over fifty were identified in the present analysis) but by the 1890s many companies had combined fire and life insurance into a composite business and the industry came to be 'increasingly dominated by multi-divisional big businesses'.[100] This trend is clearly visible in the four towns. Overall, in both 1861 and 1871 there were forty-six individual insurance agents identified and, of those listed in both years, thirty-eight (82.6 per cent) had at least one other occupation. In dramatic contrast, by 1891 only twelve insurance agents were identified, 6 in Royston, 3 in Baldock, 2 in Buntingford and just a single agent in Ashwell, and of those only two had other occupations. This finding suggests that by then for most agents there was sufficient business to make it a full-time job, undoubtedly helped by the fact that the majority were employed by some of the largest companies in the insurance world at that time, including Guardian, Norwich Union, Pearl and Phoenix.

---

[96] *Post Office Directory Six Home Counties, 1862*, p.335; *Post Office Directory Six Home Counties, Pt 1* (1870), p. 411.

[97] *Kelly's Directory Six Home Counties, Pt 1* (1882), p. 648; 1881 Census (Royston).

[98] *Post Office Directory Six Home Counties, 1851*, p. 173.

[99] *Post Office Directory Six Home Counties, 1851*, p. 216.

[100] Supple, 'Insurance in British History', p. 7.

Provision of domestic services between 1851 and 1891 in Baldock, Buntingford and Royston was largely restricted to that of chimney sweeps (20 entries in total) and hairdressers (23 entries in total) with laundries (only 5 entries) identified just in Baldock. Apart from Royston's widowed Isabella Wall, 'Mistress hairdresser', who in 1851 continued her husband William's business, all the listed hairdressers were male.[101] There was no provision of any of these domestic services listed for Ashwell, the smallest town, over the entire forty-year period.

Changing roles of the small numbers of road carriers identified and the coming of the railways to north-east Hertfordshire in the second half of the nineteenth century are discussed in detail later. The latter event created the post of Station Master at Baldock and Royston by 1861, at Buntingford by 1871, and finally at Ashwell by 1881. The only other PTPSs identified in the transport sector were Benjamin Ballard a publican, coal merchant and 'fly proprietor' in Buntingford from 1882 to 1890, and the Stamford family of Royston. James Stamford, publican at the *Catherine Wheel* in 1871, was also the agent for the Great Northern Railway and responsible for the booking office for cabs and parcels. After his death, his widow Elizabeth continued as railway agent and 'cab proprietress' but by 1890 the role had been taken on by their son James.[102]

The above evidence highlights how, in terms of the number of PTPSs identified, dealing and trading activities were a major driving force behind the successful regional economy of north-east Hertfordshire. It further shows the importance of specialist manufacturing activities; malting and brewing in Ashwell, Baldock and Royston, tanning in Buntingford. Over the forty-year period the growth of educational establishments, the advent of local health authorities and the running of the two Poor Law unions in Buntingford and Royston also created a large number of professionals and public servants confirming their town status.

The role of women

Nineteenth-century middle-class society was clearly uncomfortable with the concept of its women working on the assumption, as Leonore Davidoff and Catherine Hall stated, that 'a woman engaged in business was a woman without either an income of her own or a man to support her', compelled out of necessity

---

[101] 1851 Census (Royston).

[102] *Post Office Directory Six Home Counties, Pt 1* (1870), p. 479; *Post Office Directory Six Home Counties, Pt 1* (1882), pp. 586, 650; *Kelly's Directory Six Home Counties, Pt 1* (1890), pp. 732, 810. A cab or hackney-coach was a two-horse four-wheeled coach for hire, a fly was a lightweight covered carriage drawn by one horse.

to work.[103] They were not considered educated for business. Few would have agreed with Erasmus Darwin's enlightened view that a girl's education at school ought to include mathematics and science, most believing they should properly concentrate on drawing, piano playing and a knowledge of languages.[104] Yet, in order to avoid penury, Jane Humphries suggested many widows chose 'to escape the ghetto of poorly paid feminised jobs by taking up the occupation and/or business activities of their deceased spouses'.[105] Between 1851 and 1891 in north-east Hertfordshire 'principal' providers of goods and services, the manufacturers, retailers and professional classes identified from the selected directories and CEBs, were predominantly male, on average accounting for around 85.0 per cent of the total. In contrast, throughout the second half of the century, the proportion of women identified from directories and CEBs ranged from as few as 6.8 per cent in Ashwell (1851, n = 5) to as many as 18.9 per cent in Royston (1881/2, n = 46) of the total individual PTPSs. The numbers of individual women identified were, proportionately, significantly higher in the three larger towns of Baldock, Buntingford and Royston. Whilst the lowest proportions found in Baldock and Buntingford were 11.3 per cent (1851) and 11.0 per cent (1870/71) respectively over the five decades, in Royston they never fell lower than 16.3 per cent (1861/62). These figures are at the higher end of Davidoff and Hall's range reported in their trade directory study of Birmingham and parts of Essex and Suffolk. They calculated that from 1780 to 1850 in both rural and urban areas, 'women made up between 5 and 15 per cent of the economically active population' but with a narrowed range of activities by the mid-nineteenth century.[106]

Usually among the female PTPSs identified, with the exception of Ashwell where the proportion was somewhat lower, around two-thirds were to be found listed in the trade directories while the other third were only identifiable from the census returns. It is important to note that although trade directories do not provide a complete picture of women's importance to the local economy they are, as Sheryllynne Haggerty recently observed, 'one of the few sources available in which women are listed on their own terms' regarding their occupation and not as 'wife' or 'widow' as found in parish registers and census records.[107]

---

[103] L. Davidoff and C. Hall, *Family Fortunes: Men and Women of the English Middle Class, 1780–1850* (London, 1987), p. 272.

[104] Davidoff and Hall, *Family Fortunes*, p. 290.

[105] J. Humphries, 'Female-headed Households in Early Industrial Britain: the Vanguard of the Proletariat', *Labour History Review*, 63 (1998), p. 38.

[106] Davidoff and Hall, *Family Fortunes*, p. 312.

[107] S. Haggerty, 'Women, Work, and the Consumer Revolution: Liverpool in the late Eighteenth Century', in J. Benson and L. Ugolini (eds), *A Nation of Shopkeepers: Five Centuries of British Retailing* (London, 2003), p. 106.

Davidoff and Hall, in their 1851 census sample, estimated that 69.0 per cent of female heads of household were widows and 21.0 per cent single women.[108] Similarly, in the four centres under discussion here, a sizeable proportion of the female PTPSs, identifiable from CEBs, were widows: 23.3 per cent in the case of Royston, 24.4 per cent in Buntingford, 27.8 per cent in Baldock and 34.0 per cent in Ashwell.[109] Surprisingly, in the light of the traditional Victorian view of middle-class working women, 80.3 per cent of these widows were listed in the trade directories. Overall, the evidence illustrates the benefit of utilizing two complementary data sources to investigate the numbers of working women. Among the 474 entries of female PTPSs, almost half (n = 206) were identified in both trade directory listings and CEB entries, 91 (19.2 per cent) were found only in the selected directories, and the remaining 177 (37.3 per cent) were present only in the CEBs. Hannah Barker argued that trade directories attempted to record, in its entirety, that part of the urban business community deemed important and 'therefore provide better coverage of the urban middling sort' than alternative sources.[110] That two-thirds of the identified female PTPSs were listed in trade directories is a measure of their status in the regional economy of north-east Hertfordshire.

Many in society expressed alarm at 'the idea of middle-class women using their skills or property to establish independent careers'.[111] Thus widows, as Pat Jalland together with Davidoff and Hall observed, had few opportunities to embark on the challenge of a career since many inherited the use of their husband's property only when either they remarried or their children reached the age of majority.[112] In the early nineteenth century the growing unacceptability of women 'working publicly for profit', argued Cynthia Curran, explains the frequent willingness of widows to remarry 'often to a journeyman or competitor who would take over their deceased husband's business affairs'.[113] Yet, argued Alistair Owens, women 'were frequently and routinely placed in positions of proprietorial responsibility'. Widowed beneficiaries were principally 'custodians' of their late husband's estates which were frequently gifted 'for the remainder of

---

[108] Davidoff and Hall, *Family Fortunes*, p. 273.

[109] If an allowance is made for those numerous directory entrants not located in the corresponding census, then the proportion of widows increases to 29.3 per cent in Royston, 31.0 per cent in Buntingford, 33.7 per cent in Baldock and 40.5 per cent in Ashwell.

[110] H. Barker, *The Business of Women: Female Enterprise and Urban Development in Northern England, 1760–1830* (Oxford, 2006), p. 54.

[111] Davidoff and Hall, *Family Fortunes*, p. 275.

[112] P. Jalland, *Death in the Victorian Family* (Oxford, 1996), p. 231; Davidoff and Hall, *Family Fortunes*, p. 276.

[113] C. Curran, 'Private Women, Public Needs: Middle-class Widows in Victorian England', *Albion*, 25 (1993), p. 224.

their [wife's] natural life'.[114] Although, as Owens noted, in some wills restrictions prevented the widow selling, disposing or wilfully wasting the estate and in a fifth of his sample the will would be revoked if the widow re-married. Contrary to the foregoing views, Maxine Berg's examination of early nineteenth-century wills and inventories from Birmingham and Sheffield indicated that men had expected 'their wives would at least share in the management of [their] property'. Furthermore, many of these women 'did own real property [including shops and workshops] and in most cases, they disposed of it as they wished' to both male and female kin.[115] In the case of married women, prior to 1870, the common law 'doctrine of coverture' gave a husband legal ownership over his wife's personal property. This included managerial rights over any land and property that she might have inherited, although as Mary Beth Combs observed, 'not all marriages followed the law in practice'. However, efforts by social reformers and their proposals to 'ameliorate the abuses suffered by poor women', argued Ben Griffin, led to the 1870 Married Women's Property Act which finally gave wives the right to own and control property.[116]

According to Davidoff and Hall, among women in 'active occupations' (sic) the category of 'professional', usually that of school mistress, was the most common, followed by 'trade', then inn keeping and farming.[117] In contrast, the present analysis indicates that in the four towns, 50 per cent of the stated occupations of the 476 identified female PTPSs were in the dealing sector (See Figure 2.10 below). A further 41.0 per cent (194 in total) were found in the 'public and professional' category including 134 school mistresses and other assorted 'specialist' teachers and 41 governesses.[118] Manufacturing accounted for a modest 4.0 per cent (21 individuals) of female PTPSs together with a mere 1.5 per cent (7 individuals) involved in agricultural activities.

By 1851, women in Davidoff and Hall's sample 'made up 64.0 per cent of the teaching force in Essex and 79.0 per cent in Birmingham'.[119] These figures were matched in Ashwell and Royston where across the second half of the nineteenth

---

[114] A. Owens, 'Property, Gender and Life Course: Inheritance and Family Welfare Provision in Early Nineteenth-century England', *Social History*, 26, 3 (2001), pp. 299, 310.

[115] M. Berg, 'Women's Property and the Industrial Revolution', *J. Interdisciplinary History*, XXIV, 2 (1993), pp. 238, 243.

[116] M.B. Combs, 'Wives and Household Wealth: The Impact of the 1870 British Married Women's Property Act on Wealth-holding and Share of Household Resources', *Continuity and Change*, 19, 1 (2004), p. 143; B. Griffin, 'Class, Gender, and Liberalism in Parliament, 1868-1882: The Case of the Married Women's Property Acts', *Historical Journal*, 46, 1 (2003), p. 60.

[117] Davidoff and Hall, *Family Fortunes*, p. 293.

[118] Among the 'specialist' teachers were ten music teachers, Francois Frechet (aged 74), a widow from Savoy, a 'teacher of French' (Royston, 1871) and Charlotte Francis (aged 20) a 'teacher of drawing' (Royston, 1891).

[119] Davidoff and Hall, *Family Fortunes*, p. 293.

century the school mistresses accounted respectively for 63.0 and 77.0 per cent of the total school teachers. Figures for Baldock and Buntingford were somewhat lower at 46.0 and 50.0 per cent respectively. Numerous women, single, married

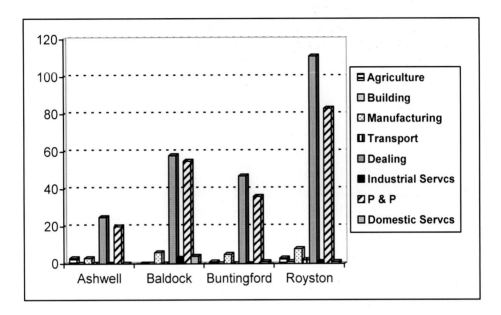

Figure 2.10: Numbers of 'principal' women by occupational sector
Source: Post Office Directories, 1851, 1862, 1870; Kelly's Directories, 1882, 1890; Census enumerations, 1851–1891.

and widowed, entered teaching. It had a relatively high status among the professions and, argued Curran, 'fostered an illusion that the [female] teacher was merely providing an extension of child-care instead of working at a paying job', pursuing part of 'the only correct and decent manner of life' for a woman.[120] Plotting the age profile of 108 school mistresses, identified from CEBs (Figure 2.11 below), shows that the majority (58.3 per cent) were under the age of thirty and single. Only seven were identified as married (aged between 44 and 66) and ten widowed (aged between 31 and 74). A similar age profile was obtained for the forty governesses and one 'private tutor'; all appeared single apart from Helene Walther (aged 48) from Paris, a widowed 'school governess' employed in Baldock (1891). A related occupation was that of widowed Maria Bacon (aged 45) employed as 'matron' at Buntingford Grammar School (1881).

Two examples of working women not exactly fitting the Victorian mould for the middle-classes were Sarah Stocken and the Pickering sisters, Clara and Lucy.

---

[120] Curran, 'Private Women', p. 230.

William Stocken was listed in Pigot's 1839 directory as Baldock's '*Post Master* (and general newspaper agent.)' but in the 1851 directory, and confirmed by the census, the 'postmistress' is the widowed Mrs Sarah Stocken (aged 59); both

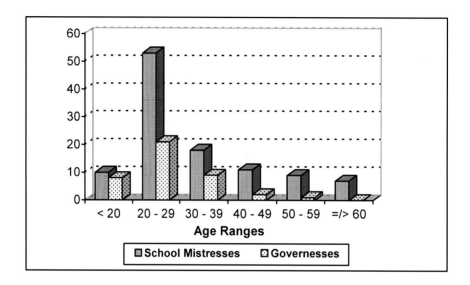

Figure 2.11: Age profile of school mistresses and governesses, 1851–1891
Source: Post Office Directories, 1851, 1862, 1870; Kelly's Directories, 1882, 1890; Census enumerations, 1851–1891.

husband and wife were agents for the '*County Fire & Provident Life*' insurance company.[121] By 1862, George Davies had become the 'postmaster' in Baldock.[122] The case of Sarah Stocken is clearly contrary to Curran's expressed view that 'widows were hampered by their age' for admission to the Post Office and other Civil Service positions.[123] In the directory of 1862, Thomas Pickering a widower (aged 64) was described as a book, print and music seller, stationer and secretary of Royston's '*Public Subscription Library & Reading Room*'; a year earlier the census enumerator recorded his daughter Clara (aged 28) as a 'librarian'.[124] By 1871 she is recorded as a 'bookseller and librarian'.[125] In 1882, after the apparent death of her father, Miss Clara Pickering appeared in Kelly's directory as 'stationer & bookseller' while the census recorded that she employed a news

[121] *Pigot's Commercial Directory, Essex, Hertfordshire, Middlesex* (1839), p. 95; *Post Office Directory Six Home Counties, 1851*, p.173.
[122] *Post Office Directory Six Home Counties, 1862*, p. 321.
[123] For entry into the Post Office as a telegraph operator, or into the Civil Service, the usual age of admission was between 14–18 and 17–20 respectively, Curran, 'Private Women', p. 229.
[124] *Post Office Directory Six Home Counties, 1862*, p. 378; 1861 Census (Royston).
[125] 1871 Census (Royston).

boy.[126] Meanwhile Clara's elder unmarried sister Lucy (aged 58), formerly a teacher of languages and music, had become the secretary and librarian of the town's library and reading room.[127]

Between 1851 and 1890 the Buntingford and Royston workhouses provided additional opportunities for women as 'Matron of Union Workhouse', usually being married to the 'Master'.[128] Mrs Mary Ann Croft (Buntingford, 1862 to 1870) and Mrs Elizabeth Ann Bryant (Royston, 1862 to 1870) provide two examples of middle-class women beginning, as Steven King observed, 'to apply their "domestic skills" to the task of "municipal housekeeping" '. This language, he argued, was utilized to reduce the hostility to their public work by 'effectively portraying such roles as a natural extension to their role as home-keepers'.[129] In addition, the Royston Union showed foresight by employing Miss Sarah Dade as workhouse school mistress in 1882, and Miss Lucy Dyball as an 'Industrial Trainer' in 1890. Such appointments were, according to King, attempts to 'change the long-term prospects of poor children through education and training' though critics argued it might give paupers an advantage over others.[130]

Remarriage of widows, suggested Curran, dropped during the nineteenth century as middle-class women moved away from a 'property-based income toward small earnings' resulting in a move toward professions which earned incomes.[131] Nevertheless, a majority earning their own livelihood were in trade, since being a woman responsible for a manufacturing enterprise was still viewed as an anomaly. Furthermore, argued Davidoff and Hall, due to a virtual 'prohibition on manual skills (outside of the domestic) which was so closely tied to their feminine status' certain occupations were, to the middle-class mind, closely associated with one or other gender and, for example, meant the exclusion of women from anything associated with the building trades.[132]

Hannah Barker, in her more recent study of Manchester, Sheffield and Leeds, disputed this 'traditional historical consensus' of unfeminine occupations

---

[126] *Kelly's Directory Six Home Counties, Pt 1* (1882), p. 649; 1881 Census (Royston).

[127] *Kelly's Directory Six Home Counties, Pt 1* (1882), p. 649.

[128] *Post Office Directory Six Home Counties, 1851*, p. 184; *Post Office Directory Six Home Counties, 1862*, pp. 335, 378; *Post Office Directory Six Home Counties, Pt 1* (1870), pp. 428, 477; *Kelly's Directory Six Home Counties, Pt 1* (1882), pp. 585, 648; *Kelly's Directory Six Home Counties, Pt 1* (1890), pp. 732, 808.

[129] S. King, ' "We Might be Trusted": Female Poor Law Guardians and the Development of the New Poor Law: The Case of Bolton, England, 1880-1906', *Int. Rev. Social History*, 49, 1 (2004), p. 29.

[130] *Kelly's Directory Six Home Counties, Pt 1* (1882), p. 648; *Kelly's Directory Six Home Counties, Pt 1* (1890), p. 808; King, ' "We Might be Trusted" ', p. 38.

[131] Curran, 'Private Women', p. 227.

[132] Davidoff and Hall, *Family Fortunes*, p. 308.

believing that, by the early nineteenth century, businesswomen were 'central characters in a story of unprecedented social and economic transformation'.[133] The present analysis supports Barker's assumption in identifying twenty-one trade directory entries for women involved in a variety of manufacturing activities and one in the building trade. These entries, some continuing over a twenty or thirty year period, involved a total of sixteen women. Census returns allowed the identification of one married and two unmarried women together with nine widows.

In 1870, for example, Thomas Whitehead (aged 55) was a master 'stonemason & carver' in Royston employing thirteen men and boys. While Kelly's 1882 directory still listed Thomas, the business had passed to his wife since the 1881 census showed Lydia Whitehead (aged 67) to be a 'Stonemason's widow'. Her exact role then and later is unclear, for by 1890 the directory listed 'Whitehead & Son, stone, marble, granite & monumental masons & general contractors' while the census showed son William (aged 52) as the employer and widow Lydia, now aged 77, 'Living on own means'.

The manufacturing businesses included 4 blacksmiths, 2 braziers, 2 millers, 2 wheelwrights, a bacon smoker, an ironmonger, a linen manufacturer and a saddler. All eight identified widows were involved, to some degree, in the continuation of what had been their husbands' businesses.[134] In two cases, Hannah Swaine (Baldock, 1851 – 62) and Sarah Wilson (Royston, 1881/2), the widows are both interestingly identified in the CEB as 'Mistress blacksmith'.[135] While it is doubtful that either was qualified to wield the smith's hammer, the title probably indicates that they were 'managing' the businesses, an interpretation supported by the fact that Sarah Wilson was shown as 'employing 2 men'.[136] There were three other cases of widowed female employers. For example, Maria Hamilton (Buntingford, 1870/71 – 1881/82) was listed in the directory as an 'ironmonger, brazier & smith' and shown in the census to be employing '5 men' in 1871 and '8 men & 1 boy' in 1881.[137] However, Kelly's 1882 directory listed 'Hamilton, John & Charles, ironmongers' perhaps suggesting that their 78 year old mother was taking a less active role in the business.[138] Another example was Mrs Emily/Elizabeth Hankin (Baldock, 1870 – 91) a 'saddler' (directory) and 'harness maker' (census) shown as 'employing 1 man' in the 1881 census and

---

[133] Barker, *Business of Women*, p. 3.

[134] Ascertained by reference to earlier directory entries.

[135] 1861 Census (Baldock); 1881 Census (Royston).

[136] 1881 Census (Royston).

[137] *Post Office Directory Six Home Counties, Pt 1* (1870), p. 429; 1871 Census (Buntingford); 1881 Census (Buntingford).

[138] *Kelly's Directory Six Home Counties, Pt 1* (1882), p. 586.

having the status 'E' for employer in 1891.[139] Finally, also with the census status 'E', was widow Eliza Wilson (aged 60) of Royston listed in 1890/91 as both a 'wheelwright' (directory) and 'coach builder' (census).[140] The only example of a married woman in business was Mrs Catherine Baker (aged 57) listed 1861/62 as a 'brazier &c' in Royston (there were no occupational details in CEB for her husband Robert).[141] Two unmarried young women, Mary Ann Hyde (aged 22) from Hitchin and Lydia Harrison (aged 25), Mary's 'partner', from Cambridge had a 'baby linen wareho[use].' under the name of 'Hide & Harrison (Misses) in Melbourne Street, Royston. The 1871 census records them both as 'Under linen manufacturer'.[142]

The 'middling sort' of women, argued Hannah Barker, were prominent in the rapidly expanding urban economies of three northern towns particularly those embarking on new business ventures such as 'buyers and sellers of goods and providers of services'.[143] She identified the highest numbers of women as unspecified shopkeepers followed by dressmakers, victuallers or innkeepers, milliners, grocers, straw hat makers, butchers and confectioners.[144] Similarly, the evidence presented here shows that exactly half of the entries (n = 240) relating to female PTPSs were involved in the dealing and distributive sector. Those engaged in the retailing of food and the twenty-one unspecified 'shopkeepers' accounted for 33.8 per cent of these dealers. Perhaps, not surprisingly, the commonest services being provided were those of baker (16 entries), confectioner (10 entries) and grocer (10 entries). However, given the prevailing attitudes, the butchers (6 entries) and fishmongers (6 entries), for instance, may have caused something of a stir among polite society in the four towns.

Christine Wiskin has illustrated many of the problems faced by female businesswomen in the late eighteenth century and suggested that most of their enterprises were short-lived. However, for those that survived five years, she thought it reasonable to assume that 'suppliers and customers alike had confidence in the proprietor'. After operating ten years or more, she felt it likely that the business was certainly profitable and that 'its proprietor was active in developing new lines of production, stock, or services offered to the public … and

---

[139] *Post Office Directory Six Home Counties, Pt 1* (1870), p. 411; *Kelly's Directory Six Home Counties, Pt 1* (1882), p. 564; *Kelly's Directory Six Home Counties, Pt 1* (1890), p. 704; 1871-1891 Census enumerations (Baldock).

[140] *Kelly's Directory Six Home Counties, Pt 1* (1890), p. 810; 1891 Census (Royston).

[141] *Post Office Directory Six Home Counties, 1862*, p. 377; 1861 Census (Royston).

[142] *Post Office Directory Six Home Counties, Pt 1* (1870), p. 478; 1871 Census (Royston).

[143] Barker, *Business of Women*, p. 4.

[144] Barker, *Business of Women*, p. 66.

developing its standing in the community'.[145] Two examples among the female butchers and fishmongers of Royston demonstrate that longevity of business was definitely achievable with minimal intervention by men. Firstly, in 1862, Miss Sarah Kefford (unmarried, aged 37) was listed as a 'fruiterer' in the High Street and some years later she had moved to Melbourn Street expanding her business to that of 'fruiterer & fishmonger'. By 1881, still unmarried, she was again listed as 'fruiterer & fishmonger' but additionally the CEB identified her as 'Greengrocer'; this last combination continued for at least another ten years.[146] Secondly, Mrs Mary Ann Barnes (widow, aged 52) is first listed in 1862 as a 'pork butcher'. The CEB of 1871 shows her to be a 'Pork butcher & dealer' assisted by her two daughters Mary Ann (aged 35) and Susanna (aged 34). A decade late, the two sisters (Mary Ann, Head of the household) had taken on the business. It appears to have been successful for by 1891 the elder sister (unmarried, aged 55) is 'Living on her own means', neither employed nor an employer.[147]

A further 30.0 per cent of female traders (72 entries) were operating services in the dealing sub-category 'dress'. These were predominantly milliners (28 entries), dressmakers (15 entries) and drapers (10 entries). An unusual example is that of Mrs Hope Ellis in Baldock, not only a 'stay & corset maker' but a married women (aged 40) running a separate business from that of her husband. In the 1881 census Albert Ellis is described as a carpenter employing a joiner while his wife's business was listed in the 1882 trade directory. By 1891 the census shows her to be widowed but still making corsets and employing her two daughters, Alice (aged 20) and Frances (aged 19) as assistants.[148] Mrs Ellis was not alone in this respect. Jane Dodd (aged 33) married to Samuel was listed in the 1861 census as a 'Leather cutter's wife' yet the 1862 directory showed her to be a 'haberdasher' in Buntingford High Street. Ten years later she appears as 'haberdasher' (directory) and 'Fancy shopkeeper' (census) but still a 'Leather cutter's wife'. By 1882 the now widowed Jane (aged 53) is listed in the directory

---

[145] C. Wiskin, 'Urban Businesswomen in Eighteenth Century England', in R. Sweet and P. Lane (eds), *Women and Urban Life in Eighteenth-century England: On the Town* (Aldershot, 2003), p. 100.

[146] *Post Office Directory Six Home Counties, 1862*, p. 377; 1861 Census (Royston); *Post Office Directory Six Home Counties, Pt 1* (1870), p. 478; *Kelly's Directory Six Home Counties, Pt 1* (1882), p. 649; 1881 Census (Royston); *Kelly's Directory Six Home Counties, Pt 1* (1890), p. 810; 1891 Census (Royston).

[147] *Post Office Directory Six Home Counties, 1862*, p. 377; 1861-1891 Census enumerations (Royston).

[148] 1881 Census (Baldock); *Kelly's Directory Six Home Counties, Pt 1* (1882*)*, p. 564; 1891 Census (Baldock).

as running a 'berlin wool repository' as well as the shop and in 1891 the CEB indicates her to be an 'employer'.[149]

Almost a quarter of the female dealers identified were involved in the 'wine, spirit and hotels' sub-category of the dealing sector being publicans (44 entries) or 'beer retailers' (12 entries). Wiskin has noted that whereas the male victualler was often seen as a 'businessman or entrepreneur', his female counterpart was 'depicted as caring and cooking in an environment only slightly removed from the domestic', almost respectable! She estimated that in late eighteenth-century Birmingham and Liverpool nearly 30.0 per cent of victuallers were women, while Koditschek found that in Bradford in 1850 women accounted for 13.0 per cent of the city's innkeepers and beer sellers.[150] In contrast, there were no women publicans listed in Ashwell between 1851 and 1891, just the very occasional 'beer retailer', while Baldock and Buntingford had only one or two women running public houses in each decennial period. However in Royston, the figures were much higher, 6 out of 19 in 1861, 4 out of 20 in 1871, 7 out of 24 in 1881, and 7 out of 26 in 1891.

The above examination of the role of women in the regional economy of north-east Hertfordshire has revealed examples of a significant number of them engaged in business activities that do not fit with the conventional wisdom regarding middle-class working Victorian ladies.

Conclusion

This chapter demonstrates some of the inherent problems encountered in seeking to identify changes in the business communities of four small towns across the nineteenth-century. Trade directories between 1800 and 1851 can only provide an incomplete picture of a town's commercial and professional community as their publishers were still evolving the format, and potential contributors still assessing their commercial value. From 1851 onwards, the CEBs of the decennial censuses allow for a more complete assessment. In order to fully appreciate the towns' business activities, nominal record linkage between these two sources is essential for the second half of the century. Results support an observation by Dennis Mills that a problem exists in interpreting the differences between single or multiple directory entries for individuals and their occupation(s) as listed by a census enumerator. He argued that 'it is evident from nominal record linkage

---

[149] 1861 Census (Buntingford); *Post Office Directory Six Home Counties, 1862*, p. 335; *Post Office Directory Six Home Counties, Pt 1* (1870), p. 429; 1871 Census (Buntingford); *Kelly's Directory Six Home Counties, Pt 1* (1882), p. 586; 1881 Census (Buntingford); 1891 Census (Buntingford).

[150] Wiskin, 'Urban Businesswomen', p. 104; T. Koditschek, *Class Formation and Urban Industrial Society: Bradford, 1750–1850* (Cambridge, 1990), p. 222.

exercises that a directory could leave out as much as it included' and questioned whether a change in the description of a given occupation is of real significance or 'merely a whim on the part of the subject or the scribe concerned'.[151] It was not uncommon however in this Hertfordshire study to find the converse of Mills's argument where the directory listed far more information about an individual than could be gleaned from the corresponding census enumeration.[152] The findings agree with Mills's further comment that 'most of those who were economically 'significant' appear' but 'how accurate were the [directory] lists is a matter for careful consideration'.[153] Having identified those individuals, who in the main, were probably business owners or master craftsmen, the record linkage work utilising relevant census returns confirmed that the majority were indeed listed in the trade directories.

Many previous socio-economic surveys of urban centres have, like Church's study of Nottingham and Koditschek's work on Bradford, focused on a single large town. Some, like Vigne and Howkins's work on small shopkeepers, investigated a narrower business aspect of towns in general. Others, like Gourvish and Wilson's study of brewing have examined a particular industry.[154] The comprehensive methodological approach utilized here for a comparative regional study of the entire business communities of four small urban centres would not be readily applicable to a comparative study of large urban centres. Unfortunately, while many clusters of similar small towns might benefit from this approach, the methodology is probably not applicable to large urban centres on account of the time and human resources that would be necessary.

The large numbers of public houses and beer retailers together with a few commercial inns and hotels are evidence that the towns' nineteenth-century business communities thrived on trade generated by the plethora of passing stagecoaches, mail coaches, carts and wagons. Others that benefited from this traffic were the blacksmiths, saddlers, harness makers and wheelwrights. All four towns were surrounded by fertile farmland producing high quality cereals, notably

---

[151] D.R. Mills, Rural *Community History from Trade Directories: A Local Population Studies Supplement* (Aldenham, 2001), p. 44.

[152] *Post Office Directory of Six Home Counties, 1851*, pp. 172–3.

[153] Mills, *Community History from Trade Directories*, p. 14.

[154] R. A. Church, *Economic and Social Change in a Midland Town: Victorian Nottingham, 1815-1900* (London, 1966); T. Koditschek, *Class Formation and Urban Industrial Society: Bradford, 1750–1850* (Cambridge, 1990); T. Vigne and A. Howkins, 'The Small Shopkeeper in Industrial and Market Towns', in G. Crossick (ed.), *The Lower Middle Class in Britain, 1870-1914* (London, 1977); T. R. Gourvish and R. G. Wilson, *The British Brewing Industry, 1830–1980* (Cambridge, 1994).

barley. This factor led to a major concentration of malting and brewing activities in three of the centres, Ashwell, Baldock and Royston.

Successful exploitation of the foregoing two factors appears to have created increased business opportunities and middle-class consumer demand leading to an expansion of local retailing. The coming of the railway to north-east Hertfordshire allowed for mass produced china, earthenware and glassware, produced in midland and northern industrial centres, to be transported to the region; dealers in such wares were most prevalent in Royston. Thus consumer demand in turn created, as Clark intimated, an emerging class of modestly affluent shopkeepers.[155] Furthermore, the presence of tea dealers, tobacconists and an 'Italian Warehouse' suggests that even small towns, with good road and rail connections, could integrate with a wider international economy.

The New Poor Law requirements of 1834 led to the creation of Poor Law Unions in Buntingford and Royston but not in Baldock which became part of the Hitchin Union. From the data gathered here, it is obvious that such organisations created a substantial local bureaucracy of public officials. Growth of these administrative functions in Buntingford and Royston enhanced their status of towns, a point illustrated by McCormack in his study of Lutterworth.[156]

Large numbers of school teachers were identified, not just working in 'National' or 'British' elementary schools, but in a significant number of private boarding schools in Baldock, Buntingford and Royston which each had three such educational establishments. Here again better roads and, especially, the railways played an important role in making boarding schools increasingly accessible to middle-class families.

Among the professionals listed for all four towns under consideration were the physicians, surgeons and general practitioners. Medical provision, according to Steven Cherry, reflected 'the pull of market forces, as the poor were irregular consumers of doctors' services'.[157] Between 1851 and 1891, the approximate ratio of one doctor to between 400 and 1000 of the population in Baldock, Buntingford and Royston was comparable to some of the best rates in Britain. Clearly the market forces here were driven by the substantial middle-class populations of these towns coupled with the presence of Union workhouses in both Buntingford and Royston.

---

[155] Clark, 'Small Towns 1700 – 1840', pp. 752–54.

[156] J. McCormack, 'Lutterworth: A Comparative Study of Economic and Social Structure in Leicestershire' (Certificate Dissertation, Centre for Urban History, University of Leicester, 1992), p. 2, cited in Clark, 'Small Towns 1700–1840', p. 754.

[157] S. Cherry, *Medical Services and the Hospitals in Britain, 1860–1939* (Cambridge, 1996), p. 42.

Despite the negative views of working middle-class women that prevailed in the Victorian period, this chapter demonstrates significant numbers of female PTPSs prepared to advertise alongside men in the local trade directories. As well as those in the traditional roles of school mistress and governess, that were considered more 'respectable', 50 per cent of all the female PTPSs identified were engaged in the dealing sector, and a few in manufacturing businesses.

Overall analysis of trade directory and census data relating to these business and professional communities indicates a clear hierarchy among the four towns. Ashwell lacks many of the activities found in the other three and perhaps ought to be viewed as a large satellite village of nearby Baldock. Their manufacturing base, the breadth of their dealing and retailing activities, and the large numbers of public servants and professionals, identify Baldock and Royston as the two most thriving small towns in the region. Buntingford, not at a major crossroads and only seven miles south of Royston on the Old North Road, occupies a mid-position in the hierarchy. These findings support Marshall's hypothesis that clusters of small towns will exhibit a hierarchy because of a combination of complementary functions existing alongside specialist manufacturers and retailers.[158] Furthermore, by the second half of the nineteenth century, the presence of a post office, a railway station and schools confirms these four small urban centres as significant 'central places' according to Christaller's criteria. That Baldock and Royston both sit on major crossroads and Royston possessed a library and newspaper publisher are further 'central place' criteria that help reinforce the observed hierarchy between the four small towns.[159] Analysis of the provision of goods and services available from craftsmen-retailers in sixteen villages within the towns' immediate hinterlands, as we shall see in chapter four, confirms the obvious dependence of these smaller centres on Baldock, Buntingford and Royston.

These towns were clearly not 'failing' but with populations remaining well below 2,500 neither had they become behemoths of industrialization. The evidence presented shows that they avoided substantial decline and thrived at this time as a result of their multi-functional nature, specialized manufacturing and improved transport infrastructure. Clearly, the findings from this regional survey of north-east Hertfordshire suggest the need for a re-evaluation of some of the earlier negative portrayals of the small nineteenth-century towns of England. They were small but certainly flourishing.

---

[158] Marshall, 'Cumbrian Market Town', p. 132.

[159] Christaller, *Central Places*, pp. 139–41, 154.

3

Ancillary providers of goods and services

It is important to establish the ancillary roles played by skilled and semi-skilled workers engaged in the provision of goods and services within the regional economy of north-east Hertfordshire. Such workers, in the main being employed by the PTPSs, cannot be ascertained from trade directories and obtaining a comprehensive view of the four business communities is not therefore possible before the 1841 census. Examination of the four towns' census returns between 1851 and 1891 enables the identification of 2937 of these 'ancillary traders professionals and service providers' including the journeymen and both male and female assistants and apprentices, whose employment opportunities were usually created by the PTPSs.[1]

Unskilled labourers are deliberately excluded from this analysis because of the frequently vague occupational descriptions applied to them by the census enumerators and their occurrence in very large numbers. Domestic servants, once again considerable in number and not viewed here as being part of the 'business community', are likewise ignored. Two particular groups of ATPSs, however, required some differentiation; these were people in charge of horses and those in charge of carts and wagons. In the first group, 'grooms' and 'coachmen', where it is sometimes difficult to identify those who were not simply domestic servants, are excluded. In contrast, 'ostlers' who were usually employed by inns or hotels, are included. In the second group, 'carters', persons simply in charge of a cart, are excluded while commercial 'carriers', 'draymen' and 'wagoners' are included. 'Carriers' transported either their own or other people's goods, 'draymen' carried goods by horse and dray cart (especially beer barrels for breweries), and 'wagoners' were carriers or horse and wagon operators.[2] Additionally, 'visitors'

---

[1] A journeyman was a fully qualified craftsman or tradesman who had served an apprenticeship but had not yet set himself up as a 'master'. He was employed and paid as a day labourer, often working away from home, in contrast to a 'master' who had his own business where he set his own rates and employed others. An apprentice was indentured to a 'master', with a premium paid to the 'master' by the boy's (to a much lesser extent the girl's) parents or, in the case of paupers, by the overseer of the poor. The unpaid apprentice received board and lodging and training for several years.

[2] C. Waters, *A Dictionary of Old Trades, Titles and Occupations* (Newbury, 1999), pp. 54, 89, 112, 161, 244.

to households listed in the CEBs, whatever their relationship to the 'Head of the Household' or occupation, were excluded though most working 'boarders' and 'lodgers', apart from labourers and other non-skilled persons, were included.[3]

Identifying the female skilled and semi-skilled 'ancillary' providers of goods and services from the census return entries has its problems. Edward Higgs has argued that the distinctions enumerators drew, especially in the case of women, 'between making and dealing, employers and employees, and those economically active and those unemployed and retired, are all obscure'.[4] From 1851 to 1881 enumerators were instructed to record the 'occupations of women who are regularly employed from home, or at home, in any but domestic duties' and in 1891 to record the 'occupations of women ... if any'. However, suggested Higgs, women's work at home, was still 'not regarded as an "occupation" and went unrecorded'. A farmer's wife was usually assumed to help with her husband's agricultural tasks and was thus listed as 'Farmer's Wife' but this led to some enumerators making entries regarding other types of wife that clearly, according to Higgs, confused 'remunerative work, kin relationships or multiple occupations (cotton spinner *and* wife?)'.[5]

Royston enumerators for the 1871 census, James Dillistone, Henry Smith and James Smith, provide several interesting examples of this practice. Charlotte Evans, 'Fishmonger's Wife', may well have assisted her husband John, as may Mary Jude, 'Retailer of Beer's Wife' in *The Griffin Inn* run by husband Alfred. It seems less likely that Grace Cass, 'Inland Revenue Officer's Wife', Elizabeth Woods, 'Railway Labourer's Wife' or Mary Cockayne, 'Solicitor's Conveyancing Clerk's Wife', would have been helping their husbands. In the case of William Hinkins, a House Decorator, Plumber and Painter, not only was Maria listed as a 'House Decorator's Wife' but Clara as a 'House Decorator's Daughter'.[6] In the period before the 1891 census which introduced the occupational classifications 'employer', 'employed' or 'neither' it is difficult to ascertain the exact role of the many women apparently involved in the clothing trade. For example was a 'dressmaker' making dresses for her immediate family, for her neighbours, to sell

[3] A 'boarder' is a paying guest receiving daily meals in addition to accommodation in a (boarding) house. A 'lodger' pays for accommodation (sleeping-quarters) in a hired room within a lodging-house, inn or hotel.

[4] E. Higgs, *Making Sense of the Census Revisited: Census Records for England and Wales, 1801–1901: A Handbook for Historical Researchers* (London, 2005), p. 99.

[5] Higgs, *Census Revisited*, pp. 101, 102.

[6] 1871 Census (Royston).

in her shop or was she employed in the 'sweated trades'? [7]

An important issue in seeking to establish detailed patterns of employment and the identification of the four towns' major employers is the occurrence and reliability of 'employee' data recorded by census enumerators. In north-east Hertfordshire, as elsewhere, the enumerators assiduously listed acreages and employees of every farmer, ranging from William Smith (Baldock, 1851) who employed one man on his twenty-four acres, to William Sale (Baldock, 1881), with twenty-four men and nine boys employed on 655 acres.[8] However, in the case of non-farming PTPSs, the enumerators appear to be less consistent in the recording of either the number or type of employee. Their varied terminology probably reflected what Higgs described as 'the difficulties inherent in trying to pin down fluid nineteenth-century employment practices' as the General Register Office moved from an economic model based on 'master', 'apprentice' and 'journeyman', to one 'structured around the polarity of 'employer' and 'worker' '.[9] Data from Ashwell, Baldock, Buntingford and Royston clearly demonstrate this variation, with employees or 'workers' variously recorded as men, boys, lads, women, females, girls, apprentices, artisans, assistants, labourers and persons.

Sectoral distribution of ATPSs and semi-skilled workers

The identified ATPSs as a proportion of the four towns' total populations are shown in Figure 3.1 below. In each case, the proportion of the ATPSs was approximately the same as the proportion of their PTPSs. Between 1851 and 1891 the proportion of ATPSs in Baldock fluctuated marginally but increased in

---

[7] This latter term applied to many wage-earners working at home in 'domestic' workshops as part of the 'outwork system' defined by Duncan Bythell as an 'industry controlled by urban merchant-manufacturers who, through the medium of agents [the "bagman", "putter-out" or "fogger"], "put out" the most labour intensive parts of the process of manufacturer to the poor of the surrounding countryside'; D. Bythell, *The Sweated Trades: Outwork in Nineteenth-century Britain* (London, 1978), p. 17.

[8] 1851 Census (Baldock); 1881 Census (Baldock).

[9] Higgs, *Sense of the Census Revisited*, p. 110. Instructions to enumerators in 1851 stated that 'In TRADES the master is to be distinguished from the Journeyman and Apprentice, thus – '(*Carpenter, master employing [6] men*)'; inserting always the number of persons of the trade in his employment on March 31st. Furthermore, 'In trades where women or boys and girls are employed, the number of each class should be separately given'. In 1861 the instructions defined the master as an employer: 'IN TRADES, MANUFACTURES, or other business, the employer must, in all cases, be distinguished; Example: '*Carpenter – master, employing 6 men and 2 boys*'; inserting always the number of persons of the trade in his employ'. In 1871 and 1881 the instructions reverted to talking of a 'Master' as opposed to an 'Employer'. Finally in 1891 the CEBs incorporated three new columns for employment status headed 'Employer', 'Employed' and 'Neither employer nor employed, but working on own account'.

Ashwell from 4.2 to 6.3 per cent, in Buntingford from 5.6 to 8.9 per cent and in Royston from 11.2 to 14.1 per cent.

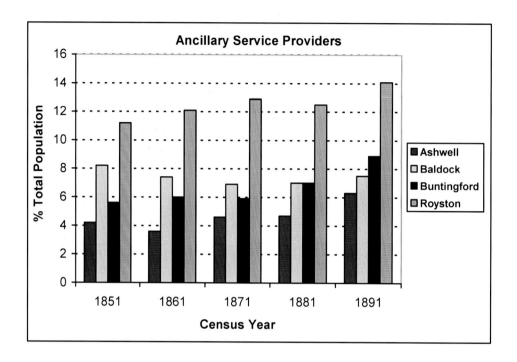

Figure 3.1: ATPSs as proportion of total population
Source: Census enumerations, 1851–1891.

Based upon the same occupational analysis that was utilised for the PTPSs, the majority of ATPSs between 1851 and 1891 were employed or self-employed in the four business sectors of 'building', 'dealing', 'manufacturing', and 'transport' (Figure 3.2 below). Smaller numbers of ATPSs were identified in the 'domestic services', 'industrial services', and the 'public and professional' sphere. The sectoral distribution of employment opportunities for ATPSs in Royston, with the not surprising exception of the public and professional sector, largely mirrored the proportional distribution of PTPSs in the sense that it was dominated by 'dealing' (*ca* 40–50 % in both groups). In Baldock and Buntingford the predominance of 'dealing', while still the largest employment sector for ATPSs (*ca* 30–40 % of total), was proportionately less than that observed for the PTPSs. This lower proportion was due to the considerable work opportunities afforded ATPSs by the building and manufacturing sectors in the two towns (*ca* 15–25 % combined). In contrast to the other three towns, Ashwell's major source of employment for the ATPSs during this period was in the manufacturing sector (*ca* 30–35 % of total) almost double that provided by 'dealing' (*ca* 15–25 % of total). The proportion of Ashwell's ATPSs employed in the building sector matched the number of those in 'manufacturing' from 1851 to 1861 (*ca* 30–35 %) but fell back to be on a par with 'dealing' in the last decades of the century. Work for ATPSs in the transport sector grew considerably in Baldock and Buntingford reaching 17.0 and 13.0 per cent respectively by 1891. In contrast, in Ashwell and Royston the proportion of ATPSs involved in transport never exceeded 9.0 per cent of the total.

Significant levels of activity in the building sector suggest that the second half of the nineteenth century was a period of regeneration and/or growth in both the commercial and domestic arenas of these towns. Regeneration was an absolute necessity in Ashwell which suffered a calamitous fire in the High Street (Plate 3.1 below) on the night of Saturday 2 February 1850 resulting in 200 people being made homeless.[10]

Plate 3.1: Post-fire regeneration, Ashwell High Street

---

[10] 'The material damage was catastrophic; the flames had destroyed seven of the largest farms, half-a-dozen craftsmen's houses and premises, some large public buildings, including the Bull's Head Inn, a school and two independent chapels … and 30 labourers' cottages.'; B.J. Davey, *Ashwell 1830–1914: The Decline of a Village Community. Dept of English Local History, Occasional Papers. Third Series, No. 5* (Leicester, 1980), p. 35.

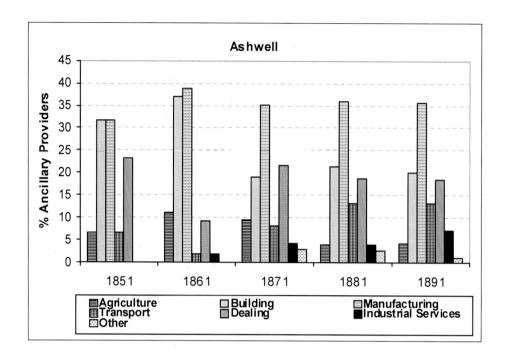

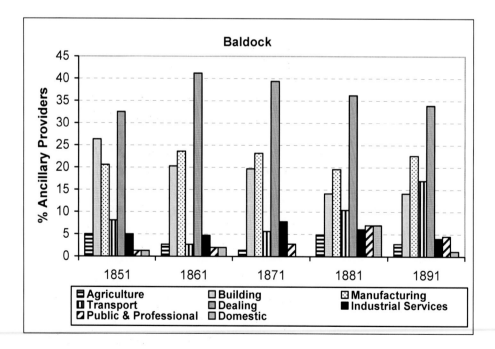

Figure 3.2: Changing sectoral proportions of ATPSs in four towns
Source: Census enumerations, 1851–1891.

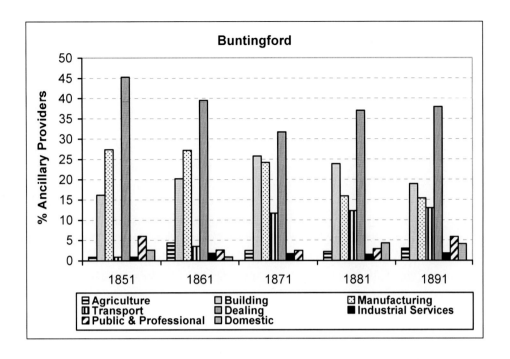

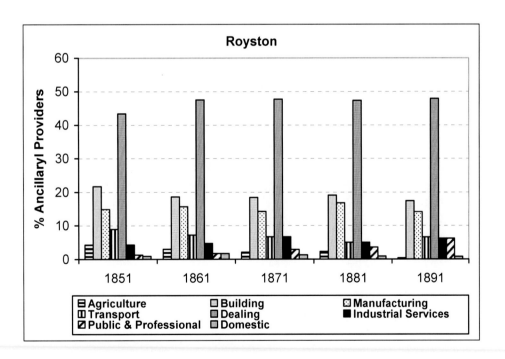

While each sector offered some employment opportunities in all four towns the dominant sector(s) varied within each locality. In Royston it was 'dealing', in Ashwell 'manufacturing', while in Baldock and Buntingford there was a more even distribution of these opportunities between the 'building', 'dealing' and 'manufacturing' sectors. Overall the number of PTPSs in the regional business and service communities offered work for a great many skilled and semi-skilled ATPSs.

According to the CEBs, only a tiny minority of the identified ATPSs had two roles compared to the 20.0 to 25.0 per cent of PTPSs who had dual or multiple occupations. There were no ATPSs found with more than two roles. In Ashwell, Baldock and Buntingford the level of dual occupation was usually between only 0.7 and 1.4 per cent of the total number of ATPSs while in Royston it was double that at 2.2 to 3.5 per cent. Among those few individuals (41 in total) with dual occupations about 40.0 per cent were involved in the 'dress' dealing category where the most common combinations found were those of dressmaker and either milliner (n = 11) or mantle maker (n = 3).[11] Examples of some more unusual combinations included those of James Coote, 'gardener and coal seller' (Royston, 1851), Thomas Morton, 'brick maker and rail carter' (Royston, 1851), Sarah Craft, 'tailor and earthenware factor's assistant' (Royston, 1871) and William Fisher, 'general carpet fitter and upholsterer' (Royston, 1891).[12] The limited number of ATPSs identified with multiple roles is a reflection of the fact that the majority of them were specialist tradesmen and women.

The changing sectoral employment scene, 1851 – 1891

Agriculture provided many job opportunities for large numbers of farm labourers. John Nunn (Royston, 1881), for example, employed twenty-three men, nine boys and five women on his 730 acre farm but, for the purposes of this analysis, these largely unskilled members of the regional workforce are excluded.[13] A very limited number (96 entries), a mere 3.3 per cent of the total ATPSs, were identified as belonging to the agricultural sector across all of the four towns. These skilled individuals were largely employed in two groups: gardeners, market gardeners and nurserymen (54.2 per cent of the sector); farm bailiffs, foremen and assistants (27.1 per cent). Among additional entries there were: 5 gamekeepers, 3 hedgers, 2 agricultural machinists, 2 veterinary assistants and James Fletcher (Ashwell, 1861), 21 year old 'farming apprentice' from Staffordshire.[14] Nearly

---

[11] A mantle was a loose sleeveless cloak.

[12] 1851 Census (Royston); 1871 Census (Royston).

[13] 1881 Census (Royston).

[14] 1861 Census (Ashwell).

all of the 'gardeners' were employed in Baldock and Royston (17 entries each) compared with Ashwell (10 entries) and Buntingford (5 entries). It should of course be noted that many skilled ATPSs employed by farmers would have lived in the region's villages rather than in the four towns.

Apart from agriculture, employment in the manufacturing sector (Figure 3.3 below) was most prevalent in the sub-categories of 'food and drink', 'leather and tallow', 'metalwork', 'carriage' and 'furniture'. Different sub-categories were found to dominate the manufacturing scene in each of the four locations.

		1851	1861	1871	1881	1891
Ashwell	Milling	6	3	2	2	3
	Brewing	3	2	1	5	6
	Malting	2	6	6	4	4
	Mineral Water	-	-	-	-	1
Baldock	Brewing	3	3	7	4	7
	Malting	9	6	4	11	9
Buntingford	Milling	1	4	1	1	2
	Malting	5	5	2	-	-
Royston	Milling	-	5	2	2	-
	Brewing	-	-	1	2	1
	Malting	2	2	1	3	3

Table 3.1: ATPSs engaged in the brewing and malting industry
Source: Census enumerations, 1851–1891.

In two of the towns, Ashwell and Baldock, the major manufacturing activities offering employment to ATPSs were in the sub-category 'food and drink' and were dominated by brewing and malting (Table 3.1 above) which to a lesser extent was the case in Buntingford and Royston. Flour milling provided jobs in all four towns.

Between 1851 and 1881 the census enumerators were instructed to distinguish 'master' from 'journeyman' or 'apprentice' by 'inserting always the number of persons of the trade in his employment'.[15] Yet attempting to link the afore-

---

[15] Higgs, p. 111.

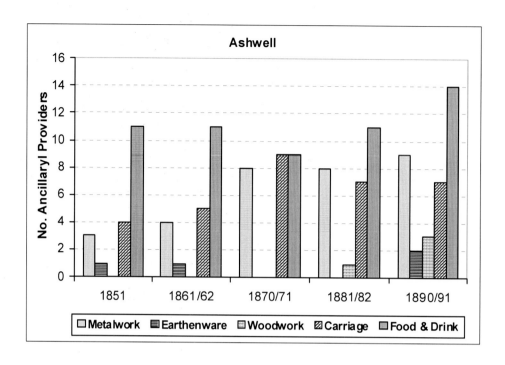

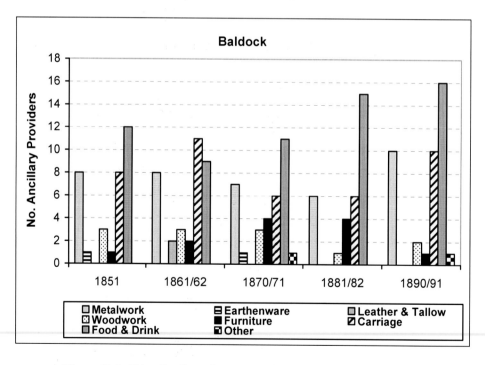

Figure 3.3: Distribution of ATPSs within manufacturing sector
Source: Census enumerations, 1851–1891.

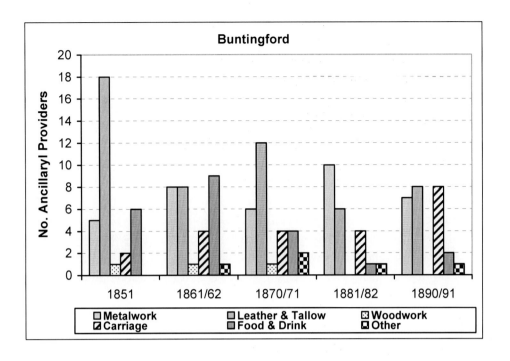

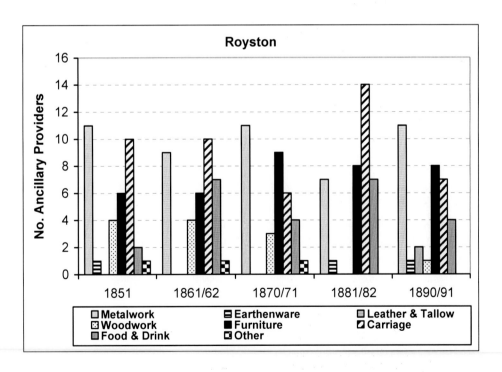

mentioned ATPSs in the brewing and malting industry to the opportunities provided by previously identified employers in this sector is not straightforward as the following three examples show. Firstly, the census of 1851 provides no employment figures for Baldock 'maltster' Joshua Page but in 1861 he is shown as 'employing 17 men and 2 boys'. Frustratingly, the 1871 CEB shows his son, Joshua Richmond Page, employing a cook and two housemaids but provides no detail of the malting's workforce. For this latter Joshua in 1881 the enumerator wrote 'employing [blank] men' suggesting his good intentions might have been thwarted in some way![16] Secondly, a frequent problem is that of brewers and/or maltsters who were also farming. An example is that of Edward King Fordham from Ashwell, 'brewer and maltster' described in the CEB of 1851 as farming 220 acres and employing 30 unspecified labourers but by 1861 his brother and partner Oswald is shown employing 17 men at their brewery. No employment figures for the Fordham's brewery appeared in 1871 but in 1881 Edward King is shown employing 12 men, 2 clerks and 1 brewer.[17] Finally, John Steed, 'brewer and maltster' of Baldock, employed '9 persons' in 1851, '18 men and 1 boy' in 1861 but no numbers listed in 1871. In 1881, Oliver Steed continued the business as well as farming 200 acres but is shown with '28 men and 3 boys' entered as unspecified employees.[18] Despite the instructions it is very clear, as Higgs has suggested, that such employment figures 'were plainly imperfect' with many employers and/or the enumerators failing to indicate the number of persons who were employed in a given business enterprise.[19] One major brewer and maltster who did provide more reliable statistics from 1851 to 1871 was John Phillips of Royston. According to the CEBs he employed '34 men' in 1851, '36 men and 5 boys' in 1861, and '34 men and 10 boys' in 1871 but even he, in partnership with his brother Joseph, gave no indication of their 1881 workforce.[20]

In Buntingford the major manufacturing activity was in the sub-category 'leather and tallow' where George Mickley's local tannery was one of the town's largest businesses. It employed, according to the CEBs, '33 men' in 1861, '23 men and 7 boys' in 1871, '20 men and 2 boys' in 1881. Unfortunately, there are no figures for 1891 because, by then, the census enumerator was simply required to indicate whether Mickley was an employer or not.[21] Although, according to Clarkson, the production of leather between 1750 and 1850 was 'by value, the second or third largest manufacturing industry in Britain', East Anglia and the East Midlands were not areas with a high density of tanneries; so why was there a successful

[16] 1861-1881 Census enumerations (Baldock).
[17] 1851-1881 Census enumerations (Ashwell).
[18] 1851-1881 Census enumerations (Baldock).
[19] Higgs, p. 112.
[20] 1851-1881 Census enumerations (Royston).
[21] 1861-1881 Census enumerations (Buntingford).

business in Buntingford? [22]   The most likely answer is probably related to Buntingford's position on a major north-south road and its relative proximity to London, which Clarkson pointed out 'had a high concentration of tanners by virtue of its importance as a meat-consuming and leather-demanding centre'. Hence the capital's meat markets would have provided Mickley with a readily available supply of hides.[23]

Plate 3.2: The Master Tanner's House, High Street, Buntingford

It is reasonable to assume that probably all the 'tanners' and 'curriers' identified in Buntingford's census returns did in fact work for George Mickley (Plate 3.2 above); their combined numbers totalling 17 (1851), 6 (1861), 11 (1871), 6 (1881) and 7 (1891) respectively.[24] His 1882 trade directory listing for Buntingford read 'currier, leather seller & tanner; & at Hertford, Royston, Biggleswade & Hitchin'. His 1890 entry for Royston read 'carrier, leather seller & tanner, Market Hill

---

[22] L.A. Clarkson, 'The Manufacture of Leather', in 'The Agricultural Servicing and Processing Industries', in G.E. Mingay (ed.), *The Agrarian History of England and Wales, Vol. 6, 1750–1850* (Cambridge, 1989), pp. 466, 478.

[23] Clarkson, 'The Manufacture of Leather', p. 478.

[24] A tanner or leather curer used tannic acids derived from oak tree barks to cure animal hides and preserve them as leather. A currier or curryer was a leather trade finisher who greased the cured/tanned dry leather to make it flexible before it was cut for sale.

(attends Weds)' while the town's 1891 census revealed Simius Camps, 'Leather cutter', and Robert Humphrey, 'Leather worker', both presumably employed by Mickley.[25] Roy Church has discussed how 'throughout the [nineteenth] century, boot and shoemakers and the makers of saddlery and harness provided the major demand for leather' and the above establishments would have been wholesale outlets supplying that local demand.[26]

In Baldock and Royston, and to a lesser extent in Buntingford, the three other regularly occurring manufacturing activities where PTPSs might have employed skilled labour were in the sub-categories of 'metalwork', 'carriage' and 'furniture'. While Ashwell had some businesses in 'carriage' work, unlike the other three towns, its 'metalwork' was limited to that of the blacksmith. Both Chartres and Turnbull believed that these particular craftsmen 'retained their importance to 1900 and beyond, for even in 1914 England was still essentially a horse-drawn society'.[27] Journeymen blacksmiths were the predominant group among ATPSs

Metal Workers		1851	1861	1871	1881	1891
Royston	Blacksmith	8	7	8	6	7
	Copper Workers	3	1	3	1	2
	Iron Workers	-	1	-	-	2
Baldock	Blacksmith	3	3	3	5	7
	Copper Workers	4	3	3	1	3
	Iron Workers	1	2	1	-	-
Buntingford	Blacksmith	1	4	3	8	5
	Copper Workers	4	4	3	2	2
Ashwell	Blacksmith	3	4	8	8	9

Table 3.2: ATPSs engaged in metalworking in the manufacturing sector
Source: Census enumerations, 1851–1891.

working with metal (Table 3.2 above) but their modest number reflects the limited opportunities for employment in all four towns. Between 1851 and 1891, apart

---

[25] E.R. Kelly (ed.), *Kelly's Directory of the Six Home Counties, Part I: Essex, Herts & Middlesex* (London, 1882), p. 586; *Kelly's Directory of the Six Home Counties, Part I: Essex, Herts & Middlesex* (London, 1890), p. 732; 1891 Census (Buntingford).
[26] R.A. Church, 'The Shoe and Leather Industries', in R. A. Church (ed.), *The Dynamics of Victorian Business: Problems and Perspectives to the 1870s* (London, 1980), p. 200.
[27] J.A. Chartres and G.L. Turnbull, 'Country Craftsmen', in G.E. Mingay (ed.), *The Victorian Countryside, Vol. 1* (London, 1981), p. 314.

from in Ashwell, the majority of master blacksmiths apparently working alone ranged from 60.0 per cent in Royston to 87.5 per cent in Buntingford. It is of course quite possible, given the frequent under-enumeration of employees noted in the breweries, that these figures are exaggerated. For example, James Pack of Ashwell employed '4 men & 2 lads' in 1851, and '7 men' in 1871 but he had no employees listed in 1861.[28] Some journeymen found employment with widows. Two examples are Mrs Hannah Swaine, 'Mistress blacksmith' of Baldock who employed '2 men' from 1851 to 1861, and Sarah Wilson, 'Mistress blacksmith' of Royston who employed '2 men' in 1881.[29] Surprisingly, only three apprentice blacksmiths were identified all bound to Royston masters and all towards the end of the century: George Robinson (aged 16, 1881), John Reeve (aged 15, 1891) and Robert Bing (aged 12, 1891). Robert was the son of an employed blacksmith, Alfred Bing, originating from Great Mongeham, near Deal in Kent.[30] A further noticeable quirk of the data from directories and CEBs is an almost total absence of reference to farriers, i.e. blacksmiths who specialize in horse-shoeing. Over the forty-year period only two farriers occurred in the directory trade listings, George Neale in Baldock (1870) and Thomas Watts in Ashwell (1870/1882). However, in the corresponding 1871 CEBs, Neale is recorded as a 'Veterinary Surgeon' and Watts a 'Horse Doctor' though he too is described as a 'Veterinary Surgeon' by 1881.[31]

Carriage Workers		1851	1861	1871	1881	1891
Royston	Saddle/Harness Maker	4	5	3	5	3
	Wheelwright	5	3	1	4	1
	Coach Builder/Painter	1	2	2	5	3
Baldock	Saddle/Harness Maker	4	3	1	2	3
	Wheelwright	3	2	5	3	3
	Coach Builder/Painter	1	6	-	1	4
Buntingford	Saddle/Harness Maker	-	1	-	1	2
	Wheelwright	1	1	2	2	5
	Coach Builder/Painter	1	2	2	1	1
Ashwell	Saddle/Harness Maker	1	1	4	1	2
	Wheelwright	3	4	5	6	5

Table 3.3: ATPSs in the manufacturing sub-category 'carriage & harness'
Source: Census enumerations, 1851–1891.

---

[28] 1851-1871 Census enumerations (Ashwell).

[29] 1851 Census (Baldock); 1861 Census (Baldock); 1881 Census (Royston).

[30] 1881-1891 Census enumerations (Royston).

[31] *Post Office Directory Six Home Counties, Pt 1* (1870), pp. 409, 411; *Kelly's Directory Six Home Counties, Pt 1* (1882), p. 561; *1871 Census* (Ashwell); *1871 Census* (Baldock); *1881 Census* (Ashwell).

In addition to farm traffic, much business remained throughout the second half of the nineteenth century for coach proprietors and especially road hauliers with the amount of freight carried short distances by road to and from railway stations. Theo Barker and Christopher Savage estimated that there were actually 'more horses pulling many more vehicles on Britain's roads in the heyday of the railway than there had ever been in the heyday of the stage coach'.[32] This meant that, in addition to the blacksmiths, there were other frequent employment opportunities for the journeymen saddlers, wheelwrights and coach builders (Table 3.3 above). According to Barker and Dorian Gerhold, the wealthier classes with their private yards 'used their own coaches (Plates 3.3 – 3.5 below), which gave greater privacy …

Plate 3.3: Carriage entrance, Upper King Street, Royston

---

[32] T.C. Barker and C.I. Savage, *An Economic History of Transport in Britain* (3rd edn, London, 1974), p. 124.

prosperous farmers showed off their new gigs; less prosperous ones travelled in locally-made spring carts'.[33]   This demand was met by the carriage businesses identified earlier and created opportunities for suitable ATPSs.   For example, Baldock's John Crawley, 'Coach maker', employed '6 Men & 3 boys' in 1861 while Thomas Cane of Royston, 'Coach builder', employed '3 Men' in 1851, '3 Men & 1 boy' in 1861, and '4 Men' in 1871.[34]

Plate 3.4: Carriage entrance, High Street, Baldock

---

[33] T. Barker and D. Gerhold, *The Rise and Rise of Road Transport, 1700–1990* (Cambridge, 1995), p. 44.
[34] 1861 Census (Baldock); 1851 Census (Royston); 1861 Census (Royston); 1871 Census (Royston).

Plate 3.5: Carriage entrance, High Street, Buntingford

Opportunities for the employment of cabinet-makers and upholsterers in Baldock and Royston between 1851 and 1891, though quite small in total (n = 12 and 36 respectively), closely reflect the number of PTPSs engaged in the furniture trade. For example, journeymen William Hankin, George Seymour, Thomas Spicer and John Webster listed in Baldock's 1871 census may very well have worked for William Richardson, builder and cabinet-maker (1851 – 1881), who according to the CEB of a decade earlier employed '7 men, 4 lads & 1 boy'. Thomas Spicer went on to better things for in 1891 he was identified as an undertaker, cabinet-maker and furniture dealer employing staff of his own.[35] Perhaps surprisingly, in contrast to the numbers working alongside the cabinet-makers in Royston, the only example found of an upholsterer in Baldock was the aforementioned George Seymour listed as such in 1851.[36] Harper Potter, a young French-polisher from Kentisbeare in Devon was the only such craftsman in either town.[37]

David Blankenhorn found that, during the second half of the nineteenth century, a number of cabinet-makers' trade societies began to complain that the increased sophistication of woodworking machinery was 'depressing their wages and threatening their status as skilled craftsmen'.[38] In fact, 'most of the power-driven woodworking tools that we have', according to Aubrey Burstall, 'were in general use before 1850'.[39] In London, craft societies tried to restrict the numbers of apprentices and boy labourers employed in increasingly mechanized furniture workshops. However, despite there being no apprentices identified in Baldock, their numbers found in Royston's CEBs between 1861 and 1891 (1, 2, 2 and 4 respectively) clearly support the view expressed by Blankenhorn that, as late as the 1890s, 'a system of apprenticeship in the cabinet trade generally prevailed in the areas outside London, especially in the smaller towns'.[40] In the case of Royston, seven of the nine apprentice cabinet-makers identified were born locally. Three, William Green (1861), Alfred Jerrard (1891) and Harold Miller (1891) were the sons of cabinet-makers while Frederick Willers's (1871) father was a butcher and publican at the *Black Swan*. The two apprentices from outside the town hailed from nearby Cambridgeshire villages, Ernest Baker (1881) from Chishill and Alfred Hoy (1891) from Wimpole.[41]

As was noted earlier, the dealing sector dominated the distribution of ATPSs within these four business communities. Within the dealing sector itself, in all four towns, the greatest preponderance of ATPSs was found to be involved in the two sub-categories of 'dress' and 'food' (Figure 3.4 below). Numbers of ATPSs

---

[35] 1851 – 1891 Census enumerations (Baldock and Royston).

[36] 1851 Census (Baldock).

[37] 1881 Census (Royston).

[38] D. Blankenhorn, ' "Our Class of Workmen": The Cabinet-makers Revisited', in R. Harrison and J. Zeitlin (eds), *Divisions of Labour: Skilled Workers and Technological Change in Nineteenth-century England* (Brighton, 1985), p. 34.

[39] A.F. Burstall, *A History of Mechanical Engineering* (London, 1963), p. 224.

[40] Blankenhorn, 'Cabinet-Makers Revisited', p. 32.

[41] 1861-1891 Census enumerations (Royston).

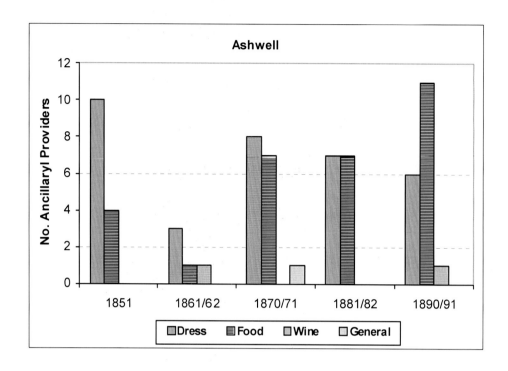

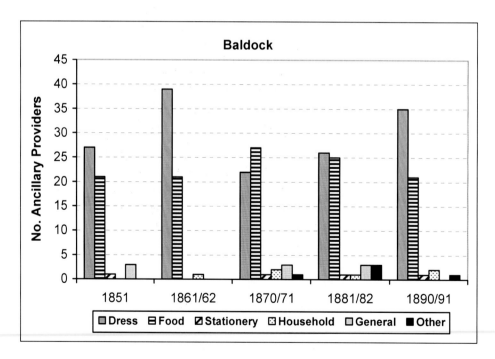

Figure 3.4: Distribution of ATPSs within dealing sector
Source: Census enumerations, 1851–1891.

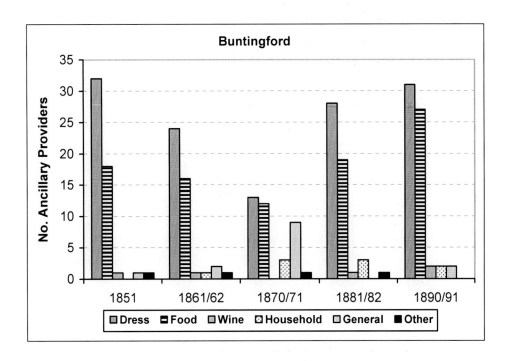

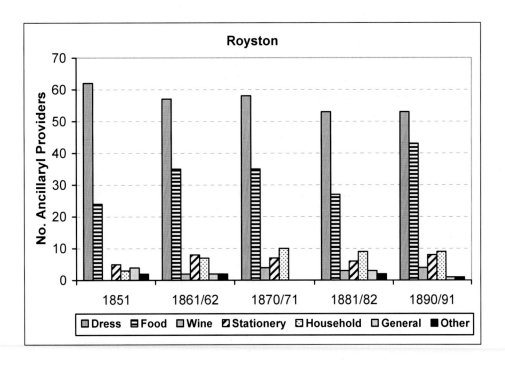

identified in other sub-categories such as 'household', 'stationery' or 'wine', never exceeded ten individuals per group in any decade.

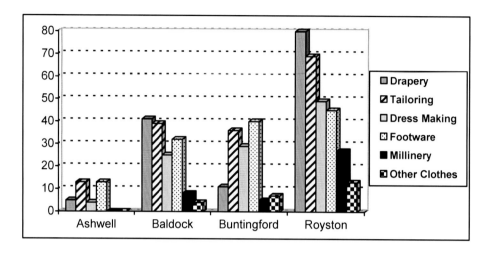

Figure 3.5: ATPSs engaged in the 'dress' trade
Source: Census enumerations, 1851–1891.

Many of the individual ATPSs engaged in the 'dress' trade (Figure 3.5 above) were identified by the enumerators simply as a draper, dressmaker, milliner or tailor without further elaboration or indication that they might in fact be PTPSs. A few others were labelled 'journeyman', others as 'Draper's assistant', 'Tailor's shopman' or 'Boot & shoemaker's shop assistant', and many were identified as apprentices. The analysis for Royston (Table 3.4 below) is typical of the three

	Craftsmen/ Craftswomen	Journeymen	Assistants	Apprentices
Boot/ Shoemaker	29	3	1	3
Draper	12	-	41	19
Dressmaker	32	-	5	12
Milliner	15	-	2	8
Tailor	47	9	3	10
Totals	135	12	52	52

Table 3.4: Types of ATPS engaged in the Royston 'dress' trade
Source: Census enumerations, 1851–1891.

larger towns. Craftsmen and women accounted for over half (53.8 per cent) of the ATPSs working in this sector, while both the assistants and apprentices each accounted for a further fifth of the total; journeymen were very few in number.

According to Alexander, the nineteenth century experienced a massive 'disentangling of production and distribution' of many commodities.[42] Fraser further suggested that the revolution in retailing was the 'displacement of hawkers, fairs and street markets by the fixed shop; the growth in the size of shops and in the variety of their stock'.[43] Analysis reveals quite a number of traders in the 'dress' sub-category employing numerous ATPSs suggestive of substantial specialist enterprises. For example Richard Brown, a Master tailor and draper of Royston, employed '4 Men & 2 apprentices' in 1851, increasing to '7 Men & 1 boy' in 1861; John Phillips, a Master tailor and woollen draper of Baldock, employed '6 Men' in 1881; Widowed Mrs Sarah Farrington, Mistress cordwainer and boot & shoemaker, employed '3 Men & 1 apprentice' in Buntingford in 1851, and '4 Men & 3 boys' in 1861.[44] Alexander argued that from the mid-nineteenth century bespoke tailoring 'was being challenged by the new "clothier and outfitter" who retailed the ready-made goods produced in the city sweatshops'.[45] The size of Richard Brown's tailoring business in Royston may well have reflected the need to compete with the challenge from Philip Craft, a tailor & clothier (employed only two to three men) and William Stone, a tailor, draper & clothier (employed only one to two apprentices).[46]

Contrary to Fraser's belief, hawkers were not completely displaced in the region, even by the end of the nineteenth century. A small number (24) of these itinerant salesmen and women were identified from CEBs as mostly lodging in Baldock, Buntingford and Royston on census nights between 1851 and 1891. This may well indicate an underestimate in view of Martin Phillips's argument that 'many itinerant traders were illiterate and could not (or would not) complete the census returns'. Additionally, he believed the census enumerators frequently ignored those who 'at times of hardship took temporarily to hawking'.[47] Neil McKendrick identified hawkers who 'operated in the depth of the provinces' from the end of

---

[42] D. Alexander, *Retailing in England During the Industrial Revolution* (London, 1970), p. 235.

[43] W.H. Fraser, *The Coming of the Mass Market, 1850–1914* (London, 1981), p. 94.

[44] 1851 Census (Buntingford); 1861 Census (Buntingford); 1851 Census (Royston); 1861 Census (Royston); 1881 Census (Baldock).

[45] Alexander, *Retailing in England*, p. 235.

[46] 1851 Census (Royston); 1861 Census (Royston).

[47] M. Phillips, 'The Evolution of Markets and Shops in Britain', in J. Benson and G. Shaw (eds), *The Evolution of Retail Systems, c. 1800-1914, Part 2, Fairs, Markets, Pedlars and Small-scale Shops* (Leicester, 1992), p. 54.

the eighteenth century onwards as a 'new kind of genuine retailer' who brought the latest products of the mills and factories to their customers' door.[48] Specialist hawkers, often selling on credit, were the 'Scotch Drapers' who McKendrick described as bringing the 'prevailing fashions announced in the advertising columns of the provincial press' to their customers.[49] Three possible examples in 1871, were John Laventhall, 'Hawker in drapery', lodging at the *Chequers Inn*, Royston with his young assistant Stephen Springate, and William Laver and William Lufman each described as 'Travelling draper' boarding at the *Crown & Dolphin*. A fourth 'Travelling draper', Thomas Carmichael, although born in Scotland, appeared to have been based in Royston for some considerable time as nine of his children were born in the town.[50]

Opportunities for ATPSs to find work in the sub-category of food closely reflects the relative numbers of the three largest groups of retailers discussed earlier. Across the four towns between 1851 and 1891 the number of census entries for those employed in this sector was predominantly found in the grocery, bakery and butchery trades (Figure 3.6 below). Instances of employment in the fish trade and confectionery shops were largely confined to Buntingford and Royston.

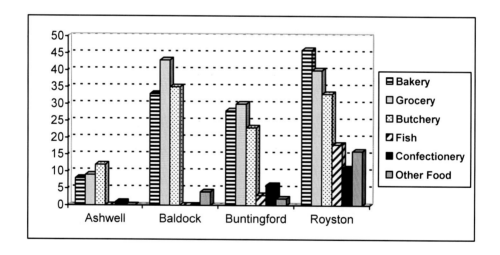

Figure 3.6: ATPSs engaged in food retailing
Source: Census enumerations, 1851–1891.

---

[48] N. McKendrick, 'The Commercialization of Fashion', in N. McKendrick, J. Brewer and J.H. Plumb, *The Birth of a Consumer Society: The Commercialization of Eighteenth-century England* (London, 1982), pp. 86, 88.

[49] McKendrick, 'Commercialization of Fashion', p. 88.

[50] 1871 Census (Royston). Because of their largely itinerant nature, hawkers in this study have been classified as ATPSs.

Before the end of the nineteenth century, in many areas of the country, baking was still seen as a domestic task. Without defining the term, Ian McKay argued that taking those listed as 'bakers' in the census gave a general English ratio of 2.36 bakers per thousand of population in 1851 rising to 2.60 in 1871. Simply taking the number of 'master' bakers identified in the four towns produces ratios of 1.94 (Buntingford and Royston) to 2.81 (Ashwell) in 1851 and 1.90 (Ashwell) to 3.44 (Baldock) in 1871. Adding in just the 'journeyman' bakers, but excluding the apprentices and any 'unspecified' bakers, increases the ratios to between 3.4 (Buntingford and Royston) and 5.21 (Baldock) in 1851 and to between 3.33 (Royston) and 4.47 (Buntingford) in 1871.[51] McKay cited the great contrast between London, the south-east and the South Midlands (all with over four bakers per thousand) and Yorkshire, the North and Wales with only one baker per thousand arguing that this difference arose from disproportionately large male workforces, as in the mines of Yorkshire, exhibiting 'working-class traditionalism which stresses home baking'.[52] The findings above suggest that many households of north-east Hertfordshire were content to buy their bread from retail bakeries rather than bake it themselves.

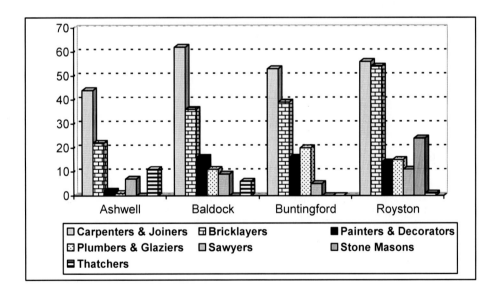

Figure 3.7: ATPSs engaged in building trades
Source: Census enumerations, 1851–1891.

---

[51] For Ashwell, Baldock, Buntingford and Royston the numbers of master bakers/journeymen in 1851 were 4/1, 5/5, 4/3 and 4/3 respectively and in 1871, 3/3, 7/1, 4/5 and 3/3 respectively.
[52] I. McKay, 'Bondage in the Bakehouse? The Strange Case of the Journeymen Bakers, 1840–1880', in R. Harrison and J. Zeitlin (eds), *Divisions of Labour: Skilled Workers and Technological Change in Nineteenth Century England* (Brighton, 1985), p. 49.

Bricklayers, carpenters and joiners together made up the largest group of ATPSs (60.9 per cent) engaged in building and construction (Figure 3.7 above) in all four towns. In the mid-nineteenth century most building firms across the country, according to Richard Rodger, employed fewer than ten workers but from around the 1870s there was a gradual move towards larger concerns.[53] An example of this trend is that of Gimson's of Royston, ironmongers, builders and contractors, who for over twenty years from 1861 employed on average thirty-nine men and ten boys.[54] As well as the staple housing market, opportunities for work would have been provided by the brewers, maltsters, tanners, railways and emerging public utilities of gas, water and sewerage works. It is very noticeable that the numbers of painters, decorators, plumbers and glaziers being employed were significantly higher in Baldock, Buntingford and Royston than in Ashwell, a probable indication of a greater number of wealthier householders in the three larger towns.

Opportunities for ATPSs in the growing transport sector (Figure 3.8 below) fell into four main categories: transport of goods by road, passenger coaches, the railways and various other engine drivers. Among those ATPSs (n = 72) being

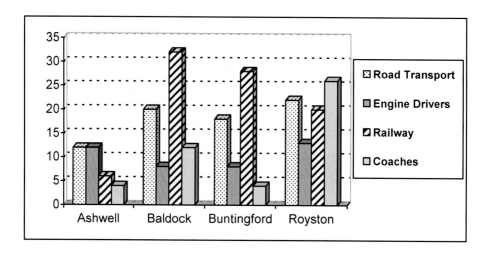

Figure 3.8: ATPSs engaged in transport activities
Source: Census enumerations, 1851–1891.

employed in the transport of commercial goods by road, 34.7 per cent were variously identified, non-specifically, as 'carman', 'carrier', 'carter', 'drayman'

---

[53] R. Rodger, *Housing in Urban Britain, 1780-1914* (Cambridge, 1995), pp. 20-21.
[54] 1861-1881 Census enumerations (Royston).

and 'wagoner'.[55]   A further 41.7 per cent were specifically identified as either 'brewer's carman' or 'brewer's drayman'.   Other examples included Izzard Bray 'Coal carter' (Baldock, 1861), Edward Pipkin 'Tanner's carman' (Buntingford, 1871), George Searle 'Timber carter' (Buntingford, 1881) and George Watson 'Builder's carman' (Buntingford, 1891).   Among those ATPSs (n = 46) identified under coaching, 43.5 per cent were non-domestically employed coachmen and a further 45.7 per cent were ostlers.   The majority of the latter group were found in Royston and in 1881 and 1891 were specifically listed by the enumerator as employed at an inn or hotel, for example in 1891 Frederick Racher was an ostler at *The Angel*, and George Ward was an ostler and groom at *The White Horse*.   The above figures for the second half of the nineteenth century show that the transport of goods by road reflected the needs of specialist manufacturers and dealers together with the role of general carriers operating services to and from the towns' railway stations.

Between 1851 and 1891 the railways offered many employment opportunities for ATPSs in the four study towns.   Plate layers, mostly in Baldock and Royston, accounted for almost a third of all ATPSs identified as working for the railway companies (n = 86), a further quarter were station porters, 14.0 per cent railway clerks, and 7.0 per cent signalmen.   However, only three railway engine drivers were specifically identified by the census enumerators along with two firemen and four guards, all living in Buntingford, the northern terminus of the Ware Hadham & Buntingford Railway, where services would have started and finished. Crews of trains passing through Baldock, Ashwell and Royston would have been based in London or Cambridge.   Barker and Gerhold argued that in Britain from the late 1850s the world's 'specialists in steam power in general' were 'busily applying steam to road vehicles'.[56]   There were twenty-four ATPSs described enigmatically by the enumerators as 'engine driver' without any indication of a railway connection and these might have been either agricultural or road steam traction engines designed to draw heavy loads.   In addition to these there were another fourteen engine drivers identified with specific roles, for example, Lewis Eversden 'Engine driver coprolites' (Ashwell, 1871), John Bloom 'Engine driver at brewery' (Baldock, 1881), Herbert Catts, 'Engine driver sewerage works' (Baldock, 1881), Frederick Anderson 'Engine driver waterworks' (Royston, 1891).

As a result of the uniform postal service developed after 1840 and its additional responsibility for telegraph services from 1870 the Post Office provided numerous

---

[55] A carter or carman was a man in charge of a horse-drawn cart. A drayman was responsible for the carriage of goods by horse and dray-cart, i.e. a low cart without sides used especially by brewers for carrying heavy loads.
[56] Barker and Gerhold, *Rise of Road Transport,* p. 53.

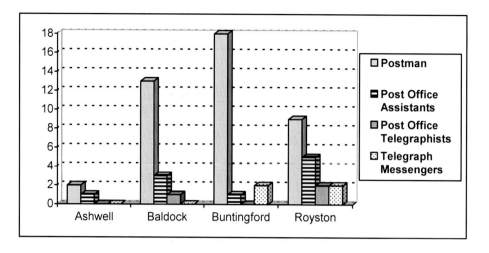

Figure 3.9: ATPSs engaged in Post Office services
Source: Census enumerations, 1851–1891.

employment opportunities for ATPSs in the public and professional sector (Figure 3.9 above). Those identified as delivering the mail, predominantly in the three larger towns, were variously described as postman (19), post boy (1), letter carrier (18), letter boy (1) and post messenger (3). Telegraphists (3) or telegraph messengers (4) were listed in Baldock and Royston from 1871, and in Buntingford in 1891, were apparently totally absent from Ashwell. Clerical 'post office assistants' were noted in all four towns while in 1891 John Earnshaw (aged 19), lodging at the *Coffee Tavern* in Royston, was employed as a 'Sorter in Post Office'. Instances of other ATPSs identified in the public and professional sector included male assistants (10) and apprentices (6) employed by chemists and druggists together with matrons and nurses at the Royston Cottage Hospital in 1881 and 1891.[57]

Apart from those being employed at Royston's small hospital, the ATPSs working in the public and professional sector were predominantly male. However, such tendencies were to change according to Diane Balser who suggested that the 'sex composition of jobs was modified during different stages of industrialization in order to meet the needs of production and maximize profits'.[58] She cites a study of the changing composition of the clerical workforce that found 'there were relatively few clerks' almost invariably men in 1870. In contrast in north-east Hertfordshire, of the 130 ATPSs of the industrial services sector identified, there were 110 assorted 'clerks' and three 'bookkeepers' employed across the whole

---

[57] It is generally agreed that few women were employed as chemists and druggists on account of the long and expensive period of training involved.

[58] D. Balser, *Sisterhood & Solidarity: Feminism and Labor in Modern Times* (Boston, 1987), p. 20.

period between 1851 and 1891. However, only six of this group were women. For example, in 1861 Agnes Day (aged 16) was employed as a 'bookkeeper' by her father Robert at his butcher's shop in Baldock and Martha Heath (aged 21) was similarly employed by her brother Thomas, a Baldock baker. Jane Fox (aged 23) from Dorset was a 'clerk' in 1881 at Wenham & Co., the Buntingford linen drapers. Another example from Buntingford is Ethel Aylott (aged 16) employed as a 'Post Office clerk' in 1891. Clearly these young women were well ahead of changes like the introduction of typewriters which meant that by the 1920s the 'entire clerical force had been feminized', based, according to Balser, on 'a myth ... that clerical work was well suited to the "female nature" '.[59] Apart from a number of non-specific 'clerks' (6), 'commercial clerks' (4) and 'merchants' clerks' (2) almost two thirds of those in clerical posts, all male, were employed in either the brewing industries of Ashwell, Baldock and Royston or by members of the legal profession practising in Baldock and Royston.[60]

Employment opportunities for women

Considerable variation exists in the number of female ATPSs and other skilled or semi-skilled women identified from the CEBs between 1851 and 1891 (see Table 3.5 below). In Ashwell between 1851 and 1891, the proportion of female ATPSs

Census Year	Ashwell	Baldock	Buntingford	Royston
	No. (%	No. (%	No. (%	No. (%
1851	3 (4.8)	6 (3.8)	19 (16.4)	30 (13.0)
1861	-	13 (8.8)	10 (8.8)	28 (12.3)
1871	1 (1.4)	5 (3.5)	8 (6.7)	33 (14.2)
1881	1 (1.4)	19 (11.7)	23 (16.7)	42 (19.6)
1891	7 (7.1)	21 (12.1)	26 (15.5)	47 (19.7)
Total 1851/	12 (3.3)	64 (8.2)	86 (13.1)	180 (15.7)

Table 3.5: Female ATPSs and others identified from CEBs
Source: Census enumerations, 1851–1891.

---

[59] Balser, *Sisterhood & Solidarity*, p. 21.
[60] Census descriptions included 'Brewer's clerk' (22 occurrences), a 'Brewery clerk', a 'Brewhouse clerk', a 'Brewery commercial clerk', a 'Mercantile clerk, brewery', a 'Maltster's clerk', Attorney's or Solicitor's 'clerk' or 'general clerk' (33 occurrences), 'Solicitor's writing clerk' (4 occurrences), Attorney's or Solicitor's 'articled clerk' (2 occurrences), an 'Attorney's managing clerk', a 'Solicitor's conveyancing clerk' and a 'Solicitor's copying clerk'.

ranged from none to only 7.1 per cent of the total. In comparison, the proportion in Baldock varied between 3.8 per cent (1851) and 12.1 per cent (1891) while in Buntingford the range was between a low of 6.7 per cent (1871) and 16.7 per cent (1881). In contrast, Royston consistently had the highest proportion of female ATPSs from 1861 onwards, rising from 12.3 per cent to 19.7 per cent (n = 47) by the end of the nineteenth century. One can speculate that, apart from having the smallest population among the four towns, it is Ashwell's lack of opportunity of 'suitable' employment for women that limits the number of ATPSs. For example, in 1881/82 the number of either food or dress retailers that might have provided waged employment for women, 11 and 9 respectively, was considerably lower in Ashwell compared to the other three towns where the comparable numbers of these traders were 15 and 14 in Buntingford, 22 and 26 in Baldock and 34 and 33 in Royston. A closer look at the latter in 1881 reveals that, in addition to the numerous jobs offered by its manufacturing drapers, the town provided a wide range of other employment opportunities for women. For instance, Fannie Beale and Emily Craft were baker's shop assistants, Lucy Pryor was a 'confectioner's assistant', Agnes Hagger worked for a greengrocer while Martha Porter was a 'bookseller's assistant'.[61]

However, low figures given for the number of female ATPSs must be treated with caution since, as Jane Humphries suggested, mid nineteenth-century 'censuses seriously under-enumerated wives' employment'. Kathryn Gleadle reasoned that such data was 'highly unreliable and exaggerates the trend towards domesticity' in addition to ignoring part-time, temporary and seasonal work. Edward Higgs advised researchers to note the biases and styles of individual enumerators as some 'appear to have been less willing than others to regard the work of women as an "occupation".[62]

The mid-Victorian retailer was a small-scale specialist trader, Lee Holcombe argued, doing much of his own processing such as blending tea, grinding sugar and roasting coffee. They gave personal attention to their regular clientele and 'relied for labour mainly upon apprentices whom they paid little or nothing' and hence employed few women as they had no need of additional shop assistants. Industrialization, mass production, improved transport and communication in the later nineteenth century 'revolutionized the character of retailing by helping to destroy its craft tradition'.[63] Gleadle saw these changes as responsible for the

---

[61] 1881 Census (Royston).

[62] J. Humphries, 'Female-headed Households in Early Industrial Britain: The Vanguard of the Proletariat', *Labour History Review*, 63 (1998), p. 36; K. Gleadle, *British Women in the Nineteenth Century* (Basingstoke, 2001), p. 96; Higgs, *Making Sense of the Census Revisited*, p. 102.

[63] L. Holcombe, *Victorian Ladies at Work: Middle-class Working Women in England and Wales, 1850–1914* (Connecticut, 1973), pp. 104, 105.

'growing avenues for educated working-class girls' in the retail services as the number of shops, estimated by Louise Tilly and Joan Scott, 'increased by 56 per cent between 1875 and 1907' and created a massive demand for female shop assistants.[64]

Analysis indicates (Figure 3.10 below) that, across most of the second half of the nineteenth century, between 80.0 and 90.0 per cent of all the identified female

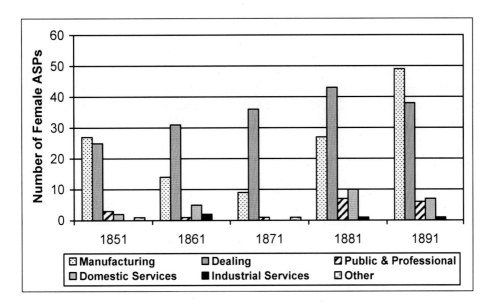

Figure 3.10: Sectoral distribution of four towns' female ATPSs, 1851-1891
Source: Census enumerations, 1851–1891.

ATPSs (n = 347) were consistently employed in either the manufacturing or dealing sector. In both these sectors, it was women working in the clothing trade who figured prominently, 74.6 per cent in manufacturing and 31.2 per cent in dealing. However, in attempting this distinction, it has to be acknowledged that many, including the assistants and apprentices, enumerated as 'dressmaker' (77), 'dress and mantle maker' (11), and 'milliner and dressmaker' (6) were probably employed by some of the manufacturer/retailer PTPSs, for example the two linen drapers, Wenham & Co. (Buntingford, 1881–91) and Whittaker & Co. (Royston,

---

[64] Gleadle, *British Women in the Nineteenth Century*, p. 106; L.A. Tilly and J.W. Scott, *Women, Work and Family* (London, 1989), p. 156.

1881–91).[65] In addition to several boot and/or shoe binders, examples of other women on the manufacturing side of the clothing trade were Jane Ellis a straw bonnet maker (Royston, 1851–1861), Sarah Latchford a shirt maker (Baldock, 1871), Eliza Mckenzie a waistcoat maker (Buntingford, 1871), and the young Ellis sisters, Alice (aged 20) and Francis (aged 19), who were both employed as corset maker's assistants (Baldock, 1891).[66]

Examples of less usual manufacturing occupations were those of widowed Ann Clifton an upholsterer (Royston, 1871), unmarried Harriett Hyde employed as a carpet maker (Baldock, 1891), and the Boddy family of Buntingford who were millers. This last case demonstrates some of the confusions that can arise in trying to categorize the work of women. According to the 1851 CEB, William Boddy was a 'Master miller', i.e. a PTPS, at the Old Windmill but it was his wife Margaret who appeared in the Post Office Directory; was she a PTPS or an ATPS? By 1861, Margaret was widowed but still listed and ten years later, then aged 71, appeared in the directory as 'Boddy Margaret (Mrs.) & Wm. Millers', William being her son. To add to the confusion, in 1861, Mrs Jane Knight (married, aged 34), 'miller', had appeared in the CEB with her brother Joseph Boddy at the Water Mill. Were they too part of the same Boddy family milling business, i.e. ATPSs or, if this was a separate enterprise, who was the PTPS? [67]

While many historians, like Holcombe, were of the opinion that Victorian society considered the work of many traders, such as butchers, fishmongers, grocers and ironmongers, too rough and heavy for the employment of women shop assistants, this appears not always to have been the case in the four towns.[68] Besides those employed by retailers as assistants or apprentices in the clothing trade, especially drapers (27) and milliners (23) where customers were chiefly other women, 12.7 per cent of the female ATPSs identified in the dealing sector were working as

---

[65] 1881 Census (Buntingford and Royston); 1891 Census (Buntingford and Royston). It should be noted that that women members of an extended family enumerated as 'dressmaker', etc, are excluded from the compilation of Figure 3.11 on the basis that they may well have been engaged simply in domestic affairs rather than paid employment. In 1881, the two Wenham sisters, Martha and Mary, linen drapers in Buntingford's High Street, employed two dressmakers, a dressmaker's assistant, a dressmaker's improver, a 'machine worker, dress', a milliner and a milliner's apprentice, all listed in the CEB as 'servant'. Similarly, in 1891, Caroline Whittaker, linen draper at The Cross in Royston, employed a first dressmaker, a second dressmaker, a dressmaker's apprentice, two draper's assistants, a milliner, a milliner's apprentice and a mantle maker, all listed in the CEB as boarding at Caroline Whittaker's. Eleven of these women were aged between 14 and 25 years old, the four others between 33 and 36 years old.

[66] 1851 and 1861 Census (Royston); 1871 Census (Baldock and Buntingford); 1891 Census (Baldock)

[67] 1871 Census (Royston); 1891 Census (Baldock); 1851–1871 Census (Buntingford); *Post Office Directory Six Home Counties, 1851*, p. 184; *Post Office Directory Six Home Counties, 1862*, p. 334; *Post Office Directory Six Home Counties, Pt 1* (1870), p. 429.

[68] Holcombe, *Victorian Ladies at Work*, p. 107.

assistants to grocers (8), butchers (4), greengrocers (4), fruiterers (2), fishmongers (2) and ironmongers (2). Others employed in the dealing sector were working in stationers, book or music sellers (13) and confectioners (11), both outlets being considered far more suitable for women, or identified as the rather ambiguous 'shopkeeper's assistant' (2) or simply 'shopwoman' (4). Finally, there were opportunities for working class girls to be employed in the drinks trade as inn keepers' and beer retailers' assistants (7) or barmaids (9).

Apart from the few female book keepers and clerks mentioned earlier, the Post Office offered women clerical opportunities in the public and professional sector. According to Holcombe, the great expansion of Post Office services after 1840 saw the number of its employees increase six-fold between 1851 and 1891, and by 1914 it had become the 'greatest single employer of middle-class women in the country, and accounted for more than 90.0 per cent of the women employed by central government'.[69] The earliest identified examples of female Post Office assistants in north-east Hertfordshire were those of 30 year old Maria Nicholls (Buntingford, 1851) and 28 year old Emma Daintry (Royston, 1861); others followed in Ashwell and Baldock by 1881.[70]

The above discussion has clearly shown that despite prevailing Victorian attitudes towards women working outside the domestic arena, they were an important and growing factor in the four towns' economies. However, the one major exception was the number of opportunities for young women to undertake apprenticeships which were either far fewer than was the case for their male counterparts or such employment was not deemed suitable for them. Analysis of the occupations of female ATPSs revealed just forty-two of them (12.0 per cent) to be apprentices compared to the 236 young men identified as such.

Opportunities for apprenticeship

The tradition of apprenticeship, according to Joan Lane, failed when it became a 'device of the Poor Law officials to be rid of large numbers of pauper children' indentured to reduce the poor rate. Premiums demanded by the master were essentially fixed at what the parent or parish overseers could be persuaded to pay although premiums varied according to the trade. Theoretically a larger premium, she argued, 'ensured the child would be taught occupational skills and be at least tolerably well treated'.[71] Evidence of this parish activity in Ashwell, especially during the 1820s and 1830s, is provided by the surviving *Ashwell Register Book*

---

[69] Holcombe, *Victorian Ladies at Work*, p. 165.

[70] 1851 Census (Buntingford); 1861 Census (Royston); 1881 Census (Ashwell and Baldock).

[71] J. Lane, *Apprenticeship in England, 1600-1914* (London, 1996), pp. 1, 11.

of Parish Apprentices which details seventeen young boys, all between twelve and eighteen years old, being sent by their parish overseers to a number of the surrounding villages and towns including Baldock and Royston.[72] A typical example is that of Mary Covington's illegitimate son John (aged 13) apprenticed to William Winters, a shoemaker in nearby Steeple Morden, 'until he attains the age of twenty one years' for a premium of £14. The commonest trades listed were those of shoemaker (5), blacksmith (4) and tailor (3) with premiums usually from £10 to £20; the one exception being that of only £5 to a carpenter. The above premiums, with the exception of that single £5, were considerably higher than Pamela Sharpe noted for pauper boys apprenticed in the Devon parish of Colyton where for example only '£5. 5s. 0d. was paid to a stonemason, £11. 0s. 0d. to a cordwainer and £6. 0s. 0d. to a ropemaker'.[73] It has been generally assumed that this practice had virtually died out by the 1820s but Kay Parrott's recent work has confirmed that parish children from industrial schools 'were still being apprenticed from Liverpool as late as 1870'.[74]

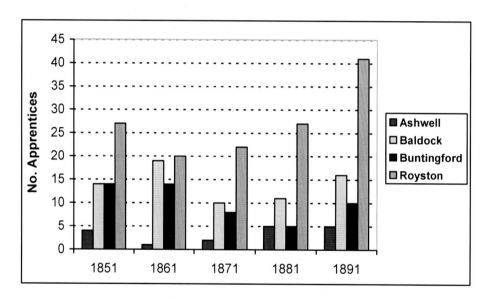

Figure 3.11: Apprentices in the four towns, 1851–1891
Source: Census enumerations, 1851–1891.

---

[72] Ashwell Register Book of Parish Apprentices, 1817-1842, HALS, D/P7/14/2. This register is laid out in the 'Form of Register of Parish Apprentices Under the Statute 42nd Geo. III. Chap. 41' giving details of date of indenture, name of apprentice, sex and age, the parents' names, parents' place of residence, name of the person to whom bound, his trade, his residence, term of apprenticeship, premium, name of parish officers and assenting magistrate.

[73] P. Sharpe, 'Poor Children as Apprentices in Colyton, 1598-1830', *Continuity and Change*, 6, 2 (1991), p. 256.

[74] K. Parrott, 'The Apprenticeship of Parish Children from Kirkdale Industrial Schools Liverpool 1840-70', *The Local Historian*, 39, 2 (2009), p. 122.

Expressed in relation to the total number of ATPSs, the proportion of persons apprenticed in the three largest towns between 1851 and 1891 was between 6.0 and 13.0 per cent. In comparison, the proportion in Ashwell, the smallest town, barely reached 7.0 per cent during the same period. Among the four towns, only Royston showed significant growth in the number of its apprentices (Figure 3.11 above) doubling from their 1861 level to reach a total of forty-one by 1891. Lane argued that into the nineteenth century apprenticeship was devalued by the 'vast numbers of children … sent to work in factories and domesticated sweated trades' but conceded that it 'remained effective and even expanded' for the more skilful careers.[75] Evidence presented here suggests that, especially in Baldock and Royston, opportunities for apprenticeship were numerous.

Examination of the CEBs enabled the identification of 275 apprentices employed in the four towns. A breakdown by occupational type (Table 3.6 below) reveals that a considerable range of training existed for those wishing to avail themselves of the apprenticeship system. PTPSs in the dealing sector, especially grocers, drapers and tailors, provided 60.4 per cent of the total opportunities (n = 166) for youngsters to undertake apprenticeships. In the building sector (n = 50, 18.2 per cent total) it was most frequently carpenters, and in the manufacturing sector (n = 44, 16.0 per cent total) saddlers, who were willing to take on apprentices. Among the forty-two female apprentices listed (only 14.2 per cent of all apprentices) almost all were engaged in the dress category of the dealing sector and of those 26 were apprentice dressmakers, 9 apprentice milliners and 4 apprentice drapers. The three exceptions were Sarah Boar, a seventeen year old from Chichester in Sussex, apprentice stationer and bookseller (Royston, 1871), Caroline Newman, a fourteen year old from Hackney in London, apprentice stationer (Royston, 1891), and the unusual case of Nellie Radford, aged fifteen, apprenticed to her harness-maker father, Samuel (Ashwell, 1891).[76] As exemplified by two of the aforementioned girls, many apprentices were employed far from their homes. A detailed analysis of their origins reveals a number moving considerable distances from as far away as Cornwall, Lancashire, Yorkshire, Cumberland and Scotland.

Lane observed that while in theory apprenticeship was 'available to boys and girls, poor or affluent, educated or illiterate', in reality the recruitment into it was strongly influenced by 'parental status, prospering occupations, consumer demand and population numbers'. In her study of Warwickshire pauper apprentices to 1834 she found very few bound to grocers, saddlers or cabinet makers compared

---

[75] Lane, *Apprenticeship in England*, pp. 245, 247.
[76] 1871 Census (Royston), 1891 Census (Ashwell and Royston).

Sector & Trade	Ashwell	Baldock	Buntingford	Royston	Total
Dealing					
Grocer	1	10	5	15	31
Draper	1	9	2	18	30
Dressmaker	1	8	7	12	28
Tailor	1	5	9	10	25
Shoemaker	-	4	7	3	14
Butcher	2	5	1	1	9
Ironmonger	-	2	-	5	7
Milliner	-	-	2	4	6
Stationer	-	-	-	6	6
Baker	-	-	2	2	4
Watchmaker	-	-	1	3	4
Printer	-	-	-	3	3
Building					
Carpenter	3	11	4	4	22
Painter	-	-	1	9	10
Bricklayer	-	3	-	3	6
Builder	-	1	-	2	3
Millwright	-	1	1	-	2
Plumber	-	2	-	-	2
Stonemason	-	-	-	2	2
Manufacturing					
Saddler	1	2	1	6	10
Cabinet Mk.	-	-	-	9	9
Coach Bld.	-	2	1	3	6
Cooper	1	-	3	1	5
Wheelwright	3	-	2	-	5
Blacksmith	-	-	-	3	3
Brazier	-	-	-	3	3
Engineer	-	1	-	2	3
Public & Prof.					
Chemist	-	1	-	5	6
Transport					
Engine Driver	2	-	-	-	2
Misc. Other	1	3	2	3	9
Total	17	70	51	137	275

Table 3.6: Four towns' apprentices, 1851–1891
Source: Census enumerations, 1851–1891.

with numbers, 31, 10 and 9 respectively, identified here. Grocers tend to be concentrated in towns and according to Lane they required a higher premium than either butchers or bakers.[77] This, along with the number of apprentice chemists, coach builders and stationers (Table 3.6 above), all commanding high premiums, suggests that in the four study towns, especially Royston, there were positions available for respectable, better educated apprentices from more affluent families.

As suggested by Lane, in the absence of satisfactory personal recommendations, to fill these positions 'notices by masters ... and parents seeking places for their children were regularly inserted in local newspapers with a regional readership'.[78] Here local manufacturers and traders placed such notices for apprentices in the *Royston Crow*. For example T. Goodman, grocer, advertised 'respectable Youth wanted', T. Whitehead, mason and stone carver, had a vacancy for a 'Strong Active Lad, about 16 years old', and J. Moger, watch and clock maker, wanted a 'quick active Youth as an Out-door Apprentice'. In contrast to Lane's view that women who 'ran their late husbands' or fathers' firms, shops and practices' did not usually take on apprentices themselves, was the example of Miss Margaret Gosling of Royston. She advertised locally, in 1862, 'vacancies for two or three Apprentices In-door or Out-door' in millinery and dress making.[79] Miss Gosling continued to employ apprentices as is clear from the 1871 census which shows Sarah Moor (aged 22) from Wigtown, Scotland, employed by her as dressmaker's apprentice.

Overall view of regional economy

Figure 3.12 below shows the combined totals of PTPSs and ATPSs expressed as a proportion of total population between 1851 and 1891. In Ashwell the proportion of providers of goods and services rose modestly (9.5 per cent to 13.0 per cent) as did its population over the same period. Buntingford also experienced a modest rise (11.7 per cent to 15.3 per cent) against a small decrease in its population. In Baldock, despite a considerable increase in population after 1871, the proportion remained constant at around 15.0 per cent. Among the four towns it was Royston that experienced the largest increase in the proportion of its service providers (21.7 per cent to 29.5 per cent) in spite of its population decreasing steadily from 1851 onwards. The significantly increased level of service provision in Royston

---

[77] Lane, *Apprenticeship in England*, pp. 241, 83, 119.

[78] Lane, *Apprenticeship in England*, p. 10.

[79] *The Royston Crow*, 1 March 1855, p. 21; *The Royston Crow*, 1May 1861, p. 334; Lane, *Apprenticeship in England*, p. 39; *The Royston Crow*, 1 January 1862, p. 365; 1871 Census (Royston).

can be linked in part to the rise in the number of PTPSs operating in the dealing sector, especially in the sub-categories of 'food' and 'domestic services', plus those of the public and professional sector. This growth appears to reflect an increase in wealth creation on the part of the business community that led to more

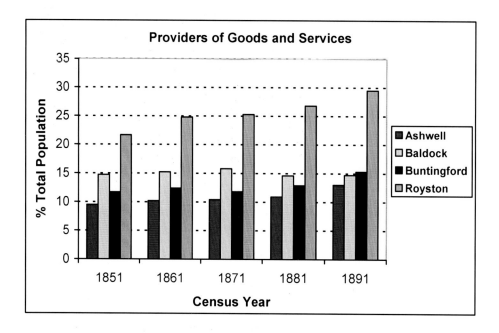

Figure 3.12: Combined totals of PTPSs and ATPSs as proportion of population.

sophisticated and fashionable demands by the town's 'middling' classes. The range and increased scale of goods and services provided in Royston, and to a lesser extent in Baldock and Buntingford, is indicative of these small towns' ability to function as central places within the region, a role explored at length in chapter four.

Conclusion

An examination of the four towns' census enumerations between 1851 and 1891, deliberately excluding the large numbers of unskilled labourers and domestic servants, identified considerable numbers of skilled and semi-skilled ATPSs. These men and women, including apprentices, amounted to approximately 4.0 to 8.0 per cent of the total population of Ashwell, Baldock and Buntingford, and between 11.0 to 14.0 per cent that of Royston, proportions remarkably similar to those of the four towns' PTPSs.

In Ashwell by far the largest numbers of ATPSs were found working in the manufacturing and building sectors especially bricklayers and carpenters in the latter case from 1851 to 1861, the decade after the town's major conflagration. The dominant manufacturing activities were malting and brewing. In Baldock, Buntingford and in particular Royston it was the dealing sector, especially the food and dress sub-categories that provided most employment opportunities for ATPSs. As in the case of Ashwell, malting and brewing also dominated the manufacturing sector in Baldock but in Buntingford it was the tanning industry that provided work for skilled ATPSs such as tanners and curriers. While there was the large *Royston Brewery,* it was metal working, carriage building, harness making and furniture making that were the town's main sub-categories employing ATPSs in manufacturing.

This chapter has emphasized some of the problems emanating from the attitude of nineteenth-century census enumerators towards working women and from the variable terminology found in the CEBs. Nevertheless, the evidence presented has shown the importance of skilled and semi-skilled women to the region's manufacturing and dealing sectors. Analysis has also revealed that between 1851 and 1881 all of the four towns' Post Offices had started to employ women as assistants, a trend that by the early twentieth century was to make the Post Office the nation's largest employer of middle-class women. Furthermore, it has identified a number of women working as assistants to butchers, fishmongers and ironmongers, etc., some of the trades traditionally viewed as 'unfeminine' by Victorian society.

Three of the towns investigated, Baldock, Buntingford and Royston, offered a wide range of opportunities for young apprentices in the 'dealing', 'building' and 'manufacturing' sectors. In total, approximately one in ten of the ATPSs were apprentices including a small number of women training as dressmakers, milliners and drapers.

Considerable numbers of ATPSs including apprentices had geographical origins well beyond the immediate hinterlands of the four towns. A detailed discussion of the appeal of north-east Hertfordshire to opportunity-seeking migrants follows in Chapter 5. Given that over the half-century, between approximately 10.0 and 15.0 per cent of the populations of Ashwell, Baldock and Buntingford, and roughly 20.0 to 30.0 per cent of that of Royston, were skilled or semi-skilled providers of goods and services is evidence that these small towns were vibrant employment centres that had evolved beyond just servicing the needs of their surrounding rural population.

Small but Flourishing

4

North-east Hertfordshire's urban hierarchy

This chapter examines the spatial relationship and urban-rural interface that existed between the four towns and the surrounding villages of their immediate hinterlands. Their provision of significant levels of both goods and services are compared, using trade directory data alone, with the relatively insignificant provision of such goods and services by a number of nearby villages with nineteenth-century populations ranging between 200 and 1200. After considering the general facets of Walter Christaller's central place theory, a detailed evaluation of goods and services utilizing more recent statistical approaches to his original theory raises a number of questions. Firstly, is it possible using this particular methodology to identify a clear regional urban hierarchy in north-east Hertfordshire? Secondly, does this type of spatial analysis allow for the identification of discrete ranks of centre, within the central place hierarchy, or does it show that the centres formed more of a continuum? Thirdly, can these four very small towns with nineteenth-century populations of less than 2500, because of the considerable range of goods and services they offered, be considered as significant high order 'central places' for the inhabitants of north-east Hertfordshire? Fourthly, does the analytical approach described here allow for the exploration of the differences between relying either on a centre's population as the prime indicator of its importance, or alternatively on the availability of goods and services for its population and that of its immediate environs? Finally, by looking at the towns' indices of centrality between 1851 and 1891, does the present analysis suggest that the degree of provision of goods and services is more significant than either population level, or even population stagnation, in the measurement of their 'centrality'? The chapter concludes by introducing the concept of an *extra-urban matrix* in which is located a network of smaller settlements which, although they fall below the generally-recognized lower threshold of centrality identified by Christaller's theory, nonetheless satisfy the criteria of urban centres.[1]

---

[1] In this particular context the word *extra* can be interpreted as meaning either in addition to and/or lying outside the usually accepted urban centres.

Services in Hertfordshire villages, 1851- 91

Sixteen villages lie roughly within and around a triangle bounded by Baldock, Buntingford and Royston (Map 4.1 below). In 1871 these villages fell into two groups, five larger settlements with populations ranging from approximately 800 to 1200, and eleven smaller settlements with populations between 200 and 600.[2]

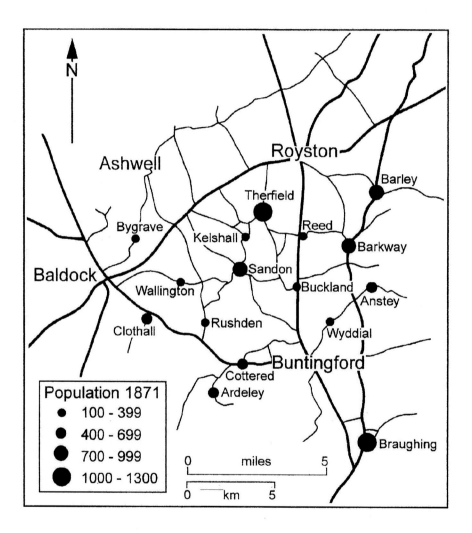

Map 4.1: Towns and villages in north-east Hertfordshire's extra-urban matrix
Source: Phillip Judge

---

[2] Hertfordshire Populations, 1801–1991 (Hertfordshire County Council, 1996), HALS 31 109 4103.

The changing range of goods and services available to the populace in each village was determined by analysing their trade directory listings for 1851, 1870 and 1890. Despite the limitations of this selective dataset, from the picture gained of local service provision, it is possible to gauge their dependence on the three nearby small towns to which villagers would have travelled for access to a wide range of high order goods and service functions. In conjunction with the three towns' hierarchical positions and functional indexes it becomes possible to estimate the degree to which villagers would have needed to travel considerable distances to larger urban centres beyond their region's immediate extra-urban matrix.

In line with general nineteenth-century rural depopulation in the south-east of England, the average population across the selected eleven smaller villages fell from 371 in 1851 to 352 in 1871 and again to only 289 by 1891. Against this picture of decline, the number of PTPSs identified in these villages (Table 4.1 below) actually changed very little as a proportion of their total populations,

	Anstey	Ardeley	Buckland	Bygrave	Clothall	Cottered	Kelshall	Reed	Rushden	Wallington	Wydiall
1851	n/a	10	9	4	2	9	6	4	6	3	n/a
1870	11	9	7	3	3	12	7	6	8	7	2
1890	13	6	8	1	2	11	6	5	6	5	2

Table 4.1: Numbers of PTPSs in eleven small villages [3]
Source: Post Office Directories, 1851, 1870; Kelly's Directory, 1890.

increasing only from an average of 1.7 to 2.0 per cent over the same forty-year period. This is a significantly lower proportion than that found for either Baldock and Buntingford (5.9 – 8.9 per cent) or Royston (10.5 – 15.5 per cent).

Michael Harverson carried out a similar but limited survey, using only data from the 1851 census, of a block of ten rural parishes in north-central Hertfordshire bounded by Baldock, Buntingford and Stevenage to the south-west. He wanted to ascertain how far a villager had to go 'to find a practitioner of a craft, trade or profession to supply one's needs'. Harverson concluded that with regard to

---

[3] Neither Anstey nor Wyddial were listed in the 1851 directory.

acquiring 'daily needs' unavailable in their own parish, 'a walk of no more than two hours … would have linked a villager in any of these [ten] parishes with a supplier in another'.[4] A very similar picture emerges here where in 1851, 'publicans' and non-specific 'shopkeepers' were the most commonly occurring PTPSs (12 and 14 respectively) found in the small villages.[5] Five of them boasted two public houses each but there were no publicans in either Kelshall or Reed, only a single 'beer retailer'.

Plate 4.1: Village of Wallington

John Chartres estimated that a settlement in Norfolk in 1836 needed a population of at least 377 before it was likely to contain a publican.[6] In comparison, the present data shows four of the seven villages with publicans in 1851 had populations above that threshold while Rushden (318), Wallington (274) and

---

[4] M. Harverson, 'Ten Hertfordshire Parishes in 1851: A Survey of Occupations', *Herts Past & Present, 3rd Series*, 8 (2006), p. 16. The villages of Ardeley, Clothall and Cottered are common to both studies.

[5] *Post Office Directory of the Six Home Counties: Essex, Herts, Middlesex, Kent, Surrey & Sussex, 1851* (London, 1851).

[6] J.A. Chartres, 'Country Tradesmen', in G.E. Mingay (ed.), *The Victorian Countryside, Vol. 1* (London, 1981), p. 304.

Bygrave (154) were considerably lower; Bygrave, the smallest, actually supported two publicans. Only Bygrave was without a 'shopkeeper' while Cottered had three. Both shopkeepers in Clothall, and two of the three in Cottered, were either publicans or 'beer retailers'. Apart from one butcher and one baker, both in Buckland, there were no other food retailers at this time and only a single outlet in the clothing sector, a shoemaker in Cottered. The majority of the villages had either a blacksmith and/or wheelwright; only Clothall, Reed and Wallington had neither. Schoolteachers, the sole 'professionals' identified, were present in only four villages, Ardeley (1), Buckland (1), Cottered (2) and Kelshall (1). This lack of other 'middle-class professionals' was similarly noted by Harverson who found that in his village cluster there were no solicitors, doctors, chemists or dentists.[7]

Plate 4.2: Church of England School in Wallington

Twenty years later, in 1870, the total numbers of publicans (10), 'shopkeepers' (14), blacksmiths (7) and wheelwrights (3) had changed little though the distribution had altered. At this time, schoolteachers (9 in total) were present in eight of the villages: Anstey, Buckland, Clothall, Cottered (n = 2), Kelshall, Rushden, Wallington (Plate 4.2 above) and Wyddial. Although Ardeley no

---

[7] Harverson, 'A Survey of Occupations', p. 20.

longer had a schoolteacher, the trend clearly shows that educational provision had increased for these small rural communities. By then, Kelshall and Reed had acquired a public house but the two in Bygrave, along with its 'shopkeeper', were no longer listed. However, the number of 'beer retailers' (13) had grown considerably. Ten of the villages had at least one such trader; only Cottered (with two public houses) and Kelshall (one public house) were without one. At this time a butcher was to be found in Anstey, Buckland and Kelshall. These apart, there were still no other village PTPSs in food retailing but in the clothing sector there were shoemakers present in Ardeley, Cottered, Kelshall and Wallington, tailors in Cottered and Wallington, and a draper in Anstey.

Plate 4.3: Village of Cottered

An important development for at least two of these small communities was the presence of a Post Office in Buckland and in Cottered (Plate 4.3 above). In terms of service provision at this time, Cottered (population 470 in 1861 census), lying on the road between Baldock and Buntingford (six miles from the former and three miles from the latter) appears to have been the most developed. It had three 'shopkeepers', two publicans, two schoolteachers, a blacksmith/wheelwright, a carpenter/joiner, a shoemaker, a tailor and a Post Ofice. Cottered, especially with the arrival of its Post Office, would obviously have been an important centre for Ardeley and Rushden and the nearby hamlets of Cromer, Luffenhall and

Throcking. Least developed were: Bygrave (population 195 in 1861 census) with a 'beer retailer', a blacksmith and a miller; Clothall (population 492, second largest of the eleven small villages) with a publican/'shopkeeper', a 'beer retailer' and a schoolteacher; and Wyddial (population 213, smallest of the small villages) with only a 'beer retailer' and a schoolteacher. These three villages were clearly dependent for the majority of goods and services on the nearby centres of Baldock in the case of Bygrave (situated 1.5 miles to the north-east) and Clothall (situated 1.5 miles to the south-east), and Buntingford in the case of Wydiall (situated 1.5 miles to the north-east).

Plate 4.4: Village of Buckland

By 1890 the numbers of PTPSs had declined somewhat in two-thirds of these small villages though overall the numbers of publicans (12), 'beer retailers' (11), 'shopkeepers' (11), blacksmiths (5) and wheelwrights (3) had changed little. There were now butchers trading in Anstey, Buckland (Plate 4.4 above), Kelshall, Wallington and Rushden (also a publican) and a baker in Anstey but still no other specialist shopkeepers such as grocers. Chartres's calculation that, in 1879, the population threshold for the appearance of a grocer in the North Riding of Yorkshire was 489 explains this lack as, apart from Ardeley (population 495 in 1881), all these Hertfordshire villages were still under that threshold.[8] Nine of the

---

[8] Chartres, 'Country Tradesmen', p. 304.

small villages now had schoolteachers (two each in Ardeley and Cottered) with only Bygrave and Reed lacking such a resource. Four villages now had a Post Office and in each location the Post Master offered a second service, being a carpenter in Anstey, a 'shopkeeper' in both Buckland and Reed, a plasterer in Cottered. If one excludes Anstey where over a third of its PTPSs were either publicans or 'beer retailers', Cottered and Buckland were the two best developed small service-providing villages in the regional hierarchy explored below.

Chartres argued that during the nineteenth century the markets in rural settlements, for both craftsmen and tradesmen, were 'often too small to permit total specialization'. Thus 'duality of occupations' was common, extending their markets and helping 'to sustain more specialized occupations' in small communities.[9] Provision of dual services was not uncommon among the PTPSs identified here but only in 1851 was the total level across all nine villages (17.0 per cent) approaching that found in the four study towns. Thereafter the incidence of dual occupations fell until, in 1890 across the eleven villages, the level (13.8 per cent) was half that of Ashwell, Baldock, Buntingford and Royston. Given that between 1870 and 1890 the population in all these small villages fell, the observed low level of occupational duality at the end of that period is not what might be expected. Analysis shows that while overall numbers of publicans (unchanged), 'shopkeepers' (+1) and wheelwrights (-2) changed little, the number within these three groups that had dual occupations was halved from fourteen to seven. Perhaps the reduced size of their markets forced these village PTPSs to concentrate on their core business activities. It is interesting to note that in 1890 the Postmasters at the four recently established village Post Offices all had need of a second occupation, carpenter (Anstey), plasterer (Cottered) or general 'shopkeeper' (Buckland and Reed).

The selected five larger villages lay either side of the Old North Road: Sandon and Therfield to the west; Barley, Barkway and Braughing (Plates 4.5 – 4.7 below) to the east, the last a little to the south of Buntingford. As we have seen with the small villages, rural-urban migration also caused the average population of these larger villages to fall from 1066 in 1841 to 984 in 1861, and again to 871 by 1881. Similarly, the number of PTPSs identified in these villages (Table 4.2 below) changed relatively little as a proportion of the population between 1851 and 1890. In 1851, the number of PTPSs in three of the larger villages, Barley, Braughing and Sandon, averaged 2.4 per cent as a proportion of their total populations; in a fourth, Barkway, the proportion was 3.3 per cent. By 1890 this average had risen to 3.9 per cent for all four of these villages, roughly double that

---

[9] Chartres, 'Country Tradesmen', p. 304.

	Barkway	Therfield	Braughing	Sandon	Barley
1851	42	21	27	22	19
1870	40	32	29	28	28
1890	36	19	33	27	27

Table 4.2: Numbers of PTPSs in five large villages
Source: Post Office Directories, 1851, 1870; Kelly's Directory, 1890.

of the eleven small villages but still a considerably lower proportion than that found for Baldock, Buntingford and Royston. In the fifth large village, Therfield, the proportion of PTPSs over the forty-year period rose only from 1.7 per cent in 1851 to 2.6 per cent in 1870 before it fell back to 1.6 per cent in 1890. Thus, in spite of having the biggest population among the five large villages (1175 in 1881

Plate 4.5: Village of Barley

Plate 4.6: Village of Barkway

Plate 4.7: Village of Braughing

census), the proportion of Therfield's PTPSs was less than that found for seven of the small villages (population range only 189 - 391) at the end of the period. The comparison of the breakdown of service provision by business sector between three of the selected villages, Barley, Barkway and Therfield, and the nearby town of Royston reveals that in all four locations the dominant sector was that of dealing (Figure 4.1 below). Proportionately, the dealing sector in the three large villages (55 – 70 per cent) is actually greater than that found in Royston (approximately 45 per cent) due to the presence of a larger public and professional sector in the town (> 20 per cent) coupled with the total absence of an industrial services sector in the villages (4.0 – 8.0 per cent in Royston).

In common with the small villages, the five larger settlements' alcohol trade again dominated service provision (Plates 4.8 – 4.9 below). In each of the three periods analysed, approximately one quarter of all available services were those of publicans (59 identified in total) and 'beer retailers' (71 identified in total). Numbers across the forty-year period varied but none of the five villages ever had fewer than two public houses, indeed Barkway actually had seven in 1851 as did Braughing in both 1870 and 1890. David Brown in his study of 218 Staffordshire villages, using data from an 1851 trade directory, estimated the mean number of 'beer outlets' to be 3.7 per village.[10]   In the five selected large Hertfordshire villages the mean number of such outlets (public houses and beer retailers) in 1851, 1870 and 1890 was significantly higher at 8.0, 10.0 and 8.0 respectively (for the small villages the mean values were 2.0, 3.0 and 3.0). Perhaps the proximity of major breweries in Ashwell, Baldock and Royston coupled with the relative ease of distribution over short distances encouraged a high rate of consumption in these villages.

Plate 4.8: Fox & Hounds Pub, London Road, Barley

---

[10] D. Brown, 'The Rise of Industrial Society and the End of the Self-contained Village, 1760–1900?', in C. Dyer (ed.), *The Self-contained Village?: The Social History of Rural Communities, 1250–1900* (Hatfield, 2007), p. 129.

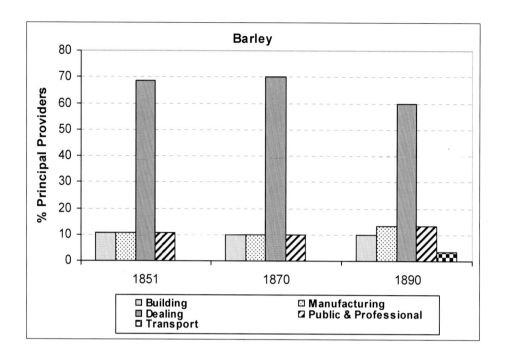

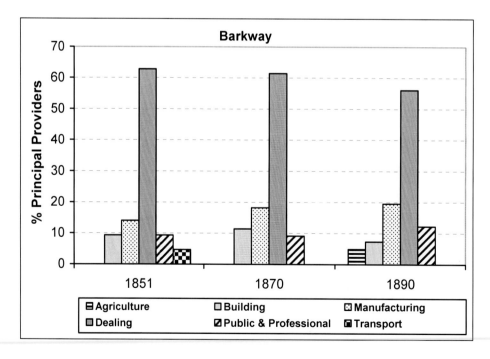

Figure 4.1: Business sector proportions in three villages and Royston
Source: Post Office Directories, 1851, 1870; Kelly's Directory, 1890;
Census enumerations, 1851, 1871, 1891.

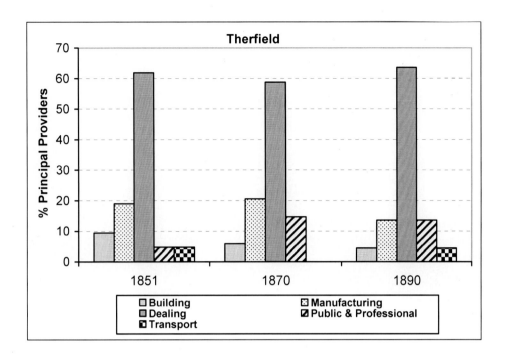

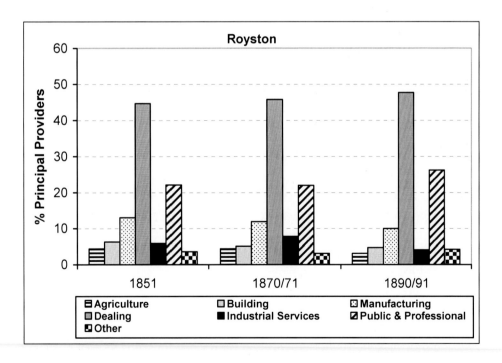

Plate 4.9: Fox & Duck Pub, The Green, Therfield

Compared with the smaller centres there was consistently, between 1851 and 1890, a considerably larger number (173 in total) of PTPSs involved in food, clothing and general retailing activities. This was approximately one third of all the service providers in the five large villages. In 1851 there were, in addition to bakers (6), butchers (5) and the general unspecified 'shopkeepers' (9), seven traders designated as 'grocer & draper' plus one other plain grocer. At this particular time, only Braughing lacked a 'shopkeeper', Sandon a grocer, and both Barley and Therfield were without a baker. In the clothing sector each of the villages had at least one 'boot and shoe maker' and only Sandon lacked the services of a 'grocer & draper'. Only Barkway, Barley and Therfield, where in the latter there were two, had the services of a tailor.

Twenty years later, when their level of service provision was at its peak, there was at least one baker, butcher, grocer and 'shopkeeper' in each of these five large villages. There were several examples of grocers offering a second service, that of butcher (Braughing), baker (Braughing and Therfield), and as in the earlier period, six also operated as drapers. Each of the villages in 1870 had at least two 'boot and shoe makers' (both Barkway and Barley had four) and at least one tailor (Barkway had three). Purveyors of alcohol had grown in number, up by 20.5 per cent, but an increased number (34.0 per cent combined total) of publicans (7) and 'beer retailers' (9) in these larger villages still appeared to need a second trade to survive; these ranged from 'boot & shoemaker' (3), baker (2), tailor (2) and wheelwright (2) to a blacksmith, a carrier, a saddler and a 'pig dealer'. The level of service providers with dual occupations peaked in 1870, across these five larger villages, at 21.0 per cent of the identified PTPSs, falling back slightly to 19.7 per cent over the following twenty years; an intermediate level between that found in the small villages and the four towns. Over the forty-year period the most frequently occurring dual occupation combination was that of the village grocer/draper with 7 in 1851, 6 in 1870 and 6 in 1890. By 1890, publicans and beer retailers apart, the level of retail provision was starting to decline despite the arrival of a fishmonger in both Barkway and Barley, and a sausage maker in Sandon. Therfield and Sandon, even with stable populations, no longer had the services of a butcher and the latter had lost its grocer too. There was also a general reduction in the number of bakers and 'shopkeepers'.

Chartres and Turnbull observed that because of the 'intensive forms of husbandry and more extensive application of machinery' during the nineteenth century, the two principal country craftsmen, the blacksmith and wheelwright, 'retained their importance to 1900 and beyond'.[11] That importance is reflected here in the five larger villages. Over the forty year period the three selected directories listed the entries of traditional service providers in the building and transport sectors, i.e. blacksmiths (22), wheelwrights (20), carpenters (16), bricklayers (7), builders (7), carriers (7), plumbers and glaziers (7), ironmongers (6) and saddlers (6). However, these services were not evenly distributed among the five villages for Braughing and Therfield never appeared to possess a bricklayer or plumber, there were no ironmongers listed under Barley or Sandon, and Barkway appeared to lack a builder. Unlike Chartres and Turnbull's assertion that in addition to the above craftsmen, 'the Victorian countryside contained … thatchers and masons', the present analysis identified only one thatcher (Barkway, 1870) and no masons in any of the sixteen villages.[12] This apparent lack probably stems from having only used trade directories as the data source for the current village analysis.

By 1870 all five villages had schoolteachers; there were at least two present in all bar Sandon. Later, as a direct result of Forster's 1870 Elementary Education Act, new 'Board Schools' with increased capacity had opened at Therfield in 1876 (Plate 4.10 below) and at Braughing in 1877 while 'National' Church of England

---

[11] J.A. Chartres and G.L. Turnbull, 'Country Craftsmen', in G.E. Mingay (ed.), *The Victorian Countryside, Vol. 1* (London, 1981), p. 314.
[12] Chartres and Turnbull, 'Country Craftsmen', p. 315.

schools continued to operate in Barkway, Barley and Sandon.[13] As Brown suggested, this increased educational provision, noted both here and in the smaller villages, increased 'literacy rates and knowledge of the world' allowing 'the villager's imagination to travel beyond the parish's physical and social confines'. This would have encouraged migration to the nearby towns and beyond leading to

Plate 4.10: Board School, Therfield

decreased village populations but some would have returned 'when opportunities allowed, bringing outside ideas into the settlement'.[14] Furthermore, by 1895 two of the larger villages, Barkway and Braughing, had acquired that nineteenth-century institution, the reading room. In Braughing's case it was a 'public hall, seating about 250 persons, with reading and coffee rooms'.[15] Such centres used

---

[13] The Elementary Education Act, 1870, 33 & 34 Vict. c. 75; Bysouth, P.T., 'Elementary Education in North East Hertfordshire during the Late Nineteenth Century and the Effect of the 1870 Education Act on Literacy' (Advanced Certificate Dissertation, University of Cambridge, Board of Continuing Education, 1996), pp. 31 – 37.

[14] Brown, 'Self-Contained Village', p. 126.

[15] *Kelly's Directory of Hertfordshire with Large Map, 1895* (London, 1894), p. 55.

for social and educational purposes were, argued Carole King, attractive to local authorities as 'a direct alternative to the public house', i.e. an answer to the social problems of poverty and drunkenness.[16] An answer perhaps needed in Braughing where a population of 974 (in 1891) had the choice of seven public houses; the *Adam & Eve*, *Axe & Compasses*, *Bell*, *Brown Bear*, *Golden Fleece*, *Old Bull*, and the *Rose & Crown*.[17]

Others in the public and professional sector were surgeons in Barkway (1851 – 1890), veterinary surgeons in Braughing (1870 – 1890), and from 1890 there were assistant overseers in Barley and Barkway (two parishes within the Royston Union), post-masters in Barley and Therfield, and a chemist in Braughing.[18] For one village, Braughing, the inclusion in the 1890 directory of a railway Station Master suggests that life for its inhabitants had probably changed considerably with the arrival of the railway station sometime after 1863.[19]

Among the PTPSs identified in the larger villages there was an increase in the incidence of Chartres's 'duality of occupation' from 12.2 to 20.4 per cent between 1851 and 1890. This was in contrast to the smaller villages where the incidence was considerably lower from 1870 onwards having declined from 17.0 per cent in 1851 to reach only 13.8 per cent by 1890. An analysis of Lincolnshire inventories and trade directories convinced Holderness that nearly all rural tradesmen also 'followed some form of agriculture, either as a major or subordinate source of income'. In addition to that 'inevitable connexion' with agriculture he found that many 'shopkeepers and craftsmen diversified their businesses in other directions'. Stobart later concurred that most 'rural craftsmen-retailers were far from being divorced from the land'.[20] While many of the craftsmen-retailers identified, in both the large and smaller villages surrounding the study towns, had dual occupations there was very little evidence in the trade directories examined that many were involved in agricultural activities across the second half of the nineteenth century. In contrast to the above views of Holderness and Stobart, there were in fact only five examples; a beer retailer and pig dealer (Barley,

---

[16] C. King, 'The Rise and Decline of Village Reading Rooms', *Rural History*, 20, 2 (2009), p. 164.

[17] *Kelly's Directory of Hertfordshire, 1895*, p. 55.

[18] Barley and Barkway were parishes situated within the Royston Poor Law Union.

[19] Trains first ran on the Ware Hadham & Buntingford branch of the Great Eastern Railway from St Margarets, Ware, to Buntingford on 3 July 1863. The 13.75 mile line ran from St Margarets through Mardock, Widford, Hadham, Standon, Braughing, West Mill and terminated at Buntingford. Braughing's call to fame was that a nearby bridge, over the River Rib, initially 'failed to come up to the requirements of the Board of Trade Inspector'. F.G. Cockman, *The Railways of Hertfordshire, Hertfordshire Local Studies, No. 1* (Hertford, 1978), p.4.

[20] B.A. Holderness, 'Rural Tradesmen, 1660-1850. A Regional Study in Lindsey', *Lincolnshire History and Archaeology*, 7 (1972), pp. 77, 82; J. Stobart, 'The Economic and Social Worlds of Rural Craftsmen-retailers in Eighteenth-century Cheshire', *The Agricultural History Review*, 52, 2 (2004), p. 143.

1870), a publican and flour dealer (Buckland, 1870), a shopkeeper and cattle dealer (Rushden, 1870), a carrier and hay/straw dealer (Barley, 1890), and a beer retailer and hurdle maker (Barkway, 1890).

Evidence presented earlier has shown that Ashwell, the smallest of the four towns, provided a wider range of goods and services than any of the villages surveyed above. Its provision was, however, more limited in terms of penetrating and satisfying the needs of its surrounding hinterland than the three other study towns. Perhaps late nineteenth-century Ashwell should be viewed as on the cusp between being as large a village, or as small a town, as commonly considered for that period.

As shown, the analysis of locally provided goods and services clearly demonstrates that for all sixteen villages, even the five larger ones, the range available to residents was very restricted when compared to those available in Baldock, Buntingford and Royston. Most villages had bakers, butchers and grocers but there were no confectioners, fruiterers or greengrocers though it is probable that many villagers grew their own fruit and vegetables. There were 'boot and shoemakers', drapers and tailors but villagers would have had to travel to one of the towns to find a clothier, dressmaker, haberdasher, hosier, milliner or outfitter; in the villages, dressmaking would still have been a 'cottage industry' performed by wives and daughters. Local carpenters might have made furniture but the villages lacked the services of skilled cabinet makers and upholsterers. There were no banks, policemen or solicitors. Finally, if any of the villagers had wanted and could have afforded a few luxuries, they would have needed one of the towns for a bookseller, china and glass dealer, photographer, tobacconist, watch and clockmaker, or a wine and spirit merchant to provide something a little different from the routine fare sold by all those 'beer retailers'. Furthermore, there was a range of attractions available in the towns that villages could not provide. As Thomas Hardy observed in *Tess of the d'Urbervilles*, village youngsters found their 'chief pleasures' every Saturday night through the 'weekly pilgrimage' when they had finished the week's work 'to Chaseborough, a decayed market-town two or three miles distant'.[21] It can be seen through the pages of its own local newspaper that Royston offered other villagers more sophisticated entertainments ranging from 'SELECT READINGS FROM SHAKSPEARE (sic)' by Miss Poole at the Bull Inn's Assembly Room, to either 'A SELECT BALL' with 'A CAPITAL BAND IN ATTENDANCE' or 'GRAND VOCAL &

---

[21] T. Hardy, *Tess of the d'Urbervilles. A Pure Woman* (Heron Books Edn, London, 1970), p. 75.

INSTRUMENTAL CONCERTS' by Dr. Mark and his Little Men at the Lecture Hall of the Royston Institute.[22]

Thus beyond the basic needs of life, all sixteen villages, small and large, were obviously very dependent on the wide range of goods and services available in Baldock, Buntingford and Royston, clearly their nearest significant urban centres. As Brown observed, this dependence would have been greatly facilitated by the fact that since the eighteenth century 'improving transport and the progress of consumerism brought villages increasingly within a regional and national economy'.[23]

Central places

The following section examines the long tradition of studies, derived from Walter Christaller's seminal work of the 1930s, based on his concept of centrality providing a significantly clearer theoretical distinction between an urban centre's degree of service provision and its size, than one relying simply on demographic relationships.

Harold Carter has more recently argued that the nature and significance of urban experience was influenced by 'location or position' and 'form or internal structure'. He suggested that 'location can only be understood through function; what a town does, or did in the past, determines its location and controls its growth'.[24] There existed across England and Wales, in response to nineteenth-century industrialization, a developing network of towns that included the principal centres of population growth. Why, asked Walter Christaller, looking at similar developments in southern Germany, 'are these, then, large and small towns, and why are they distributed so irregularly?'. The proliferation and expansion of these urban centres can be seen as a response to economic pressures. As Christaller argued, 'economic factors are decisive for the existence of towns' since demand must exist for services which the towns can offer and for the variety of goods that can be distributed from them. In examining the hierarchical regional distribution of towns in southern Germany, he put forward the notion of 'place' as the 'localization of the functions of a center' with the functions of a 'central place' extending 'over a larger region in which other central places of less importance' existed. These 'places' extend into the surroundings as far as the influence of their central professions and services are felt, i.e. the importance of a

---

[22] *The Royston Crow*, 1 June 1855, p. 44; *Royston Crow*, 2 January 1860, p. 268; *Royston Crow*, 1 October 1860, p. 305.

[23] Brown, 'Self-Contained Village', p. 115.

[24] H. Carter, *The Study of Urban Geography* (4th edn, London, 1995), p. 5.

'centrality' can be defined as the extent to which the 'combined economic efforts of the inhabitants' satisfies the demands of the smaller places within their region.[25] Beguin argued that it was Christaller's pioneering vision of the 'explicit integration of geography and economics' to explain the spatial structure of a central place system that led to the later development of modern spatial analysis.[26]

Christaller's theory of centrality, according to Richard Preston, includes a number of static relations such as the structure of the population and the range of available central goods and services that are supported by the means of transport for passengers and goods.[27] The latter of these, Carter observed, was clearly closely associated with central place functions since 'by their nature general services for a hinterland demand local distributive networks'.[28] Preston suggests, however, that such 'descriptions of the structure of Christaller's central place theory might be improved' if more geographers and regional scientists were to recognize that it also includes a number of dynamic historical processes.[29] These processes include changes in supply and demand for central goods and services and the influence of improved communications and technical progress on a regional economy.[30]

Christaller devised a hierarchy of seven types of urban centre each with a particular range of influence which Carter described as being 'the maximum distance over which people will travel to purchase a good or derive a service'. The major conurbations were identified by Christaller as L, P and G centres with ranges of 108, 62 and 36 km respectively.[31] The four smaller types of settlement in the hierarchy, in descending order of the range of their *complementary region*, are B-places (regional centres, range 20.7 km), K-places (district towns, range 12.0 km), A-places (commercial towns, range 6.9 km) and M-places (market towns, range 4.0 km).[32] Historians have largely ignored the late-

---

[25] W. Christaller, 'Central Places in Southern Germany' ([Unpublished Doctoral Dissertation, Friedrich-Alexander University of Erlangen, Nuremberg, 1933] trans. C.W. Baskin, New Jersey, 1966), pp. 1, 3, 17, 18.

[26] H. Beguin, 'Christaller's Central Place Postulates: A Commentary', *Annals of Regional Science*, 26 (1992), p. 215.

[27] R.E. Preston, 'Christaller's Neglected Contribution to the Study of the Evolution of Central Places', *Progress in Human Geography*, 9, 2 (1985), p. 181.

[28] Carter, *Study of Urban Geography*, p. 25.

[29] Preston, 'Christaller's Neglected Contribution' p. 189.

[30] Preston, 'Christaller's Neglected Contribution', pp. 181-85.

[31] Christaller's hierarchical identifiers were taken from the German descriptors *Landstadt, Provinzstadt, Gaustadt, Bezirksstadt, Kreisstadt, Amstort* and *Marktort*.

[32] Keith Beavon identified the 'complementary region' as that region served by a central place in which the 'service limit of each central activity was described by the *outer limit of the range of the commodity* in which it dealt', K.S.O. Beavon, *Central Place Theory: A Reinterpretation* (London, 1977), p. 18; Carter, *Study of Urban Geography*, p. 28.

nineteenth-century urban significance of small centres such as Ashwell, Baldock, Buntingford and Royston as they seemingly sit beneath the above hierarchy.

Leland Burns and Robert Healy in their American study of 185 metropolitan areas criticized empirical testing of central place theory, chiefly by geographers, for simplifying 'the hierarchy to one based on demographic size as the determinant of ordering in space'.[33] They argued that there are 'several economic reasons why occupations should vary with city size' and suggested that 'the principal tenet of central place theory is founded on the existence of minimum market size for activities of different kinds'.[34] While geographers have made much of the range of the demand for a centre's goods and services from its surrounding hinterland, it should be obvious that the diversity of provision must also be a response to the demands and requirements of the centre's own populace. A study of eighteenth-century consumption by Jon Stobart, Andrew Hann and Victoria Morgan found that there was indeed 'a close correlation between town population and overall service provision, suggesting that internal markets were important in determining the level of provision in a town'.[35]

The evidence presented here regarding the range of goods and services available in four small towns clearly indicates significant internal markets and supports Burns and Healy's view that 'a hierarchy which takes explicit account of demand and other economic determinants' is more powerful than the traditional symmetrically geometric basis of central place theory.[36] Despite their modest populations, the towns under consideration such as Baldock (population rose from 1920 to 2301 between 1851 and 1891) and Buntingford (population fell from 2058 to 1887 between 1851 and 1891), when judged by the diversity of business, financial, public and professional services they offered, clearly rank as significant 'central places' of a type that characterizes the extra-urban matrix but which have been too frequently ignored by urban historians examining the second half of the nineteenth century.

---

[33] L.S. Burns and R.G. Healy, 'The Metropolitan Hierarchy of Occupations: An Economic Interpretation of Central Place Theory', *Regional Science and Urban Economics*, 8, 4 (1978), p.381.

[34] Burns and Healy, 'Metropolitan Hierarchy', p. 382.

[35] J. Stobart, A. Hann and V. Morgan, *Spaces of Consumption: Leisure and Shopping in the English Town, c. 1680-1830* (Abingdon, 2007), p. 47.

[36] Burns and Healy, 'Metropolitan Hierarchy', p. 393

North-east Hertfordshire's central place hierarchy

The notion of a 'hierarchical arrangement of service centres', Wayne Davies argued, lay 'at the heart of central place theory'. He devised, and applied to an early 1960s study of a South Wales mining area, a technique of measuring centrality that was objective, could be tested, allowed comparability between different areas, and incorporated all central functions of a given place.[37]

Davies identified this measure of centrality, or 'degree of focality', of a single outlet of any functional type (t) as its location coefficient (C) where $C = t/T \times 100$ when T equals the total number of outlets of the functional type (t) in the whole hierarchy. Multiplying C by the number of that functional type's outlets in a given settlement produces the centrality value (or 'degree of centrality') imparted to that settlement by each functional type (t). Finally, totalling all its centrality values gives the functional index for each settlement in the hierarchy.[38] Compared to the uniformity of Christaller's original theory, Davies believed 'the precise relationships existing in the case study area must be the result of local circumstance' but the structure of the results is important in determining 'whether or not a hierarchical structure is present'.[39]

Using Davies's approach to the establishment of hierarchies, as Carter has pointed out, poses the difficult problem of exactly what to count. Given three shops: A, a grocer/greengrocer/wine and spirit merchant; B, a greengrocer/fishmonger; C, a grocer/butcher, should one count three establishments (i.e. A, B and C), five functions (i.e. butcher, fishmonger, greengrocer, grocer and wine and spirit merchant), or seven functional units (i.e. 2 greengrocers, 2 grocers, 1 butcher, 1 fishmonger and 1 wine and spirit merchant)? He also argued that the full range of 'such data [functions/functional units] are seldom available from the censuses'.[40] Where an establishment performed two very different functions it was, in Davies's original study, allocated to both functions. A similar approach was used here for the analysis of data, obtained from trade directories and CEBs, relating to people with dual or multiple roles.

Whereas Davies confined his original analysis to retail functions, Roy Lewis in his study of mid-Wales extended it to include social services and professional functions. A later regional study of early eighteenth-century north-west England by Jon Stobart, utilizing data from urban probate records, classified central place

---

[37] W.K.D. Davies, 'Centrality and the Central Place Hierarchy', *Urban Studies*, 4, 1 (1967), p. 61.
[38] Davies, 'Centrality', p. 63.
[39] Davies, 'Centrality', p. 77.
[40] Carter, *Study of Urban Geography*, p. 40.

functions under the broad headings of dealing, public service, professional activities and craftsman-retailers.[41] In this present analysis, the regional hierarchy of central places was determined for the building, dealing (including craftsmen-retailers but excluding wholesalers), domestic services (e.g. chimney sweeps, laundresses and hair dressers), public and professional, and transport (e.g. carriers & railway agents) sectors as described in detail previously. In order to determine whether the hierarchy had changed over time it was assessed using data from the 1851, 1870 and 1890 trade directories for all twenty locations supplemented, in the case of the four study towns, by additional data from the 1851, 1871 and 1891 national censuses.

The calculated functional indices for the twenty centres (Table 4.3 below) clearly show on that basis an attenuated hierarchy. Their individual values range from a miniscule 7 to a considerable 3143 in 1851, from 3 to 4688 in 1870/71, and similarly from 2 to 4976 by 1890/91. Over the forty-year period, twelve of the centres show an overall increase of their functional index, most significantly in Ashwell (111.5%), Royston (58.3%) and Baldock (25.5%), three of the four most populous centres in 1891. Apart from Barkway, one of the larger villages, the six centres showing an overall decrease in their functional index over the same period included five of the smallest centres in the hierarchy. These six centres had all suffered serious population decline during this time ranging from 15.1 per cent in Rushden to 39.4 per cent in Barkway, a state of affairs that mirrors the finding of Lewis that 'consistent depopulation' caused a 'lowering in demand for central place functions'.[42]

A place's centrality, i.e. the level of goods and services provided, and 'the degree to which it served a tributary area' was, according to Carter, carefully distinguished by Christaller from the secondary notion of a town's importance 'which was reflected in its population' but not measureable by that alone. However, Davies argued that centrality values of each type of establishment 'revealed that centrality varied according to the size of centre'. More recently, Stobart, Hann and Morgan noted a close correlation 'between town population and overall service provision' in north-west England and the west Midlands by the mid-eighteenth century, and suggested that 'internal markets were important in determining the level of provision in a town'.[43] In the present analysis the

---

[41] C.R. Lewis, 'The Central Place Pattern of Mid-Wales and the Middle Welsh Borderland', in M. Carter and W.K.D. Davies (eds), *Urban Essays: Studies in the Geography of Wales* (London, 1970), p. 242; J. Stobart, 'The Spatial Organization of a Regional Economy: Central Places in North-west England in the Early-eighteenth Century', *J. Historical Geography*, 22, 2 (1996), p. 149.

[42] Lewis, 'Central Place Pattern', p. 246.

[43] Carter, *Study of Urban Geography*, p. 26; Davies, 'Centrality', p. 78; Stobart, Hann and Morgan, *Spaces of Consumption*, p. 47.

order of the hierarchy by 1890/91 clearly demonstrates a close correlation between the centres' populations and their level of service provision as indicated by their functional indexes. Centres 1 and 5 had populations above 1000, centres

Settlements in the NE Herts Hierarchy	Functional Indices		
	1851	1870/71	1890/91
1. Royston	3143	4688	4976
2. Baldock	1756	2518	2203
3. Buntingford	1274	1438	1363
4. Ashwell	340	446	719
5. Braughing	207	176	336
6. Sandon	141	156	302
7. Barley	115	165	268
8. Barkway	341	293	234
9. Anstey	n/a	44	142
10. Cottered	32	49	136
11. Buckland	42	86	132
12. Therfield	69	154	98
13. Kelshall	18	17	22
14. Reed	38	108	20
15. Rushden	25	70	19
16. Ardeley	38	63	11
17. Wallington	6	14	10
18. Clothall	9	6	5
19. Wyddial	n/a	3	3
20. Bygrave	7	5	2

Table 4.3: Functional indices of NE Hertfordshire's hierarchy [44]
Source: Each Functional Index, corrected to whole numbers, is based on data extracted from Post Office Directories, 1851 and 1870, Kelly's Directory, 1890, and additional data from the 1851/1871/1891 censuses for Ashwell, Baldock, Buntingford and Royston.

6 to 8 between 600 and 800, centres 9 to 11 between 300 and 400, centres 13 to 20 between 100 and 300 (with the exception of centre 16, Ardeley, population

[44] Neither Anstey nor Wyddial were listed in the 1851 directory. The above functional indices were calculated from the analysis of a total of 76 functional types in 1851, 105 in 1870/71 and 110 in 1890/91.

495, functional index 11). Therfield, centre 12 with a population of 1175 but a functional index of only 98, is the other exception to the general trend. Ardeley and Therfield are among seven examples of centres whose functional index increased from 1851 to 1870 but fell back by 1890, the others being Baldock, Buntingford, Reed, Rushden, and Wallington. Only Braughing exhibited the opposite effect where its functional index fell from 207 in 1851 to 176 in 1870 but, increased twenty years later, to 336, well above its 1851 level.

Integral to Christaller's theory is 'a stepped hierarchy of central places' but in reality, Keith Beavon argued, the 'postulation of continua' appears more logical as the identification of groups 'remains subjective and unresolved'. This concern was echoed by Carter who felt that having established measures of centrality, the 'critical problem still remains – do these demonstrate a set of discrete ranks or a continuum'?[45] Distinguishing the within-group distances, that is the 'differences between the centrality indexes of members of the same order' from the between-group distance to the next order, according to Stobart, can define clusters of towns when 'this between-group distance … [is] greater than each individual difference within an order'.[46] The diagrammatic representation of the central place groupings identified by this present analysis (Figure 4.2 below) clearly shows an attenuated hierarchy of central places in north-east Hertfordshire that has both elements of Beavon's continuum and Stobart's discrete ranks or clusters.

In 1851, the nine lower-order centres all with functional indices below fifty lie along the 'Continuum V' (Anstey and Wyddial having no data are located on the baseline) followed by Therfield (W), the cluster of Barley and Sandon (X), Braughing (Y), and the cluster Ashwell and Barkway (Z) with functional indices of 340 and 341 respectively. The centrality values of the remaining three study towns of Buntingford, Baldock and Royston, 1274, 1756 and 3143 respectively, clearly confirms their high order status in this regional hierarchy. By 1890/91, Stobart's method of distinguishing orders is clearly demonstrated. 'Continuum A' is now clearly of a different order to that of 'Cluster B' made up of Therfield, Buckland, Cottered and Anstey, which in turn is clearly differentiated from 'Cluster C' comprising Barkway, Barley, Sandon and Braughing. Ashwell's centrality value has doubled over forty years from 340 to 719 elevating it towards the increasingly high order centres of Buntingford, Baldock and Royston whose indexes had risen to 1363, 2203 and 4976 respectively.

---

[45] Beavon, *Central Place Theory: A Reinterpretation* (London, 1977), pp. 1, 51; Carter, *Study of Urban Geography*, p. 46.
[46] Stobart, 'Spatial Organization of a Regional Economy', p. 149.

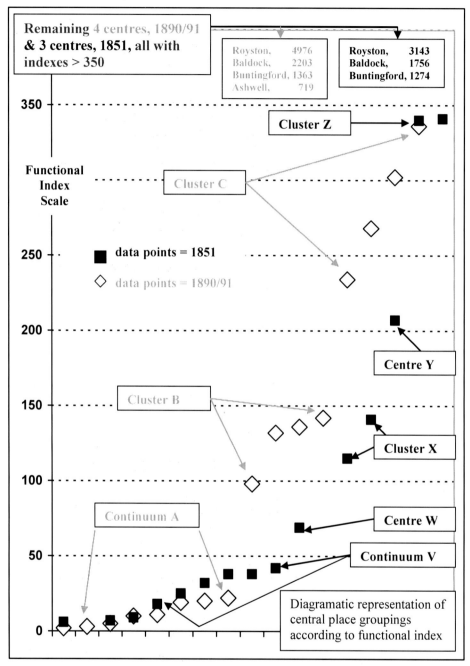

Figure 4.2: Alignment of the central place hierarchy, 1851 and 1890/91

Source: Each Functional Index is based on data extracted from the Post Office
Directory, 1851 and Kelly's Directory, 1890 with the 1851 and 1891 censuses
providing additional data for Ashwell, Baldock, Buntingford and Royston.
Note: Functional indices are plotted from left to right in ascending order of value
(apart from Anstey and Wyddial for which there is no 1851 data).

Using Stobart's 'within-group' and 'between-group' distance approach it is possible, calculating those figures from Table 4.3 above, to identify a changing hierarchical relationship among the four study towns between 1851 and 1891. In 1851, Ashwell was in Cluster Z alongside Barkway with almost identical functional indexes and a 'between-group' distance from Buntingford of 934. A figure of only 482 between Buntingford and Baldock suggests that they should be clustered as a pairing distinct from Ashwell and especially Royston where the 'between-group' distance between it and Baldock was 1387. By 1891, Ashwell's distance from Braughing, now the leading village, was 383. By the same time, Ashwell's distance from Buntingford had reduced by one-third to 644. Although the 'within-group' distance between the latter and Baldock was now 840 (a doubling), they can be considered a cluster of three distinctly separated from the fourth town Royston whose 'between-group' distance from Baldock had by then doubled to 2773.

Dynamic towns, according to Margaret Noble, drew on influences from 'other than its own inhabitants' and exhibited a degree of 'externality'. For example, improvements in rail links in the latter half of the nineteenth century led to external support that she argued resulted 'in higher trade flows and greater participation in intra- and inter-regional trade'.[47] The substantial growth of the study towns' functional indexes suggests that Noble's concept is operating here. The degree to which they were 'outward-looking towns' can be estimated using Stobart's 'externality rating' which he 'calculated by dividing its functional index by its population [then multiplied by 100]'.[48] On this basis Royston's rating in 1891 was 292.5 (doubled since 1851) compared with Baldock's 95.7 (little changed), Buntingford's 72.2 (increased modestly) and Ashwell's 46.2 (doubled). This provides further confirmation of the hierarchy of these small towns and re-emphasises the pre-eminence of Royston.

In considering the characteristics of hierarchical ordering, Wayne Davies argued that a fundamental tenet, giving an order its distinctiveness, was that 'centres of each higher order perform all the functions of lower orders as well as carrying on a set of central functions that differentiates them from the lowest order centres'.[49] These marginal hierarchical goods and services define a grade that has access to a sufficient population to make the distribution of those goods and services profitable, whereas there are not enough people in the hinterland of the grade below to support their distribution. Analysis of the current data (Table 4.4 below)

---

[47] M. Noble, 'Growth and Development in a Regional Urban System: The Country Towns of Eastern Yorkshire, 1700-1850', *Urban History Yearbook* (1987), p. 18.

[48] J. Stobart, *The First Industrial Region: North-west England, c. 1700-60* (Manchester, 2004), p. 166.

[49] Davies, 'Centrality', p. 73.

Royston	Baldock	Buntingford	Ashwell	Barkway
				Barley
Artist	-	-	-	Braughing
Bird Stuffer	-	-	-	Sandon
China Dealer	-	-	-	-
Art Teacher	-	-	-	-
Dentist	-	-	-	-
Dining Room	-	-	-	-
Librarian	-	-	-	-
Music Seller	-	-	-	-
Newsagent	-	-	-	-
Photographer	-	-	-	-
Stone Mason	-	-	-	-
Toy Dealer	-	-	-	-
Umbrella Mk	-	-	-	-
2	Auctioneer	-	-	-
1	Coffee Tavern	-	-	-
2	Fireman	-	-	-
1	Florist	-	-	-
3	Greengrocer	-	-	-
4	Milliner	-	-	-
2	Music Teacher	-	-	-
4	Solicitor	-	-	-
2	Upholsterer	-	-	-
2	1	Banker	-	-
6	1	Cabinet Maker	-	-
2	2	Coach Builder	-	-
6	2	Confectioner	-	-
2	1	Printer	-	-
1	1	Tobacconist	-	-
4	4	2	Coal Merchant	-
2	2	1	Commercial Inn	-
6	3	2	Insurance Ag	-
3	2	4	Police Officer	-
2	2	2	Wine Merchant	-
9	7	5	3	Boot/Shoe Mk
11	5	3	4	Grocer

Table 4.4: Marginal goods in NE Hertfordshire's high order centres, 1890/91

Source: Kelly's Directory, 1890 plus the 1891 census providing additional data for Ashwell, Baldock, Buntingford and Royston.

Note: The values under each centre are the number of the lower orders' marginal goods found in that particular centre.

clearly supports Davies's tenet. The four larger villages (Barkway, Barley, Braughing and Sandon) of 'Cluster C' are differentiated from all the other lower order villages by the presence of a boot and/or shoemaker and a grocer. Similarly, Ashwell has five high order activities that distinguish it from 'Cluster C', Buntingford six that distinguish it from Ashwell, Baldock nine that distinguish it from Buntingford, and Royston a further thirteen that distinguish it from Baldock. However, the present data reveals a number of exceptions to the idea of marginal hierarchical activities that Stobart called 'an incremental basket of goods'. Some goods and services (Table 4.5 below) that were only found in Baldock, Buntingford and Ashwell were not available in Royston, the study town with the highest functional index.[50]

Services unavailable in Royston, 1890/91	Baldock	Buntingford	Ashwell
General Dealer	3	1	1
Clothier	1	1	-
Undertaker	1	1	-
Domestic Machine Dealer	1	-	-
Provident Friendly Institution	1	-	-
Hosier	1	-	-
Laundry	1	-	-
Optician	1	-	-
Reading Room	1	-	-
Stone & Sand Dealer	1	-	-
Fly Proprietor	-	1	-
Wallet Maker	-	1	-

Table 4.5: Number of services unavailable at the hierarchy's apex, Royston
Source: Kelly's Directory, 1890 and the 1891 census.

Note: The values under each centre are the number of particular services in that centre

At the heart of Christaller's original central place theory was the distribution of places in a symmetrical lattice of hexagons. Places at each level of a hierarchy (e.g. A centres) were arranged in a hexagonal pattern (Figure 4.3 below) with

---

[50] Stobart, 'Spatial Organization of a Regional Economy', p. 153. The absence of general dealers in Royston is explained by Davies's argument that their various goods were 'being sold in specialist outlets in the larger centres', Davies, 'Centrality', p. 76. The fact that something as basic as an undertaker was not identified in Royston from either trade directory or census is surprising but time did not permit the seeking of an explanation.

places of the next level down the hierarchy (e.g. M centres) situated at the centres of equilateral triangles joining the former and producing a smaller hexagon.[51]

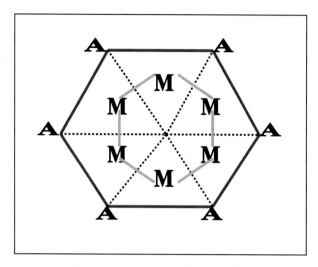

Figure 4.3: Christaller's hexagonal lattice of A and M-places

Regarding these supposed spatial patterns of central places, there appears to be general agreement with Davies's expressed view that 'nothing remotely connected with a hexagonal structure with precise nesting relationships has been found'. Later work, Carter argued, has revealed 'little of the regularity which Christaller's model predicted' and while there might be a hierarchy of central places in a given area he believed 'its spatial distribution does not conform to central place theory'.[52]

In this present analysis Baldock, Buntingford and Royston lie at the points of a regular triangle (Figure 4.4 below). At the centre of that triangle (see Map 4.1 on p. 158), further down the hierarchy, is Sandon (Cluster X, 1851 and Cluster C, 1890/91). However, apart from two other triangles formed with centres of similar population (Baldock, Royston and Potton to the north; Baldock, Buntingford and Welwyn to the south) there is little further evidence of geometric symmetry in the region. On the basis of such triangulation, one might reasonably expect Barley, Barkway or Braughing, with similar functional indexes to Sandon, to resemble it in respect of their locations but they do not, all being situated a short distance east of the Royston/Buntingford axis along the Ware to Cambridge road (see Map 4.1 on p. 158). It should be noted that Sandon, at the epicentre of the Baldock,

[51] Carter, *Study of Urban Geography*, pp. 29-30.
[52] Davies, 'Centrality', p. 77; Carter, *Study of Urban Geography*, pp. 61, 62.

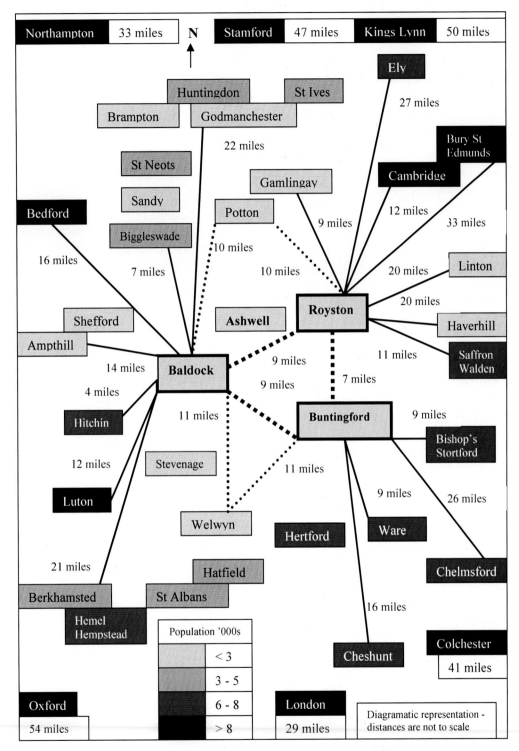

Figure 4.4: Proximity of significant urban centres to the study towns, 1851
Source: Population figures provided by Beds, Cambs and Herts County Archives

Buntingford and Royston triangle, exemplifies one problem associated with Christaller's theory that was identified by John Everson and Brian FitzGerald. They believed that dependent places could be 'divided in their allegiance to the central place one higher in the hierarchy'.[53] This must have been the case with some of the other villages within the triangle, for example, Rushden equidistant between Baldock and Buntingford.

Apart from London, the nation's 'central place' lying twenty-nine miles to the south of Buntingford, there are only three centres within twenty miles of any of the study towns, possessing populations above 8,000 in 1851, that could probably be considered as B-places in Christaller's hierarchy. These are Bedford and Luton, north-west and south-west of Baldock respectively, and Cambridge, north-east of Royston. Six other similar-sized centres, Bury St Edmunds (33 miles), Colchester (41 miles), Kings Lynn (50 miles), Northampton (33 miles), Oxford (54 miles) and Stamford (47 miles), are at considerably greater distances from any of the three towns. These centres are widely scattered in a non-geometric fashion and frequently at distances from each other greater than that predicted by Christaller (22.5 miles). Using population as a guide, Hitchin situated four miles south-west of Baldock is the nearest centre that could probably be considered as belonging to Christaller's K-places (those with populations between 6,000 and 8,000 in 1851). There is a rather surprising absence of any other K-place north of the study towns until reaching Ely at a distance of twenty-seven miles. Yet, to the south and east there are seven such centres; Saffron Walden, Bishop's Stortford, Chelmsford, Ware, Hertford, Cheshunt and Hemel Hempstead. In the case of A- and M-places, populations of between 3,000 to 5,000, and below 3,000 respectively, the great majority are located north and south of Baldock on or near the Great North Road. Others relate to Royston, Gamlingay 9 miles to the north, and Linton and Haverhill 14 and 20 miles respectively to the east. To the south and east of Buntingford there is an inexplicable absence of either A- or M-places within twenty miles of the town. The geographical spread of urban centres around the north-east Hertfordshire triangle of Baldock, Buntingford and Royston (Figure 4.4 above) clearly does not match the more evenly distributed geometric spatial patterns in Christaller's original thesis or those described by Everson and FitzGerald.[54]

---

[53] J.A. Everson and B.P. FitzGerald, 'The Theoretical Basis of Central Place', in J.A. Everson and B.P. FitzGerald, *Concepts in Geography: 1. Settlement Patterns* (London, 1969), p. 108.

[54] Everson and FitzGerald, 'Theoretical Basis of Central Place', pp. 101–11.

The extra-urban matrix

There is, interspersed between the seven ranks of Christaller's urban hierarchy, a continuous weft of land much of which is rural in nature, the traditional countryside. In addition to its many villages and hamlets, this extra-urban landscape contains within it numerous towns that were very small by late nineteenth-century standards. Measuring the size of the extra-urban landscape in demographic terms is not simply a matter of counting the apparently rural population living in settlements below the thresholds of urbanity usually applied by historians. Depending on that particular benchmark, the size of the apparent non-urban population will vary but it is important to realise that a considerable proportion of these people were not living in the villages, hamlets and isolated farms of the countryside but in a matrix of small towns embedded within it. While many might expect these towns to be of less consequence than Christaller's M-places some of them were, despite their modest size, centres of commercial significance with high functional indexes.

Figures compiled by Brian Mitchell and Phyllis Deane show that in 1801 the population of greater London, including the county of Middlesex, was 1.03 million or 11.6 per cent of the total population of England and Wales (8.89 million).[55] At this time, according to Chris Cook and Brendan Keith, the fifty-three principal towns of England and Wales (excluding London) accounted for a further 1.11 million people.[56] These towns ranged in population between 9,000 and 10,000 in Cambridge, Carlisle, Dudley and King's Lynn, to over 50,000 in Birmingham, Bristol, Manchester, Leeds and Liverpool. By 1851, greater London's population (England's 'Landstadt' in Christaller's hierarchy) had more than doubled to 2.5 million and that of sixty-two other principal towns more than trebled to a combined population of 3.67 million people or 20.5 per cent of the total for England and Wales (17.93 million). This latter group now ranged in population from 11,000 in Luton to 19,000 in Colchester and King's Lynn, and over 100,000 in the seven major urban areas of Birmingham, Bradford, Bristol, Manchester, Leeds, Liverpool and Sheffield. These seven major centres, included among those identified by Joyce Ellis as the 'largest provincial towns' in 1841, approximate to Christaller's regional 'B' centres.[57] At the turn of the century, in 1901, the combined population of London and Middlesex had reached 5.33 million (16.4 per cent of total 32.53 million in England and Wales). Another sixty-four principal towns accounted for a total of 8.97 million people (27.6 per

---

[55] B.R. Mitchell and P. Deane, *University of Cambridge Dept of Applied Economics Monographs, 17: Abstracts of British Historical Statistics* (Cambridge, 1962), pp. 20–23.

[56] C. Cook and B. Keith, *British Historical Facts, 1830–1900* (London, 1975), pp. 232–36.

[57] J. Ellis, 'Regional and County Centres 1700-1840', in P. Clark (ed.), *The Cambridge Urban History of Britain, Vol. 2, 1540-1840* (Cambridge, 2000), p. 679.

cent of total). The population of these major centres ranged from 20,000 in King's Lynn, 28,000 in Shrewsbury and 29,000 in Southend-on-Sea, to the above mentioned 'seven major urban areas' each now having over 250,000. It is true that the agricultural population fell during this period and consequently many rural workers migrated to the expanding urban industrial centres. However, while the proportion of the total population of England and Wales living in the extra-urban landscape, based on the above figures, fell from 75.9 per cent (1801) to 56.0 per cent (1901) in real terms its population continued to increase and actually tripled from 6.75 million at the start to 18.23 million at the close of the nineteenth century.

Unfortunately, this simplistic attempt at estimating the size of the extra-urban landscape fails to take account of the number of 'small towns' in England and Wales. A more meaningful calculation can be based on Lynn Hollen Lees's estimate for England and Wales in 1851 that the overall urban population was 9.7 million (54.0 per cent of the total) including 1.8 million (10.0 per cent of the total) living in towns with populations of under 10,000. Her figures for 1891 showed that the total urban population had risen to 21.6 million (74.5 per cent of the total) and the proportion found living in the towns with populations under 10,000, to 2.96 million (10.2 per cent of the total).[58] Similarly, Stephen Royle's figures suggested that in 1851 there were 2.33 million people (13.0 per cent of the total) living in 786 towns with populations under 10,000 and that by 1901 there were 2.31 million (7.1 per cent of the total) living in 695 towns.[59] Within these 'small towns', the probable equivalents of Christaller's K-, A- and M-places, we find Robson's smallest category of those with populations of between only 2,500 and 4,999 still well above the size of the four towns under consideration. While this category rose in total from 234 places in 1851 to 290 places in 1901 he argued that it became proportionately less important 'falling from 49.9 per cent of the total urban places in 1851 to 32.8 per cent in 1901'.[60]

By reconciling the differing estimates of Hollen Lees, Royle and Robson one can achieve a much more accurate view. Their figures suggest that the extra-urban proportion of the total population of England and Wales, i.e. those residing in settlements with fewer than 2,500 inhabitants, dwindled from approximately 45 per cent of the total in 1851 to only 25 per cent by 1891. Yet in real terms this country-wide matrix still contained around 8.2 million people in 1851 and 7.4

[58] L. Hollen Lees, 'Urban Networks' in M. Daunton (ed.), *The Cambridge Urban History of Britain, Volume 3, 1840–1950* (Cambridge, 2000), p. 70.

[59] S.A. Royle, 'The Development of Small Towns in Britain', in Daunton, *Urban History of Britain, Volume 3*, pp. 153-61.

[60] B.T. Robson, *Urban Growth* (London, 1973) cited in Royle, 'Development of Small Towns', p. 166.

million people in 1891 who, in order to service their daily lives, were dependent on even smaller towns such as those examined in this study.

The levels of productivity in agriculture, argued Tony Wrigley, 'necessarily govern the growth opportunities of other industries'. There is no doubt that the proportion of the rural labour force engaged in agriculture declined but he noted that by the end of the eighteenth century the emergence of 'specialist employments not previously encountered' was commonplace.[61] Despite the decline of Hertfordshire's agricultural workforce during the nineteenth century, its efforts in producing top-quality barley created increased employment in specialist malting and brewing industries in many of the county's small towns.

Despite the lack of regular general-purpose markets, it is reasonable to suggest that such small, late nineteenth-century towns might otherwise correspond to Christaller's M-places, the lowest rank of his seven-tier hierarchy of 'central places' engaged in the exchange of goods and services.[62] In addition to weekly markets 'central places' in this rank not only had breweries, mills, agricultural brokers and all types of traders and retailers but commonly possessed 'central institutions' such as Registrar's offices, schools, libraries, physicians and veterinary surgeons. They were further characterized by nearly always having a railway station, an intersection of major roads, a postal agency, a local newspaper and various social clubs.[63] According to James Bird, the relationship of 'central places' to major roads was governed by the *principles of traffic* that say their distribution is 'at an optimum where as many important places as possible lie on one traffic route between larger towns'.[64] Three of the towns in north-east Hertfordshire fit that theory by lying on either the Great North Road or Old North Road connecting London to the north of England. The many other remaining modest habitations, of limited central importance beyond their own confines and possessing few central functions, probably equate to those identified by Christaller as 'auxiliary central places'.[65]

In the early sixteenth century Hertfordshire was, according to Nigel Goose and Terry Slater, 'replete with small towns, maintaining one of the densest urban networks of any English county'. By the end of the following century, 'it was

---

[61] E.A. Wrigley, *People, Cities and Wealth: The Transformation of Traditional Society* (Oxford, 1987), pp. 167, 169.

[62] By the second half of the nineteenth century Buntingford had just one annual fair. Ashwell had lost its small weekly market for corn and cattle by the 1870s but retained two annual stock fairs. Baldock held a Friday market for the sale of straw plait and five annual fairs for cheese and horses. Royston held Wednesday markets for corn and cattle plus a further five annual cattle fairs.

[63] Christaller, *Central Places*, pp. 139 – 41, 154.

[64] J.H. Bird, 'Of Central Places, Cities and Seaports', *Geography*, 58, 2 (1973), p. 105.

[65] Christaller, *Central Places*, p. 17.

those in the Lea Valley or in close proximity to London' that, they argued, 'had fared best, while in the very north ... Baldock had declined substantially in terms of its rank order, while Ashwell was already well on the way to village status'. By 1801, although sharing the urban growth witnessed across England, Goose and Slater argued that Hertfordshire had still 'failed to produce a single town of truly regional significance' and remained a county of small towns.[66] This absence of any significant regional urban centres within thirty to forty miles of the study area was still the case in 1851, especially to the south and east. It resulted in an extra-urban matrix consisting of very modest sized late nineteenth-century towns, as exemplified here by Baldock, Buntingford and Royston. This particular cluster in north-east Hertfordshire exemplifies the proposed model portrayed opposite in Figure 4.5.

Despite their modest populations of less than 2500 inhabitants these were centres of significant commercial importance. Because of their geographical locations far from major towns, and their utilization of improved communications, this matrix of very small urban centres, outside or additional to those normally recognized by urban historians, were able to flourish. Possessing specialist manufacturers and providing an extensive range of goods and services to satisfy consumers across a large catchment area they created considerable local employment opportunities while many of their entrepreneurial citizens could afford the fashionable developments of the late nineteenth century.

The location of these towns also matches some of the features of Charles Phythian-Adams's construct of frontier 'borderlands', a development of his earlier theory of 'cultural provinces'. These 'borderlands', he argued, most frequently lie 'along and across under-populated watershed zones' or along 'lowland/upland juncture[s]'.[67] In the present case the 'borderland' is represented by the north-eastern sweep of the Chiltern ridge separating Hertfordshire from the fenlands to the north. Phythian-Adams observed that these 'borderlands' were often 'marked out by ragged lines of usually modest market towns' that could occasionally 'be found along major inter-regional routeways' and 'function as mediators between adjacent economies'.[68] Again, it is possible to suggest that, because of a paucity of major regional centres, not only would the study towns have served the economy in and around the Baldock-Royston-Buntingford triangle but also the

---

[66] T. Slater and N. Goose, 'Panoramas and Microcosms: Hertfordshire's Towns through Both Ends of the Telescope', in T. Slater and N. Goose (eds), *A County of Small Towns: The Development of Hertfordshire's Urban Landscape to 1800* (Hatfield, 2008), pp. 9, 10, 11.

[67] C. Phythian-Adams, 'Differentiating Provincial Societies in English History: Spatial Contexts and Cultural Processes', in B. Lancaster, D. Newton and N. Vall (eds), *An Agenda for Regional History* (Newcastle, 2007), p.12.

[68] Phythian-Adams, 'Spatial Contexts and Cultural Processes', p. 13.

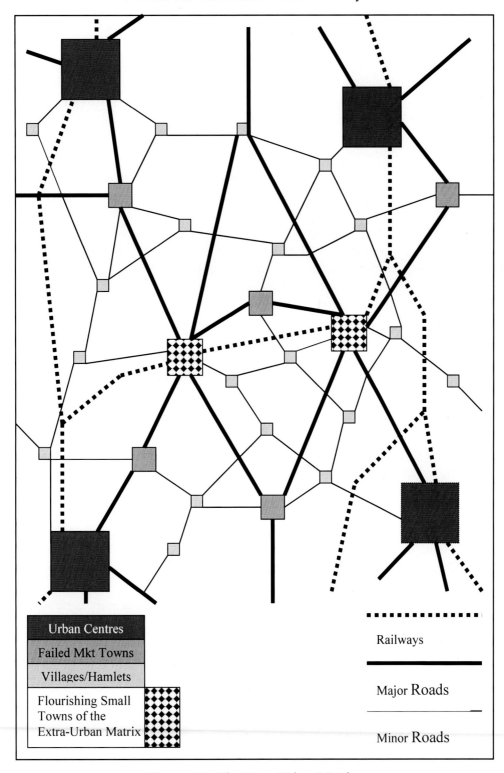

Figure 4.5: The Extra-Urban Matrix

economies of small centres within the wider extra-urban landscape extending into adjacent 'cultural provinces' to the north of Baldock into Bedfordshire and Cambridgeshire, and to the east of Royston into Cambridgeshire and Essex. In summary, these strategic settlements formed an extra-urban matrix that was, as Joyce Ellis so succinctly observed of very small Georgian towns, 'set apart from the surrounding villages by distinctive patterns of employment and activity; they were in the countryside but not part of it'! [69]

Conclusion

The foregoing evaluation of the urban-rural interface between the towns and the smaller settlements in and around the Baldock-Buntingford-Royston triangle clearly establishes that beyond the day-to-day necessities of life, all sixteen villages, small and large, were clearly reliant on these three larger centres for the provision of many other goods and services.

Using more recent statistical interpretations of Christaller's central place theory to calculate each centre's functional index establishes the existence of an obvious regional urban hierarchy in north-east Hertfordshire. Plotting the results (Figure 4.2 above) reveals an attenuated hierarchy featuring elements of a continuum with regard to the smaller villages and a number of discrete ranks or clusters of the larger villages and the four study towns.

The earlier detailed analysis of the extensive range of goods and services offered by these towns coupled with their significant functional indexes confirms them as high-order 'central places' for the region's populace. Furthermore the method deployed confirms that whether one simply takes population figures, estimates the number of PTPSs, or uses the statistical approach to measuring centrality, the order of the resultant regional hierarchies is very similar, confirming that central place theory cannot be divorced from demography.

As might be expected against the background of nineteenth-century agricultural decline and diminishing rural populations, the statistical indicator of centrality, i.e. the functional index, fell in six of the smaller and one of the larger villages between 1851 and 1890. However, an intriguing finding of this current analysis is that functional indexes, albeit modest values, rose in nine of the remaining villages despite falls in their populations over the same forty years. For example, Cottered's population fell 18.5 per cent (465 to 379) yet its functional index rose 325 per cent (32 to 136) while Braughing's population fell similarly by 16.2 per cent (1220 to 1022) and its index increased 62.3 per cent (207 to 336). In 1851,

---

[69] J.M. Ellis, *The Georgian Town 1680-1840* (Basingstoke, 2001), p. 12.

Ashwell had a very similar population and functional index to that of Barkway but while the latter fell four places down the hierarchy, Ashwell's population by 1891 had risen modestly (+ 9.2%) and its index more than doubled from 340 to 719. The most significant finding is that the already high functional indexes of the three larger study towns, Buntingford, Baldock and Royston, all increased over the forty-year period by 7.6, 25.5 and 58.3% respectively, despite falls in population in the case of Buntingford (- 8.3%) and Royston (- 17.5%).

So, despite the overall demographic downturn across the region, the analysis clearly demonstrates that business and service activities as reflected by the changing functional indexes were certainly not in decline. In the north-east corner of Hertfordshire bordering on Bedfordshire, Cambridgeshire and Essex, the three small towns of Baldock, Buntingford and Royston were clearly high-order central places servicing the nearby lower order villages. Their success owed much to their strategic frontier town locations enabling the range for their goods and services to be extended north and south along the Great North Road and Old North Road. Given its location four miles north-east of Baldock, Ashwell the smallest of the four towns considered here would have been heavily reliant on the provision of its near neighbour. However, the location of this Hertfordshire centre in the 'borderland' south of Bedfordshire and Cambridgeshire would have produced an economic benefit from its ability to service the villages of Newnham, Hinxworth, Steeple Morden, Guilden Morden and others in the south-west corner of the Baldock-Potton-Royston triangle (Figure 4.4 above). In this way, even very small urban settlements might easily supply a range of goods and services to satisfy consumers across a substantial hinterland.

Modestly populated and geographically located far from major urban centres, Baldock, Buntingford and Royston were flourishing centres during the second half of the nineteenth century. Possessing specialist manufacturers, an extensive range of service providers and excellent transport links, they exemplify the very small towns of the extra-urban matrix.

Part II

Changing communities in nineteenth-century Hertfordshire

5

Occupational mobility and stability

Many of the principal and ancillary providers of goods and services found in the four towns were born in those towns and, on the available census evidence, seemed never to have left them. Take the case of Thomas Daintry, Royston's Post Master and keeper of the Falcon Inn on Melbourn Street. According to the 1851 census both he, aged 44, and his wife Betsy, aged 40, were born in Royston and they had seven children (Thomas, 20, an ostler; Emma, 18; William, 16, a solicitor's writing clerk; Ellen, Louisa, Edward and Frederick aged 11, 8, 5 and 2 respectively) all born in Royston and still living at home.[1] Yet nineteenth-century Britain experienced a period of increased internal migration when migrants motivated by economic forces generally moved in a series of relatively short steps, often from declining rural to developing industrial and commercial regions. Their progress was greatly aided by improved means of transport, especially the rapidly expanding railway network during the second half of the nineteenth century.

This chapter seeks to address a number of questions relating to the possible effect that this migratory stream might have had on the small towns of north-east Hertfordshire. Did their expanding service provision, for example in retailing and education, offer John Marshall's *attractive* factors' of higher wages for parents and apprenticeships for youngsters?[2] According to Peter Clark, it was migration that 'integrated towns with the villages of their hinterlands' but did the four towns under consideration here have a wider appeal beyond that of their immediate surroundings?[3] How many of the migrants who settled in towns like Baldock and Buntingford viewed it as a long-term or even permanent relocation or were these towns merely stepping-stones on the way to somewhere else? Particular attention is paid to long-distance migrants who settled, however briefly, in the four towns.

---

[1] 1851 Census (Royston).

[2] J.D. Marshall, 'The Lancashire Rural Labourer in the Early Nineteenth Century', *Transactions of the Lancashire and Cheshire Antiquarian Society*, 71 (1961), p. 95.

[3] P. Clark, 'Migration in England during the Late Seventeenth and Early Eighteenth Centuries', in P. Clark and D. Souden (eds), *Migration and Society in Early Modern England* (London, 1987), p. 214.

The respective contributions of organic growth and inward migration to the increased scope of principal and ancillary service provision are explored. Relevant individuals are identified from trade directories and CEBs. Detailed examination of the geographical origin, i.e. the place of birth listed by the census enumerator, of individuals, their wives and particularly their children provides an insight into the migratory patterns of those who had moved into the four towns from elsewhere. Some like Edward Stredder, for example, a master upholsterer living in Royston in 1851 but born at Folkingham in Lincolnshire, appear from the evidence of the census to have settled there in just one migratory step. Edward aged 54 was married to Mary aged 59. She and their six children (Mary, 30; William, 28, another upholsterer; Ann, Sarah, Eleoner (sic) and Harriet aged respectively 24, 22, 18 and 13) had all been born in Royston.[4]

Edward Stredder therefore provides a straightforward example but can more complex migratory wanderings be identified by this approach? Most migration data, according to Pooley and Turnbull, comes from sources, such as marriage registers and census returns, which were not designed with migration studies in mind. Therefore 'the amount of explanatory and contextual evidence relating to migration is always limited'.[5] Census returns record only 'gross movement of people from their place of birth to their residence at an arbitrary point of their life on census night'.[6] Consequently this source, they believe, does not allow us to distinguish between people who have made a single migration and those who may have moved several times, or indeed others who are temporary visitors. However, many examples from the information gathered here clearly contradict Pooley and Turnbull's argument and reveal the true potential of the source, since some indication of the migration pathways of specific families can be seen by analysing the different recorded birthplaces of their offspring. Examination of these examples suggests that the census returns have the potential for both quantitative and qualitative analysis in the study of migration pathways.

For instance, the 1881 census for Buntingford lists Frederick Crouch (aged 37) and originally from Hertford married to Eliza (aged 40) from Wimborne, Dorset. They had five children: Eliza (11) born in Hertford; Frederick (9) born in Braintree, Essex; Louisa (6) born in Hertford; Grace (4) and Herbert (2) both born in Buntingford. The data suggest that Frederick, a railway engine driver, had moved at least twice before he settled in Buntingford.[7] The same 1881 census lists George Nind, a 48 year old widowed grocer, born in Cavendish, Suffolk.

---

[4] 1851 Census (Royston).

[5] C. Pooley and J. Turnbull, *Migration and Mobility in Britain Since the 18th Century* (London, 1998), p. 24.

[6] Pooley and Turnbull, *Migration and Mobility*, p. 24.

[7] 1881 Census (Buntingford).

The data here suggest that he and his family had moved at least four times before settling in Buntingford. There were nine children: Lawrence (23), a grocer's assistant, born a British Subject in St Charles, North America; Arthur (19), also a grocer's assistant, born in Hoddesdon, Hertfordshire; Elizabeth (16), Frank (14), Herbert (11) and Edith (11) all born in Edmonton, Middlesex; Margaret (9) born in Bishops Stortford, Hertfordshire; Eleanor (7) and Ernest (5) both born in Buntingford. It should be noted that tracking the birthplace of offspring does not preclude the possibility that families had other migratory pauses along the way where either no children were born or any that were died prematurely. Hence by reason of the 'snapshot' nature of the censuses the data gleaned from them for the number of migratory steps is undoubtedly an underestimate for many families.

Using census data is not without its problems for identifying the origins of 'incomers' in this way. A few individuals, like Benjamin Edwards an Ashwell blacksmith, appear very confused about their place of birth; in 1851 (aged 36) he appeared in the CEB as born in Ashwell, this changed in 1861 (aged 45) to Weston, a village 5.5 miles to the south, and by 1871 (aged 56), Benjamin, now also publican at the Rose & Crown, gave his birthplace as the town of Baldock, 4 miles away. Another Ashwell publican, Abraham Berry, in 1871 (aged 58) gave his origin as Welwyn but ten years later in 1881 (aged 67), he was also a farmer and his birthplace was listed as Stevenage, 6 miles further north on The Great North Road. Some of these confusions may have arisen from poor memory or could have occurred if an enumerator asked 'Where are you from?' rather than 'Where were you born?' and the respondent simply gave the name of the previous place they had lived. A further problem, one suspects, arises from a limited knowledge of English geography on the part of some enumerators. The 1851 census for Royston includes George Godderd, a painter, apparently from Bristol in Norfolk. A check of an index to place names suggests that this is probably Briston, a Norfolk village 8 miles east of Fakenham, rather than the port of Bristol which is the only place with that name in Britain.[8] In spite of such problems, which in truth occur relatively infrequently, the census is still a vital research tool for migration studies.

An important caveat regarding the following analysis is that it is, perforce, based only on those PTPSs who, as well as being listed in a trade directory, were also identifiable in the censuses between 1851 and 1891. Notwithstanding the above limitation, the data used here is very much a viable entity as it still contains 2357 entries i.e. 77.4 per cent of the total number of entries, directory and census, identified as PTPSs (n = 3047). Over the forty-year period, significantly more of Ashwell's PTPSs appeared in the census (87.4 per cent) compared with those of

---

[8] 1851-1881 Census enumerations (Ashwell); 1851 Census (Royston).

the other three towns (73.0 – 78.6 per cent). Also in all four towns there was a significant reduction from 1851 to 1891 in the proportion of directory-listed PTPSs that were identifiable by nominal linkage in the CEBs. This reduction ranged from 7.5 per cent in the case of Ashwell to 18.8 per cent in Royston.

Inward migration from towns' immediate hinterlands

Analysis of identifiable birth-places, given in the relevant CEBs for the period 1851 to 1891, proves that a substantial proportion of all service providers, both principal and ancillary, were born outside the four towns (Figure 5.1 below).[9] In Baldock and Royston the proportions, across the forty-year period, were found to be consistently between 53.0 and 61.0 per cent of the total while in Buntingford they were above 65 per cent until 1871 after which they fell back to only 56.0 per cent. A different pattern was identified in Ashwell where the 'town-born' service

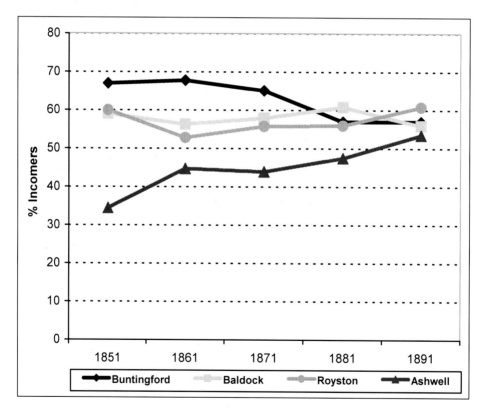

Figure 5.1: Combined proportion of PTPSs & ATPSs born outside the four towns
Source: Census enumerations, 1851-1891.

---

[9] Figures are based on total number of entries not the number of individually identified PTPSs or ATPSs who might have appeared in more than one decennial CEB.

providers were in the majority until the end of the century when migrant service providers had reached 53.5 per cent of the total. Analysis shows that, overall, 61.1 per cent of all PTPSs and 54.1 per cent of all ATPSs were born elsewhere.

Over the forty-year period, the proportion of PTPSs originating from outside three of the towns remained fairly consistent at around 70.0 per cent in the case of Buntingford and around 60.0 per cent in the case of Baldock and Royston. By contrast, the proportion in Ashwell grew steadily from a low of 36.6 per cent in 1851 to a figure by 1891 almost comparable, at 58.6 per cent, to that of Royston. A different picture emerges from an analysis of the origins of the towns' ATPSs which in all cases revealed the proportion of 'incoming' ATPSs over the same period to be significantly lower. The proportions in Baldock, Buntingford and Royston, which in 1851 were approximately 60.0 per cent in all three cases, fluctuated somewhat until 1881 when the proportions of their ATPSs born outside the towns ranged between 55.0 and 65.0 per cent. However, the next ten years saw contrasting changes when the proportion of such ATPSs in Baldock and Buntingford fell to below 50 per cent while Royston's rose from 54.5 per cent in 1881 back to just over 60 per cent by 1891. As in the case of Ashwell's 'incoming' PTPSs, the proportion of its ATPSs coming from outside the town in 1851 was just under one-third of the total. The proportion had risen by 1861 (42.3 per cent) only to fall back again by 1871 (35.6 per cent), and then rise again to reach approximately the same level by 1891 (49.0 per cent) as that seen in Baldock and Buntingford.

Each decennial census allows for the identification of a substantial proportion of the identified PTPSs born in the four towns themselves. Baldock and Royston show a very similar picture where the proportion of 'town-born' PTPSs was found to be consistently over one third of the total entries. Both exhibited relatively minor fluctuations between 1851 and 1891 with the proportion ranging from 34.9 to 38.6 per cent in Baldock and from 37.0 to 44.1 per cent in Royston. In contrast, the proportion of 'town-born' PTPSs in Buntingford, while also relatively stable over the same period, accounted for only between one quarter and one third of the total entries. A significantly different situation was revealed in Ashwell where in 1851 its 'town-born' PTPSs represented 63.4 per cent of the total entries. The size of this group then fell by a third over the next forty years and stood at 41.4 per cent in 1891, just above the proportion of 'town-based' PTPSs identified in Baldock and Royston.

Between 1851 and 1891 Ashwell's population grew by 9.2 per cent and Baldock's by 19.8 per cent while the number of their PTPSs increased from 84 to 123 and from 156 to 195 respectively. Figures above relating to the number of 'town-born' PTPSs indicate that, among the total of PTPSs representing 5–8 per cent of the towns' total population across the same period, approximately 60.0 per cent were 'incomers' who had migrated to these centres from elsewhere. This finding suggests Ravenstein's theory that 'Towns grow more by migration than by natural increase' is clearly applicable to the maintenance of this particular segment of a small town's population.[10] At the same time, though Buntingford and Royston's overall populations fell by 8.3 and 17.5 per cent respectively, the proportion of PTPSs was maintained in Buntingford and actually rose from 10.0 to 15.0 per cent of the total in Royston. In both towns 'incoming' migrant PTPSs again accounted for at least two-thirds of that business sector. David Grigg, while acknowledging the important contribution of migration to growth of large towns such as Liverpool in the first half of the nineteenth century, suggested that during the latter half of the century 'natural increase had become far more important than migration in accounting for urban growth'. Plainly, this is not the case regarding the skilled and professional communities identified in the four considerably smaller towns of this corner of Hertfordshire.[11]

Further analysis identified 'incoming' master craftsmen, retailers and professional people whose geographical origins were within a ten-mile radius of each of the four towns (Figures 5.2 and 5.4 to 5.6 below). The combined sub-total of these 'incomers' with the 'town-born' accounted for between 53.0 and 64.0 per cent of all PTPSs identifiable from the CEBs for Baldock, Buntingford and Royston between 1851 and 1891. In Ashwell's case, the same combination encompassed over three-quarters of all PTPSs. Beyond this core, the origins of the remaining PTPSs were scattered over the adjacent counties and the rest of Britain. Although the total number of PTPS entries (n = 565) originating from these four hinterlands was less than the corresponding 'town-born' PTPS entries (n = 917) the relative proportions varied considerably between the towns. For example, in Buntingford, the total number of entries for PTPSs born in the town was almost identical to the number originating from its hinterland, 132 and 128 respectively. In contrast, the total entries for PTPSs from the hinterlands of Baldock and Royston, 137 and 182 respectively, were only just over half the number of entries for PTPSs born in the two towns, 231 and 352 respectively. Ashwell provides a totally different scenario where, in contrast to the steady fall in the proportion of 'town-born' PTPSs noted previously, the proportion of entries for PTPSs originating in the town's hinterland almost doubled from 21.1 per cent in 1851 to 36.8 per cent by 1891.

---

[10] D.B. Grigg, 'E.G. Ravenstein and the "Laws of Migration" ', *J. Historical Geography*, 3, 1 (1977), p. 50.

[11] Grigg, 'Ravenstein', p. 51.

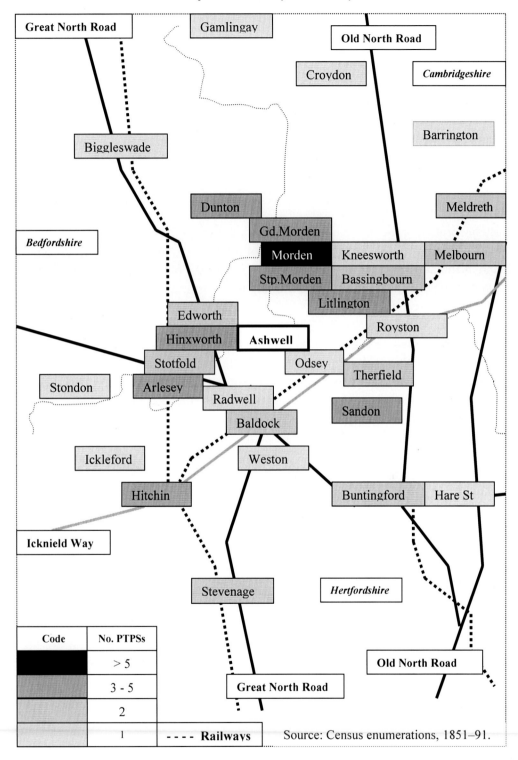

Figure 5.2: Ashwell's PTPSs born within 10 miles of Ashwell (n = 71)

Figures 5.2 (above) and 5.4 to 5.6 (below) illustrate the geographical origins, taken from birth-places given in censuses, of 'incomers' to the four towns from their immediate hinterlands. Total numbers are based only on the original appearance of an individual PTPS in a census and do not take account of that person's subsequent entries in later censuses.[12] In line with two of Ravenstein's migration theories, that 'the majority of migrants go only a short distance' and that 'the major direction of migration is from the rural areas to the towns', the majority of 'incomers' to all four towns were born in rural settlements situated in their immediate vicinity.[13] However, each town exhibited a different directional emphasis regarding those originating from the periphery of the ten-mile radius. These patterns of migration were also encountered by Cathy Day in her recent study correlating the occupations and geographical mobility of marriage partners in Wiltshire. She found that 49 per cent of a group of 'non-agricultural' dealers and manufacturers had been born within ten miles of the parish where they married with a further 19 per cent travelling from further afield.[14]

In relation to theories regarding the distance between origin and destination, George Boyer and Timothy Hatton emphasised the effects of potential migrants' friends and relatives already having moved to the destination region. As they put it, rather enigmatically, 'distance is a proxy for the monetary and psychic costs of migration and for information on destination labour markets' that is alleviated by the 'friends and relatives effect'.[15] This close-by 'relative' effect can obviously be frequently facilitated through the effect of marriages spreading particular families within an area, as evidence of marriage partners' horizons in a cluster of rural parishes in this region has earlier demonstrated. For example, 'Stoten or Stoton, the two most frequent spellings of this [unusual] surname, appear ... forty-four times between 1838 and 1897' in the marriage registers of a line of villages that stretches between Baldock and Royston (Figure 5.3 below).[16] This cluster may well have influenced journeyman tailor Thomas Stoten's decision to migrate from St Neots in Huntingdonshire to Baldock.[17]

---

[12] Widows and children continuing a family business were not considered as 'incomers'.

[13] Grigg, 'Ravenstein', pp. 44, 52.

[14] C. Day, 'Geographical Mobility in Wiltshire, 1754-1914', *Local Population Studies*, 88 (2012), pp. 70-72.

[15] G.R. Boyer and T.J. Hatton, 'Migration and Labour Market Integration in Late Nineteenth-century England and Wales', *Economic History Review*, 50, 4 (1997), p. 699.

[16] P.T. Bysouth, *Hertfordshire's Icknield Way: 19th Century Migration Frontier and Marriage Obstacle* (Cambridge, 2010), p. 26.

[17] 1851 Census (Baldock).

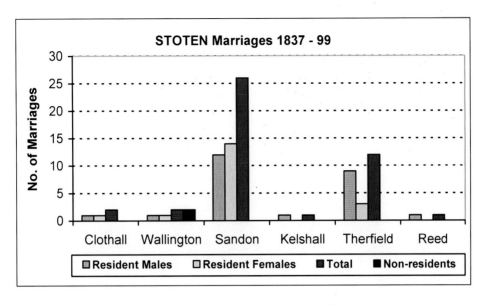

Figure 5.3; Distribution of Stoten marriages in adjacent rural parishes

Clearly, for Ashwell (Figure 5.2 above), the Cambridgeshire border was no barrier to migration with almost one third of its 'incoming' PTPSs originating from the three villages immediately to the east: the two Mordens (18) and Litlington (4).[18] A further fifth of Ashwell's 'incomers' came from the adjacent Hertfordshire village of Hinxworth (5) and from Hitchin (5) a large town beyond Baldock on the Icknield Way. The directional emphasis of Ashwell's 'incomers' was largely from Bedfordshire and Cambridgeshire with only 15.5 per cent (n = 11) having migrated northwards from the Hertfordshire side of the Icknield Way. In contrast, reflecting its location at the junction of several major roads, Baldock (Figure 5.4 below) had no clear directional bias in relation to the origins of its 'incoming' PTPSs. As was the case at Ashwell, the several villages surrounding Baldock provided over one quarter of its 'incoming' PTPSs: Norton (7), Clothall (6), Stotfold (4), Weston (4), Bygrave (2) and Willian (1). The influence of major roads and the railway link between Hitchin and Royston is demonstrated by the number (25.3 per cent, n = 22) of migrant PTPSs coming to Baldock from Biggleswade (4) and Stevenage (4), north and south respectively on the Great North Road, and Hitchin (9) and Royston (5), west and east respectively on the Icknield Way and linked from 1850 by the Great Northern Railway.

---

[18] The CEBs refer to Guilden Morden (4), Steeple Morden (5) and the non-specific 'Morden' (9).

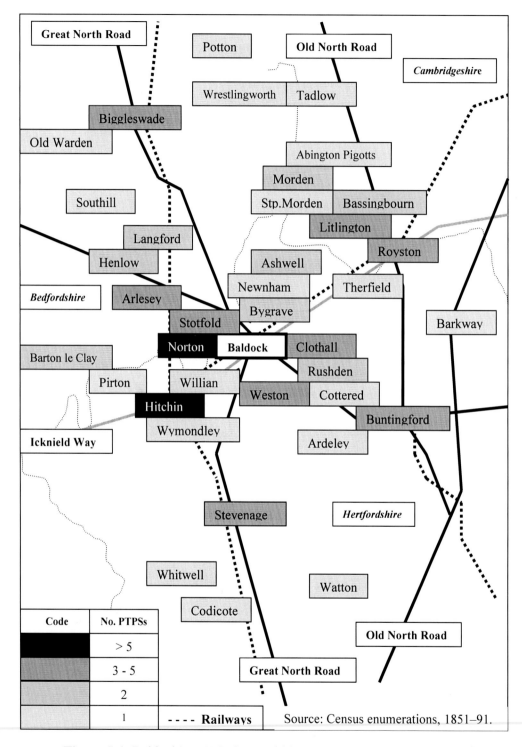

Figure 5.4: Baldock's PTPSs born within 10 miles of Baldock (n = 87)

Four villages surrounding Buntingford provided almost one fifth of the incoming PTPSs: Aspenden (7), Throcking (1), Westmill (4) and Wyddial (2).[19] The geographical origins of PTPSs migrating into Buntingford (Figure 5.5 below) from its immediate hinterland were heavily concentrated (72.6 per cent) along the corridor created by the Old North Road and the road from Braughing up through Barkway and Barley to Cambridge. Migration was largely from northerly and easterly directions though three came from the town of Baldock seven miles to the west. Royston, seven miles to the north, was the birthplace of nine migrants yet only a single person had moved to Buntingford from Ware, nine miles to the south on the Old North Road. Perhaps more surprisingly, was the limited number of migrants from villages on or near the road heading east from Buntingford into Essex. Only one person came from both Great Hormead and Brent Pelham while not a single 'incomer' to Buntingford was identified as moving from Essex despite the county border being only six miles away.

One possible explanation might be that the Essex-Hertfordshire county border defines the margins of two 'cultural provinces'. Charles Phythian-Adams argued that such areas display certain distinguishable cultural traits and inter-parochial marriage patterns.[20] If the county boundary lying to the east of Buntingford does delimit two such areas, it is probable that it discouraged cross-border marriages as shown in Phythian-Adams's study. Analysis further suggests that, in relation to Buntingford's 'incoming' PTPSs, it might also have inhibited economic migration from nearby Essex settlements. Earlier research examining origins of marriage partners in a number of north-east Hertfordshire rural parishes suggested that 'in the nineteenth century a localised "cultural province", with the Icknield Way forming its northern boundary ... [was] centred around a triangular area bounded by the three market towns of Baldock, Royston and Buntingford'.[21] This latter finding could be a contributory factor in helping explain the surprisingly limited

---

[19] The town of Buntingford includes portions of four ecclesiastical parishes: Aspenden, Layston, Throcking and Wyddial. Three of these parishes actually contain small settlements. Throcking is a hamlet 1.5 miles north-west of Buntingford, Wyddial a village 1.5 miles to the north-east and Aspenden juxtaposes the southern edge of the town. In 1891, Buntingford had a population of 1336 of which 739 lived in the parish of Layston (reciprocal locations for the purpose these analyses). Trade directories for 1851 and 1862 listed traders under 'Buntingford and Neighbourhood'. The former edition identified some as from Aspenden, Throcking and Wyddial. Between 1870 and 1890 traders were listed under 'Buntingford with Layston' without specifically noting those from the other villages. Included in the current data set are all PTPSs and ATPSs whose census address clearly identified them as residing in part of Buntingford or Layston, and others with joint Aspenden/Buntingford addresses. Those clearly from the settlements of Throcking, Wyddial and the more distant parts of Aspenden are excluded.

[20] C.V. Phythian-Adams, *Re-thinking English Local History, Occasional Papers, Fourth Series, No. 1* (Leicester, 1987); C.V. Phythian-Adams (ed.), *Societies, Cultures and Kinship, 1580–1850. Cultural Provinces and English Local History* (London, 1993)

[21] Bysouth, *Hertfordshire's Icknield Way*, p. 96.

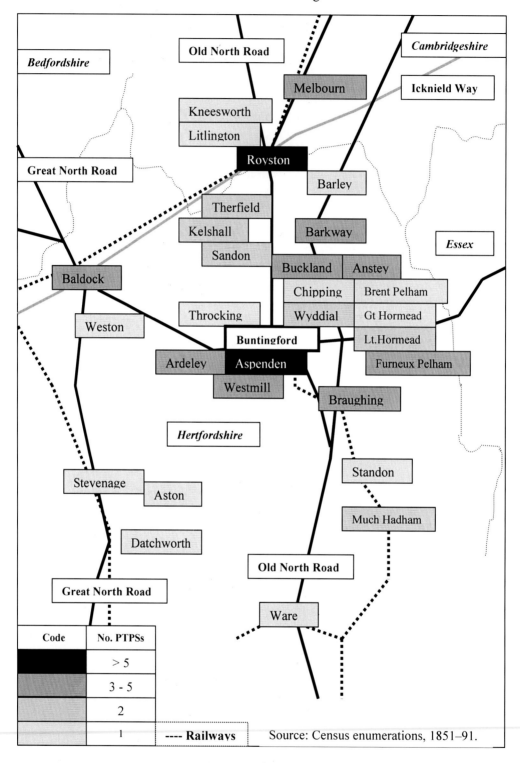

Figure 5.5: Buntingford's PTPSs born within 10 miles of Buntingford (n = 73)

number of migrants in the present analysis who had migrated south from Cambridgeshire to Buntingford. However, the earlier study had noted that, in contrast to the rural parishes, the two towns actually situated on Icknield Way, Baldock and Royston, 'fulfilled their roles as "hubs", acting as a focus for their surrounding hinterland and attracting people from all directions in almost equal measure'; at least regarding those centres' exogamous marriage partners.[22] It is possible that Royston simply acted as a filter for migrants moving south from Cambridgeshire.

Although similarly situated on a major road junction at the crossing of the Icknield Way and the Old North Road with a further road heading for Cambridge to the north-east, Royston, in contrast to Baldock, demonstrated a clear directional bias with regard to the origins of its 'incoming' PTPSs in contrast to that of 'outsiders' marrying there. A total of 63 migrant PTPSs (61.8 per cent) originated from Cambridgeshire villages to the north of the Icknield Way (Figure 5.6 below) with well over one third (n = 25) coming from the immediately adjacent villages of Litlington (6), Bassingbourn (8) and Melbourn (11). There was a clear pathway along the road from Cambridge with 'incomers' migrating to Royston from, in addition to Melbourn, the villages of Meldreth (3), Shepreth (4), Barrington (2) and Hauxton (1). It is also noticeable that, in spite of its obvious business and employment opportunities, only a very limited number of Royston's incoming PTPSs actually came from Cambridge itself (see later discussion of migrants from larger urban centres, p. 217). From the south of Royston migrant PTPSs (n = 17) moved north from a cluster of Hertfordshire villages that included Therfield (5), just off the Old North Road and Barley (4) and Barkway (4) situated on the parallel route northwards from Braughing. Further afield, the two Hertfordshire towns of Baldock and Buntingford were the source of three and four 'incoming' PTPSs respectively. Unlike the case in Buntingford, a few intrepid migrants (n = 5) did make the journey to Royston from the neighbouring county of Essex.

Migration of PTPSs between the four towns themselves was, surprisingly, very limited. In all, between 1851 and 1891, only thirty-two individuals (9.6 per cent of 333 PTPSs identified as born within 10 miles of their current residence) moved between the towns. Julian Wolpert's behaviourist approach stressed the notion of 'place utility', which he defined as an individual's degree of 'satisfaction or dissatisfaction with respect to that place'.[23] The limited movement of PTPSs between the four towns suggests that the business opportunities each offered

---

[22] Bysouth, *Hertfordshire's Icknield Way*, p. 56.
[23] J. Wolpert, 'Behavioural Aspects of the Decision to Migrate', *Papers and Proceedings, Regional Science Association*, 15 (1965), p. 162.

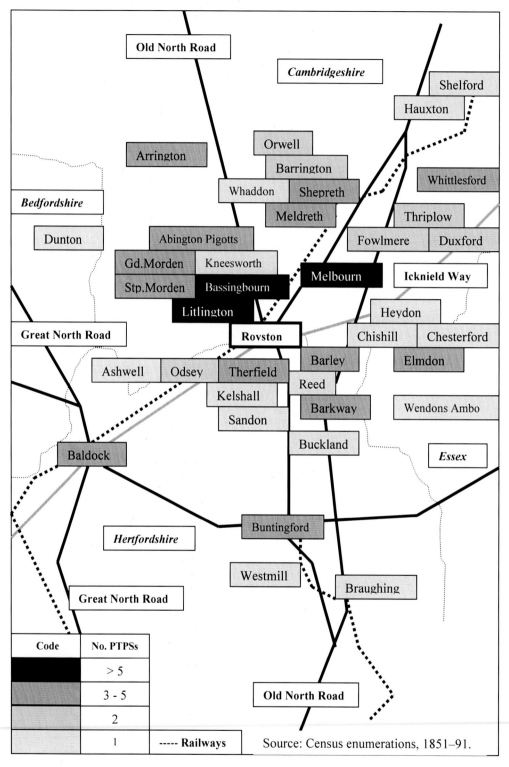

Figure 5.6: Royston's PTPSs born within 10 miles of Royston (n = 102)

were sufficient to encourage most to stay. Ashwell, Baldock and Royston all managed to attract at least one migrant PTPS from each of the other three towns. However, Buntingford, in spite of two PTPSs moving across to Ashwell, only attracted 'incoming' PTPSs from Baldock and Royston, three and eight respectively (Figure 5.7 below). A wide range of dealers and manufacturers were represented among the occupations of the migrating PTPSs including 4 bakers, 2 beer retailers, 2 brewers, 2 coach builders, 2 corn dealers, 2 publicans and 2 shoemakers. Noticeably absent were members of the 'public and professional' sector apart from Benjamin James, a 25 year old policeman who left Royston for Buntingford in 1881.[24]

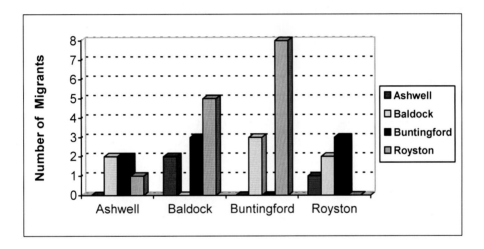

Figure 5.7: Migration of PTPSs between the four towns, 1851–91
Source: Census enumerations, 1851–1891.

Between 1851 and 1891 proportionately more of the four towns' ATPSs (45.9 per cent) were born in the towns themselves compared with the proportion of their 'town-born' PTPSs (38.9 per cent). While the proportion, over the forty-year period, of 'town-born' ATPSs in Baldock remained between 40.0 and 50.0 per cent, that in both Buntingford and Royston rose from around 40.0 per cent to just over 51.0 per cent in the former and to just under 57.0 per cent in the latter. In contrast, the proportion of ATPSs born in Ashwell fell from almost 70.0 per cent to approximately 50.0 per cent by 1891, whilst for those originating in Ashwell's immediate hinterland it rose by a third from almost 17.0 per cent to a little over 22.0 per cent during the same period.

---

[24] 1881 Census (Buntingford).

Further analysis identified the skilled journeymen, retail assistants, clerical workers and apprentices whose geographic origins were within the same ten mile radius of each of the four towns as that used for the earlier identification of migrating PTPSs. Over the period 1851 to 1891, the combined total of these 'incomers' (698 entries) and the 'town-born' ATPSs (1340 entries) was between 65.0 and 75.0 per cent of all ATPS entries identified from the CEBs for Baldock, Buntingford and Royston. Ashwell's combined total was somewhat higher ranging between 72.0 and 85.0 per cent over the same four decades. As in the earlier case of the PTPSs' origins, beyond the four towns and their core catchment areas, the remainder of the 'incoming' ATPSs had travelled from far and wide across Britain and beyond.

Not surprisingly, the patterns of birth-places given in censuses for the 'incoming' ATPSs from the four towns' immediate hinterlands closely resemble those identified for the PTPSs (Figures 5.2 and 5.4 to 5.6 above). Compared with the absence of any PTPSs moving to Buntingford from east of the Hertfordshire county boundary, a total of six ATPSs were identified as having their origins in three nearby Essex villages. Three from the village of Clavering all had the surname Bush and were probably related. These were James (aged 65), a miller (1851), Allen (aged 35), a painter and glazier (1851) and Alfred (aged 40), a coach painter (1871). The others were James Sampson (aged 33), a journeyman baker (1851) and John Pateman (aged 17), another painter (1891) both from Elmdon, and Elijah Mott (aged 24), a brass founder from Rickling (1861).[25] If there was a 'cultural boundary' in the vicinity of Buntingford then it would seem, for these few migrants, that 'propulsive' and/or 'attractive' factors outweighed other considerations. For each of the towns, the same villages in their immediate vicinities that were the origins of a substantial number of PTPSs also provided large numbers of ATPSs.[26] For example, thirty-seven and twenty-two ATPSs respectively migrated from the two Cambridgeshire villages of Litlington and Bassingbourn into the four towns of north-east Hertfordshire. Similarly, twenty-eight and sixteen ATPSs respectively moved to the nearby towns from Therfield and Barley, two Hertfordshire villages near Royston. These same four villages were identified as the geographic origins of forty-two of the towns' 'incoming' PTPSs.

---

[25] 1851-1871 and 1891 Census enumerations (Buntingford).

[26] In Ashwell, 38.1 per cent (24 ATPSs) came from six surrounding villages, Guilden and Steeple Morden (12), Litlington (6), Hinxworth (4) and Bassingbourn (2). In Baldock, 35.3 per cent (59 ATPSs) came from seven villages, Weston (16), Norton (12), Clothall (11), Stotfold (10), Bygrave (5), Willian (3) and Rushden (2). In Buntingford, 40.7 per cent (63 ATPSs) came from 9 villages, Aspenden (29), Great and Little Hormead (7), Wydiall (7), Braughing (5), Furneux Pelham (5), Westmill (5), Throcking (4) and Ardeley (1). In Royston, 57.0 per cent (110 ATPSs) came from ten villages, Bassingbourn (29), Therfield (17), Barley (13), Litlington (13), Melbourn (11), Guilden and Little Morden (10), Kneesworth (6), Reed (6) and Barkway (5).

Given the generally accepted view, that during the nineteenth-century 'the major flows of migrants were from the [depressed] rural districts to London and the industrial and commercial towns of the Midlands and the North', the pattern of movement observed here has two possible explanations.[27] It could be that this was the initial break by these migrants from their rural origins and they later moved on to London, just thirty-five miles to the south, or that the developing regional economy of north-east Hertfordshire provided them with enough 'attractive' reasons to stay. In the latter case it is also possible, in line with Jason Long's views on rural-urban migration, that potential migrants would consider a move to these small towns because 'they anticipated economic gains' that would 'improve their socio-economic status'. For those drawn to the range of new opportunities available, Long believed that leaving the countryside and moving to a town, 'offered migrants a better chance to escape the intergenerational career trajectory inherited from their father'. He calculated that the average son of an agricultural labourer 'was 26.0 per cent more likely to improve the quality of his occupation over that of his father' if he decided to move rather than remain in a rural area.[28] Many, according to Richard Perren, reluctant to follow their fathers onto the land chose instead 'the police, railway service and various industrial jobs' while daughters left for domestic service.[29]

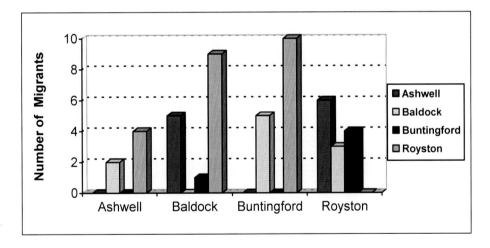

Figure 5.8: Migration of ATPSs between the four towns, 1851–91
Source: Census enumerations, 1851–1891.

---

[27] Grigg, 'Ravenstein', p. 53.

[28] J. Long, 'Rural-Urban Migration and Socioeconomic Mobility in Victorian Britain', *Journal of Economic History*, 65, 1 (2005), pp. 3, 24, 28.

[29] R. Perren, *Agriculture in Depression, 1870–1940* (Cambridge, 1995), p. 23.

Migration of ATPSs directly between the four towns was found to be on a limited scale, very similar to that of the PTPSs. A total of only forty-nine individually identified ATPSs (8.5 per cent of 578 ATPSs identified as born within 10 miles of current residence) migrated between the four towns (Figure 5.8 above) from 1851 to 1891. Here there was no apparent movement of ATPSs between Ashwell and Buntingford in either direction suggesting that for the potential migrant there were sufficient employment opportunities to be found in the nearer intervening towns of Baldock and Royston. Two-thirds of these migrants were from the 'dress' (13), 'food' (7) and 'building' sectors (4). Also among them in 1851 were two 14 year-old apprentices, both from Royston, Moses Humphry apprenticed to a butcher in Ashwell and James Trudgett apprenticed to a tailor in Baldock.[30]

The wider appeal of north-east Hertfordshire

John Marshall argued that reasons such as improved employment opportunities coupled with the possibility of higher wages were '*attractive*' reasons for a person to migrate especially when reinforced by '*propulsive*' reasons such as rising agricultural unemployment, depressed wage rates and poor housing conditions in their present location.[31] More recently, Boyer and Hatton agreed that a 'wage gap favouring the destination region' is an obvious incentive when coupled with the 'probability of gaining employment in the individual's occupation'. However, they accepted that individuals' different preferences, their lack of 'ability to exploit opportunities', and the cost of moving resulted in many staying put.[32] Substantial numbers of both PTPS and ATPS migrants living in the four study towns but originating from beyond their immediate hinterlands suggest that the regional economy of north-east Hertfordshire in the later half of the nineteenth century did in fact offer sufficient 'attractive' inducements for people to move into the area.

In Ashwell, the smallest town, approximately 15.0 to 20.0 per cent of its PTPSs had migrated from locations that were situated further than ten miles away (Figure 5.9 below).[33] Between 1851 and 1871, the majority of these had come from either

---

[30] 1851 Census (Ashwell); 1851 Census (Baldock).

[31] Marshall, 'Lancashire Rural Labourer in the Early Nineteenth Century', p. 95.

[32] Boyer and Hatton, 'Migration and Labour Market Integration', pp. 698, 699.

[33] Although the county of Middlesex is adjacent to Hertfordshire, here people born in Middlesex are grouped together with those born in London as the distinction between the two areas in the latter part of the nineteenth century is somewhat confused with parts of Middlesex obviously lying within the city conurbation. Dudley Baines has previously commented on this 'serious confusion between London and Middlesex born' and adopted the same single unit approach in, D. Baines, *Migration in a Mature Economy: Emigration and Internal Migration in England and Wales, 1861–1900* (Cambridge, 1985), p. 97. It is obvious from the CEBs that the distinction also confused the enumerators.

further afield in Hertfordshire, the bordering counties of Bedfordshire, Buckinghamshire, Cambridgeshire and Essex, or the 'London and Middlesex' region. However, after 1871, these numbers declined and almost 10.0 per cent of Ashwell's PTPSs originated from other counties in England and Wales. Migrants originating further than ten miles from either Baldock, Buntingford or Royston consistently represented between 25.0 and 35.0 per cent of the PTPS census entries between 1851 and 1891. The decennial proportions of those moving into the three larger towns from either wider Hertfordshire or the adjacent counties (9.0 – 16.5%), and those from further afield in Britain (10.0 – 19.5%), exhibited relatively modest changes across the forty-year period.

Those migrants moving north from London and/or Middlesex to Buntingford, presumably having travelled along the Old North Road, regularly provided between 6.0 and 8.5 per cent of the town's resident PTPSs. Fewer appear to have travelled the further seven miles north to Royston where migrant PTPSs from London and/or Middlesex only made up between 2.5 and 5.0 per cent of the total. Surprisingly, in comparison with Buntingford and despite being on the Great North Road out of London, Baldock in 1851 had only 1.6 per cent of PTPSs born in or around the metropolis. That proportion rose a little between 1861 and 1871 but fell back to 1.7 per cent by 1881 before finally climbing to just over 6.0 per cent by 1891. Given the relative proximity of these Hertfordshire towns to London and its business attractions, the aforementioned migrations might seem to be in the opposite direction to that expected. However, this observation provides a clear example of another of Ravenstein's 'laws of migration', that 'Each current of migration produces a compensating counter current'. David Grigg asserted that, given the few studies of in- and out-migration for an individual location during the nineteenth century, Ravenstein was 'remarkably perceptive in calling attention to the existence of these counter-currents'.[34] Migration from London that reached as far north as Buntingford and Royston is a true counter-current as it is clearly well beyond what Ravenstein meant when he observed that migrants moving to the suburbs in adjacent counties 'can hardly be said to have left the metropolis'.[35]

Another 'counter current' identified by the present analysis is that of a number of migrants leaving much larger urban centres such as Bedford, Cambridge and Hertford for small towns like Baldock and Royston. Although Ravenstein's suggestion that 'natives of towns are less migratory than those of rural districts' has, according to Grigg, been largely discredited, it is perhaps surprising to find

---

[34] Grigg, 'Ravenstein', pp. 43, 48.

[35] E.G. Ravenstein, 'The Laws of Migration', *Journal Statistical Society*, 48 (1885), p. 185, cited in Grigg, 'Ravenstein', p. 53.

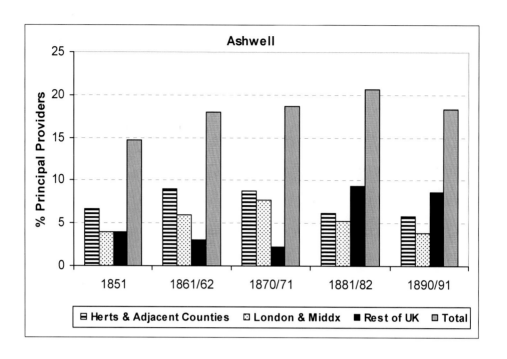

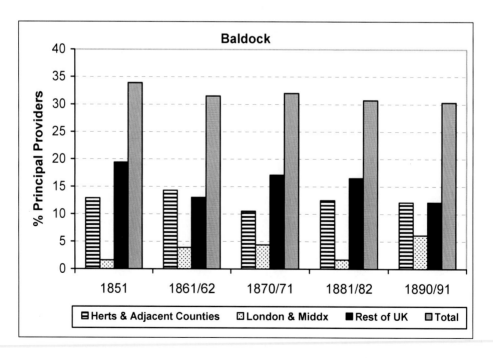

Figure 5.9: PTPSs from beyond 10 miles of the four towns
Source: Census enumerations, 1851-1891.

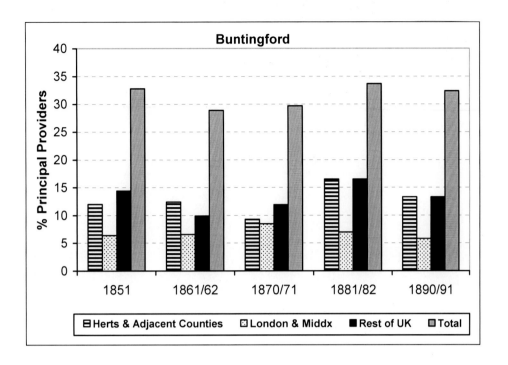

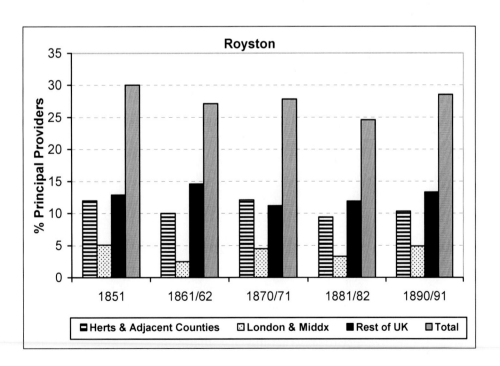

them 'downsizing'.[36] Two towns, Baldock and Royston, attracted the majority (84%) of such PTPSs (Figure 5.10 below) with almost half of them migrating from Cambridge, twelve and nineteen miles north-east of Baldock and Royston respectively. Though their occupations ranged widely, from Conrad Baker a veterinary surgeon who left Chelmsford for Baldock to Lydia Harrison an 'under linen manufacturer' who moved to Royston from Cambridge, almost half of these PTPSs were either publicans (n = 6) or school mistresses (n = 6).[37]

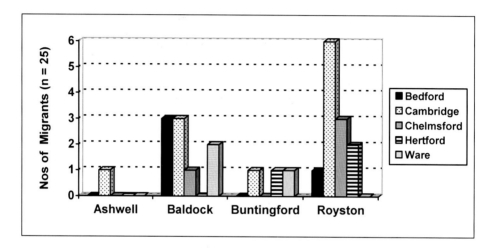

Figure 5.10: PTPSs 'incoming' from the region's larger urban centres, 1851–91
Source: Census enumerations, 1851–1891.

All four towns attracted similar numbers of ATPSs from the region's larger urban centres (Figure 5.11 below) with the great majority (72.3%) moving from either Bedford, fifteen miles north-west of Baldock, or Cambridge. Again the occupations were very varied but a fifth of these ATPSs were employed in the dress sector and almost a quarter of them were apprenticed to masters in Baldock (n = 2), Buntingford (n = 2) and Royston (n = 7).

A substantial number (n = 369) of individual PTPSs working in the four towns had been born, according to the CEBs, in a wide range of counties across England and Wales as well as in 'Scotland' and 'Ireland'; in the case of the latter two countries no further geographical detail was given. As Edward Higgs explained, these latter broad locations arose from the instructions given to the enumerators from 1851 onwards, a set of instructions that interestingly omitted Wales until

[36] Grigg, 'Ravenstein', p. 48.
[37] 1871 Census (Baldock); 1871 Census (Royston).

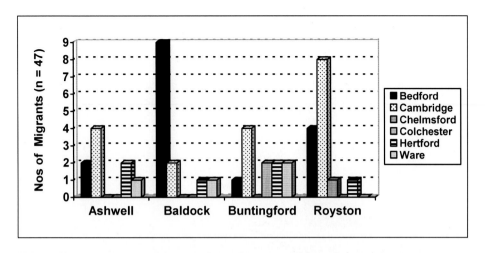

Figure 5.11: ATPSs 'incoming' from the region's larger urban centres, 1851–91
Source: Census enumerations, 1851–1891.

1891.[38] In addition to the 'London & Middlesex' entity, the analysis identified PTPSs who had originated in twenty-seven English and six Welsh counties as well as the 'Isle of Man', 'Scotland' and 'Ireland'. This picture is very much in line with Grigg's observation that 'even in areas suffering from heavy net out-migration there is always some in-migration' as with his example of Huntingdonshire where the population fell at every census from 1861 yet, in 1901, had 'natives of every English and Welsh county living in the county'.[39]

The dominant flow of incoming PTPSs (Figure 5.12 below), accounting for over a quarter of the total (n = 98) was northwards out of the London and Middlesex conurbation. A second major flow, accounting for a further third of incoming PTPSs (n = 121) was from six counties of eastern England: Huntingdonshire (26); Norfolk (24); Suffolk (21); Lincolnshire (15) and two from south of the Thames; Kent (21) and Surrey (14). A third major migratory stream (62, 16.8%) was that from nine counties in south-west and southern England among which the largest numbers of migrants actually originated from the most distant counties, Devon (10) and Somerset (8). Among the final quarter, thirty-seven incoming PTPSs had origins scattered across the Midlands and twelve across Wales while a further

---

[38] E. Higgs, *Making Sense of the Census Revisited: Census Records for England and Wales, 1801–1901: A Handbook for Historical Researchers* (London, 2005), p. 88. 'In the case of those born in England, householders were to indicate first the county, and then the town or parish of birth.', 'In the case of those born in Scotland, Ireland, the British Colonies, the East Indies or Foreign Parts, the country of birth was to be stated.'

[39] Grigg, 'Ravenstein', p. 48.

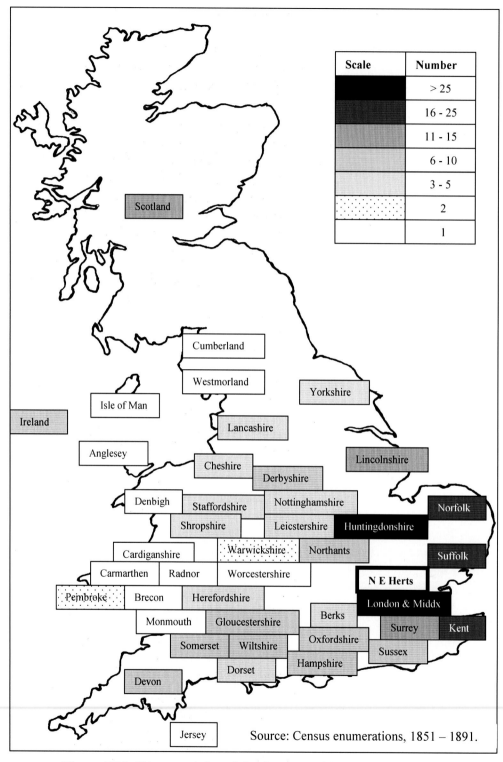

Figure 5.12: Distant origins of the four towns' PTPSs (n = 369)

thirty-five originated from four more distant sources, Scotland (15), Ireland (10), Lancashire (5) and Yorkshire (5).

Although industrial expansion created opportunities in many areas of Britain, a number of previous studies have identified London as the great magnet to migrants. For example, C.T. Smith examined the Census Commissioners' 'Notes to the Census' of 1851 and 1861 and concluded that for every county 'south of a line from Lincolnshire to the Severn' migration from them to London exceeded migration to them from the capital. He further noted little 'movement in other directions as one approaches the capital' but expressed surprise at not finding more evidence of stepwise migration between neighbouring counties.[40] Dov Friedlander, using decennial inter-county migration data, has looked specifically at migration patterns relating to London. He stated that up to 1881 these were 'characterised by heavy population concentration movements into London, and early signs of population dispersal movements mainly to the Home Counties', largely to Surrey and Middlesex. It was not until between 1881 and 1901 that dispersal from London greatly increased as the growing urban middle classes moved out mainly to the capital's developing suburbs in Essex, Middlesex and Surrey.[41] This observation by Friedlander is in direct contrast to the present findings which identified migrants born in London and Middlesex moving to the four small Hertfordshire towns from 1851 onwards. However, this evidence is in line with David Souden's belief that 'London acted as an overwhelmingly important migration node' with its effects 'felt throughout the economy, and personal contacts with it were ubiquitous'.[42]

While one might argue that the migrants identified from East Anglia were making steps towards the capital, it is perhaps less obvious why those in the observed migratory stream from south-west England should divert northwards into north-east Hertfordshire. Also less obvious is why those migrants originating from Sussex, Surrey and Kent should have either 'leap-frogged' the capital or stopped-off there along their way north to Hertfordshire. Evidence from the towns considered here contrasts with Smith's argument, in relation to larger industrial centres, that each 'recruited by far the greater part of its labour in a zone of which the radius was rarely more than fifty miles'. It also counters his claim that, apart from Irish migrants to Lancashire, London alone drew migrants from over a

---

[40] C.T. Smith, 'The Movement of Population in England and Wales in 1851 and 1861', *Geographical J.*, 117 (1951), p.206.

[41] D. Friedlander, 'London's Urban Transition, 1851–1951', *Urban Studies*, 11(1974), pp. 135, 136.

[42] D. Souden, 'Pre-industrial English Local Migration Fields' (PhD thesis, University of Cambridge, 1981), p. 324.

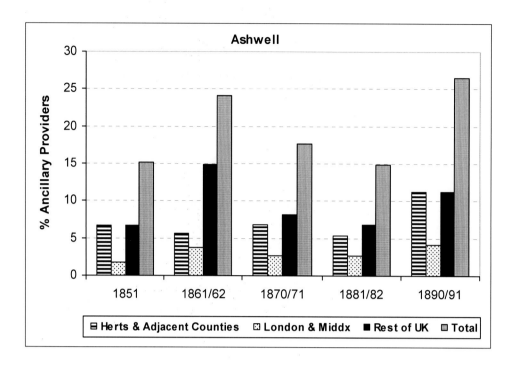

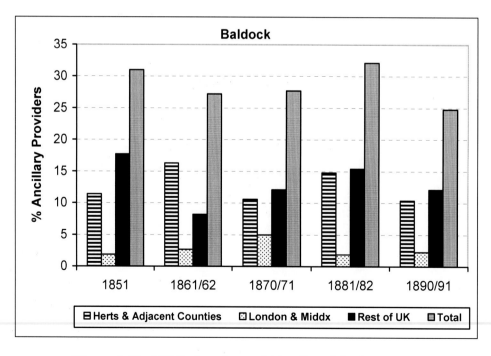

Figure 5.13: ATPSs from beyond 10 miles of the four towns
Source: Census enumerations, 1851-1891.

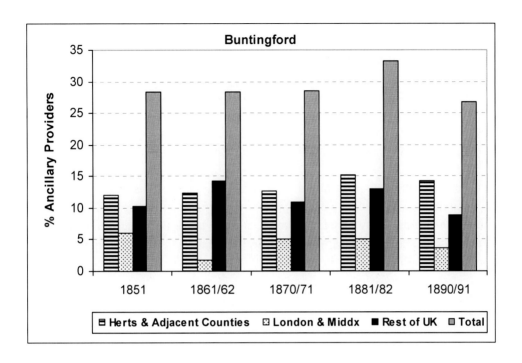

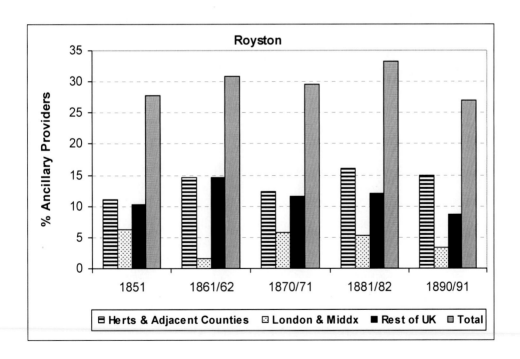

hundred miles away.[43] Even small centres like Baldock and Royston received migrants from as far afield as Devon, Pembrokeshire, Yorkshire, Scotland, Ireland and Jersey, proving that they could overcome Friedlander's observation of the 'extremely high costs to the individuals or families who moved [long distances] from their former social environment'.[44] These findings relate to the fact that, unlike so many analyses of migration which are concerned with late nineteenth-century rural depopulation and/or industrialization's demand for largely unskilled labour, the evidence presented here is concerned with the skilled, semi-skilled and professional members of a regional business community.

In a similar pattern to that found with their PTPSs, analysis of the origins of ATPSs residing in Baldock, Buntingford and Royston in the second half of the nineteenth century shows that between a quarter and a third had migrated from further afield than the immediate ten-mile hinterlands. The proportion of these three towns' ATPSs born in the rest of Hertfordshire and the neighbouring counties of Bedfordshire, Buckinghamshire, Cambridgeshire and Essex was regularly between 10.0 and 16.0 per cent across the period (Figure 5.13 above). Migration northwards along the Old North Road was again very apparent but here the proportions of ATPSs from London and Middlesex were virtually identical in Buntingford and the more northerly Royston. Apart from 1871, Baldock on the Great North Road again attracted fewer migrants than might be expected from the capital and its environs, with only 2.0 per cent of the total ATPSs having been born there. In the three larger towns, apart from Baldock in 1851 (17.7 per cent), the proportion of ATPSs born elsewhere across Britain was reasonably stable at between 10.0 and 15.0 per cent of the total. However, figures do suggest a general decline in the numbers of these long-distance migrants by 1891 when their proportions had fallen to only 8.6 per cent in Royston, 9.9 per cent in Buntingford and 12.1 per cent in Baldock. Ashwell, the smallest of the four towns, has similar numbers of 'incoming' ATPSs from wider Hertfordshire and its adjacent counties to those found for its PTPSs. Those ATPSs moving to Ashwell from London and/or Middlesex formed a much lower proportion, only 2.0 to 4.0 per cent of the total, than that found for the corresponding PTPSs. What is striking here is the more than doubling by 1861, from 6.7 to 14.8 per cent, of ATPSs moving into Ashwell from the rest of the UK. This proportion then fell back, between 1871 and 1881, to 8.2 and 6.8 per cent respectively suggesting that there had been a window of opportunity for semi-skilled workers, especially bricklayers and carpenters, as noted earlier, following the disastrous Ashwell fire of 1850.

---

[43] Smith, 'Movement of Population', p. 210.

[44] D. Friedlander, 'Occupational Structure, Wages, and Migration in Late Nineteenth-century England and Wales', *Economic Development and Cultural Change*, 40, 2 (1992), p. 315.

The patterns of flow of ATPSs from distant origins (n = 439) looks remarkably similar (Figure 5.14 below) to that found for the PTPSs. The dominant flow (n = 87) was still that of migrants moving out from London and Middlesex although the proportion, at 19.8 per cent, is less than that of the PTPSs. This decrease is balanced by the fact that the second major flow (n = 163), from the east of England, is somewhat higher at 37.1 per cent due largely to the significant numbers of incomers originating from Norfolk (40) and Suffolk (37). The proportion of migrants from the south and west at 17.1 per cent is virtually identical to that found among the PTPSs although half here originate from Hampshire (15), Sussex (12) and Oxfordshire (10). While the proportion of ATPSs originating from the Midlands (13.9%) is significantly more than that of the PTPSs, it is mostly attributable to the twenty-three migrating from Northamptonshire. Very few ATPSs had their origins in Wales, two from Glamorgan and one each from Cardiganshire, Denbighshire and Herefordshire, while their numbers from Scotland (7) and Ireland (8) are far fewer than with the PTPSs. However, the proportion of ATPSs from Yorkshire (14) and Lancashire (12) is double compared with that of PTPSs.

It is interesting to compare these migrant flows, of both PTPSs and ATPSs, with those described by Friedlander and Roshier in their large-scale study of internal migration in England and Wales. These authors used census data to 'estimate the volume of inter-county migration [between all 53 counties] in each of the inter-censal periods' from 1851 to 1951.[45] They identified four major migration streams from the counties of 'the North Midlands', 'the Southern Region', 'the Eastern Region' and 'the South-Western Region', the last pair corresponding to two of the major streams seen here. However, unlike the present findings, Friedlander and Roshier identified the destinations of these migrants between 1851 and 1891 as mainly 'London and the home counties, particularly to Surrey and Middlesex' with no indication of Hertfordshire being a major recipient.[46] The current data includes a number of migrants from the south-west that had reached north-east Hertfordshire before 1861 (Devon, 8; Somerset, 6; Dorset and Wiltshire, each 3, and Cornwall, 1). This finding contrasts with that of Friedlander and Roshier whose analysis only identified such migrants after that date. Again, they argued that the 'County of London began to lose population through internal migration after the 1871–81 decade'. They saw this migration, most frequently to Sussex, Berkshire, Buckinghamshire and Hertfordshire, as part of a 'continuing process of population dispersal from the old residential centres of

---

[45] D. Friedlander and R.J. Roshier, 'A Study of Internal Migration in England and Wales: Part I', *Population Studies*, 19 (1966), p. 239.
[46] Friedlander and Roshier, 'A Study of Internal Migration', p. 256

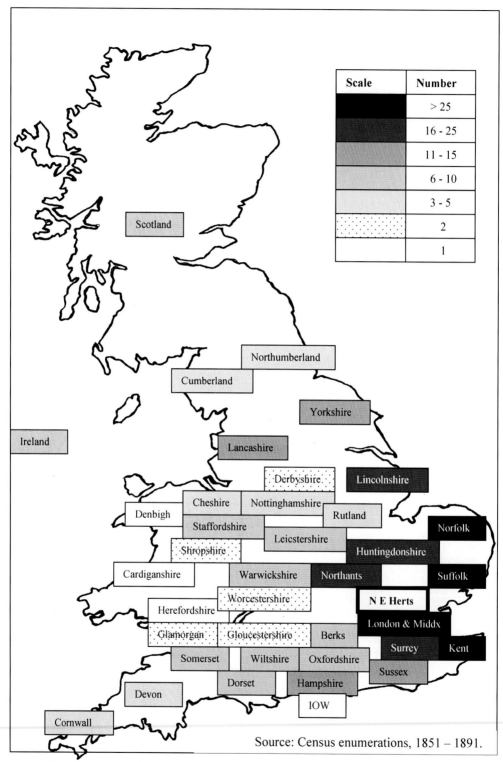

Figure 5.14: Distant origins of the four towns' ATPSs (n = 439)

inner London'.[47] Yet, in contrast, the present analysis of migrants reveals a steady stream (4.0 – 7.0% in the case of PTPSs, see Figure 5.11 above) arriving from London and/or Middlesex across the period 1851 to 1891.

Profile of 'incomers' from distant origins

In all four towns, PTPSs and ATPSs migrating from distant origins were found to be overwhelmingly men, 79.5 and 86.4 per cent of the total respectively. While female PTPSs consistently accounted for only around 20.0 per cent of the total migrants, the proportion of female ATPSs varied widely from not one in Ashwell to almost 19.0 per cent in both Buntingford and Royston. Overall, 52.8% of 'incoming' PTPSs were unmarried but there was considerable variation between the four towns: over one-third in both Ashwell and Baldock, almost half in Buntingford, and nearly three-quarters in Royston. A considerably higher proportion of all 'incoming' ATPSs were single (74.1%) but again there was a sizeable difference between the four towns: over half in both Ashwell and Baldock, almost three-quarters in Buntingford, and nearly 90.0 per cent in Royston. Within both migrating groups there was a small number of widows and widowers accounting for 5.1 per cent of 'incoming' PTPSs and 3.2 per cent of 'incoming' ATPSs.

According to Friedlander and Roshier, 'there is no doubt that migrants form a highly selective group in their age structure' and that this group contains an excess of adolescents and generally young adults.[48] Similarly, Dudley Baines, using the Registrar General's reports to calculate migration by county of birth between 1861 and 1900, concluded that 'the evidence that current migrants contained a disproportionate share of young adults is overwhelming'. He speculated that marriage, leaving the parental home and high expectations from their investment in migrating, motivated this group.[49] Baines's analysis suggested an age profile of 19.0 per cent aged below 15 (young children), 53 per cent aged 15 to 24 (unattached adults) and 28 per cent aged 25 to 34 (parents of the young children).[50] A similar young-adult bias was reported by Jeffrey Williamson whose investigation of the age distribution of city immigrants in the 1860s found two-thirds to be aged between 15 and 29 with the rest largely children.[51]

---

[47] Friedlander and Roshier, 'A Study of Internal Migration', p. 257, 263.

[48] Friedlander and Roshier, 'Study of Internal Migration', p. 246.

[49] Baines, *Migration in a Mature Economy*, p. 100.

[50] Baines, *Migration in a Mature Economy*, p. 104.

[51] J.G. Williamson, *Coping with City Growth During the British Industrial Revolution* (Cambridge, 1990), p. 43.

In contrast to the age profiles established by both Baines and Williamson the one shown below (Figure 5.15) is based only on 'incoming' PTPSs and ATPSs identified as having long-distance origins, not the total number of migrants to the four towns. Also, in contrast to these other more complex calculations, this age profile is simply based on the individual's first appearance in a CEB which is not necessarily the age at which the migrant actually arrived. As Williamson acknowledged, 'the census takers never asked when the respondent moved' to their present location.[52]

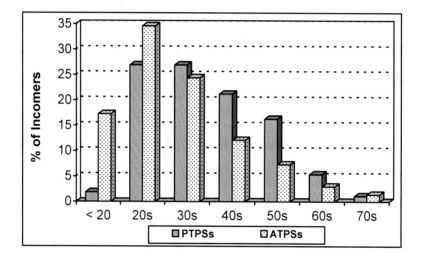

Figure 5.15: Age profile of 'incoming' migrants, 1851–91
Source: Census enumerations, 1851–1891.

There is a clear difference between the profiles of the two groups of service providers studied here. A little over half of all PTPSs were between twenty and thirty-nine years of age with more than a further one-third (37.5%) being aged between forty and fifty-nine. Less than 2.0 per cent of PTPSs were under twenty years of age in contrast to the ATPSs where almost a fifth was found in that youngest age group. While over half (59.0%) of all ATPSs were aged between twenty and thirty-nine, in contrast to the identical spread of PTPSs (26.9 % of both 20 year olds and 30 year olds), the proportion of ATPSs fell from 34.6 per cent in their 20s to 24.4 per cent in their 30s. Unlike the age profile of the PTPSs, the numbers of ATPSs in their 40s and 50s were significantly fewer at only 12.1 and 7.3 per cent respectively. Overall, the analysis clearly identifies a younger age profile for ATPSs migrating from distant origins to north-east Hertfordshire

---

[52] Williamson, *Coping with City Growth*, p. 9.

compared to that of the 'incoming' PTPSs. However, compared with the findings of Baines and Williamson's two studies, substantial numbers of PTPSs (44.0 %) and ATPSs (23.8 %) here were aged 40 and above.

Occupation	No.	% Total
School Teacher	93	25.2
Publican/Innkeeper/Hotelier	45	12.2
Surgeon/G.P	20	5.4
Grocer	17	4.6
Tax Official	17	4.6
Draper	12	3.3
Police Officer	11	3.0
Brewer/Maltster	8	2.2
Boot &/or Shoemaker	6	1.6
Clock &/or Watchmaker	6	1.6
Chemist & Druggist	5	1.4
Farmer	5	1.4
Plumber & Glazier	5	1.4
Solicitor	5	1.4
Tailor	5	1.4
Sub-Totals =	**260**	**70.5**

Table 5.1: Major PTPS groups 'incoming' from distant origins
Source: Census enumerations, 1851-1891.

A very wide range of occupations was represented among the 369 'incoming' PTPSs but the two largest groups of migrants (Table 5.1 above) were the school teachers (n = 93) and those associated with public houses, inns and hotels (n = 45). In addition to school teachers, other professionals included surgeons, tax officials, police officers, chemist and druggists, solicitors, plus two accountants and two relieving officers not included in the table above; these professionals (n = 155) accounted for 42.0 per cent of the total 'incoming' PTPSs. A further group (n = 51) were the typical high street traders, the grocers, drapers, tailors and a variety of other retailers from the food and dress sectors not included in the table above, who accounted for a further 13.8 per cent of the total 'distant' incomers.[53]

Similar findings to the above have been noted for another cluster of small towns with good road and rail communications in the latter half of the nineteenth

---

[53] These other retailers included 3 bakers, 3 butchers, 3 confectioners, 3 fishmongers, 3 milliners and 2 clothiers.

century. Appleby (population 1680), Brough (population 1520) and Kirkby Stephen (population 4116) featured in Margaret Shepherd's study of the Upper Eden Valley. While the majority of shopkeepers and shopworkers were from local parishes and some from nearby counties (Yorkshire, Cumberland and Durham), she found 'birthplaces in Scotland, Ireland, Shropshire, Derbyshire [and] Cambridgeshire'. Shepherd also noted that those 'in professional occupations had the highest proportion with distant birthplaces, apart from the railway construction workers in 1861 and 1871'.[54]

Among the more unusual PTPSs in the present dataset were two umbrella makers, James Lee from Macclesfield in Cheshire, trading in Melbourn Street in Royston, and William Kingston from Taunton in Somerset, operating a rival establishment in Kneesworth Street.[55] Other unusual trading rivals were two Royston soot dealers, Edward Ewen from Langham, Norfolk, on the High Street, and Isaac Roe from Norwich, who had the advantage of being next door to a sweep, John Mann, on Market Hill.[56] However, perhaps the most unusual 'incoming' PTPS was William Brown a racehorse owner and trainer from Chatham in Kent living at Heath House in Back Street, Royston.[57]

A similar wide range of occupations (Table 5.2 below) was identified among the 439 'incoming' ATPSs. After various clerks and apprentices, the most common ATPSs were the journeymen and various types of shop assistant associated with high street traders. Those employed in the clothing, grocery and butchery trades plus five in bakery not included in the table above (n = 105) amounted to 23.9 per cent of the total 'incoming' ATPSs. Those skilled craftsmen working in the building trade (n = 53), the bricklayers, carpenters, painters and plumbers plus four stonemasons and two plasterers not included in the table above, accounted for a further 12.1 per cent. Among the less common occupations were those of Thomas Williams a bookbinder from Chester, and Harper Potter a French polisher from Kentisbeare in Devon.[58] There were also two young 'mantle makers', Emma (aged 21) and Edith (aged 20) Baker from Shipdham in Norfolk, boarding with Alfred Cheshire a partner in Whitaker & Co., linen drapers.[59]

---

[54] M.E. Shepherd, *From Hellgill to Bridge End: Aspects of Economic and Social Change in the Upper Eden Valley, 1840–95. University of Hertfordshire, Studies in Regional and Local History, Vol. 2* (Hatfield, 2003), pp. 310, 314.

[55] *Kelly's Directory of the Six Home Counties, Part 1: Essex, Herts & Middlesex* (London, 1882), p. 649; 1881 Census (Royston).

[56] 1871 Census (Royston).

[57] *Kelly's Directory of the Six Home Counties, Part 1: Essex, Herts & Middlesex* (London, 1890), p. 809.

[58] 1851 and 1881 Census enumerations (Royston).

[59] 1881 Census (Royston); *Kelly's Directory Six Home Counties, Pt 1* (1882), p. 650.

Occupation	No.	% Total
Clerks, various	33	7.5
Apprentices, various	32	7.3
Drapery Trade	32	7.3
Dressmaking/Millinery Trade	29	6.6
Railway Worker	28	6.4
Leather Trade	18	4.1
Bricklayer	16	3.6
Brewery Trade	15	3.4
Grocery Trade	13	3.0
Hawker	13	3.0
Blacksmith	12	2.7
Painter	12	2.7
Carpenter	11	2.5
Tailoring Trade	10	2.3
Butchery Trade	8	1.8
Ironmonger	8	1.8
Plumber	8	1.8
Shoemaker	8	1.8
Sub-Totals =	306	69.7

Table 5.2: Major ATPSs groups 'incoming' from distant origins
Source: Census enumerations, 1851-1891.

Long distance apprenticeship

While it might be expected that skilled traders and 'professionals' would migrate some distance in search of business opportunities, it is perhaps more surprising to find young people being apprenticed to 'masters' at considerable distances from their homes. Indeed, such long distance placing of apprentices had supposedly been prohibited by the Factory Act of 1816 which stated that 'a maximum of 40 miles from home was the greatest distance children might be sent and nine the youngest age at which they might be bound'.[60] This provision, explained Joan Lane, was to address the concerns of officials and parents as to how well, or otherwise, apprenticed children were treated by their masters. For by the nineteenth century, she suggested, the traditional scheme of apprenticeship was 'degenerating into the scandal of the factory child and the pauper apprentice,

---

[60] 1816 Factory Act, 56 Geo. III c.139, cited in J. Lane, *Apprenticeship in England, 1600–1914* (London, 1996), p.7.

bound far away from home to save the poor rate'.[61]

Although apprenticeship was supposed to be in the interest of trade and manufacturing, Sara Horrell, Jane Humphries and Hans-Joachim Voth in their work on nineteenth-century intergenerational poverty traps agreed with Lane that it was seen as 'a partial solution of the problem of pauperism'. However, those apprenticed by the parish, they argued, generally went on to practice the trade they had been taught and believed the 'the system generally provided training in a humane context for otherwise deprived children'.[62]

Clearly, the provision of the 1816 Act was not strictly adhered to by the PTPSs of the four study towns. While most of the 275 apprentices identified in this analysis were born either in one of the four towns or elsewhere in Hertfordshire, just over a third of them came from outside the county. Among the latter group, twenty-one apprentices (Figure 5.16 below) came into the towns from beyond the five counties (including London & Middlesex) that immediately surround Hertfordshire. This finding is very different from that of Malcolm Kitch whose work on Sussex apprentices, albeit an eighteenth-century study, suggested that the average distance travelled was only 10.9 miles, even when migrants to places in adjacent counties were included. He observed that few apprentices from Sussex would have 'travelled outside their own and neighbouring counties, except for those who went to London'.[63] However, by the late nineteenth century, Sarah Boar (apprentice stationer, aged 17) from Chichester and Robert Tailor (apprentice chemist, aged 15) from St Leonards (both towns on the Sussex coast, 50 miles from London) were in Royston, 40 miles north of the metropolis.[64] There is also some evidence that the Poor Law officials of Ashwell, in addition to placing pauper apprentices in the surrounding locality, as we have seen in chapter 3, were prepared in some instances to send them long distances away from the town. For example, a letter from William Jowett, curate of Silk Willoughby near Sleaford in Lincolnshire written on behalf of Mr Gale a shoemaker (dated 16 December 1850) to Henry Morice, vicar of Ashwell, asked 'whether it will be convenient to settle about the boy Picking (who was Apprenticed to him [Mr Gale] last year) on the 26th of this month'.[65]

---

[61] Lane, *Apprenticeship in England*, p.9.

[62] S. Horrell, J. Humphries and H-J Voth, 'Destined for Deprivation: Human Capital Formation and Intergenerational Poverty in Nineteenth-century England', *Explorations in Economic History*, 38, 3 (2001), pp. 358, 359.

[63] M. Kitch, 'Population Movement and Migration in Pre-industrial Rural England', in B. Short (ed.), *The English Rural Community: Image and Analysis* (Cambridge, 1992), p. 78.

[64] 1871 and 1891 Census enumerations (Royston).

[65] Ashwell: Miscellaneous Papers re Apprenticeship, 1790-1850, HALS, D/P7/14/3.

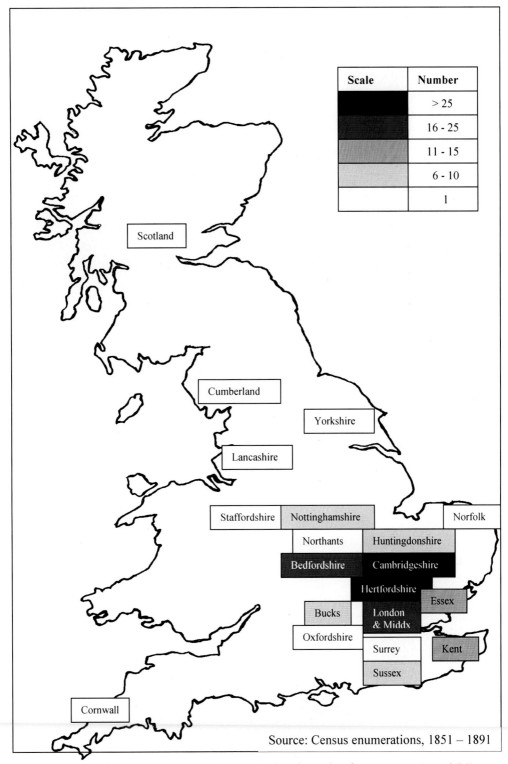

Figure 5.16: Origins of apprentices coming into the four towns (n = 275)

Long-distance apprentices were bound to sixteen different types of master that included four drapers, two stationers, and two chemist and druggists. Those farthest from home were, farmer's apprentice James Fletcher from Staffordshire (Ashwell, 1861), apprentice draper John Bell from Staithes in Yorkshire (Baldock, 1861), dressmaker's apprentice Sarah Moor from Wigtown in Scotland (Royston, 1871), apprentice horse-trainer James Brown from Southport in Lancashire (Royston, 1891), grocer's apprentice Walter Storbeck from Carlisle in Cumberland (Royston, 1891) and apprentice draper Alfred Hestell from St Kew in Cornwall (Royston, 1891).

Out of the twenty-one long-distance apprentices, seventeen were bound to masters in Royston, three in Baldock and just one in Ashwell; there were no long-distance apprentices in Buntingford. Furthermore, it is interesting to note the eight apprentices that by-pass London and move to north-east Hertfordshire along with a further eleven that move out of London itself. Four of the five apprentices from Kent (blacksmith, draper, saddler and smith-fitter) along with the two from Sussex (chemist and stationer) and one from Surrey (stationer) were all bound to masters in Royston. The apprentices originating from London and Middlesex were more evenly distributed with four in Buntingford, three each in Baldock and Royston, and just one in Ashwell. In the early part of the nineteenth century, as Katrina Honeyman noted, 'a large proportion [of factory apprentices] originated in the poor London parishes and was bound northwards'.[66] By the end of the century it is clear that north-east Hertfordshire was attracting apprentices from far and wide, including London, into trades that perhaps gave them a greater opportunity for employment after their period of apprenticeship had ended, compared to those earlier pauper parish apprentices bound to mill owners. For example, in 1881, Frederick Firenden (aged 16) from New Cross was a draper's apprentice in Royston. Ten years later, William Green (aged 19) from Dollis Hill and Caroline Newman (aged 14) from Hackney were respectively apprenticed to a joiner and stationer in the same town.[67]

Contrary to Lane's arguments, as noted above, the picture in Royston at the end of the nineteenth century provides little evidence of a lessening in demand for traditional apprenticeships. There were forty-one apprentices found listed in the 1891 CEB for Royston (see Table 5.3 below) covering nineteen different trades and skills. The majority were in the 'dealing' and 'manufacturing' sectors (21 and 12 respectively) with very limited numbers in the 'building' and 'public and professional' sectors (5 and 2 respectively), plus the single horse trainer's

---

[66] K. Honeyman, *Child Workers in England, 1780-1820. Parish Apprentices and the Making of the Early Industrial Labour Force* (Aldershot, 2007), p. 89.

[67] 1881 and 1891 Census enumerations (Royston).

Apprentice	No.	Ages	Origins
Draper	5	14, 16, 16, 17 & 19	Cambs (1), Cornwall (1), Essex (1), Royston (2)
Dressmaker / Milliner	5	14, 14, 15, 16 & 18	Cambs (3), Herts (1), Royston (1)
Cabinet Maker	4	15, 15, 15 & 16	Cambs (1), Royston (3)
Grocer	4	14, 15, 16 & 18	Cumberland (1), Cambs (2), Royston (1)
Blacksmith	3	12, 15, 15	Kent (2), Royston (1)
Carpenter / Joiner	2	15 & 19	London (1), Norfolk (1)
Coach Builder	2	14 & 21	Herts (1), Oxfordshire (1)
Chemist	2	15 & 17	Herts (1), Sussex (1)
Painter	2	14 & 17	Royston (2)
Saddler / Harness Maker	2	14 & 16	Cambs (1), Herts (1)
Stationer	2	14 & 14	London (1), Surrey (1)
Architect	1	18	Royston
Baker	1	13	Cambs
Butcher	1	16	Herts
Engineer	1	16	Royston
Horse Trainer	1	17	Lancashire
Ironmonger	1	16	Huntingdonshire
Tailor	1	15	Royston
Watchmaker	1	16	Nottinghamshire
Total	41	31.7% Royston, 22.0% Cambridgeshire, 12.2% Hertfordshire, 34.1% Elsewhere	

Table 5.3: Geographical origins of Royston's apprentices, 1891
Source: Royston census enumeration, 1891.

apprentice. While thirteen came from Royston itself, and seventeen came from elsewhere in Hertfordshire or the surrounding adjacent counties, eleven others (26.8 per cent) were long-distance apprentices. This continued demand suggests a vibrant economy in a town that was clearly identified from afar as a place of opportunity.

Migratory behaviour of 'incomers'

There is evidence, using the birthplace data of their children provided by the CEBs, of a few PTPSs who moved away from the town of their birth and then returned at a later date. In total, only twenty such individuals were identified over the forty-year period 1851 to 1891. Twelve of these PTPSs were from Royston and five from Buntingford; these are levels representing less than 4.0 per cent of each town's local-born PTPSs listed in any of the five censuses.[68]

Nearly all (n = 16) of the returning PTPSs had, on the evidence of their children's origins, settled in only one other location before their return; in most cases a location within their original town's hinterland. For example, Frederick Bryant (aged 40) an Ashwell blacksmith living in the High Street in 1881 with his wife Mary Ann (Aged 40) from Barley, a village three miles south-east of Royston, had three children, Annie (aged 12) and George (aged 10), both born at Great Chishill in Essex, a village two miles east of Barley, and Constance (aged 6) born in Ashwell.[69] The remaining four examples had migrated twice or three times before their return.[70] An interesting case is that of William Croft, a master tailor and beer retailer from Baldock. In the 1881 census he (aged 53) and his wife Mary (aged 49), also from Baldock, had four children: Clara (aged 15) born in Stony Stratford, Buckinghamshire, Rosa (aged 12) born back in Baldock, and Derek (aged 9) and Frank (aged 5) both born in 'London, Middx'.[71] The three other PTPSs eventually all returned to their 'home town' after spells in London: George Tottman (aged 53) returned from 'Holborn, London' as licensed victualler at the *Crown* in Buntingford in 1891; Charles Andrews (aged 48) an ironmonger, brazier and gunsmith returned to Royston after a period in 'St Pancras, Middx'; Benjamin Goslin (aged 52) a master tailor returned to Royston by 1871 having

---

[68] This kind of analysis obviously excludes any returning migrants who were unmarried along with the married and widowed who were either without a family or any children were no longer living at home with their parents.

[69] 1881 Census (Ashwell).

[70] In all these analyses the number of identified steps should be viewed as a minimum since childhood deaths were common at this time and create potential gaps in a family's migratory history. Furthermore, where elderly parents return, their older children may already have left home, again creating gaps in the number of migratory steps.

[71] 1881 Census (Baldock).

spent some years in 'London, Middx'.[72] One can only speculate why these PTPSs returned to north-east Hertfordshire from the metropolis. On the one hand, it might have been kinship ties that were responsible; on the other, it could have been the effect of Everett Lee's 'push and pull' argument regarding social and economic opportunities or obstacles that were crucial factors influencing these people's decisions to stay, to move on or indeed return to their origins.[73]

Again, among resident ATPSs, the number of those born in the study towns that had ventured elsewhere and returned to the town of their birth was very limited. Here another twenty-four examples were identified over the same forty-year period. Twelve of these ATPSs were from Royston, seven from Buntingford and five from Ashwell; these are levels averaging less than 4.0 per cent of each town's local-born census-listed ATPSs. Among the returning ATPSs, there were again a few coming back from London and its environs, one to Buntingford and three to Ashwell. Thomas Austin (aged 42), a baker and beer seller had returned to Ashwell by 1871 with his wife Sarah (aged 45 and originally from Wimbledon, Surrey) and their six children (aged between 5 and 18) all born in 'London, Middx'. Data from the 1891 census showed that Agnes (aged 13), Percy (aged 6), William (aged 3) and their parents Julius (a blacksmith) and Emma Eversden all originated in Ashwell but that their older brothers Harry (aged 11) and Julius (aged 8) were born in 'Finsbury Park, London'. Beer retailer Arthur Westerman's daughter Louisa (aged 3) was born in 'Islington, Middx', but he and his wife Georgiana then settled in Potton, Bedfordshire, where Frank (aged 3 months) was born before Arthur returned to Ashwell in 1891 to run the *Fox* public house.[74]

Over half of the ATPSs that left Royston went no further than either Bassingbourn, Buntingford, Stapleford (Cambs), Therfield or Whittlesford in its immediate hinterland before returning. Occasionally, as in the case of John Tookey, a Royston sawyer, a migrant left and returned to his home town more than once. The 1861 CEB shows John and Eliza (from Tunbridge Wells) had their first son Walter (aged 12) in Rembury, Kent. They returned to Royston, where Susan (aged 11) was born, before migrating again to nearby Guilden Morden. Here they had twins Elizabeth and John (aged 8) before moving a few miles south to Barley from where, after the births of Ann (aged 4) and Alice (aged 2), they again returned to Royston.[75] Strangely and inexplicably, the data does not contain one family of an ATPS that had left Baldock then later returned, a

---

[72] 1891 Census (Buntingford); 1851 and 1871 Census enumerations (Royston).

[73] E.S. Lee, 'A Theory of Migration', in J.A. Jackson (ed.), *Migration, Sociological Studies, Vol. 2* (Cambridge, 1969), pp. 285–90.

[74] 1871 Census (Ashwell); 1891 Census (Ashwell); 1891 Census (Ashwell).

[75] 1861 Census (Royston).

situation similar to that of William Croft being the only migrant PTPS from Baldock to return.[76]

Further analysis of the census birthplace data reveals that over half (57.5%) of all PTPSs moving to the four towns from various locations within their immediate hinterlands did so directly (Figure 5.17 below) but for a third of them the move to these towns was actually their second migratory step. A very limited number (n = 23) of these PTPSs had made between two and four moves to reach the towns of

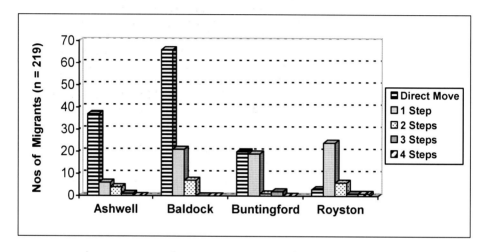

Figure 5.17: Stepwise moves by 'incoming' migrants from towns' hinterlands
Source: Census enumerations, 1851–1891.

north-east Hertfordshire. Grigg has argued that Ravenstein's hypothesis that 'migration proceeds step by step' has eluded modern research and proved 'difficult to confirm'.[77] However, this present survey provides evidence that at least some families' migratory patterns were stepwise in nature. An individual's profession or occupation clearly explains some long-distance progressions. For example, John Phillips, a Baldock J.P., and his wife Elizabeth had sons Ian (aged 8) and Eric (aged 7) before leaving Baldock for Kirklington in Nottinghamshire where Edwin (aged 6) was born. Widower John (aged 55) finally returned to Baldock from Filey in Yorkshire in 1891 with twin girls Ella and Kath (aged 1). A second example is that of Frederick Jennings (aged 65), a maltster and brewer's agent in Royston in 1881. The CEB shows he and his wife Ann (aged 55) had three daughters, Ann Eliza (aged 22) born in Burton upon Trent, Staffordshire, the centre of British brewing, together with Ellen (aged 19) and Bertha (aged 17) both

---

[76] See p. 246 above.
[77] Grigg, 'Ravenstein', p.47.

born in Cambridge which must also have provided numerous opportunities for a maltster.[78]

Among a few other PTPSs, originating from the hinterlands of the four towns, five just migrated to the London area (Chelsea, Hackney, London, Southwark and Clerkenwell), one to London (Paddington) and then Kingston upon Thames, and one to Tonbridge in Kent and then London (Kensington), before returning to Baldock (2), Buntingford (3) and Royston (2). The occupations of these migrant PTPSs ranged from fishmonger and innkeeper to that of insurance agent and schoolmaster.

Among the 142 PTPSs with long-distance origins that migrated with a family to the four towns between 1851 and 1891, well over a third moved without any intermediate steps; just under a further third had made a single intermediate migratory step before reaching their destinations (Figure 5.18 below). This

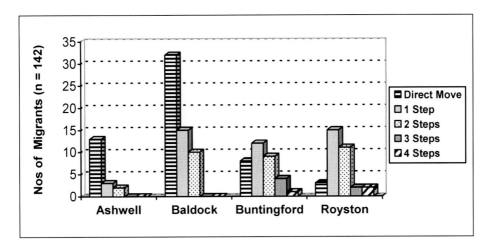

Figure 5.18: Stepwise moves by 'incoming' long-distance PTPS migrants
Source: Census enumerations, 1851–1891.

compares to the pattern of the ninety ATPSs with families, among whom just over a quarter moved directly to one of the four towns while just under a half had settled at one intermediary location *en route* (Figure 5.19 below). In both of these categories around a quarter (28.8% PTPSs and 24.4% ATPSs) had migrated to one of the study towns via two to four intermediary settlements. The CEB entries of the remaining married or widowed long-distance migrants, thirty-two PTPSs

---

[78] 1891 Census (Baldock); 1881 Census (Royston).

and twenty-four ATPSs, provided no data regarding children and are excluded from these calculations.[79]

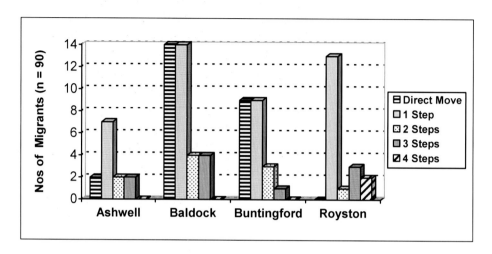

Figure 5.19: Stepwise moves by 'incoming' long-distance ATPS migrants
Source: Census enumerations, 1851–1891.

Stability, Continuity and Family Businesses

The following discussion examines the stability of the business communities within the four towns and the continuity of family-run enterprises. Nominal record linkage allows for the identification of businesses or business owners which between 1839 and 1890 were listed in at least two consecutive trade directories within the chosen series of publications.[80] Combining this evidence with subsequent examination of the corresponding CEBs from 1851 onwards allows the identification of successive family members continuing to run a given business.

In addition to the aforementioned groups, the proportion of businesses appearing for the first time in each town's directory listing indicates that generally in all four

---

[79] CEBs are a more relevant, comprehensive and readily available source of data for providing clues to an individual's migratory path than settlement certificates, removal orders or settlement examinations. Where records of poor relief exist in sufficient quantity and quality they can show interesting details of migration. However, even the majority of ATPSs identified in the above analysis were probably well above the level of pauper and certainly none were identified as such by the census enumerators.

[80] For the purposes of this analysis the assumption is made that among the traders, retailers and other directory-listed PTPSs it is unlikely that few, if any, would have migrated elsewhere and returned during the period between their two successive appearances in the given town's directory listing.

towns there was a decennial influx of between 32.0 and 42.0 per cent of new business enterprises. This level of newcomers, while not surprising in Royston where the total number of directory-listed PTPSs rose by 35.8 per cent over the fifty-year period, suggests a rather high turnover of businesses in Baldock and Buntingford where the numbers of listed PTPSs only increased by 10.7 and 8.4 per cent respectively over the same period.

An indication of business stability, i.e. those enterprises run by the same given individual over a period of time, can be gauged in the case of Baldock from the analysis of successive directory entries between 1823/4 to 1890. Here, thirty-eight businesses listed in 1851 (37.6 per cent total) had appeared in previous directories. The results show that among this 1851 group of PTPSs, seven had been trading at least since 1823/24. This latter group consisted of two publicans (William Dear at the *Plume of Feathers* and John Little at the *White Lion*), two shoemakers (George Emery and John Malein), a butcher (Robert Day), a cooper (William Thurgood) and a glover and tailor (John Hankin). Among the rest, nineteen had traded since 1833/34 and twelve since 1839. Looking beyond 1851, nine of this group of PTPSs were still trading in Baldock until at least 1862, seven until 1870 and two each until 1882 and 1890. Among those twenty businesses still trading after 1851, ten had operated for around thirty years, four for almost forty years, and five for almost fifty years.

A second measure of business stability is provided by analysing the seventy-five PTPSs (56.4 per cent total) listed in Baldock in 1890 who had appeared in some earlier editions of Hertfordshire directories. The results, based on their earliest directory entries, indicate that a considerable number of this group (n = 44) had been trading since at least 1882, a further eighteen since 1870, eight since 1862, three since 1851 and two since 1839.

As was noted above, five PTPSs provided their services to the people of Baldock for approximately fifty years. Based on their trade directory entries, Thomas Harvey a clock and watchmaker and John Trolley a boot and shoe maker ran their businesses for fifty-one years between 1839 and 1890; Trolley was also victualler at the *George Inn* in 1862. An example of the long-term development of a family business is provided by Samuel Veasey, solicitor, first listed in the 1833/34 directory. From 1851 (aged 54) he was partnered by Thomas Veasey (then aged 36) until at least 1862 but by 1870 Samuel's partner was Charles Veasey (aged 32). This second partnership lasted until 1882 when, after forty-eight years in the business, Samuel would have been aged 84. Finally, the 1890 directory lists Charles Veasey in partnership with Herbert Warren at 'Veasey, Balderston & Warren, Solicitors'. William Thurgood, mentioned above, a cooper (1823/4 to 1870) and William Thody a butcher (1833/34 to 1882) were in business for at least forty-six and forty-eight years respectively. In both cases the businesses carried on under the name of their sons: Robert Thurgood from 1882 and William Thody junior from 1890.[81]

For businesses to be continued by family members (widows, sons, daughters and other family relatives) was not uncommon. In Buntingford and Royston from 1851 to 1890 between approximately 6.0 and 13.0 per cent of businesses were in the hands of relatives of their founders. For Baldock, the proportion in 1851 was much higher at 22.8 per cent but from 1862 onwards at between 4.5 and 11.6 per cent the situation more closely resembled that found in Buntingford and Royston. In Ashwell, the proportion of businesses carried on by family relatives was still 20.3 per cent in 1870 but thereafter dropped to levels seen in the other three towns.

Migratory behaviour of PTPSs leaving the four towns

A small but instructive sample of twenty-five PTPSs of a relatively young age (those in their 20s to 40s) who appeared to have moved away from the four towns between 1851 and 1881, i.e. were not listed in the succeeding directory or CEB for that particular town, but unlikely to have died, were sought on a wider basis using the relevant succeeding national census.[82] Their moves away were then examined for any obvious geographical trends. It might be expected, given their proximity to London, that in order to seek betterment for themselves and their families many of the four towns' service providers would have chosen to migrate to the capital. However, analysis of the whereabouts of those who had left shows no such pattern of behaviour.

Among PTPSs born in one of the four towns some, like James Goodchild, simply moved elsewhere in Hertfordshire. In 1871 (aged 34), he was a 'gas-fitter' and

---

[81] *Pigot's Commercial Directory, 1833-34*, p. 726; *Pigot's Commercial Directory, Essex, Hertfordshire, Middlesex (1839)*, pp. 95, 96; *Post Office Directory Six Home Counties, 1851*, pp. 172, 173; *Post Office Directory Six Home Counties, 1862*, p. 320; *Post Office Directory Six Home Counties, Pt 1* (1870), pp. 411, 412; *Kelly's Directory Six Home Counties, Pt 1* (1882), p. 564; *Kellys Directory Six Home Counties, Pt 1* (1890), p. 704; Census enumerations, 1851-1881 (Baldock).
Unfortunately the relationships of Thomas and Charles either to Samuel or to each other could not be determined from the CEBs. In the 1851 census Samuel (aged 54, born in Huntingdon) was living with his wife Margaret but there were no children at home. They continued to live in Baldock's High street throughout. In the same 1851 census, Thomas (aged 36, also born in Huntingdon) was living in Hitchin Street, apparently alone. In the 1881 census, Charles (aged 32, again born in Huntingdon) was living in White Horse Street with his wife and 8 month old baby. Given their ages, it is probable that Thomas and Charles were Samuel's son and grandson respectively.
[82] UK Census Collection, www.ancestry.co.uk/search/rectype/census/uk, © 2008 (April 2008). This source was used to determine the whereabouts of all the examples discussed on pp. 265-68.

ironmonger in Baldock but by 1881 James had moved to St Albans where the CEB described his occupation as 'Master Tin, Zinc, Copper & Iron plate worker &c'. Others migrated as far as the adjacent counties; for example George Gentle (aged 23) a Baldock butcher in 1851 was, by 1861, similarly trading in Luton, Bedfordshire. Similarly in 1881, William Wale (aged 18) was then a miller's apprentice in Royston, the town of his birth. Ten years later, employed as a miller, William was living in Cambridge with his wife Priscilla and two year-old son William born in that town.

A few took the chance to move south into the capital. Richard Holder (aged 30), was working as a Royston 'carrier' in 1871 but a decade later he was a 'carman' living on the Borough Road in Southwark. Another example, Walter George Hood (aged 29), was in 1881 a 'Master builder' and undertaker plying his services in Royston. However, by 1891, Walter was reduced to lodging in Newington in north London and being employed simply as a carpenter.

Other local-born PTPSs migrated a considerable distance from north-east Hertfordshire. John Westrope (aged 24) for example was in 1871 trading as a corn merchant in Ashwell. A decade later he had become a merchant and farmer in Newark, Nottinghamshire but his apparent 'improvement', judged by his ability to employ a housekeeper, cook and housemaid, must have been tempered by the fact that he was widowed with two young daughters (aged 5 and 3). Another example, Martin Luther Sanders from Buntingford, went from the position of a clerk (aged 22) in 1871 to that of station master in Harwich, Essex ten year later. Finally, George Edward Walker (aged 25), working in 1881 as a 'medical dispenser' in Royston migrated to the city of York where in 1891 he was employed as a 'chemist and druggist'. By this time he was married to Kate from Earswick in Yorkshire and had a month-old daughter, Constance.

Similarly, a number of 'incoming' PTPSs appeared to have later migrated away from the four towns. Among the large number of PTPSs identified earlier as migrating from East Anglia into Hertfordshire during the second half of the nineteenth century some decided, after a relatively short stay, to return to the county of their birth. For example in 1851, George Sharpe (aged 37) a surgeon and general practitioner originating from Weassenham in Norfolk was practising in Baldock. By 1861 he had returned to Norwich where he was superintendent at the Infirmary Asylum for Pauper Lunatics. Others, such as William Thomas Raven from Fincham in Norfolk, moved on to another East Anglian county. In 1881, William (aged 26) was hotelier of the *Rose and Crown Commercial Hotel* in Baldock but by 1891 he had become Manager of the *Temperance Hotel* in Peterborough, Northamptonshire. The ages of his three sons (8, 7 and 6 years respectively), all born in Baldock, suggest that he had left there sometime after 1885.

The migratory stream identified as coming from the south-west of England into Hertfordshire clearly had its counter-current. 1851 found Edward Heath Sanders (aged 27) from Totnes in Devon working as an insurance agent and solicitor's general clerk in Royston but ten years later he had moved on to Chesterton on the edge of Cambridge, still working as a solicitor's clerk. Conversely, in 1871, Josiah William Parker (aged 33) from Rushden in Northamptonshire was working as an insurance agent, grocer, glass and china dealer, and an ale porter and wine merchant in Buntingford. By 1881, Josiah had moved away to set up business as a wine merchant in Liskeard, Cornwall.

The survey found evidence of migrants settling for a while in one of the towns either on their way to or from London. For example, Charles Wilson (aged 23) from Sudbury in Suffolk was a teacher at the British School in Baldock in 1861. He had moved on by 1871 and was a schoolmaster in Lambeth in south London. The reverse pattern was exhibited by Edward Keen (aged 37) born in Spitafield in Middlesex who in 1871 was a plumber, glazier and gas-fitter in Royston. A decade later, Edward had moved to Sturton in Nottinghamshire with Charles, his fourteen year-old Royston-born son, his apprentice plumber.

A few of the migrants moving into north-east Hertfordshire found alternative opportunities near to where they first settled. For example, John Blackley (aged 36) from Bluntisham in Huntingdonshire was, in 1851, the licensed victualler of the *White Hart* in Buntingford. However, by 1861 he had moved to the hamlet of Bradfield near Throcking, just to the north-west of the town, where he was farming 108 acres and employing three men and two boys. Another migrant to move away, albeit rather further, and forge a completely new life, was Charles Jones who was born in Norwich, Norfolk. In 1871, Charles (aged 38) was Buntingford's railway station master but in 1881 he had established himself as a grocer in Kettering, Northamptonshire, employing a shop assistant and an apprentice.

Some migrants, it seems, wandered incessantly. George Quartermain who was born in Marlborough, Oxfordshire had married Anne from Thame in the same county and, by 1881 (aged 42), was a 'watch and clockmaker' living in Baldock. The birthplaces given for their five children in the 1891 CEB provided evidence of the couple's wanderings. It appeared that after they left Oxfordshire: their daughter Minnie (aged 21) had been born in Bournemouth in Hampshire; Thomas (aged 14) and Joseph (aged 13) were both born in St Pancras, Middlesex; William (aged 9) was their one child to be born in Baldock and, before the family reached

Kingston in Surrey, their youngest daughter Dora (aged 6) had been born at Clacton on the Essex coast. Thus the evidence of the census shows that the Quartermains had settled in at least five locations across southern England over a twenty-year period.

One example was found of a PTPS who emigrated to Australia only to return to England. Louis Minchen born in Cirencester, Gloucestershire had moved to Royston by 1881 where (aged 22) he was a 'Master draper' employing two female assistants. A decade later, Louis and his wife Sarah (aged 34), originally from Burbage, Leicestershire were living in Leyton, Essex where he was there employed as a 'cabinet salesman'. The 1891 census revealed two children, Lionel (aged 10) born in Royston and Reginald (aged 8) born in 'Sydney, New South Wales'. This evidence suggests that the Minchens had probably left for Australia in 1882 but had returned sometime after 1883 too impoverished to be able to re-establish a drapery business.

Seemingly there were no particularly popular destinations or any obvious geographical flows of the PTPSs who decided to seek opportunities away from the four towns. For many, like Charles Wilson, the services they offered remained the same; others, like Josiah Parker, became more specialized while some, like Charles Jones and Martin Sanders, changed their occupations totally. From the evidence of Walter Hood and Louis Minchen it seems that the apparent opportunities offered by a new location sometimes failed to materialize.

Conclusion

There are several facets of the observed migratory behaviour among service providers migrating to, and from, the four towns that are contrary to the generally held tenets of migration theory. For instance, these locations certainly cannot be considered as major nineteenth-century commercial or industrial centres and yet they clearly attracted migrants from considerable distances and from agricultural regions. Furthermore, the number of families who moved into, or away from, this corner of Hertfordshire suggests that the migration of families out of their county of birth is not as rare as has been previously suggested. However, the pattern here, as Ravenstein proposed, is one of migrants proceeding in a stepwise fashion, and Ashwell, Baldock, Buntingford and Royston were clearly stepping-stones in that process. Additionally, it is a pattern that includes a number who returned to their geographical origins and others who engaged in migratory meanderings with no clear directional bias; neither of these behaviours being clearly implied in general migration theory.

Using identifiable birth-place data extracted from CEBs clearly shows that the majority of service providers, principal and ancillary, were born outside the three largest towns. By contrast, Ashwell, the smallest centre, had proportions that were much lower from 1851 to 1871 but were approaching the levels of the other three between 1881 and 1891.

Surprisingly, given their modest populations and proximity to London and its suburbs, the pattern of inward migration to these four towns clearly vindicates many of Ravenstein's migration theories. Over the forty-year period, around 20.0 to 35.0 per cent of all PTPSs and ATPSs were 'incoming' migrants from the towns' immediate hinterlands. In all four cases a majority of migrants travelled only short distances from the surrounding small rural villages, but there was some evidence of the triangle bounded by Baldock, Buntingford and Royston being a 'cultural province' whose boundaries sometimes modified the migratory pattern.

Numbers of PTPSs and ATPSs (consistently between 25.0 to 35.0 per cent of the three larger towns' totals) that had migrated to the towns, from the four counties immediately adjacent to Hertfordshire, from London and Middlesex, and from much farther afield in the U.K., suggest that they were clearly viewed as centres offering business and employment opportunities. Compared to the large number of apprentices whose movements and appointments were regulated by trade unions and local authorities, the traders, professionals and semi-skilled workers that migrated to these small towns were able to do so of their own free will. The attraction was such that the evidence gathered here identified a considerable number of migrants who were prepared to leave the London area and other major urban centres of the home-counties, such as Bedford, Cambridge and Chelmsford, to seek the wealth-creating opportunities offered by this cluster of towns. This research adds to the existing large body of literature on migration by clearly demonstrating that it was feasible for very small nineteenth-century towns to offer sufficient inducements to be considered 'attractive' centres of opportunity.

Good transport links were obviously vital in the flow of migrants. Baldock and Royston had the great advantage of being situated on major crossroads astride the Great North Road and Old North Road respectively. To the south of Royston, Buntingford was also situated on an albeit lesser crossroad along the Old North Road. However, while the railways further enhanced this connectivity, it has to be recognized that it was not only people but also goods, services and information that travelled along the improved network of communications.

6

The impact of technological change

This chapter addresses a number of issues relating to the influence of improved communications and technological advances on businesses and their customers during the latter half of the nineteenth century. Firstly, what was the impact of the coming of the railway to north-east Hertfordshire and the subsequent changes to local road transport? Secondly, did improved postal services and the introduction of the electric telegraph aid the conduct of commerce in the region's towns? Thirdly, were the four towns large enough and sufficiently prosperous to warrant investment in new technological advances such as the manufacture of coal-gas? Fourthly, what use did local businesses make of developments in advertising?

Evidence of businesses availing themselves of these nineteenth-century advances to integrate into the developing national market for goods and services was gleaned by examining a number of surviving business records. These include an account book (1855–1869) of Ashwell carpenter Thomas Picking, minutes (1875 onwards) of the Baldock Gas Light & Coke Company directors' meetings, accounts and letter books (1853 onwards) of Simpson's Brewery in Baldock, and ledgers and cashbooks (1870 onwards) of the Farmers' Manure Company in Royston. Other sources utilised include copies of two local newspapers, *The Royston Crow* and the *Herts & Cambs Reporter*, and a relatively rare survival in the form of an 1895 Kelly's Directory of Hertfordshire with its many pages of advertisements still intact.

The following discussion considers first the impact of the railways on the region's passenger coach services and commercial goods carriers. It then looks at the development of postal and telegraphic services exploring how local businesses adopted and exploited these improved means of access to ideas and goods that occurred during the latter half of the nineteenth century. Finally, consideration is given to the different forms of advertising that contributed to these small towns' business activities and also provide some evidence that their shopkeepers were, as Jon Stobart concluded, not 'simply passive conduits for the transfer of goods from producer to consumer, but were active in promoting consumption'.[1]

---

[1] J. Stobart, *Spend, Spend, Spend! A History of Shopping* (Stroud, 2008), p. 86.

Coaches, carriers and the advent of the railways

Long-distance coaches and carriers

Baldock situated on the Great North Road, together with Buntingford and Royston on the Old North Road, have long been strategic centres in the nation's commercial network. Typically, for example, Baldock has been described as a place of 'considerable thoroughfare to the north of England' where its inns, especially the George, 'afford requisite accommodation to the posting or commercial traveller'.[2] This section explores the effects on such travel by the coming of the railways in the second half of the nineteenth century.

By the end of the eighteenth century the efficiency of transporting commercial goods by road had improved considerably leading to the gradual disappearance of the packhorse. According to Dorian Gerhold the key factors were 'better waggon horses, needing less provender and having greater strength' and the introduction of the 'flying waggon' which 'provided greater than packhorse speed at waggon cost'.[3] Additionally, improved road surfaces and the effects of turnpikes, meant that waggons could travel by night all year round thus further improving efficiency and cutting costs.

In contrast to earlier Hackney coaches, the stage-coaches which appeared during the mid-seventeenth century had regular schedules along fixed routes, changed horses *en route*, achieved reasonably high speeds, and carried passengers prepared to share their journeys with strangers.[4] Theo Barker and Dorian Gerhold described the final quarter of the eighteenth century as a time in which there was 'a huge increase in the number of coaches, accompanied by drastic reductions in journey times', a development that 'closely followed the peak period for setting up turnpike trusts' and improvements in road surfaces.[5] Vehicle refinements led to the even faster mail coaches that travelled with armed guards and paid no turnpike tolls. They had increased capacities of 'six insiders and up to twelve outsiders (the maximum allowed by law)'.[6]

The Old North Road and the Great North Road were two major trading and coaching routes from London that traversed Hertfordshire and headed northwards

---

[2] *Pigot's Commercial Directory & Topography of Hertfordshire, 1833–34* (London, 1834), p. 726.

[3] D. Gerhold, *Carriers and Coachmasters: Trade and Travel Before the Turnpikes* (Chichester, 2005), pp. 70, 73.

[4] Gerhold, *Carriers and Coachmasters*, pp. 80–83.

[5] T. Barker and D. Gerhold, *The Rise and Rise of Road Transport, 1700–1990* (Cambridge, 1995), pp. 36, 39.

[6] Barker and Gerhold, *Rise of Road Transport*, p. 38.

through eastern England and on to Scotland. Baldock on the Great North Road, 37 miles from London, was an important stopping point for travellers. Barker and Gerhold describe how from its beginnings coaching was 'operated by partnerships of innkeepers' that came to dominate the business by the end of the eighteenth century. They characterized it as an easily pursued sideline 'directly relevant to the innkeepers' business of providing food and accommodation'.[7]

Plate 6.1: [Old] *White Horse Inn*, Great North Road, Baldock

Pigot's 1823/24 directory listed details of ten different coach services (including two carrying mail) that passed to and from London, apparently on a daily basis. Four of these services stopped at Mrs Mary Reynold's *White Horse Inn* (Plate 6.1 above), three at Thomas Parrington's *George Inn*, and three more at James

---

[7] Barker and Gerhold, *Rise of Road Transport*, p. 40.

Norris's *Rose and Crown*.[8]   The coaches were identified as the Boston Perseverance, Glasgow Mail, Leeds Rockingham, Leeds Union, Lincoln Express, Lincoln Mail, Oundle Coach, Stamford Coach, York Express and York Highflyer. A decade later, for whatever reason, coach details were minimal in Pigot's 1833/34 directory. It simply stated that coaches, to and from London, 'pass through Baldock every hour'.[9] There were still ten coach services operating in 1839 but apart from the Boston Perseverance, which was still stopping at the *George Commercial Inn* run by Edward Smith, Pigot provided no evidence regarding the other servicing hostelries. The only daily services listed were those of the Glasgow Royal Mail and the Lincoln & Hull Royal Mail which now stopped at the Post Office run by its Post Master, William Stocken.   Other coaches ran less frequently, for example, the Regent from Stamford left for London every Tuesday, Thursday and Saturday and returned through Baldock every Monday, Wednesday and Friday.[10]

Plate 6.2: *Bell Inn*, Old North Road, Buntingford

---

[8] *Pigot's Commercial Directory for 1823–24* (London, 1824), p. 350.
[9] *Pigot's Commercial Directory, 1833–34*, p. 727.
[10] *Pigot's Royal National and Commercial Directory and Topography of the Counties of Essex, Hertfordshire, Middlesex* (London, 1839), pp. 95 - 96.

Royston on the Old North Road had similar traffic passing through the town. As Pigot's 1826/27 directory noted, coaches left to 'London, through Royston and back, eight times a day, and to Cambridge five times a day'.[11] Unlike the sketchy details provided in the case of Baldock, the 1833/34 directory entry for Royston gave a mass of evidence regarding the nine coach services that passed through, including details of the routes taken either for the north of England via Huntingdon and Stilton or southbound along the valley of the River Lea to London (see Map 6.1 below).[12] Final destinations served by these coaches operating to and from London were Cambridge, Peterborough, Wisbech, King's Lynn, Boston, Louth (mail coach), York, Newcastle and Edinburgh (mail coach). Under Buntingford, the 1833/34 directory simply noted that coaches 'To and from LONDON, and Towns on the line of road to Cambridgeshire, pass through Buntingford daily'.[13] Pigot's 1839 directory indicated that at Buntingford all coaches 'call at the *Bell Inn* (Plate 6.2 above), except the Cambridge

Plate 6.3: [Old] *Bull* 'Posting' *Inn*, High Street, Royston

---

[11] *Pigot's Commercial Directory for 1826–27, Hertfordshire* (London, 1827) p. 577.

[12] *Pigot's Commercial Directory, 1833–34*, p. 754.

[13] *Pigot's Commercial Directory, 1833–34*, p. 731.

Star, which calls at the *George*'.[14] Traffic between London and Cambridge via Royston (and Buntingford) was frequent with three services daily in both directions, Sundays excluded. The Star and the Telegraph coaches used Thomas Taylor's *Red Lion* 'Posting' Inn while the Rocket used Mary Luck's *Bull* 'Posting' Inn (Plate 6.3 above). In addition the Bee Hive coach left the *Bull Inn* on Mondays, Wednesdays and Fridays for London and returned via the *Bull Inn* to Cambridge on Tuesdays, Thursdays and Saturdays.[15]

The evidence demonstrates a considerable volume of coaching traffic passing through Baldock, Buntingford and Royston that must have created substantial and regular business for many innkeepers, blacksmiths, saddlers and wheelwrights in these towns. These good road communications which existed long before the railways were critical, as Peter Clark's recent study of Loughborough showed, to a small town's 'commercial and industrial growth'. Loughborough had similarly been a 'busy coaching station on the road between London and Manchester' with fourteen services in each direction per week in 1791.[16] Directory evidence regarding coach services not only varied from edition to edition but varied between the three towns listed within a single edition. That no services passed through Ashwell was to be expected given that this small town was not located on a major thoroughfare. Assuming that the fuller listings are complete, it is noticeable that all coach services, irrespective of their origin or destination, travelled to and from London (Map 6.1 below). Several routes that passed through Royston served towns beyond Cambridge in East Anglia and Lincolnshire. Different coach services from London passed through either Baldock or Royston en route to Stamford, Boston and York. Other services through Baldock operated as far as Lincoln, Hull, Leeds and Glasgow while others through Royston reached Newcastle and Edinburgh. Barker and Gerhold argued that most services were London-based as 'coaches could only survive on the busiest routes'.[17] Thus it would appear that the apparent lack of coaches travelling from Bedford in the west to Baldock on to Royston and then eastwards to Newmarket and beyond implies a lack of east-west business. Another notable absence is that of any service to Oxford or beyond into south-west England. These two observations illustrate that at this time the dominant direction of trade through this part of Hertfordshire was north-south along the two major roads in and out of London.

---

[14] *Pigot's Commercial Directory, Essex, Hertfordshire, Middlesex* (1839), p. 101.

[15] *Pigot's Directory for 1839, Cambridgeshire* (London, 1839), pp. 67–68.

[16] P. Clark, 'Elite Networking and the Formation of an Industrial Small Town: Loughborough, 1700-1840', in J. Stobart and N. Raven (eds), *Towns, Regions and Industries: Urban and Industrial Change in the Midlands, c. 1700-1840* (Manchester, 2005), p. 168.

[17] Barker and Gerhold, *Rise of Road Transport*, p. 35.

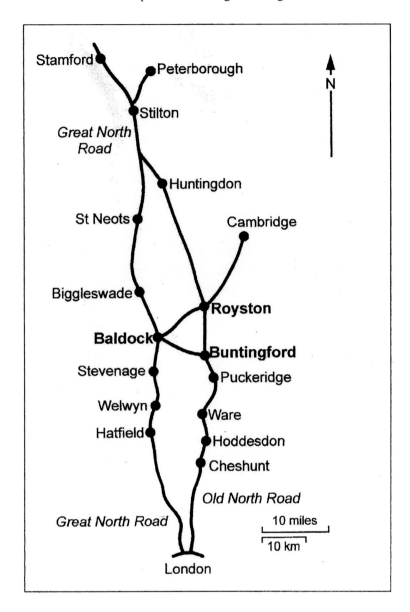

Map 6.1: Routes from London through Hertfordshire to the north of England
Source: Phillip Judge

By the time of the 1851 Post Office Directory there was a total absence of any reference to coaching services in the three larger towns. In that same year the railway had arrived in Baldock and Royston. This dramatic demise of coach services coinciding with the arrival of the railway is in line with the observation that, by 1832, of twenty-six coaches originally running between Liverpool and

Manchester 'only one coach was left and that carried mainly parcels'.[18] Although by the early nineteenth century the Post Office had introduced a network of fast mail coaches working to a fixed timetable, its inflexibility discouraged much of the passenger traffic. As Daunton commented, 'mail coaches ceased to be the most favoured form of transport' and the system 'was encountering problems even before the arrival of railways which were to sound its death-knell'.[19] As a consequence, the last London-based mail-coach service finally stopped in 1846.[20]

Before the coming of the railways to north-east Hertfordshire there is evidence, from trade directories, of some provision for long-distance road haulage, especially to and from London. Though slow, these road services were, according to Barker and Savage, 'regular, numerous and systematic', and along the main trunk routes their waggons 'left at advertised times, delivering and collecting at specified inns on the way'.[21] From the available directory evidence these long-distance carrier services appear to have peaked around the end of the 1830s. For example, from Baldock in 1839, 'Jackson & Co's *waggons*, from the *George*, daily' provided carrier services to Leeds and London, John Little's carriers went to London four days a week, while George Petty's and Woodward's went once a week. Woodward also served St Neots in Huntingdonshire, going 'from the *Chequers*, every Sunday – and another Waggon, every Thursday'. Only one local service was listed, that of William Manning who departed 'from the *George*, every Tuesday & Friday' to Hitchin.[22] Inns like the *George* and the *Chequers*, Barker and Savage suggested, had an important trading function since merchants 'could buy and sell [and store] their wares there and display their samples'.[23]

In 1839, John Biscoe, a Buntingford baker and flour dealer, ran a waggon 'from his house' to London on Tuesdays and Fridays. All Buntingford's other long-distance carrier services, according to Pigot, were provided by Deacon & Co., that is Deacon, Harrison & Co., described by Gerhold as a 'great northern firm' based in Leeds. Their waggons served London and York on a daily basis while their vans served Norwich, Bury St Edmunds and Ely less frequently. According to Pigot, all Deacon's vans and waggons called at their agent Thomas Nicholls, a tailor and draper in Buntingford.[24] Like so many carriers of the period, Deacon's

---

[18] Barker and Gerhold, *Rise of Road Transport*, p. 44.

[19] M.J. Daunton, *Royal Mail: The Post Office Since 1840* (London, 1985), p. 121.

[20] Key Dates, The British Postal Museum & Archive, www.postalheritage.org.uk/history (26 May 2008, accessed 26 May 2008).

[21] T.C. Barker and C.I. Savage, *An Economic History of Transport in Britain* (3rd edn, London, 1974), p. 45.

[22] *Pigot's Commercial Directory, Essex, Hertfordshire, Middlesex* (1839), p. 96.

[23] Barker and Savage, *Economic History of Transport*, p.45.

[24] *Pigot's Commercial Directory, Essex, Hertfordshire, Middlesex* (1839), p. 101; D. Gerhold, 'The Growth of the London Carrying Trade, 1681–1838', *Economic History Review*, 41, 3 (1988), p. 407.

would probably have been a large operation 'which benefited from economies of scale' and regularly passed through Buntingford and Royston because of those towns' situation on the Old North Road.[25] Indeed that point is made by Pigot's observation regarding a carrier service from Royston to Wakefield in Yorkshire that 'a waggon [un-named] passes thro' Royston daily'.[26]

In addition to Royston's daily services to and from London provided by 'Deacon & Co.'s Fly Vans and Waggons' (from the *Chequers*) and Day and Clement's Waggons (from the *Catherine Wheel*), there were five other carriers that only operated on Tuesdays. In contrast to all the carriers operating through or from Baldock and Buntingford, four of these Tuesday London services originated from nearby Cambridgeshire villages, two each from Bassingbourn (Docwra's and Elbourn's) and Melbourn (Bullen's and Gilly's). Royston also had services to Cambridge (four different carriers) while Day and Clement's waggons went daily to St Ives, and to Wisbeach on Thursdays and Sundays.[27]

The aforementioned long-distance carrier services were to be dramatically challenged by the arrival of the greatest revolution in nineteenth-century transport, the steam railway. Many, as Alan Everitt demonstrated in his study of Victorian Leicestershire, were 'killed off with remarkable celerity by the railways'.[28]

Advent of the railways

A revolution in travel was witnessed during the nineteenth century with the expansion of the railway from a mere novelty in 1830 to a widely accepted form of transport by 1880. Its success, according to Barker and Gerhold, was its 'overwhelming cost advantage, as well as speed advantage, when competing directly on stage coach or hauliers' routes for passengers and higher value freight'.[29] The first line to pass through Hertfordshire, in 1838, was the London & Birmingham Railway traversing the west of the county.[30] Then in 1845 a Bill was put before Parliament proposing a line from Oxford to Cambridge but according to Phil Howard, Parliament only approved the 13 mile section of double track

---

[25] Barker and Gerhold, *Rise of Road Transport*, p. 26.

[26] *Pigot's Directory, 1839, Cambridgeshire*, p. 68.

[27] *Pigot's Directory, 1839, Cambridgeshire*, p. 68. A waggon was an open, four-wheeled, horse-drawn vehicle used for carrying heavy or bulky loads. A van was a covered waggon. A fly was a lightweight, covered carriage drawn by one horse.

[28] A. Everitt, 'Town and Country in Victorian Leicestershire: The Role of the Village Carrier', in A. Everitt (ed.), *Perspectives in English Urban History* (London, 1973), p. 217.

[29] Barker and Gerhold, *Rise of Road Transport*, p. 44.

[30] F.G. Cockman, *The Railways of Hertfordshire, Hertfordshire Local Studies, No. 1* (Hertford, 1978), p. 1.

from Hitchin to Royston and the Bill for the Royston and Hitchin Railway (R&HR) received the Royal assent on 16 July 1846.[31] The Great Northern Railway (GNR) from London to Peterborough, passing north through Hitchin, obtained authority to lease the R&HR from 1 August 1850. After an application to extend the railway to Cambridge was refused, they were granted permission to build the line as far as Shepreth. The line was opened in full from Hitchin to Shepreth, via Letchworth, Baldock, Ashwell and Royston, in August 1851 and the GNR arranged to 'connect with Cambridge by using horse-drawn omnibuses'.[32]

These developments were typical of the piecemeal development of the industry and stemmed from the very competitive nature of the private capital that built the railway network, and which frequently had to overcome the lengthy objections of land owners, canal companies and turnpike trusts. Cockman identified a further sixty plans between 1834 and 1902 for railway lines that, if approved, would have been wholly or partly in Hertfordshire but in the end were never built.[33]

In 1852 the Eastern Counties Railway (ECR), already running from London to Cambridge, opened a single line south linking Cambridge to Shepreth which it leased to the GNR to work the line to Hitchin. Later, the GNR reached a compromise with the Great Eastern Railway (which had acquired the ECR 1862) to double the line from Cambridge to Shepreth and allow the GNR finally, from 31 March 1866, to run its own trains directly from King's Cross to Cambridge.[34] This development was very important to the regional economy as it gave Baldock, Ashwell and Royston access to the wider rail network (Figure 6.1 below) and distant manufacturing centres.

From Cambridge the rail network connected the three centres to the ports of King's Lynn to the north and Ipswich to the east and also, beyond Norwich, to the fish markets of Great Yarmouth and Lowestoft. Furthermore, the line westward from Cambridge directly to Huntingdon and the line to Peterborough via Ely and March provided access into the industrial centres of the Midlands. Using their rail link to either Cambridge or Hitchin provided the three centres with access to routes southwards into London.

As its name implies, the Ashwell & Morden Station also serviced the two villages of Guilden Morden and Steeple Morden just over the border in Cambridgeshire. Kelly's directory of 1890 noted that Ashwell's station was '2^{1}/2 miles south-east

---

[31] P. Howard, *Take the Train from Hitchin: A Journey into our Local Railway Heritage* (Hitchin, 2006), p. 57.

[32] Howard, *Train from Hitchin*, p. 58.

[33] Cockman, *Railways of Hertfordshire*, p. v.

[34] Howard, *Train from Hitchin*, p. 58.

from the village', a considerable distance from all three locations.[35] This was because a line out of the Vale of Baldock directly into Ashwell would have required two deep cuttings or even tunnels to negotiate two 90 metre chalk hills lying between Ashwell and Baldock. Howard describes how 'in its heyday, Royston had an extensive goods yard which included eight private sidings.' Large amounts of barley 'were dispatched to Scotland for processing in the whisky industry'. He also noted that 'other freight handled included racehorses from local racing stables, pigs and fertiliser.'[36] Further proof of the region's commercial links with whisky and benefits of long distance travel, almost certainly by rail, is provided by the 1896 marriage of Bella Gilchrist to David Graham, a distiller from the Isle of Jura, in the village of Wallington (between Baldock and Royston).[37]

A Bill to construct a new route between Ware and Cambridge, passing through Buntingford and Royston, failed in 1856. However, Buntingford became the northern terminus of the Ware Hadham & Buntingford Railway in 1863. This branch line which ran from St Margarets, just south of Ware, was an offshoot from the Great Eastern's line from London to Hertford. Here, according to Cockman, 'goods sheds and sidings were installed in 1864'; later additions were coal storage bays, cattle pens and stables.[38] The railway from Buntingford to Ware (Figure 6.1 below) provided important commercial access to the extensive maltings of Ware and onward routes to London either by train or by barges along the River Lea.

In 1839, George Bradshaw first published his national guide to railway timetables. Two years later it became the monthly guide, thereafter eponymous with the name of its publisher, which by the 1890s ran to several hundred pages. Consequently, unlike the often detailed evidence of arrival/departure times, pick-up points, routes and destinations of coach services that the earlier trade directories included, the later ones were very cursory in their approach to the railways. For example, in 1851 the Post Office directory simply described Royston as 'a market, railway, County Court, and Union town'. Eleven years later it observed that the town was '44¾ miles from London by railway' and in 1882 that Thomas Middleton was station master at the 'station on a branch of the

---

[35] *Kelly's Directory of the Six Home Counties, Part 1: Essex, Herts & Middlesex* (London, 1890), p. 699.

[36] Howard, *Train from Hitchin*, p. 62.

[37] Wallington Parish Marriage Register, 1837–1975, HALS, D/P115/1/5.

[38] N. Catford, 'Disused Stations Site Record: Buntingford', www.subbrit.org.uk/sb-sites/stations/b/ (13 February 2005, accessed 22 March 2008); Cockman, *The Railways of Hertfordshire*, p. 4.

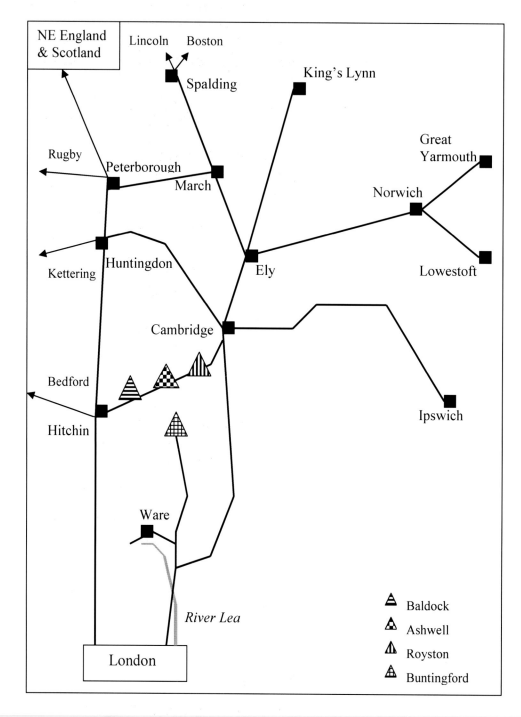

Figure 6.1: North-east Hertfordshire's C19th rail links

Great Northern railway from Hitchin to Cambridge'.[39]   Similarly, in 1882 John Cunningham was listed as the station master at Baldock 'on the Hitchin and Cambridge branch of the Great Northern railway, which places it within one hour of London'.[40] Interestingly in the case of Buntingford, before it was connected to the rail network, the Post Office directory of 1851 described it as 'on the Great North road, 31 miles from London by road, and 34¼ by the Ware Railway. It then detailed a coach service between Royston and Ware station that called daily at the Bull Inn.[41] However, after the arrival of the railway in Buntingford, Kelly's 1882 directory baldly stated that 'here is the terminal station of the Ware & Buntingford branch of the Great Eastern Railway, a single line of about 13 miles' and that William Hancock was station master.[42]   Thus, as far as north-east Hertfordshire was concerned, the directories clearly excluded any detailed evidence regarding railway timetables. One can speculate that, in addition to the specialist coverage of Bradshaw, this obvious omission was probably due to the large amount of space that such timetables would have needed, making their inclusion uneconomic from the publisher's perspective. However, this problem did not deter newspapers like *The Royston Crow* from providing timetables of local rail services.

Detailed railway timetables, for passenger services only, were published regularly in *The Royston Crow* newspaper. That of February 1855 listed four trains running each weekday between Hitchin Junction and Cambridge with only two on Sundays.   There was an additional afternoon service between Royston and Cambridge on Wednesdays, and an extra service on Saturday mornings from Baldock to Cambridge.[43] That the extra Wednesday service was to specifically benefit the local traders and their customers can be seen from the additional panel inserted by the '*Crow*'s' publisher in a railway timetable of 1860. Headed 'ROYSTON MARKET', the panel informed travellers that a train, calling at all intermediate stations, left Cambridge for Royston on Wednesday morning and that it returned to Cambridge late the same afternoon.[44]

In addition to their two obvious roles of carrying passengers and goods, the railways played a fundamental part in improving communication across Britain

---

[39] *Post Office Directory of the Six Home Counties: Essex, Herts, Middlesex, Kent, Surrey & Sussex, 1851* (London, 1851), p. 215; *Post Office Directory of the Six Home Counties: Essex, Herts, Middlesex, Kent, Surrey & Sussex,1862 (London, 1862)*, p. 376; *Kelly's Directory of the Six Home Counties, Part 1: Essex, Herts & Middlesex* (London, 1882), p. 648.

[40] *Kelly's Directory Six Home Counties, Pt 1 (1882)*, pp. 562–63.

[41] *Post Office Directory Six Home Counties, 1851*, pp. 183, 185.

[42] *Kelly's Directory Six Home Counties, Pt 1 (1882)*, pp. 585–86.

[43] *The Royston Crow*, 1 February 1855, p. 14.

[44] *The Royston Crow*, 1 February 1860, p. 274.

by carrying the nation's mail together with London and regional newspapers. Originally, newspapers incurred a stamp duty of a penny a sheet to allow free transmission through the post but, following the introduction of a book post in 1848, this duty was abolished in 1855. By 1860, in addition to 564 million letters, the Postmaster General was able to report a figure of almost 83 million books and newspapers handled by the Post Office.[45] Twenty years later the figure for newspapers alone had risen to over 134 million copies. However, Martin Daunton argued that increased postal business generally was due far more to the 'growth in population and the economy' than 'relatively minor adjustments' in tariffs after 1840.[46] Hence the typical advertisement in the *Royston Crow* of April 1858, by John Warren, for ' "THE TIMES" and other LONDON DAILY PAPERS' to be delivered by the earliest train from London to Royston and other neighbouring stations. This 'General Newspaper Agent' also regularly guaranteed that 'ADVERTISEMENTS for any of the PAPERS [would be] carefully attended to', an offer of which many local brewers and maltsters probably took advantage.[47]

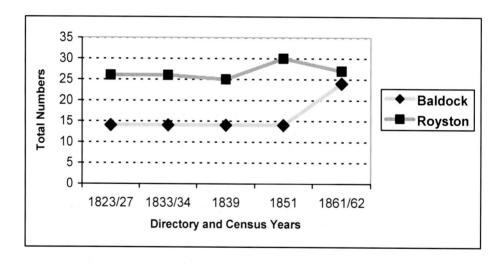

Figure 6.2: Total number of hostelries between 1823 and 1862 [48]
Source: Trade directories and CEBs

It would be reasonable to assume that the eclipse of coaching services by the railways might have reduced trade for the towns' hostelries but there is very little

---

[45] Daunton, *Royal Mail*, pp. 10, 55, 80.

[46] Daunton, *Royal Mail*, p. 79.

[47] *The Royston Crow*, 1 April 1858, p. 184.

[48] The term hostelries includes commercial inns, hotels, other inns, public houses, taverns and other named establishments plus individual PTPSs identified as 'publican' or 'victualler'.

evidence to support that view (Figure 6.2 above). In Baldock, the total number of inns and other licensed premises remained unchanged from 1823 until 1861/62 when it rose significantly. In Royston, the numbers were consistently between twenty-five and thirty across the whole forty-year period. This suggests that many hostelries were patronized by far more than just coach travellers and passing long-distance carriers. In addition to the towns' local business communities and general populace, it would have been the growth of railway traffic and short-haul carriers that rapidly helped rebuild the licensed victuallers' trade.

According to Gerhold, the share of goods (by volume) transported by road declined in the late eighteenth and early nineteenth centuries, 'reflecting a widening choice of mode of transport', and carrier companies like Pickford's and Deacon Harrison became heavily involved in canal transport.[49] Later, the coming of the railways had a further dramatic effect on the above commercial waggon services. According to the Post Office Directories, services between Baldock, London and the north of England had ceased to operate by 1862, as had those to Royston and Cambridge. All that remained between 1862 and 1890 was a daily service (Sundays excepted) to Hitchin that returned the same evening.[50] By 1862, the year before the arrival of the Ware to Buntingford line, only Levi Coxall, carrier and publican at the Angel, still operated a limited service to London which left Buntingford on Thursday afternoon and did not return until Saturday. At this time, Joseph Clayton, a local coal dealer, offered carrier services to Hitchin on Tuesdays, Royston on Wednesdays (market day), and on Thursdays and Saturdays to 'Hertford, calling at the Railway station, Ware'. Although not identifying the operator, the 1870 directory advised travellers of 'a fly to meet every train except the last'. In 1890 Webb's carrier service to London 'passes through Thurs & returns Sat' while the only local service listed was that passing through to Royston offered by Deville on Wednesdays and Saturdays.[51] By 1851 Royston's carrier services to London had been halved and none of the remaining three (Elbourne, Gilby and King) maintained a daily service, each passing through only once or twice weekly. Twenty years later only Joseph Day from the ' "*White Horse*" tuesday' and William Bullen from the ' "*Falcon*" thursday' were carrying goods to London. Both went 'to the "*Catherine Wheel*", Bishopsgate street' returning on Thursday and Saturday respectively. In 1890, only the

[49] Gerhold, 'London Carrying Trade', p. 408.

[50] *Post Office Directory Six Home Counties, 1862*, p. 321; *Post Office Directory of the Six Home Counties, Part 1:Essex, Herts, Middlesex, Kent* (London, 1870), p. 411; *Kelly's Directory Six Home Counties, Pt 1 (1882)*, p. 563; *Kelly's Directory Six Home Counties, Pt 1* (1890), p. 703.

[51] *Post Office Directory Six Home Counties, 1862*, p. 335; *Post Office Directory Six Home Counties,Pt 1 (1870)*, p. 429; *Kelly's Directory Six Home Counties, Pt 1* (1890), p. 732.

Thursday/Saturday London service survived, operated by the carrier Wedd of Melbourn.[52]

Everitt argued that, while long-distance carriers suffered, 'local traffic on the roads was certainly not brought to an end by the railways' for the simple reason that 'most rural communities had no railway station'.[53] Thus, he suggested, numbers of local carriers rapidly proliferated because of the need to connect 'outlying villages and the new railhead' by road links that 'considerably extended the market area of the town'.[54]

Short-haul carrier services

Evidence supporting Everitt's view of the changing pattern of carrier traffic after the arrival of the railways is clearly provided by the case of Royston where, in great contrast to the reduction in carrier services passing to and from London, services to and from surrounding local and regional centres increased substantially over the second half of the nineteenth century (Figure 6.3 below). A clear example of Gerhold's argument that road transport 'increasingly specialized in what it was best at, including the most urgent and highest value traffic and shorter hauls'.[55] Rather inexplicably, only two of the carriers listed in directories between 1851 and 1890 could be identified in Royston's CEBs over the same period. These were widowed Sarah Godfrey who operated a three times a week service to Cambridge in 1851, and James Stamford (cab proprietor and agent for the Great Northern Railway) who in 1890 provided daily services from Kneesworth Street to Barkway and Reed, Chishall and Heydon, and Therfield. All other carriers would appear to have been based out of the town and the business of their Royston-listed services conducted as they passed through *en-route* to their other destinations.[56]

Barker and Savage considered the doubling of Britain's population from 18.5 million in 1841 to 37 million in 1901 as responsible for the greatly swelled number of road users and the amount of freight carried short distances, especially to and from railway stations. This, they argued, led to there being 'more horses pulling many more vehicles on Britain's roads in the heyday of the railway than

---

[52] *Post Office Directory Six Home Counties, 1851*, p. 217; *Post Office Directory Six Home Counties, Pt 1 (1870)*, p. 478; *Kelly's Directory Six Home Counties, Pt 1* (1890), p. 808.
[53] Everitt, 'Village Carrier', p. 217.
[54] Everitt, 'Village Carrier', p. 218.
[55] Gerhold, 'London Carrying Trade', p. 408.
[56] *Post Office Directory Six Home Counties, 1851*, p. 217; 1851 Census (Royston); *Kelly's Directory Six Home Counties, Pt 1* (1890), p. 808-09; 1890 Census (Royston).

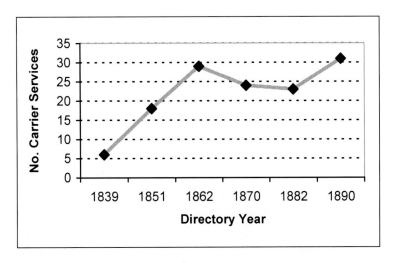

Figure 6.3: Carrier services between Royston and its hinterland
Source: Pigot's, Post Office and Kelly's trade directories

there had ever been in the heyday of the stage coach'.[57] Carriers operating through Royston in 1890 served Ashwell, Buntingford, Cambridge and an additional thirty-five villages, two-thirds of which lay within approximately ten miles of Royston. Its regional coverage was much in line with Everitt's observation that the Midland market towns of Lutterworth, Hinkley, Market Harborough and Loughborough all served between thirty and thirty-eight surrounding villages.[58] Centres served by the Royston carriers (Figure 6.4 below) were predominantly to the north of the town in Cambridgeshire and to the south-east in Hertfordshire and just over the county border into Essex. In total there were thirty-nine different services, listed in the 1890 directory, provided by thirty-one carriers. Rather surprisingly, over three-quarters of these appeared to link Royston to only a single village. The closer the village to Royston the more likely it was to be served by several different carriers operating on different days of the week; Morden, Chishall and Heydon were each served by four carriers while Barkway and Reed were each served by three.

Only the two services covering the longest distances stopped at several locations en-route. Deville's from the *Angel* on Wednesdays and Saturdays travelled along the Old North Road to call at Buckland, Buntingford, Aspe[n]den, Westmill, Braughing, Puckeridge and, finally, Sandon (distance 12 miles). Flack's from the

[57] Barker and Savage, *Economic History of Transport*, p. 124.
[58] Everitt, 'Village Carrier', p. 217.

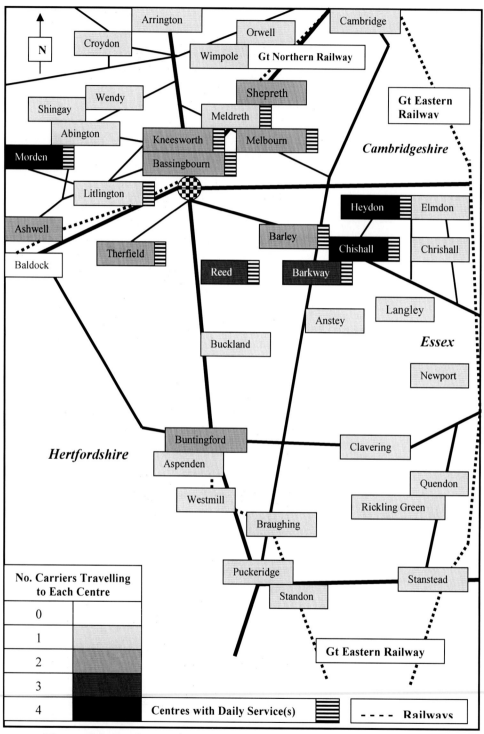

Figure 6.4: Carrier services travelling to and/or from Royston, 1890
Source: Kelly's Directory Six Home Counties, Pt 1 (1890)

White Lion on Wednesdays and Fridays travelled south-eastwards into Essex via Langley, Newport, Clavering, Quendon and Rickling Green to Stansted (distance 17.6 miles). In a dozen villages closely clustered around Royston the carriers had sufficient business to warrant the provision of a daily service. In contrast to James Bowen's recent findings that Lancaster's carriers most frequently operated on Saturdays, the day with the greatest number of carrier services via Royston was Wednesday (n = 23) followed by Saturday (n = 7); Royston held its weekly corn and cattle markets on Wednesdays.[59] This volume of business, much of it probably to and from Royston's railway station, clearly fits with Barker and Savage's argument. It also echoes Everitt's suggestion that the railway actually helped increase the prosperity of carriers because they either conveyed villagers to their local town's market or became 'shopping "agents", purchasing goods [in the town] ordered by villagers' unable or not wishing to travel.[60] Furthermore, the carrier was able to supply the town's shops with locally grown farm produce. This, argued Bowen, contributed to 'the sense of community within the carrying trade and the wider community' whilst the exchanges at inns, railway stations and markets acted as 'foci for the local population, combining business and pleasure in a distinctly informal environment'.[61] Long-distance travel was undoubtedly greatly facilitated by 'aqueducts, tunnels, viaducts, terminal stations and locomotives' but, as Barrie Trinder recently observed, 'carriers provided the unspectacular capillaries of this distribution network'.[62]

Apart from Therfield, there were no other centres lying to the south-west of Royston that were served by the above carriers. This finding is hardly surprising since Baldock with its own railway station might be expected to have a similar number of carriers operating from, or through, the town to serve the villages of its immediate hinterland. Yet, strangely, at least according to the trade directories, Baldock had very few local carrier services throughout the second half of the nineteenth century. Between 1862 and 1882, William Brown's waggon left daily (except on Sunday and Thursday) 'from his own house' for Hitchin and returned to Baldock the same evening. Additionally, in 1882, Baldock shoemaker Frederick Walman's service operated daily to nearby Clothall and Wallington. By 1890, the only Baldock-based carrier services listed were those travelling to Hitchin: George Cox on Tuesdays and Saturdays; William Hankin on Tuesdays, Wednesdays, Fridays and Saturdays. One other listed service to Hitchin was that

---

[59] J.P. Bowen, 'The Carriers of Lancaster 1824 -1912', *Local Historian*, 40, 3 (2010), p. 181.

[60] Everitt, 'Village Carrier', p. 218.

[61] Bowen, 'Carriers of Lancaster', p. 187.

[62] B. Trinder, 'Country Carriers Revisited', *Local Historian*, 42, 2 (2012), p. 145.

of Chapman and Haggar from Sandon who passed through on Tuesdays.[63] It is beyond the scope of the present evidence to ascertain whether, because Hitchin was a large railway junction, carriers serving this part of Hertfordshire operated their services from there, or that the apparent lack of carriers in Baldock was a major omission on the part of the directory publisher.

According to Barker and Gerhold the omnibus, originally developed in Paris and introduced to London in 1829, made its appearance in other towns from the 1830s onwards.[64] The only detailed reference to omnibus services identified in the present data was in the Post Office Directory of 1851 under Royston. It indicated that omnibuses operated by Stamford, and by Ginn & Co., provided a return service to Cambridge three days a week from the *White Horse* and *Catherine Wheel* respectively. The same two companies operated similar services to Baldock and Hitchin twice a week.[65] There was no mention of the above services under Baldock but its 1851 directory entry did note that Clutten's 'van or omnibus' went from the *Plume of Feathers* to Hitchin every Tuesday and Friday.[66] Thereafter there was no further mention of omnibus services under either Baldock or Royston.

By 1851 evidence provided by trade directories clearly suggests that the development of a national railway network had largely abrogated the need for long distance coach and carrier services, including those carrying the mail. As we have seen previously, increased spread and capacity of rail freight and passenger services across the second half of the nineteenth century encouraged inward migration to the towns and integrated the businesses of the regional economy into wider markets than hitherto. By speedily transporting Rowland Hill's new mail service and distributing newspapers to and from the four towns, railways dramatically increased their inhabitants' communications with the wider world.

---

[63] *Post Office Directory Six Home Counties, 1862*, p. 321; 1861 Census (Baldock); *Post Office Directory Six Home Counties, Pt 1* (1870), p. 411; 1871 Census (Baldock); *Kelly's Directory Six Home Counties, Pt 1* (1882), p. 563; 1881 Census (Baldock); *Kelly's Directory Six Home Counties, Pt 1* (1890), p. 703; 1891 Census (Baldock).

[64] Barker and Gerhold, *Rise of Road Transport*, p. 46. The early omnibus was a large vehicle drawn by two horses that carried fourteen inside passengers and others on its roof.

[65] *Post Office Directory Six Home Counties, 1851*, p. 217.

[66] *Post Office Directory Six Home Counties, 1851*, p. 173.

Nineteenth-century innovations in correspondence

David Vincent argued that if 'correspondence might be seen as the epitome of civilisation' its extent depended on literacy and 'postal flows'. He suggested that the developing postal and railway services of the nineteenth century were mutually dependent, the former requiring a 'rapid and reliable means of transport' and the latter deriving 'immense benefit from the revenue generated by carrying mail'.[67] This mutuality was crucial for the effect on potential migrants of the diffusion of information, a factor in long-distance migration flows identified by Getis and Boots.[68]

Postal services after 1840

By the early nineteenth century there was growing public dissatisfaction with successive governments using the profits from the increasingly expensive postal service to help repair the state of Britain's finances. As a result, a Committee of Enquiry was set up in 1835 to review the high postage rates that were generally paid by the recipient. Two years later, Rowland Hill proposed a uniform postage rate of 1d which he contended would lead to an increase in correspondence and substantially reduce the number of people attempting to evade existing postal charges. Hill 'argued that distance had little bearing on the cost of conveying a letter' and proposed a specially designed adhesive label to pre-pay the uniform charge. This Uniform Penny Post came into force on 10 January 1840 and the new postage stamps were introduced on 6 May. Such was the popularity of this method that 168 million letters had been posted by the end of 1840. This volume had doubled to 347 million by 1850, clearly vindicating Hill's prediction.[69] According to Daunton, Hill then argued that to encourage the growth of postal traffic a 'systematic national coverage of post offices was necessary to complete his "plan" '.[70]

Among the four towns, Baldock and Royston had Post Offices listed by Holden in 1811 and Buntingford by Pigot in 1833/34 but the first indication of a Post Office in Ashwell was not until the Post Office Directory of 1851.[71] Earlier directories

---

[67] D. Vincent, *Literacy and Popular Culture: England 1750–1914* (Pbk Edition, Cambridge, 1993), pp. 47, 48.
[68] A. Getis and B. Boots, *Models of Spatial Processes: An Approach to the Study of Point, Line and Area Patterns* (Cambridge, 1978).
[69] 'The Penny Post', The Victorian Web: Literature, History, & Culture in the Age of Victoria, www.victorianweb.org/history/pennypos.html (24 October 2006, accessed 1 May 2008).
[70] Daunton, *Royal Mail*, p. 41.
[71] *Holden's Annual London and County Directory of the United Kingdom and Wales in Three Volumes for the Year 1811, Vol. 3* (London, 1811), pp. alphabetically arranged entries.

gave details of coach services and their mail deliveries. For example, in 1839 Pigot indicated that letters from London arrived in Royston just after midnight and were dispatched every morning at 1.30 a.m. Letters from Cambridge arrived and were dispatched at 2.00 a.m. whilst those 'from Huntingdon, Northampton, Grantham, Manchester, York and Edinburgh arrive every morning at a quarter before two, and are dispatched at the same hour'.[72] Postal services were obviously considered vital to business by the publishers of trade directories who, with the demise of coach traffic and the coming of the railways, as we have seen, regularly printed detailed information of collections and deliveries. Kelly's Directory of 1851 informed readers that letters arriving in Baldock [by rail] from London in the early hours, were delivered at 7.30 a.m.; letters for London were dispatched late in the evening.[73] It should be noted that the railways made London a major distribution hub for mail. Daunton describes how each train on arrival [at Baldock for example] was met by a mail cart that transferred the mail bags to the local post office where the contents were sorted 'down to the level of the individual "walk" of a letter-carrier'.[74] In the case of Baldock, the CEBs identified (see chapter 3 above) one 'post boy' in 1851 and two 'letter carriers' in 1861/71, increasing to four in 1881/91.

Growth of postal services was a vital factor in the migration flows described earlier, influencing the comings and goings of PTPSs and ATPSs to and from the four towns by providing a key channel in the feedback process of communication. As David Souden emphasised, most movement occurs where individuals and areas experience 'a series of contacts continually being re-forged': a process that was catalyzed in the nineteenth century by the advent of the Universal Penny Post.[75]

By 1882, during the years when Simpson's letter book was being compiled, Kelly's Directory reflected the substantial growth in postal services even to a small town the size of Baldock. By this time, letters from London arrived three times throughout the day and were dispatched to London five times a day. Furthermore, Baldock was able to receive mail, morning and afternoon, from nine surrounding villages. The means of transport for these local services was not given but it is known that in 1887 the Post Office reintroduced horse-drawn services that operated in conjunction with the transport of mail on the railways.[76]

---

[72] *Pigot's Directory, 1839, Cambridgeshire*, p.66.

[73] *Post Office Directory Six Home Counties, 1851*, p. 173.

[74] Daunton, *Royal Mail*, p. 119.

[75] D. Souden, 'Pre-industrial English Local Migration Fields' (PhD thesis, University of Cambridge, 1981), p. 10.

[76] 'Key Dates', The British Postal Museum & Archive, www.postalheritage.org.uk/history (26 May 2008, accessed 26 May 2008).

Initially all deliveries and dispatches of mail went directly via the local Post Office itself but in 1855 the first street letter boxes were erected in London.[77] Kelly's Directory of 1890 indicated that the 'wall letter boxes' at the top of Baldock High Street and at the Railway Station were cleared three times each weekday. By the latter part of the nineteenth century the range of services available at the towns' Post Offices had expanded considerably. Baldock's 1870 directory description was typical: 'Post & Money Order Office, Post Office Savings Bank [first opened 1861], Government Annuity & Insurance & Telegraph Office'.[78] Thus for the business communities and 'middling sorts' they became the focus of communications and modest financial transactions.

James Watt's development of the steam engine in 1769 was followed in 1802 by Richard Trevithick's high-pressure version that led directly to the development of the steam locomotive. These crucial innovations and the subsequent development of a national rail network were pivotal to the success of Rowland Hill's Uniform Penny Post after 1840. Two other nineteenth-century scientific and technological advances that made a significant impact on communications and business activities, the electric telegraph and telephone, are discussed below.

Electric telegraph and telephone services

Charles Wheatstone developed the universal electric telegraph (the transmission of coded messages along wires by means of electrical signals) for business, domestic and personal use between 1840 and 1868. Much of the early development was carried out in conjunction with the railway companies who used the telegraph as an important part of their track signalling equipment. The Electric Telegraph Company was created in 1845 after its founders had purchased Wheatstone's early patents. It operated a communications network over the entire country. By 1854 the company had 5,070 miles of line, operated 420 telegraph stations, and handled 572,216 messages during that year. Five years later the number of messages sent had increased to over a million.[79] The Post Office was given control of telegraphic services in 1870 and trade directories added 'Telegraphic Office' to a town's listed establishments.[80] All four towns had access to the new telegraphic services through their post offices and the 1870 directory indicated that the Royston 'office is open from 7 a.m. till 9 p.m. for the

---

[77] Daunton, *Royal Mail*, p. 42.

[78] *Post Office Directory Six Home Counties, Pt 1* (1870), p. 411; 'Key Dates', The British Postal Museum & Archive, www.postalheritage.org.uk/history (26 May 2008, accessed 26 May 2008).

[79] S. Roberts, 'A History of the Telegraph Companies in Britain between 1838 and 1868', undated, www.distantwriting.co.uk (© 2008, accessed 1 May 2008).

[80] 'Key Dates', The British Postal Museum & Archive, www.postalheritage.org.uk/history (26 May 2008, accessed 26 May 2008).

sale of stamps & for telegrams on week days, & from 7 a.m. till 10 a.m. on Sundays'.[81] It is reasonable to assume that the towns' larger businesses, for example their breweries, would have wanted to exploit the commercial benefits of the telegraph as soon as it became available in their post offices but there is little direct evidence to support this assumption.

Hard on the heels of the telegraph came the telephone. This next development in communication was invented by Alexander Graham Bell in 1876 and further facilitated by Thomas Edison's development of the carbon transmitter in 1877. Exploitation of their patents in Britain led to the formation, in 1878, of The Telephone Company which after a number of mergers became The National Telephone Company in 1881 that remained in business until eventually taken over by the General Post Office in 1912.[82] Again there is little direct evidence of the four towns' businesses having utilized the convenience of the telephone. This may be, as Graeme Milne believed, a consequence of the early telephone companies initially targeting 'business districts in London and in the commercial and industrial centres of the north of England and the central belt of Scotland'.[83]

Regional businesses in north-east Hertfordshire, as exemplified by Simpson's Brewery, which were heavily reliant on the postal service for the efficient conduct of their affairs would surely have found, despite the lack of much written evidence, that the telegraph and telephone were another two vital adjuncts to their efficiency. The case studies that follow provide evidence of the impact of these nineteenth-century communication developments on local business activities.

Business strategies: Case studies

Four business case studies provide evidence of the extent that nineteenth-century improvements in communications and technological advances influenced businesses in the small towns of north-east Hertfordshire. They also provide an indication of the extent to which local businesses availed themselves of, and even became dependent on, access to the wider national market for their operation. Firstly, a carpenter from the smallest town, Ashwell, exemplifies the traditional craftsmen apparently continuing to operate successfully without any obvious evidence of recourse to developments in communication. Secondly, a major brewery in the larger town of Baldock illustrates its heavy dependence on the use

---

[81] *Post Office Directory Six Home Counties,Pt 1* (1870), p. 477.

[82] Connected Earth, 'How Communication Shapes the World', www.connected-earth.com/galleries (Undated, © BT and museum partners, accessed 21 May 2008).

[83] G.J. Milne, 'British Business and the Telephone, 1878 – 1911', *Business History*, 49, 2 (2007), p. 165.

of the reliable postal service and national railway network for conducting its business. Thirdly, the Baldock Gas Company, which utilized the railway to bring in its coal supplies, provides an example of local entrepreneurs exploiting scientific and technological advances to improve the environment and domestic comfort of the town's citizens. Fourthly, a large-scale supplier of fertilizers from its base in Royston provides evidence of integration into national and international markets for its raw materials.

Thomas Picking, carpenter, Ashwell

It is to be expected that some skilled craftsmen, like Thomas Picking of Ashwell, would be able to pursue their specialist business activities within the local environs of their town, untroubled by the nineteenth-century's changing transport services. Thomas was variously described as a carpenter and joiner (1839), builder and carpenter (1851) and plain carpenter employing between three and four other men (1861).[84] Although his accounts for the period 1855 to 1869 have survived they contain no indication of where he might have acquired his timber.[85] However, it is not unreasonable to assume that for the most part it would have been purchased locally, perhaps through the frequent sales advertised by Cockett and Nash, auctioneers of Baldock Street, Royston. For example, according to *The Royston Crow*, they were to auction '1100 straight & clean Larch POLES' at Thriplow Place and '1000 fine Scotch and other Fir POLES' at Chrishall Grange, both locations to the south of Cambridge, on 6 and 18 December 1858 respectively.[86] A list of 'bills submitted' during 1861 mentions twenty-nine individuals of whom only one, 'Mr Smyth of Bygrave', appears not to have been a resident of Ashwell; Bygrave was a tiny village just two miles to the south. Seventeen of Picking's customers were among Ashwell's identified PTPSs and included nine farmers. Others, whose occupations were listed in trade directories and CEBs, were 'Peter Bailey Junior' (Master Bricklayer), 'Mr G[eorge] Bonfield' at the *Three Tuns*, 'Mr [Jesse] Burr' (Baker), 'Mr James Flitton' (Insurance Agent for Unity Fire & Life), 'Mr [Nathan] Scott' (Butcher), 'Mr Simons' at the *Bull's Head*, 'Mr Samuel Thorne' (Tailor) and 'Mr [Edward] Tindale' (surgeon).

Apart from charging Mr [Benjamin] Christy, a farmer, £15.13s.7d for 'fencing' during the year, few other details of the actual work carried out appear in the list of bills except in the case of Picking's most important client, Mr E[dward]

---

[84] *Pigot's Commercial Director, Essex, Hertfordshire, Middlesex* (1839), p. 95; *Post Office Directory Six Home Counties, 1851*, p. 171; *Post Office Directory Six Home Counties, 1862*, p. 318; 1851 Census (Ashwell); 1861 Census (Ashwell).

[85] Thomas Picking, Carpenter, Account Book, 1855–1869, HALS, D/EFmZ1.

[86] *Royston Crow*, 1 December 1858, p. 215.

Fordham, brewer and farmer of 600 acres and employer of forty men and ten boys.[87] During 1861, Picking billed Fordham for work carried out at the 'Old Farm' between April 1860 and March 1861 worth £28 0s. 2d., for work 'At the Cottage' between March and December 1861 worth £15 11s. 9d., for work over unspecified periods at the 'Brewhouse' and 'Duck Lake Farm' worth £48 10s. 6d. and £35 0s. 7d. respectively, and for unspecified work between November 1861 and March 1861 worth £23 14s. 1^1/2d. None of these bills for a total of £150 17s. ^{1}/2d., approximately 30 per cent of Picking's annual total of £504 8s. 10d. (worth £32,423 today calculated on changing RPI [88]), appear to have been settled during 1861. Edward Fordham, described by Davey as the 'squire', was certainly not in need of credit. Perhaps Thomas Picking, glad of the regular employment and not wishing to antagonize one of the most powerful men in Ashwell, was prepared to await payment being confident that it would materialize.[89]

Simpson's Brewery, Baldock

In the second half of the nineteenth century Simpson's Brewery in Baldock High Street occupied a site where, according to Allan Whitaker, Robert Thurgood had first started commercial scale brewing in 1743.[90] Simpson's acquired the brewery from Morris Pryor in 1853. The Simpson brothers, John and Thomas, nephews of the Royston brewer John Phillips, 'bought the brewery, maltings and tied estate for £81,000'. They proved very successful brewery managers, increasing their output to over 22,000 barrels in 1867. Four years later the census listed Thomas Simpson as a brewer and maltster employing forty-one men. [91]

Surviving records suggest that Simpson's was vital to the prosperity of local barley-growing farmers. Between 1858 and 1892, during the period September to March, the brewery bought-in between 4,000 and 6,000 'quarters' of barley per annum, ie between 50 and 75 tons.[92] Richard Perren argued that during the 1870s when a run of bad seasons produced poor harvests farmers were compensated 'for

---

[87] 1861 Census (Ashwell).

[88] L.H. Officer and S.H. Williamson, 'Five Ways to Compute the Relative Value of a UK Pound Amount, 1830 to Present', www.measuringworth.com (© 2007, accessed 6 December 2007).

[89] B.J. Davey, *Ashwell 1830–1914: The Decline of a Village Community.* Dept English Local History, Occasional Papers, Third Series, No. 5 (Leicester, 1980), p. 45.

[90] A. Whitaker, *Brewers in Hertfordshire: A Historical Gazetteer* (Hatfield, 2006), p. 53.

[91] Whitaker, *Brewers in Hertfordshire*, p. 58; 1871 Census (Baldock), RG 10 1364. The 1871 CEB is the only one to provide any employment details. While the 1882 trade directory lists 'Simpson Joseph and Thomas G. & Co. brewers, High street' and 'Simpson & Co. maltsters, High street', and the 1890 lists 'Simpson Joseph and Thomas G. & Co. brewers & maltsters, High st', in neither case were the brothers found listed individually in the CEBs.

[92] In Avoirdupois Weight, 14 pounds (lbs) = 1 stone, 2 stone (28 lbs) = 1 quarter, 4 quarters = 1 hundredweight (cwt) and 20 hundredweight = 1 ton.

low yields in the high prices brought about by shortage'. However, for the rest of the nineteenth century when 'steam navigation drastically reduced the price of ocean freight' and there was huge growth in world cereal production, price reductions lead to the 'great agricultural depression of 1879 – 1896'.[93] Against this background, the price of barley per quarter paid by Simpson's varied from an average 43s. 8d. in 1860/61 to 30s. 10^1/2d. in 1890/91 while their annual expenditure on this vital ingredient fell from £11,222 in 1875/76 to only £6,221 in 1890/91.[94] Although the above prices for 'some of the best barley ... in the country' declined, they were better than the wholesale prices of barley listed by Perren of 40s. 5d. per quarter in 1873, 33s. 1d. in 1880 and 27s. 10d. in 1888.[95]

Given that the area around Baldock was renowned for growing top quality barley, it is probable that Simpson's and other local brewers purchased most of their barley from the farmers of that region. A table detailing the barley bought by the brewery between 25 September and 4 December 1860 lists fifty-three different farmers of which eleven were identified as PTPSs from the region's towns, four each from Ashwell and Baldock, two from Buntingford and one from Royston. Among the remaining forty-two, some farmers may well have come from villages in the vicinity of Baldock but others could have operated much further away. Simpson's purchased from William Sale of Baldock 17 quarters of barley (at 46s/Qtr) for 'Malting No. 4' on 6 November, 14 quarters (at 35s/Qtr) for 'Malting No. 3' on 20 November and 24 quarters (at 41s/Qtr) again for 'Malting No. 4' on 27 November. These figures suggest that the brewery was purchasing barley of different qualities for different maltings that probably produced different types of beer.[96] The quantities are modest in comparison to some of the brewery's suppliers. An unidentified farmer 'Green' supplied 128 quarters for 'Malting No. 5' on 20 November (at 43s/Qtr) and a further 95 quarters for 'Malting No. 4' on 4 December (at 42s. 6d./Qtr). By the late 1890s, Simpson's were certainly aware of the plight of their barley suppliers as a letter of 13 February 1896 to a Mr John Brown from near Royston demonstrated. It offered him only '24/- per quarter for about 50 qrs: of Barley as per sample ... weighed up 16 stone wt per sack & put on rail at Royston station in your sacks as before'. The letter, while being very clear about the brewery's requirements and agreeing to pay 'carriage' to Baldock station, apologetically noted that 'we are sorry we cannot give you a better price' for the barley. Obviously such expressions of sympathy did not prevent the brewery from paying close to the market price for their barley, 24s. being

---

[93] R. Perren, *Agriculture in Depression, 1870–1940* (Cambridge, 1995), p. 7.

[94] Simpsons Brewery, Day Book of Expenditure on Barley, 1853–1945, HALS, D/ESb/B59.

[95] L.M. Munby, *The Hertfordshire Landscape* (The Making of the English Landscape Series, London, 1977), p. 26; Perren, *Agriculture in Depression*, p. 9.

[96] The Day Book indicates that from 1856 to 1875 the brewery operated Maltings Nos 1 & 2 (always listed together), 3, 4 and 5.

just above the 22s 11d. cited by Perren as the wholesale price for that year.[97]

In contrast to its purchasing of barley from local farmers, the letter book of Simpson's Brewery, Baldock, covering the period February 1880 to June 1897, reveals a company trading far and wide across Britain for other goods and services, and one heavily dependent on the railway for carriage of its requisites. This finding agrees with that of Christina Hallas's analysis of the impact of the coming of the railway to a largely rural area. She argued that the railway opened up the area to 'the mainstream influences of Victorian England' while giving local producers, like the example of Simpson's discussed here, 'greatly improved access to the nation at large' and encouraged both traditional and new industries.[98] On 27 August 1895, Simpson's requested that Hill & Smith at the Brierley Hill Iron Works, near Halesowen in the Black Country, 'quote us your lowest price and terms for cash on delivery for 22 gauge corrugated roofing iron galvanised and of best quality delivered free at Baldock station'.[99] Two weeks later the brewery were in touch with English Brothers Ltd of Wisbech in Cambridgeshire, a firm established since 1847 and importing timber into the UK via the River Nene.[100] Simpson's wrote that they would be obliged if English Brothers could 'forward the timber as specified in our letter of the 5th Inst' as soon as possible to Baldock railway station 'consigned to us at the prices quoted in your letter of the 6th Inst:'; the exchange clearly demonstrating the speed of the postal service.[101]

Not every potential supplier met Simpson's requirements. Rands & Jeckell Ltd of Foundation Street, Ipswich, had been manufacturing tents, waterproof coverings, netting and canvas goods since 1830 but a letter to them, dated 24 September 1895 read, 'We have returned the 2 sample malt sacks you kindly sent us for inspection and as your quotation is so high we propose to place the order elsewhere', and they did.[102] Two days later, a letter to J. Clement Johnston, Station Road, Cambridge, acknowledged their recent quotation for malt sacks and the sample forwarded. It placed an order for '40 sacks as per sample at 1/0³/4 each double sewed and branded SIMPSON & CO. BALDOCK' and very generously observed that 'you can charge us with the sample sack in addition to

---

[97] Simpson's Brewery, Letter Book, February 1880–June 1897, HALS, D/ESb/B90, p.129; Perren, *Agriculture in Depression*, p. 9.

[98] C. Hallas, 'The Social and Economic Impact of a Rural Railway: the Wensleydale Line', *Agricultural History Review*, 34, 1 (1986), p. 43.

[99] Simpson's Letter Book, p.37.

[100] Mel Hubbard, 'English Brothers Timber Frame Specialists', www.englishbrothers.co.uk (2005, accessed 11 December 2007).

[101] Simpson's Letter Book, p.41.

[102] 'MERL Archive Collections: Business Records', The Museum of English Rural Life, www.ruralhistory.org (Undated, accessed 11 December 2007); Simpson's Letter Book, p.47.

the 40 now ordered.[103]

Phrases along the lines of 'delivered free at Baldock station' occur regularly in Simpson's letters to suppliers emphasising the importance of rail transport to businesses by the end of the nineteenth century. It would have been crucial in the movement of coal from the pits to the consumers. For example, on 30 August 1895, the brewery wrote to 'W[m]. H. Essery' in Swansea requesting '3 Trucks … malting coal best quality at 21/9 per ton net at Baldock station … about the middle of September'. William Essery owned the Bryn Morgan Pit in the Swansea Valley, Glamorgan.[104] Twelve months later on 28 August 1896 Simpson's, obviously aware of where Joshua Richmond Page, another Baldock 'Maltster and Brewer', was obtaining his coal, wrote to the Manager of Page's supplier the Emlyn Colliery Company in Swansea advising him of this fact. Simpson's asked them to 'kindly quote us your price for the best malting coal delivered in truck loads at Baldock station' and pointed out that 'if your price & quality suits us we shall require about 80 tons this season'.[105] The Emlyn Colliery, in the village of Penygroes, was actually connected directly to the GWR Mountain branch by its own siding which had been built in 1890.[106] Two further examples from the Letter Book make it clear that businesses depended on the speed and reliability of the late nineteenth-century postal service. The first, a letter of 16 September 1895 from Simpson's to C. French, a Hitchin builder, regarding some brickwork at one of their public houses, observed 'we shall be glad if you can let our Mr Thurnall have your estimate in Hitchin corn exchange tomorrow (Tuesd[a]y) afternoon', obviously confident of the letter's prompt delivery. The second, a letter of 28 May 1896 to the Official Receiver in Cambridge regarding the licensing of the *Three Tuns Inn*, Ashwell, was 'in reply to your [the Official Receiver] letter of the 27[th] Inst', seemingly received the day after its posting.[107]

Apart from greatly facilitating their routine business activities, the railways also benefited employers by enabling them to extend the scope of the traditional annual work's outing. For example, Simpson's wrote to the Great Northern Railway on 16 June 1896 noting that the men of the Pryor Reid Brewery in Hatfield were travelling on 'an excursion to Yarmouth on Saturday, July 4th and

---

[103] Simpson's Letter Book, p.53.

[104] Simpson's Letter Book, p. 39; 'Collieries of the United Kingdom at work in 1880', Coal Mining History Resource Centre, www.freepages.genealogy.rootsweb.com (Undated, accessed 11 December 2007).

[105] Simpson's Letter Book, p. 265; *Kelly's Directory Six Home Counties, Pt I* (1882), p. 564.

[106] 'Emlyn Colliery, Penygroes', Collieries Pg., www.welshcoalmines.co.uk (Undated, accessed 11 December 2007).

[107] Simpson's Letter Book, pp. 44, 204.

that they wished their men 'to have their usual outing that day' too. Thus Simpson's requested 'two third class saloon carriages on the [same] train [be] reserved for them as usual', adding that about forty men could be expected to travel.[108] The British seaside resort beloved of the work's outing, Nigel Agar believed, 'was largely the invention of the railways'. On the whole it was they that 'either created the resorts from nothing or turned tiny seaports or well established fishing harbours like Great Yarmouth into popular resorts'.[109]

Brewers in Britain were slow to develop bottled beers. They were possibly inhibited by the government's excise duty levied on glass between 1745 and 1845. As Corran suggested, this was one of the 'various legislative restrictions [that] inhibited the progress of technology'. However, importation of continental lagers after 1880 so improved 'the popularity of bottled beers in general' that Simpson's were eventually forced to respond to the market in spite of the 'extra expense of bottles and of closing, labelling, filling and cleansing them'.[110] Following their attendance at the 1896 Brewers and Allied Trades Exhibition their commercial correspondence, as we shall see below, demonstrates that they had decided to go into production of bottled beer.[111] Having made that decision, two letters dated 10 December 1896 clearly show that Simpson's were anxious to eliminate competition from their rivals. In the letters to Messrs Fordham in Ashwell and J. W. Green at the *Phoenix Brewery* in Luton, they announced their future intention 'to supply our tenants with bottled ales and stout', asked that the others discontinue their supplies and instructed them to 'collect your bottles from our [tied] houses at the earliest opportunity'.[112]

The size of their tied estates (Table 6.1 below) show that Simpson's and the region's other major brewers successfully utilized the period's improved communications to expand their own businesses well beyond the confines of the four towns into the surrounding counties and beyond. Simpson's Brewery in 1853 owned or leased 122 licensed premises, Steed's Pale Ale Brewery, also in Baldock, had 66 premises in 1881, Phillips's Royston Brewery had 118 establishments in 1894, and Fordham's in Ashwell had 131 licensed premises in 1897.[113] Some of these totals may well have benefited from amendments to the Beer Act in 1869 which, as discussed previously in chapter 2, crippled many of the smaller beer houses. The geographical distribution of the three breweries'

---

[108] Simpson's Letter Book, p. 206.

[109] N. Agar, 'Hertfordshire Rail Excursions in the Nineteenth Century', *Herts Past & Present (3rd Series)*, 17 (2011), p. 29.

[110] H.S. Corran, *A History of Brewing* (Newton Abbot, 1975), pp. 231, 232, 234.

[111] See pp. 324-25 below.

[112] Simpson's Letter Book, p. 92.

[113] Whitaker, *Brewers in Hertfordshire*, pp. 57, 68, 182.

	Simpson's Baldock, 1853	Steed's Baldock, 1888	Phillips's Royston, 1894
Hertfordshire	81	20	56
Bedfordshire	24	34	4
Cambridgeshire	16	9	48
Huntingdonshire	-	-	3
Essex	1	-	5
Suffolk	-	-	2
London	-	3	-
Total	122	66	118

Table 6.1: County distribution of tied estates
Source: A. Whitaker, *Brewers in Hertfordshire*

tied estates (Table 6.1 above) is interesting in that Simpson's, despite the size of its estate, had no properties in Royston where the Phillips's brewery was owned by an uncle of the Simpsons who reciprocated by having no presence in Baldock.

The letter book also provides glimpses of the brewery's involvement with the newer telegraphic and telephone developments. However, the only evidence of the former was a letter of 6 March 1896, to Messrs Benjamin Farrar & Co. of 35 Cannon Street, London, in which Simpson's urgently requested a consignment of two large 'fire lumps' (*sic*) that they wanted to fix on Monday and advised the supplier to 'wire us first thing if you cannot send them at once'.[114] Again, there is only a single contemporary reference to the latter development in a letter the brewery wrote on 16 June 1896 to Mr Jesse Watts at the *Chequers* in Bedford, part of Simpson's tied estate of licensed premises. In it they acknowledged that the 'National Telephone Company have applied to us for permission to fix a pole in the corner of the Chequers Hotel yard'. Simpson's indicated that if Mr Watts had no objections they would 'be willing to make an arrangement with them'.[115]

The selected items from Simpson's letter book reveal a company heavily dependent on the railways for the rapid delivery to their local station of a wide range of goods necessary for the successful conduct of their brewing activities. They also clearly demonstrate Simpson's reliance on a speedy and reliable postal service for business communications. It is obvious from the confident tone of many letters that Simpson's felt they commanded respect from employees and suppliers alike.

---

[114] Simpson's Letter Book, p.141.
[115] Simpson's Letter Book, p. 205.

Baldock Gas Company

Robert Millward and Robert Ward, comparing public and private gas suppliers, estimated that by 1845 'all towns with 2,500 or more inhabitants had a gas supply'.[116] In fact, it took only thirty years after the illumination of London's Pall Mall for gas street-lighting to arrive in the small towns of north-east Hertfordshire.[117] Pigot's 1839 directories informed their readers that both Royston and Baldock were well lit by gas from works erected in 1836 and 1837 respectively, shortly after the Cambridge Gas Light Company opened in its much larger town in 1834.[118] While the railways eventually facilitated the easy carrying of coal from distant collieries to these towns, it should be noted that they did not actually reach Baldock and Royston until 1850, and Cambridge in 1852.[119] Until then, these gas works must have been dependent on road haulage for supplies of coal, possibly brought up from Ware situated on the navigable River Lea along which barges would have brought coal north from the Port of London. Buntingford also benefited by being 'lighted with gas from works erected at the south end of the town in 1861' but similarly this was two years before its railway station opened.[120] Evidence of this kind of activity is provided by an 1854 advertisement for Henry Hunt, a coal merchant and lighterman of Waltham Cross, eighteen miles south of Buntingford on the Old North Road and the River Lea. Hunt claimed to receive coal 'daily from the Counties of Leicester, Derby, York, Northumberland and Durham', and to convey it on 'the various railways' to his six depots. He also sailed barges daily from the nearby Cheshunt Wharf to and from London.[121]

---

[116] R. Millward and R. Ward, 'The Costs of Public and Private Gas Enterprises in Late 19th Century Britain', *Oxford Economic Papers*, 39, 4 (1987), p. 721.

[117] Friedrich Albert Winzer, living in London, had patented coal-gas lighting in 1804. Public street lighting was first introduced on 28 January 1807 when 'flickering gaslight illuminated Pall Mall'. Parliament granted a Charter to the London-based Gas Light and Coke Company in 1812 and, by 1823, 40,000 lamps covered 215 miles of London's streets, T. Long, 'Flickering Gaslight Illuminated Pall Mall', www.wired.com/science/discoveries (28 January 2008, accessed 3 May 2008); Coal-gas is a mixture of 'mainly hydrogen, methane, and carbon monoxide, formed by the destructive distillations [heating in the absence of air] of bituminous coal'. Encyclopaedia Britannica, www.britannica.com/eb/article-9024503/coal-gas (© 2008, accessed 3 May 2008); 'Coke [a clean, light fuel] is the [brittle silver-grey] residue remaining after ... substantially all the volatile constituents have been driven off'. Encyclopaedia Britannica, www.britannica.com/eb/article-9024703/coke (© 2008, accessed 3 May 2008).

[118] *Pigot's Directory, 1839, Cambridgeshire*, p. 66; *Pigot's Commercial Directory, Essex, Hertfordshire, Middlesex* (1839), p. 94; 'National Register of Archives, Cambridge Gas Light Company, GB/NNAF/C112358', www.nationalarchives.gov.uk/nra (© 2008, accessed 12 June 2008).

[119] Cockman, *Railways of Hertfordshire*, pp. 4-6.

[120] *Post Office Directory Six Home Counties, 1862*, p. 334.

[121] *Craven & Co's Commercial Directory of Bedfordshire & Hertfordshire, 1854* (Nottingham, 1854), un-paginated advertisements.

According to Derek Matthews, gas was initially used principally for street lighting and on commercial premises such as shops because its price meant that 'domestic use was feasible only by the aristocracy'. However, he argued that the gradual fall in price 'took gas consumption on a journey down through the Victorian class structure'. By the 1850s, gaslight had entered middle-class living rooms. Growth in demand led to further price reductions which by the 1870s made 'gas cooking and heating a commercial possibility' that was slowly taken up by the same middle-classes targeted by advertisements in *The Royston Crow* for domestic gas stoves. Matthews argued that it took until the 1890s for the price of gas to have fallen sufficiently to allow 'its adoption for lighting and cooking in working-class homes'.[122]

While local supply of gas for street lighting and domestic use might be considered an indication of 'civic pride' and sufficient numbers of householders able to pay for it, it was not without its problems for the manufacturers of gas. Minutes of the meeting of the directors of the Baldock Gas Company on 9 January 1875 revealed the need to investigate 'certain complaints and rumours arising from some late stoppages or defects in the supply of Gas and its impure quality'.[123] They called for a report on any reconstruction or repair required for 'the use or supply of the Public Lamps and private consumers with pure Gas'. On 30 August of the same year the Company discussed 'a Tender to the [Local] Board for the supply of Gas to the 56 Street Lamps' in Baldock at the reduced price, compared to 1874, of £125. However, due to the additional cost of not less than £10 per lamp to supply the gas by meter, it was 'resolved to be inexpedient in so small a place as this to adopt the system'.

There were still supply problems in 1877 when the minutes of 4 August admitted that the dilapidated condition of the gas plant and coal stores meant that the works were 'certainly not equal to supplying the demand for Gas made upon it'. The Committee was of the opinion that if the supply pipes were relaid in the 'High Street & other parts of the Town where they are defective or too small for the consumption' it would 'put an end to all complaints & increase the revenue of the Company'. Their strategy obviously worked, for the minutes of 19 July 1878 revealed £255 17s. 3d available for payment to shareholders and the resolution that 'a dividend of £8 per cent be paid upon the shares in this Company's assets'. The Board were also now willing to 'supply Gas by their Posts by meter leaving it

---

[122] D. Matthews, 'Laissez-faire and the London Gas Industry in the Nineteenth Century: Another Look', *Economic History Review*, 39, 2 (1986), p. 246.
[123] Baldock Gas Light & Coke Co., Minutes of Meetings of Directors, HALS, PUG1/1/1.

to the [Baldock] Local Board to light and extinguish their lamps by their own servants'.

Much of the apparent improvement in the Company's performance occurred under the stewardship of James Gilbert Dear, identified as the Manager of the Company between 1870 and 1882. Dear was a man of many parts for the 1870 directory also listed him as an assessor and collector of taxes, an insurance agent, jeweller and watchmaker, but by 1882 his only role other than managing the gasworks was still that of a taxman.[124] It is interesting to note that a relevant scientific or engineering background was apparently deemed unnecessary for involvement in the running of the local gasworks since between 1861 and 1882 the position of Secretary at Buntingford's Gas & Coke Company Limited was held first by Henry Goodes Macklin the local Registrar of births and deaths, then by William Bray a chemist and druggist, and finally by Thomas Moore an Inland Revenue officer. A similar situation existed in Royston between 1861 and 1882 where Edward Nash, an architect and surveyor, held the post of Secretary at both the Gas Works and the Royston Water Company.[125] Perhaps because of the need to attract local investors and their ability to persuade the local populace of the long-term benefits of the inevitable disruption to their towns by the construction of these utilities, it would appear that existing officials and respected local service providers acted as secretaries to these companies.

By 2 June 1882, three Baldock Gas Company directors, T.G. Simpson, S. Veasey and J. Dear were able, 'out of the balance', to deposit £150 with Wells Hogg & Linsdale the local Baldock Bank. Like Simpson's Brewery, the minutes of 3 July 1884 indicate that the gas company also took advantage of the railways to bring in supplies of coal. The Committee resolved to estimate the 'probable quantity of coal required at the works for the current year' and ask the senders to supply it 'free from the Colleries (sic) to the Baldock Railway Station'.

Street lighting would have greatly improved the atmosphere of Baldock especially regarding the safety and security of its citizens. To this end, on 29 August 1887, the Directors proposed to tender for the town's public lighting 'at 30/- per lamp and 32/6 for all night D[itt]o. The rate of consumption to be 5 [cubic] ft per hour' and the arrangements for the lighting of the lamps to remain as previously agreed. This equates to an approximate price of 1s 9½d per 1000 cubic feet of gas which compares very favourably with Matthews's estimated averages in London of 15s

---

[124] *Post Office Directory Six Home Counties, Pt 1* (1870), p. 411; 1871 Census (Baldock); *Kelly's Directory Six Home Counties, Pt 1* (1882), p. 564; 1881 Census (Baldock).
[125] *Post Office Directory Six Home Counties, 1862*, p. 335, 377–78; *Post Office Directory Six Home Counties, Pt 1* (1870), p. 429, 478–79; *Kelly's Directory Six Home Counties, Pt 1* (1882), p. 586, 649-50.

per 1000 cubic feet in the early 1820s dropping to 2s. 4d. per 1000 cubic feet by 1914.[126] Demand for gas clearly continued to increase for on 28 July 1888 the Directors agreed to accept the £557 10s. 0d tender 'of Messrs Newton & Chambers for the extension of the Works including New Purifier'. This was an example of local industry's integration into the wider national economy, as Newton, Chambers & Co. Ltd were based in Sheffield, Yorkshire.[127] Established in 1792 they were iron founders, colliery proprietors, chemical and disinfectant manufacturers who from their smelting and casting of iron provided components for the storage gasometers.

In addition to street lighting, coal gas had two important uses for domestic customers. It replaced candles for lighting the home and it replaced the wood-fire as the source of heat for cooking. Ironmongers, such as James Goodchild of Baldock, took on the role of gas fitters while others additionally sold the very latest domestic appliances.[128] For example, Charles Andrews, ironmonger and upholsterer on Market Hill, Royston, in an advertisement of 1860 'begged to inform the Ladies, Gentlemen, and the Inhabitants generally ... that he has now engaged in his service men experienced in GAS FITTING'. Two years later Andrews was supplying 'LENI'S Patent Self-acting Blow Pipe GAS STOVE' which his advertisement explained, by mixing gas and air, produced an intense heat that 'will boil one pint of water in three minutes and one gallon in fifteen minutes' without soiling the brightest kettle.[129]

Baldock, Buntingford and Royston were all able to attract the investment necessary to provide them with street lighting, a development that must have seemed to many of their inhabitants a wonder of their age. As the numbers of the 'middling sort' grew in these successful small towns in the later decades of the nineteenth century, so too did the spread of domestic gas lighting and the development and availability of appliances for cooking; all advertised as the above examples illustrate in their local newspaper, *The Royston Crow*.

---

[126] Matthews, 'Laissez-faire and London Gas', p.247. The present calculation assumes an average, across the year, of ten night-time hours of usage per lamp. Therefore 10 x 5 x 365 = 18250 cubic feet of gas consumed annually by each lamp. At 32/6 per lamp, i.e. 390d, price per 1000 cubic feet is 390/18.25 = 21.4d or approximately 1s 9$\frac{1}{2}$d.

[127] 'National Register of Archives, Newton, Chambers & Co Ltd, GB/NNAF/C117393', www.nationalarchives.gov.uk/nra (© 2008, accessed 19 May 2008).

[128] *Post Office Directory Six Home Counties, Pt 1* (1870), p. 411.

[129] *The Royston Crow*, 1 February 1860, p. 272; *The Royston Crow*, 1 July 1862, p. 390.

Farmers' Manure Company, Royston

Nitrogenous fertilizers provide nitrogen, potassium and phosphorous necessary for healthy plant growth. In the early nineteenth century, farming remained very dependent on traditional means of manuring such as livestock and town dung. Richard Perren described how hay and straw were carried forty miles to London and 'ashes, soot, and sheep's trotters brought back'.[130] Liam Brunt claimed that before 1850 all nitrogenous fertilizers were organic substances such as dung, malt dust and ashes used in conjunction with chalk, lime and marl to adjust the acid balance of the soil; which was essential for the uptake of nitrogen. In contrast, Jonathan Brown suggested that by the 1840s vast quantities of artificial fertilizers became available, especially crushed bone containing phosphoric acid (ca 46,000 tons imported/year) which was dissolved in sulphuric acid to produce superphosphate of lime for easier spreading over fields. John Laws, who patented this process and began manufacture at Deptford Creek on the south bank of the Thames, first advertised the product in the *Gardeners' Chronicle* in July 1843. [131]

The Farmers' Manure Company's first directory appearance was under Royston in 1870 and indicated that it also had a branch near Abbey Mills at Stratford in Essex, simplified to 'London' ten years later. William T. Nash was the company secretary in 1870, and its manager between 1882 and 1890.[132] An 1871 valuation of the Company's 'Stock in Trade' indicates that their Stratford branch was considerably smaller than that at Royston with the total stock value estimated at £436 5s 0d compared to £1241 10s 0d (worth £27,912 and £79,433 respectively today calculated on changing RPI).[133] It also refers to what must have been a very small outlet in Hitchin where the stock was only valued at total of £11 12s 6d. The make-up of the listed stock (Table 6.2 below) suggests that the Farmers' Manure Company was another Hertfordshire business heavily dependent on the railways for the transport of raw materials such as salt probably brought from the Cheshire mines and used to release potassium from soil (4 ton), coal (3 ton) and coke (8 ton) for fuel, and the large 'mineral dump' (65 ton) that probably referred

---

[130] R. Perren, 'Markets and Marketing', in G.E. Mingay (ed.), *The Agrarian History of England and Wales, Vol. 6, 1750–1850* (Cambridge, 1989), p. 198.

[131] L. Brunt, 'Where there's Muck, there's Brass: The Market for Manure in the Industrial Revolution', *Economic History Review*, 60, 2 (2007), p. 341; J. Brown, 'Arable Farming Practices', in Mingay, *Agrarian History of England and Wales, Vol. 6*, p. 278; F.M.L. Thompson, 'Agricultural Chemical and Fertiliser Industries', in E.J.T. Collins (ed.), *The Agrarian History of England and Wales, Vol. 7, Pt. 2, 1850–1914* (Cambridge, 2000), p. 1019.

[132] *Post Office Directory Six Home Counties, Pt 1* (1870), p. 478; *Kelly's Directory Six Home Counties, Pt 1* (1882), p. 649; *Post Office Directory Six Home Counties, Pt 1* (1870), p. 809.

[133] L.H. Officer and S.H. Williamson, 'Five Ways to Compute the Relative Value of a UK Pound Amount, 1830 to Present', www.measuringworth.com (© 2007, accessed 6 December 2007).

to 'basic slag' brought in from iron works and commonly used as a fertilizer.[134] Evidence of involvement in the wider international fertilizer market is provided

Tons/Cwt	Commodity	Value/Ton	Total £.s.d
· -/10	½ inch Bones	7.00.00	3.10.00
1/10	Ground Coprolites	60.00	4.10.00
-/13	Blood	10.00	6.10.00
-/ 2	Sulphate of Am[mon]ia	15.00	1.10.00
15/ -	Rape Cake	6.10.00	97.10.00
-	150 New Bags	06	3.15.00
-	1000 Second Hand Bags	-	-
1/10	Dissolved Bones	5.00.00	7.10.00
9/ -	Potash	3.00.00	27.00.00
1/ 1	Dis[solve]d Guano	9.10.00	9.19.06
-	23 Empty Carboys	3.00	3.09.00
65/ -	Mineral dump	3.15.00	243.15.00
30/ -	Bone Super[phosph]ate	4.10.00	135.00.00
20/ -	Blood Manure	4.15.00	95.00.00
8/ -	Mineral Super[phosph]ate	4.00.00	32.00.00
2/ -	Rough Bones	6.00.00	12.00.00
4/10	Guano	12.00.00	54.00.00
1/ -	Nitrate Soda	15.00.00	15.00.00
3/ -	Guano	9.10.00	28.10.00
8/ -	Coke	16.00	6.08.00
3/ -	Coal	16.00	2.08.00
4/ -	Salt	22.00	4.08.00
		Total =	1241.10.00

Valuation of Stock held at Royston, 1871

Table 6.2: Valuation of Farmers' Manure Company's stock in trade
Source: Farmers' Manure Company's own 'Valuation of Stock in Trade'. [135]

by the fact that the Company's depots at Royston (7 ton 10 cwt) and Stratford (3 ton) held stocks of guano, the excrement of sea birds imported from the islands off the coast of Chile and Peru, quantities of imported bones, and nitrate of soda

---

[134] Basic slag, a waste product of iron and steel works, rich in calcium, magnesium, sulphur and phosphates was (and still is) commonly applied to pastures and arable fields once every 3 – 5 years, Wiley – VCH Staff, *Ullmann's Agrochemicals* (Wiley – VCH, 2007), pp. 354-55.

[135] Farmers' Manure Company – Ledgers, Cashbooks, Registers & Business Records, 1870–1972, Impersonal Ledger, HALS D/Eky/B1, pp. 29–30.

(1 ton) from mainland Chile. The relatively small quantities of guano and nitrate of soda, valued respectively at £12/ton and £15/ton, clearly reflect the costs involved in importing these materials, compared to that of acquiring locally mined coprolites valued at only £3/ton.

While the stock contained some of the more traditional fertilizers of the period, e.g. twenty tons of blood manure, it clearly shows that the company was also heavily into the production of the new chemical fertilizers such as bone superphosphate (thirty tons held at Royston). The twenty-three empty carboys listed would once have held the sulphuric acid used to dissolve the bones and coprolites.[136] Coprolites, fossilized animal excrement with a high phosphate content, were obtained from the 1850s by shallow mining and, according to Thompson, production peaked in 1876 at 258,150 tons but had ceased by the end of the century. Royston lies five miles to the east of Ashwell where, according to Albert Sheldrick, several companies were engaged in the hand-digging of coprolites from the greensand between 1860 and 1880.[137] However, whilst Ashwell may have supplied the Royston depot, the coprolite belt stretched as far as Soham in Cambridgeshire and in 1871 the Manure Company's branch at Stratford listed a stock of eighty-two tons of 'Wicken Coprolites', Wicken being two miles south-west of Soham but twenty-two miles north-east of Royston.

Thomas Picking excepted, the case studies presented provide ample evidence of major businesses in the region being reliant on improved road and rail transport as well as the late nineteenth-century postal service for the effective conduct of their enterprises. The final section of this chapter examines the benefits to the regional economy of advertising in terms of both a business's potential customers and of its material and service suppliers.

Marketing power of advertising

Advertisers in the markets of eighteenth- and early nineteenth-century England, according to Thomas Richards, were seen as nuisances only 'a step above derelicts and vagrants'. However, John Clapham suggested that the essential features of nineteenth-century retail distribution were improved stock control, price cutting, refashioned shop-fronts and interiors, window displays and advertising. David Alexander later agreed that, between the 1820s and 1850s, such aggressive and competitive 'entrepreneurial concepts' gradually spread from the cities across the whole country. However, W. Hamish Fraser argued that mass advertising, dismissed at the time as 'puffery' by its critics, lacked respectability

---

[136] A carboy is a large globular glass bottle, protected by a frame, for storing corrosive liquids.

[137] A. Sheldrick, *A Different World: Ashwell Before 1939* (Ashwell, 1992), p. 11.

and wall posters remained its main vehicle until the 1880s when major national newspapers first began to allow advertisements to spread over more than one column.[138]

The above views have more recently been challenged by a number of retailing historians. Fundamental changes, according to Nancy Cox and Claire Walsh, were 'triggered by new possibilities in the use of the printed word'.[139] While newspaper advertisements first appeared in London's press from the late seventeenth century, Stobart observed, they were 'in essence, an eighteenth century innovation and were an important feature of provincial newspapers, especially from the 1740s'.[140] This 'technique of sale through retail outlets linked to provincial newspapers', argued Cox and Walsh, broadened its scope during the eighteenth century. They found it particularly evident where the 'dividing line between medicaments, foodstuffs and beverages was fine' and the practise of fixed price, branded goods 'often imposed nation-wide, spread into the grocery and confectionery trades, and to some extent into the drinks industry'.[141]

This final section examines the extent to which businesses, local, regional and national, exploited that distinctive form of communication, the advertisement of goods and services. It examines the range of advertising found in two Hertfordshire trade directories of 1854 and 1895, in the local *Royston Crow* and *Herts & Cambs Reporter* newspapers, and it briefly touches on the specialized advertising role of a nineteenth-century trade exhibition.

Trade directories

It is obvious that local trade directories provided businesses and the local populace with basic details of their own and neighbouring towns' service providers. Craven's 1854 directory of Hertfordshire, published in Nottingham, also contained a very limited number of large detailed advertisements relating to two of the four towns' service providers, three in Baldock and two in Royston. Three of these advertisements were for inns and hotels, William Warner's *Crown & Dolphin Commercial Inn* 'near the railway station, Royston', John Little's

---

[138] T. Richards, *The Commodity Culture of Victorian England: Advertising and Spectacle, 1851–1914. The Great Exhibition of 1851* (London, 1991), p. 40; J.H. Clapham, *An Economic History of Modern Britain, Vol. 1, The Early Railway Age, 1820-1850* (2nd Ed., Cambridge, 1930), pp. 219–33; D. Alexander, *Retailing in England During the Industrial Revolution* (London, 1970), p. 234; W.H. Fraser, *The Coming of the Mass Market, 1850–1914* (London, 1981), pp. 134, 138.

[139] N. Cox and C. Walsh, ' "Their Shops are Dens, the Buyer is their Prey": Shop Design and Sale Techniques', in N. Cox, *The Complete Tradesman: A Story of Retailing, 1550-1820* (Aldershot, 2000), p. 114.

[140] Stobart, *Spend, Spend, Spend!*, p. 91.

[141] Cox and Walsh, 'Their Shops are Dens', p. 103.

White Horse [Commercial] *Hotel* and Posting-house in Baldock also described as being 'near the railway station' and the location for the monthly Magistrates Meetings, and William Sparks's *Rose and Crown Commercial Inn* and Baldock's Inland Revenue Office that was 'situated in the centre of the town'. Clearly the emphasis of the information provided was directed at potential travellers to the two towns and their convenience. Only two local service providers placed detailed advertisements in the directory, Edward Fossy Bally a Baldock 'Chemist, Druggist & Dentist', and Luke Gimson a Royston 'General and Furnishing Ironmonger' with a general agricultural warehouse.[142] This suggests that the vast majority of PTPSs felt that a basic listing in a directory was sufficient and preferred not to pay the cost of inserting large detailed advertisements.

In addition to the many standard entries listed under each of the four towns, Kelly's 1895 'Directory of Hertfordshire' contained specific advertising sections under the headings of banking, assurance, London, county, and a few advertisements that were from further afield. Similarly to the situation found in

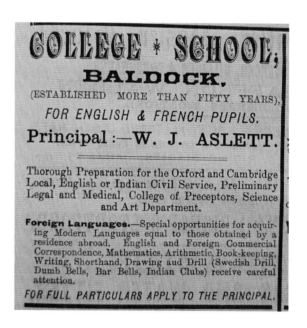

Plate 6.4: Advertisement for College School, Baldock
Source: *Kelly's Directory of Hertfordshire*, 1895

Craven's directory, only two local PTPSs, both from Baldock, placed detailed advertisements in the county section. They were both for educational establishments, W. J. Aslett's College School (Plate 6.4 above) 'for English &

---

[142] *Craven & Co's Commercial Directory, 1854*, un-paginated advertisements.

French pupils', and Mrs G. Sibley's Grove House Ladies College that advertised 'High School Teaching & Home Comforts'. Presumably, the Principals of these two colleges wished to appeal to a wider potential clientele.[143]

More importantly the detailed, and occasionally large and illustrated, advertisements placed in the five sections of the directory would have allowed businesses in the four towns to identify potentially useful suppliers ranging from W.H. Collier, 'Red and White Brick, Tile, and Pipe Manufacturer' of Marks Tey (Essex); George C. Davis, 'Stained and Leaded Glass' of Finchley (North London); Nicholl & Co., 'Timber and Slate Merchants' of Colchester (Essex) to B.S. Morse, 'The Watford Electro-Plating Works' (Hertfordshire).[144] The directory also listed a limited number of more distant traders including the 'Guest and Chrimes, Foundry & Brass Works, Rotherham' in Yorkshire, Thomas Briggs, 'Spinner and Manufacturer, Sacking and Sacks' of Manchester, and 'John Blake, Hydraulic Ram Works, Accrington, Lancashire'.[145] Perhaps most importantly, the directory contained advertisements for Kelly's own specialist national directories such as the 'now ready', seventh edition of 'Kelly's Directory of Engineers, Iron & Metal Trades and Colliery Proprietors of England, Scotland and Wales, and the Principal Towns of Ireland' and a similar 'Kelly's Directory of The Building Trades'; both were priced at 30s, more than the Hertfordshire Directory which quoted 'Price to Subscribers, Ten Shillings; Non-Subscribers, Twelve Shillings'.[146]

These directories were also an important source of information, needed by businesses, on such monetary matters as banking and insurance. While Baldock and Royston were served between 1851 to 1891 by the Wells, Hogge & Lindsell Bank (branch of the Baldock & Biggleswade) and Fordham's Bank (drawing on Barclay, Bevan & Co., London) respectively, some in business might have preferred dealing directly with the larger London banks. Kelly's 1895 directory included advertisements, three of them full-page, for four of the capital's banks including the London and County Banking Company which listed Bedford, Bishop's Stortford, Cambridge and 'Hitchin & Biggleswade' among its 'country branches'.[147] The importance attached to protecting business assets was amply demonstrated by the inclusion of twenty-one assurance and/or insurance companies that covered the usual fire, life and marine aspects of loss and sometimes also reflected the new dangers resulting from the nineteenth-century's

---

[143] *Kelly's Directory of Hertfordshire with Large Map, 1895* (London, 1894), County Advertisements, pp. 43, 53.

[144] *Kelly's Directory of Hertfordshire, 1895*, County Advertisements, pp. 50, 45, 41, 51.

[145] *Kelly's Directory of Hertfordshire, 1895*, County Advertisements, pp. 57, 58, 59.

[146] *Kelly's Directory of Hertfordshire, 1895*, County Advertisements, p. 56.

[147] *Kelly's Directory of Hertfordshire, 1895*, County Advertisements, p. 1.

Plate 6.5: Advertisement for Engine Boiler Insurance Company
Source: *Kelly's Directory of Hertfordshire*, 1895

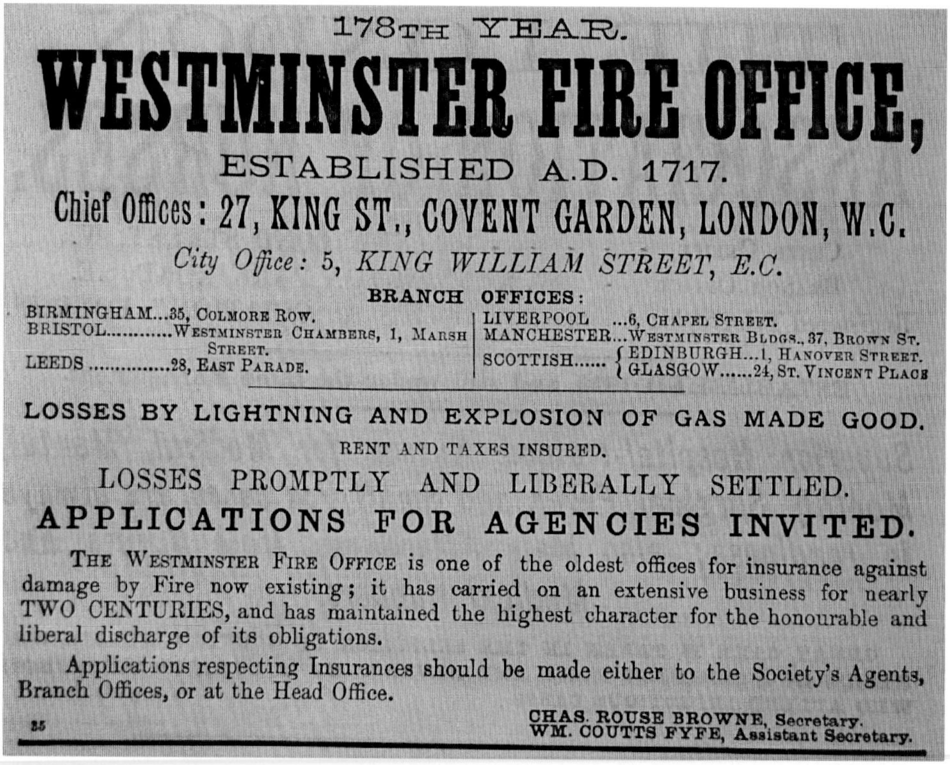

Plate 6.6: Advertisement for Westminster Fire Office
Source: *Kelly's Directory of Hertfordshire*, 1895

technical developments. For example, the Manchester-based Engine, Boiler, and Employers' Liability Insurance Company (Plate 6.5 above), offered 'Inspection and Insurance of Engines, Boilers, Gas Engines, and Steam and Hot Water Appliances in all parts of the United Kingdom' which would have been of potential interest to the Baldock Gas Company and Simpson's Brewery. Baldock's retail and domestic users of gas lighting might well have taken advantage of the Westminster Fire Office's boast (Plate 6.6 above) that it settled promptly any 'losses by lightning and explosion of gas' with liberal settlements.[148]

Clearly, newspapers saw trade directories as a means of bringing themselves to the attention of business in the hope of generating their own advertising revenue. Kelly's directory of 1895 carried advertisements for eleven different newspaper publishers, covering Essex (4), Hertfordshire (4), Middlesex and Buckinghamshire combined (2), and Essex with West Suffolk (1). The all embracing *Essex County Standard, West Suffolk Gazette and Eastern Counties Advertiser*, published every Friday night for sale the following Saturday morning, had its offices in Colchester. The publisher claimed that the *Essex County Standard* was the 'paper of Essex' and being published in Colchester (population 34,559) it 'has the advantage over its rivals in Circulation, Influence and Advertising Notice'. It was further claimed that it 'circulates amongst the very best classes in Essex and the Eastern Counties, and is consequently a most valuable medium for Advertisers'.[149]

Businesses in north-east Hertfordshire took advantage of such inducements, some advertising far and wide, including the Farmers' Manure Company of Royston. Their 'General Expenses' account included a number of items for placing advertisements in newspapers including £6.10s.0d on 14 December 1871 to the *Hertfordshire Express*, two sums of £7.10s.0d on 1 February 1872 one to the *Cambridgeshire Express* and the other to the *West Sussex Gazette*, and £2.1s.0d on 1 April 1872 to the *Hertfordshire Guardian*. Perhaps, not surprisingly given the nature of their product, the Farmers' Manure Company advertising went beyond newspapers and included an item of expense listed for 27 October 1871 of £13.5s.0d for advertising, in the *Agricultural Journal*.[150]

---

[148] *Kelly's Directory of Hertfordshire, 1895*, County Advertisements, pp. 5, 15.
[149] *Kelly's Directory of Hertfordshire, 1895*, County Advertisements, p. 29.
[150] Farmers' Manure Company – Ledgers, Cashbooks, Registers & Business Records, 1870–1972, Impersonal Ledger, HALS D/Eky/B1, pp. 49–50.

Local newspapers

In contrast to Fraser's expressed view, the evidence here suggests that bill posters were thin on the ground in north-east Hertfordshire despite the region having to wait until 1855 for the arrival of *The Royston Crow*. [151] It was a time when, according to Pat Hudson, such 'provincial newspapers depended on the dissemination of national information from London' but with the capital being the 'centre of conspicuous consumption influencing fashion and tastes far and wide' advertisements were another key component of their content.[152] John Warren, the publisher of *The Royston Crow*, was clearly determined to use his newspaper as a vehicle for advertising. Issue Number 7 on 2 July 1855 (Plate 6.7 below) abandoned the previous price of one penny and proclaimed '1,000 copies given away'.[153] The publisher explained that previous sales had not been satisfactory and, given that he saw no prospect of them becoming so, he had 'decided on circulating the publication GRATUITOUSLY in Royston and in places within fourteen miles'. Warren's editorial noted that this was the only way of providing 'An Excellent Advertising Medium for Royston and the Neighbourhood' and presumably he felt confident that traders would be willing to pay him to publish

---

[151] See p. 312 above; The present analysis found a total absence of any reference to 'bill posters' or 'bill stickers' in both Ashwell (between 1851 and 1891) and Buntingford (between 1833/34 and 1891). There were similarly none identified in Baldock until Charles Mellum was listed as 'bill poster' in Kelly's directories of 1882 and 1890. Royston was the only one of the four towns to regularly have a bill sticker/poster throughout the second half of the nineteenth century, Thomas Farr (1851 census), Robert Bidnall (1861 census) and William Stamford (1870 to 1890 trade directories) who was also Royston's Town Crier.

[152] P. Hudson, 'The Regional Perspective', in P. Hudson (ed.), *Regions and Industries: A Perspective on the Industrial Revolution in Britain* (Cambridge, 1989), p. 20.

[153] *The Royston Crow* monthly newspaper was first published in January 1855, price one penny or two pence by post. Its banner proclaimed it to be 'designed in its own humble way to promote the improvement of the Physical, Intellectual, and Moral Condition of Mankind, and to further the interests of Agriculture, Trade, and Commerce'. By Issue No. 7, 2 July 1855, its banner announced 'Published Monthly. 1,000 COPIES GIVEN AWAY'. The Friday evening edition of 29 September 1876, saw the first edition of a re-vamped weekly newspaper, *The Royston Crow* now 'Circulating (in the Counties Herts. Cambs. and Essex) throughout Royston, Baldock, Buntingford, Ashwell, Arrington, Bassingbourn … Wendy, Whaddon, Wimpole, and other adjacent places', again selling for one penny and now 'Registered for Transmission Abroad'. On 26 January 1877 the banner changed again, with Issue No. 18 of this 'New Series', to 'The Royston Crow circulating extensively in HERTFORDSHIRE, CAMBRIDGESHIRE. Also in BEDS. HUNTS. & ESSEX'. On 28 November 1877 the publisher changed the title of Issue No. 61 to that of the *Herts & Cambs Reporter* with which is incorporated *The Royston Crow*. Finally, with Issue No. 397 on 2 May 1884, still priced at one penny, the banner proclaimed it to be the '*Herts & Camb Reporter* and ROYSTON CROW. The General Advertiser for the Counties of Herts., Cambs., Beds., Hunts., and Essex'; *Kelly's Directory of Hertfordshire* (London, 1895). It should be noted that issues from January 1855 to July 1875 were paginated continuously from page 1 onwards. The new series from August 1875 was published unpaginated until 3 January 1890 when each issue from No. 693 onwards was paginated individually.

their advertisements. The following review of the paper's extensive advertisements suggests that Warren's belief was justified.[154]

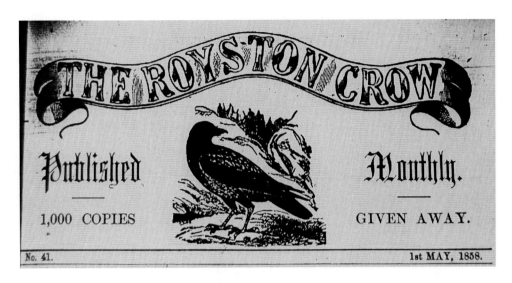

Plate 6.7: Banner for local newspaper
Source: *Royston Crow*, 1 May 1858

Advertisements placed in *The Royston Crow* newspaper from its inception in 1855 until 1890 reveal several different categories. One category is that of local Royston traders advertising their services. For example, B. Gosling, High Street tailor, thanked his 'friends and the Public in general' for their support over many years and begged 'to inform them that all the newest styles' in ponchos, cloaks and overcoats 'are made to order at his Establishment'.[155] From her investigation of menswear retailers' press advertisements, Laura Ugolini concluded that tailors, here exemplified by Gosling's (Plate 6.8 below), had by this time 'already enjoyed a long tradition of printed advertisements' that emphasised their role as an intermediary between retailer and purchaser by using 'a "common sartorial language" that encouraged and justified male consumption'. The following example illustrates another of Ugolini's observations that a common advertising ploy was one that 'emphasized as selling points both the reasonableness of the prices and the availability' of the goods.[156] Pendered and Son, linen and woollen drapers, similarly thanked their friends for 'favours received' and informed them of their 'purchase of new goods for the present season' and invited 'inspection of

---

[154] *Royston Crow*, 2 July 1855.

[155] *Royston Crow*, 1 February 1855, p. 12.

[156] L. Ugolini, 'Men, Masculinities, and Menswear Advertising, c. 1890-1914', in J.Benson and L. Ugolini (eds), *A Nation of Shopkeepers: Five Centuries of British Retailing* (London, 2003), pp. 83, 88.

their Stock' which was available 'at prices which cannot fail to give satisfaction to the purchasers'.[157] Some retailers like W[illiam] Bull, variously described as a 'Chemist', 'Family Medicine Warehouse' and 'Chemist and Druggist', advertised a surprisingly wide range of products. These ranged from cod liver oil, pure malt vinegar and Hertfordshire Sauce to tobacco, cigars, ginger beer and British wines.[158]

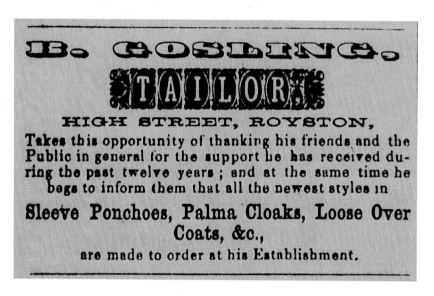

Plate 6.8: Advertisement for a Royston tailor
Source: *Royston Crow*, 1 February 1855

A second category is that of traders from other regional towns advertising their wares in *The Royston Crow*. For example, in the summer of 1857 Steed's Baldock Brewery advertised that its 'VERY SUPERIOR PORTER, ALES, & TABLE BEER, Brewed expressly for Hay Time and Harvest, may be obtained at the Brewery, in excellent condition'.[159] Neil Mckendrick, again in contrast to Fraser, argued that by 1800 the advertising columns of the press were 'vital agents in the spread of fashion'.[160] It is clear that T. W. Westrope of Ashwell thought so when he 'invited attention to his extended Assortment of New Goods suitable for THE AUTUMN SEASON, consisting of FANCY DRESS MATERIALS in all the new shades'. These goods included jackets, skirts, corsets, shawls, ribbons,

[157] *Royston Crow*, 1 February 1855, p. 12; *Royston Crow*, 1 October 1855, p. 63.

[158] William Bull, Chemist & Druggist, appeared in the *Post Office Directory Six Home Counties, 1862*, p. 377; *Royston Crow*, 1 February 1855, p. 12; *Royston Crow*, 1 March 1855, p. 21; *Royston Crow*, 1 June 1855, p. 45; *Royston Crow*, 1 June 1858, p. 191.

[159] *Royston Crow*, 1 July 1857, p. 149.

[160] N. McKendrick, 'The Commercialization of Fashion', in N. McKendrick, J. Brewer and J.H. Plumb, *The Birth of a Consumer Society: The Commercialization of Eighteenth-century England* (London, 1982), p.41.

hosiery and 'Hats and Caps in the new shapes'.[161] Some traders from other towns actually had branches in Royston. For example, W. T. Palmer, a boot and shoe manufacturer in Sydney Street, Cambridge (Plate 6.9 below), had a branch of his Cambridge Shoe Warehouse on Market Hill. Here was held 'a Stock of several Thousands (sic) Pairs of Boots and Shoes to select from suitable for all classes for the present season'.[162] These fashion advertisements provide evidence of the importance to the towns' society of 'new goods', 'new shades' and 'new shapes' for the new season and support McKendrick's view that provincial newspaper fashion advertisements were effective in spreading the word and 'encouraging imitation and emulation from below'.[163] This type of newspaper advertising, Hannah Barker has more recently argued, 'painted pictures of urban cultural refinement, albeit of a suitably measured sort' with goods being described commonly as 'fashionable and cheap' and shops offering 'up-to-the-minute fashions and top quality goods'.[164]

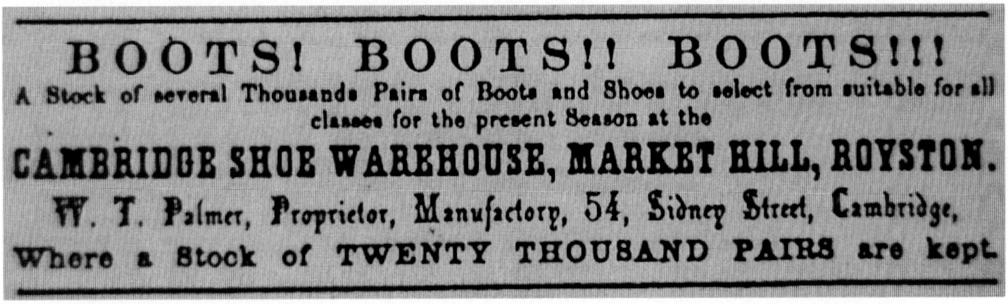

BOOTS! BOOTS!! BOOTS!!!
A Stock of several Thousands Pairs of Boots and Shoes to select from suitable for all classes for the present Season at the
CAMBRIDGE SHOE WAREHOUSE, MARKET HILL, ROYSTON.
W. T. Palmer, Proprietor, Manufactory, 54, Sidney Street, Cambridge,
Where a Stock of **TWENTY THOUSAND PAIRS** are kept.

Plate 6.9: Advertisement for a Cambridge boot & shoe manufacturer
Source: *Royston Crow*, 9 July 1880

A third category is that of the many advertisements in *The Royston Crow* illustrating how improved transport provided local retailers with an opportunity to integrate into the wider British and World markets. In 1855 for example, T. Goodman advertised himself as a 'Grocer and Dealer in Tea, Coffee, Cocoa, Chocolate, and Spices' and an agent for 'Huntley and Palmer's Reading Biscuits'.[165] William Barton, fishmonger and poulterer in Royston's High Street, would have been dependent on the railways for his advertised 'Supplies of Fish daily from London and Yarmouth'. It would have been a similar situation for Thomas Craft, on Fish Hill, who sold 'CHINA, GLASS, AND

---

[161] *Royston Crow*, 6 October 1876, un-paginated.

[162] *Royston Crow*, 9 July 1880, un-paginated.

[163] McKendrick, 'Commercialization of Fashion', p.49.

[164] H. Barker, ' "Smoke Cities": Northern Industrial Towns in Late Georgian England', *Urban History*, 31, 2 (2004), pp. 182, 183.

[165] *Royston Crow*, 1 March 1855, p. 21.

EARTHENWARE, at the most reasonable prices'.[166]   In addition to being a chemist & druggist, J[oseph] Mathews in Royston High Street was a 'Licensed Dealer in Foreign Wines' (Plate 6.10 below) able to supply champagnes, clarets, Hungarian wines, ports and sherries 'Carriage paid to any Railway Station in England'.[167]   B[enjamin] Bull, Dispensing & Family Chemist, advertised himself as an agent for The London, Birmingham, and Havana Cigar Company who 'sell their unequalled Cigars in neat cases, each case containing 6 cigars, mild, medium or full flavoured quality, guaranteed and the price moderate'.[168]

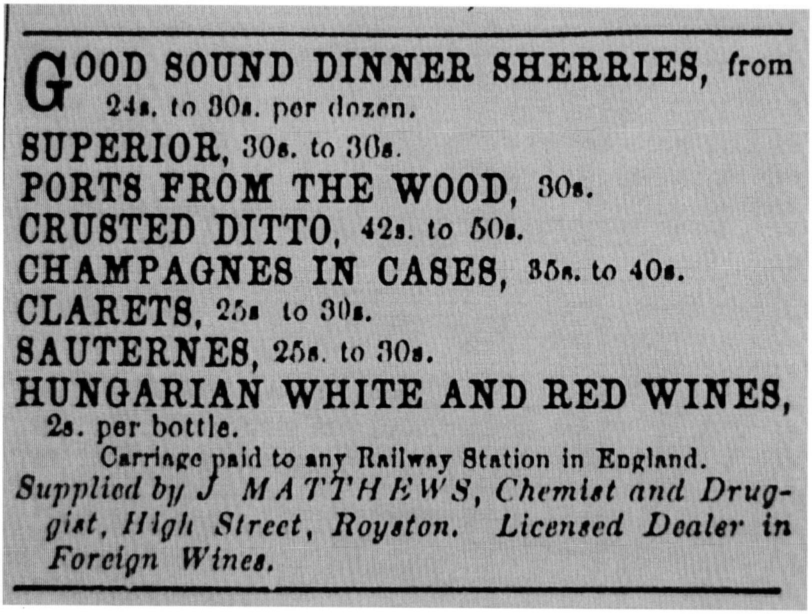

GOOD SOUND DINNER SHERRIES, from 24s. to 30s. per dozen.
SUPERIOR, 30s. to 36s.
PORTS FROM THE WOOD, 30s.
CRUSTED DITTO, 42s. to 50s.
CHAMPAGNES IN CASES, 36s. to 40s.
CLARETS, 25s to 30s.
SAUTERNES, 25s. to 30s.
HUNGARIAN WHITE AND RED WINES, 2s. per bottle.
    Carriage paid to any Railway Station in England.
Supplied by J MATTHEWS, Chemist and Druggist, High Street, Royston. Licensed Dealer in Foreign Wines.

Plate 6.10: Advertisement for a Royston wine dealer
Source: *Royston Crow*, 1 April 1863

A fourth category is that of distant manufacturers who, often with accolades to boast, felt it worthwhile to advertise their products in local newspapers such as *The Royston Crow* which suggests that they were likely to have been supplying them, either directly or indirectly via wholesalers, to the local retailers. Examples include Bryant & May's Matches winners of 'EIGHT PRIZE MEDALS', Coleman's Starch (Plate 6.11 below) claiming 'UNRIVALLED EXHIBITION HONORS – PARIS 1878', Coleman's Mustard boasting a 'SPECIAL

---

[166] *Royston Crow*, 1 December 1859, p. 264.

[167] Joseph Matthews, Chemist & Druggist, and China & Glass Dealer but not listed as a Wine Merchant, appeared in the *Post Office Directory Six Home Counties, 1862*, p. 377; *Royston Crow*, 1 April 1863, p. 433.

[168] Benjamin Bull, Chemist & Druggist, appeared in the *Post Office Directory Six Home Counties, Pt 1* (1870), p. 478; *Royston Crow*, 3 November 1876, un-paginated.

WARRANT TO THE QUEEN' and Sinclair's Cold Water Soap that was 'Awarded GOLD MEDAL, Melbourne, 1881'.[169] Occasionally the manufacturer was overseas and relied on their U.K. distributor for the promotion of their product. For example, Biller & Stevens, 110, Fenchurch Street, London, were sole importers and agents for J. S. Saccone's Gibraltar Sherries and advertised 'Manzanilla, Oloroso and Amontillado' as 'supplied throughout Her Majesty's Services, and shipped to all parts of the World'. Another, H.K. Terry & Co., 55, Holborn Viaduct, London, Wholesale Agents, placed advertisements for their 'LITTLE BEAUTIES' tipped cigarettes manufactured by Allen & Ginter of Richmond, Virginia, U.S.A.[170]

Plate 6.11: Advertisement for Colman's Mustard
Source: *Royston Crow*, 2 April 1880

Finally, one can detect evidence from some advertisements placed in *The Royston Crow* that this small town had sufficient 'middling' people with money to spend on luxuries to make their insertion in the newspaper worthwhile. This reflects, in part, Gareth Shaw's assertion that consumption in the late-nineteenth century was fuelled by the 'influences on consumer behaviour of mass advertising, price competition, fashion magazines, informed opinion and credit buying'.[171] Some

---

[169] *Herts & Cambs Reporter with which is incorporated The Royston Crow*, 8 April 1881, un-paginated; 2 April 1880, un-paginated; 1 July 1881, un-paginated; 2 December 1882, un-paginated.
[170] *Royston Crow*, 29 September 1876, un-paginated; *Herts & Cambs Reporter*, 20 January 1882, un-paginated.
[171] G. Shaw, 'The European Scene: Britain and Germany', in J. Benson and G. Shaw (eds), *The Evolution of Retail Systems, c. 1800-1914, Part 1, The Economics and Social Context of Retail Evolution* (Leicester, 1992), p. 29.

historians have argued that this 'consumer society' was encouraged by The Great Exhibition of 1851. According to Thomas Richards it erected 'a monument to the commodity' that shaped advertising for the next eighty-five years. He argued that it 'fashioned a mythology of consumerism' that like a prototype department store 'successfully integrated the paraphernalia of production into the immediate phenomenal space of consumption'.[172] For example, John Warren (Plate 6.12 below) informed the 'Ladies and Gentlemen of Royston ... that his Piano-forte Tuner and Repairer from LONDON, attends every quarter'. He also advised that

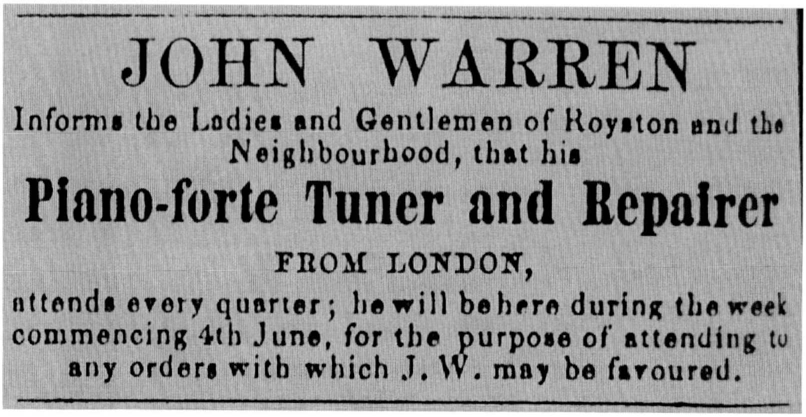

Plate 6.12: Advertisement for a Baldock piano tuner
Source: *Herts & Cambs Reporter*, 1 March 1855

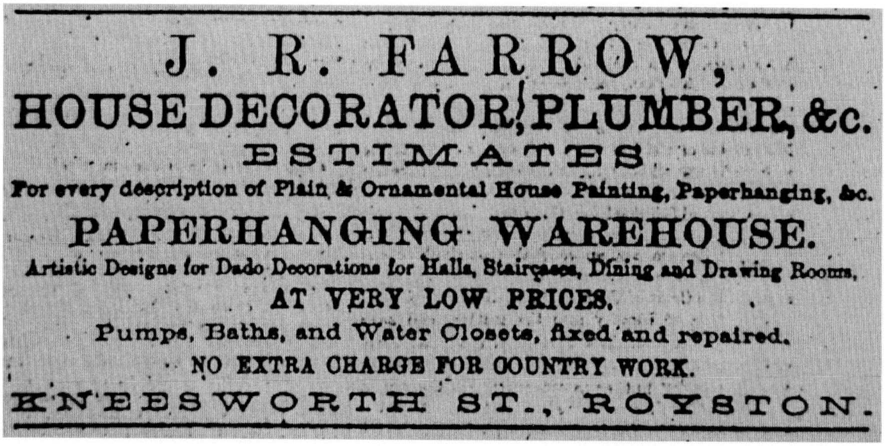

Plate 6.13: Advertisement for a Royston decorator & plumber
Source: *Herts & Cambs Reporter*, 1 July 1881

---

[172] Richards, *Commodity Culture of Victorian England*, pp. 17, 18, 30.

he was now 'appointed Agent for the London Stereoscopic Company' and invited the public to view his 'stock of Stereoscopes & Stereoscopic Pictures'. The boxed instrument and a fine collection of pictures could be purchased for 20 Guineas. T. S. Higgins assured potential customers that at the Royston Depot for 'MAPPIN & WEBB MANUFACTURING Silversmiths and Cutlers' in Kneesworth Street they would find the 'Same Prices charged as at their LONDON and SHEFFIELD SHOW ROOMS'. House decorator and plumber, J. R. Farrow (Plate 6.13 above), provided estimates for 'every description of Plain & Ornamental House Painting, Paperhanging, &c.' and in his paperhanging warehouse clients would find 'Artistic Designs for Dado Decoration for Halls, Staircases, Dining and Drawing Rooms, AT VERY LOW PRICES'.[173]

Advertisements placed in the local newspaper at this time would also have made the reader aware that improved communications were rapidly opening up a wider world. By the summer of 1863, *The Royston Crow* was able to publicise the 'Seaside and Excursion Train Arrangements' of the Great Eastern Railway which included the provision for 'journeying to and from' such places as Aldborough,

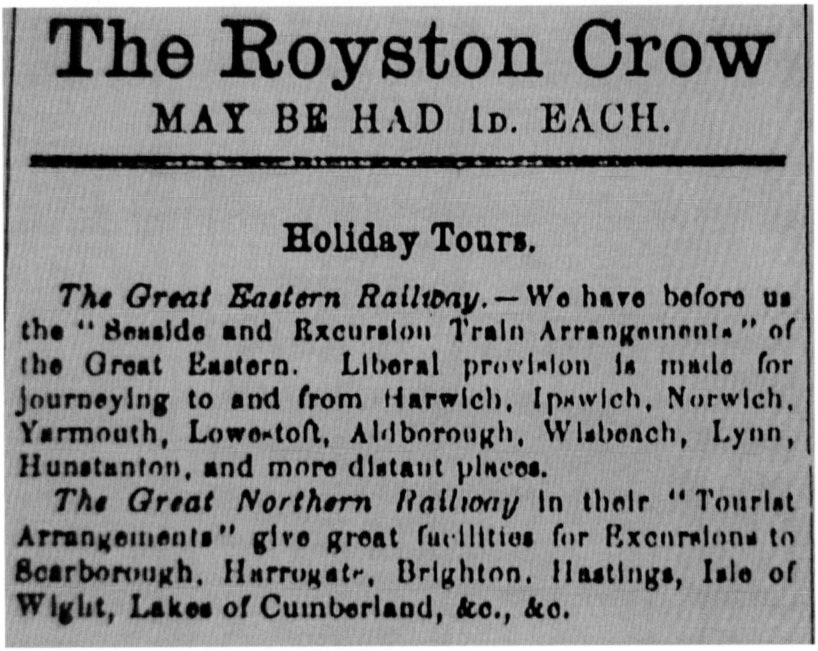

The Royston Crow

MAY BE HAD 1D. EACH.

Holiday Tours.

The Great Eastern Railway.—We have before us the "Seaside and Excursion Train Arrangements" of the Great Eastern. Liberal provision is made for journeying to and from Harwich, Ipswich, Norwich, Yarmouth, Lowestoft, Aldborough, Wisbeach, Lynn, Hunstanton, and more distant places.

The Great Northern Railway in their "Tourist Arrangements" give great facilities for Excursions to Scarborough, Harrogate, Brighton, Hastings, Isle of Wight, Lakes of Cumberland, &c., &c.

Plate 6.14: Advertisement for holiday tours by rail
Source: *Royston Crow*, 1 August 1863

[173] *Royston Crow*, 1 March 1855, p. 21; 1 December 1856, p. 121; *Herts & Cambs Reporter*, 4 April 1879, un-paginated; 1 July 1881, un-paginated.

Hunstanton, [Kings] Lynn, Lowestoft, Yarmouth and Norwich (Plate 6.14 above).[174]   For the more adventurous were the advertisements placed by the Dominion Line shipping company that, without naming the particular settlement, offered 'Free Land Grants of 160 Acres, with Bonus to Settlers'. Details of their weekly sailings from Liverpool, offering 'Special through bookings to all inland points in Canada and United States', were available from Ernest Matthews [chemist, dentist, wine & spirit merchant, and fire engine superintendent], High Street, Royston and Edwin Darville [bookseller & stationer], High Street, Buntingford.[175] So, by the latter part of the nineteenth century, the small towns of north-east Hertfordshire could be seen as part of the developing national leisure travel market, and their citizens potentially receptive to the inducements offered by the international emigration scene. Indeed, there must have been sufficient numbers of emigrants from the region for local shopkeepers like T. Goodman, a Royston grocer, to consider it worthwhile advertising goods aimed at that specific clientele, for example 'Groux' Spermaceti Navy Soap for Washing in Fresh and Salt Water, indispensable for Emigrants'.[176]

In her study of late eighteenth- and early nineteenth-century Manchester, Sheffield and Leeds, Hannah Barker found that elegantly styled newspaper advertisements catered for a readership that, at least in part, 'saw itself as refined and sophisticated'. She cited advertisements for 'polite' pastimes such as balls, concerts, playing an instrument or learning to dance that 'offer a unique insight into the cultural life of towns'.[177] Similarly, *The Royston Crow* provides such examples as Miss Poole (Plate 6.15 below) soliciting 'the patronage of the Gentry and Public in general of ROYSTON, for the FASHIONABLE ENTERTAINMENT of SELECT READINGS from SHAKSPEARE' at the Bull Inn's Assembly Room, Miss Stainton, on her return from Paris, offering 'Lessons in *Fashionable Dancing* and the CALISTHENIC EXERCISES' at the Royston Institute, and B. Waterhouse, from the Crystal Palace, declaring his intention to deliver a 'GRAPHIC LECTURE on *The Gorilla and other Monkeys Compared and Contrasted with Man*', also at the Royston Institute.[178] These activities paint a similar picture of 'middling culture … and provincial self confidence' to that which Barker noted in her study on large industrial towns.[179] Furthermore, as

---

[174] *Royston Crow*, 1 August 1863, p. 450.

[175] *Herts & Cambs Reporter*, 19 February 1892, p. 8; *Kelly's Directory Six Home Counties, Pt 1* (1890), pp. 808, 810; 1891 Census (Buntingford).

[176] *The Royston Crow*, 1 March 1855, p. 21. Spermaceti was a white waxy substance obtained from sperm whales and used in the manufacture of candles, soaps, etc.

[177] H. Barker, *The Business of Women: Female Enterprise and Urban Development in Northern England, 1760–1830* (Oxford, 2006), p. 27.

[178] *Royston Crow*, 1 June 1855, p. 45; *Royston Crow*, 1 October 1860, p. 306; *Royston Crow*, 1 April 1863, p. 433.

[179] Barker, *Business of Women*, p. 34.

Morris suggested, such performers and speakers 'often from the metropolitan centre of London, frequently provided the stimulus for activity and innovation' among the local populace.[180]

READING OF THE COURT AND DRAWING ROOM

MISS POOLE

Respectfully solicits the patronage of the Gentry and Public in general of Royston, for the

FASHIONABLE ENTERTAINMENT,

(so often commanded by Her Majesty the Queen) of

SELECT READINGS from SHAKSPEARE;

OR,

The Portraiture of the Passions from Classic Authors, Crabbe, Prior, Mrs. Hemans, &c. &c.,

Combining that pathos, feeling, and energy, which the fine and noble subject requires. It forms a pleasing performance—blending Instruction with amusement—that may be enjoyed by persons of a refined and classic taste, of all opinions and persuasions.

The design of this Entertainment is to improve the Ear, to impart a correct Pronunciation, free from Provincial Accent, and at the same time to develope the most prominent traits in the Female Characters of " The Swan of Avon," and some of our Classic living Authors.

This Entertainment will take place at

The Assembly Room, Bull Inn, Royston,

On Friday, the 8th day of June, 1855.

Admission—Reserved Seats 2s; Second Seats, 1s; Children to the Reserved Seats, 1s.

☞ Tickets may be had at Mr. Warren's, Bookseller; where the Subscribers List is open.

Doors to be open at Half-past 7. To commence at 8 o'clock.

CARRIAGES MAY BE ORDERED AT A QUARTER TO TEN.

Plate 6.15: Advertisement for fashionable entertainment in Royston
Source: *Royston Crow*, 1 June 1855

---

[180] R.J. Morris, 'Civil Society and the Nature of Urbanism in Britain, 1750-1850', *Urban History*, 25, 3 (1998), p. 294.

Trade exhibitions

Since the Crystal Palace Exhibition in 1851, the national public trade exhibition had become, according to Anne Clendinning, an 'important promotional medium for a wide spectrum of goods, from manufactured items and imported foods, to public services such as gas and electricity'.[181] This specialist alternative form of advertising was important enough to warrant detailed reporting in *The Times* newspaper. For example, it reported at length on 21 October 1895 that the '17th yearly exhibition and market organized by the brewers and allied trades' would open that day at the Agricultural Hall, Islington in north London. The reporter ventured the view that 'it will be no less comprehensive and instructive than its predecessors'. Exhibitors were to include brewers, maltsters, distillers, mineral water, and other non-alcoholic drink manufacturers, 'together with the appliances they use'.[182]

Simpson's Brewery may well have exhibited their own products but they certainly attended with a view to seeing the latest from other suppliers especially with regard to their decision, discussed above, to begin production of bottled beers as a number of letters written the following week demonstrate. For example, a letter of 26 October to Foxon Robinson & Co. of Sheffield referred to the fact that 'you quoted us at the Brewers Exhibition for Class B No 3 varnished 2 coats beer bottle boxes' and went on to place an order for several hundred of various sizes with 'inner wire binding' that were to be branded SIMPSON & CO. THE BREWERY BALDOCK. A second to Ryder & Co. in north-east London ordered '70 gross of Imperial pint beer bottles and screw stoppers as quoted to us at the Brewers Exhibition'. A third letter to G. H. Gledhill & Co. of Cambridge pointed out that Simpson's had inspected their 'bottle washing & rinsing machine' at the exhibition and would welcome a quote of the lowest price for that apparatus delivered complete plus 'the price for 20 of the 3 doz[en] pint draining crates'.[183] Simpson's would probably have agreed with the chairman of the event who was quoted by *The Times* as saying 'the object of the exhibition was the good of all who were connected with a great and staple industry in the country'.

The evidence demonstrates that, in addition to their basic advertising role for a town's service providers, trade directories included important sections on regional and national services such as banking and insurance. It is clear that local entrepreneur John Warren began promoting advertising in his publication, *The*

---

[181] A. Clendinning, ' "Deft Fingers" and "Persuasive Eloquence": The "Lady Demons" of the English Gas Industry, 1888-1918, *Women's History Review*, 9, 3 (2000), p. 504.

[182] *The Times*, 21 October 1895, p. 10, in The Times Digital Archive, 1785–1985, www.infotrac.galegroup.com/itw/infomark (2 January 2008, accessed 13 June 2008).

[183] Simpson's Letter Book, pp. 68, 67, 69.

Royston Crow, about thirty years before the date suggested by Fraser thus greatly benefiting the regional economy.

Conclusion

Apart from traditional craftsmen like Thomas Picking of Ashwell, perhaps rather insular and therefore isolated from the fast developing world outside, improved nineteenth-century communications had a great impact on the regional economy of north-east Hertfordshire. Most crucial was the replacement of long-distance horse-drawn coaches and waggons by the railways. The arrival in 1851 of the GNR at Ashwell, Baldock and Royston, and in 1863 of the Ware Hadham & Buntingford railway at Buntingford, heralded a change that integrated local manufacturers, service providers and their customers into the developing British economy of mass-produced goods and the wider global market. Examination of business records from Simpson's Brewery in Baldock, the Baldock Gas Company, and the Farmers' Manure Company of Royston provide an insight into the crucial role that the railways played in their activities.

As clearly demonstrated by Simpson's Letter Book, Rowland Hill's 'Uniform Penny Post' of 1840 was heavily utilised by the region's brewers and maltsters, as was the electric telegraph. Britain's late-nineteenth-century postal service provided a business such as Simpson's with a fast and reliable means of communication between their suppliers and the managers of their extensive estate of tied public houses.

Baldock, Buntingford and Royston, each with the benefit of the railway to bring in the essential coal, were prosperous enough to attract those entrepreneurs and investors willing to exploit the technological development of coal-gas. This meant that the citizens of these small towns benefited from well-lit pavements and shops, and a domestic gas supply for lighting and cooking in their homes.

Advertising, in trade directories and local newspapers like *The Royston Crow*, played a key-role in local and regional business activities. Furthermore, in addition to benefiting the trade of local and regional retailers and service providers, many of the advertisements demonstrated the increasing availability of foodstuffs and other products made possible by improved transport and Britain's integration into world markets. Following the enormous success of the Great Exhibition of 1851, specialist trade exhibitions, another important mode of advertising, kept industries abreast of the latest developments in their particular field of business.

Newspaper advertisements brought many wonders of the late-Victorian world to the attention of their readers. The wide range of commodities and consumables portrayed in *The Royston Crow*, many stocked and supplied by John Warren its publisher and printer, must have reflected the ability of many of the town's populace to purchase them. Royston, through the activities of its PTPSs, and no doubt Baldock and Buntingford too, were small urban centres providing a range of employment opportunities that increased individual wealth and allowed increasing numbers of their townsfolk to enter into the expanding consumer society.

McKendrick argued that while pedlars offered 'an unpredictable, if welcome opportunity to spend' and annual fairs a brief but regular chance to indulge, it was the provincial clothing shop that offered 'a permanent, regular outlet which, if well served by London and the major industrialists', could satisfy the local consumer's 'appetite for fashion'. Many of the retailers identified in the dress category of the dealing sector (chapter 2, Figure 2.7), including the aforementioned Thomas Westrope, would have acknowledged his argument that the power of newspaper advertisements to inform the public of their latest attractions, their array of fashions and their links with London, assured the provincial shopkeeper of the 'ultimate victory as the main retail outlet' for clothing.[184]

David Harvey argued that as industrialization gained momentum more business activities including distribution and the service sector were 'integrated through market exchange'. He thought that with 'adequate transport facilities' it was possible to match supply and demand relatively quickly. Harvey concluded that the 'spatial integration' of much of the world through 'market exchange' was 'contingent upon the existence of adequate means of communication'.[185] This chapter emphasises how the regional economy of north-east Hertfordshire greatly benefited from the various nineteenth-century improvements in communications to become well integrated into the developing national and international trade markets. Furthermore, evidence gleaned from the analysis of advertising as the nineteenth century progressed strongly supports McKendrick's view that 'that which had previously been looked on as a luxury for the worker was thought of in terms of being a decency or even a necessity', especially for those aspiring to join in the cultural activities of Royston's elegant society .[186] It might also suggest that for a few of the more leisured class in this small rural town, influenced by the proximity of London, expenditure was beginning 'to contribute efficiently to the

---

[184] McKendrick, 'Commercialization of Fashion', pp. 89, 90.
[185] D. Harvey, *Social Justice and the City* (London, 1973), pp. 243, 244.
[186] McKendrick, 'Commercialization of Fashion', p. 60.

individual's "good fame" ' by their ability to afford what their contemporary Thorstein Veblen labelled "superfluities", that is to engage in conspicuous consumption.[187]   Proof, as more recently Woodruff Smith argued, that demand 'for consumer goods in the nineteenth century arose from people's use of goods to signal and maintain their respectability'.[188]

Morris argued that 'an associational culture was a choice of the urbanite'. Throughout the nineteenth century, he suggested, more and more places had the 'threshold size of population to sustain a variety of [voluntary] associations' and cultural activities. This view has been supported recently by Barrie Trinder who suggested that more substantial towns were 'centres for cultural and social organisations' that might be 'centrifugal, town-based bodies like mechanics' institutes or temperance societies ... duty-bound to spread messages in the surrounding countryside'.[189]   Such was the case in Royston, where an early twentieth-century town history by Alfred Kingston explained how 'literary and artistic culture and public spirit' flourished 'first as a Mechanics' Institute, founded in 1831' and later as the Royston Institute which opened its doors in 1856.   Pigot described this in 1862 as possessing a reading room, classrooms, museum and lecture hall, and its objects 'being the instruction of its members in the various branches of useful knowledge, the rational amusement of the members, and the cultivation of their tastes'.[190]

Newspapers like *The Royston Crow* were 'essential to the activities of associational culture' as demonstrated by the sample of its advertisements discussed above. Morris also argued that by recycling information from other urban centres a town became a 'focus for information flows' which was 'important for [its] commercial advantage and success'.[191]   The range of advertisements carried by *The Royston Crow* clearly demonstrate not only the cultural life of the town but the paper's regional role as a window on the variety of goods and services available from the wider commercial world in Royston, the most important centre in north-east Hertfordshire's urban hierarchy.

---

[187] T. Veblen, *The Theory of the Leisure Class, with an Introduction by John Kenneth Galbraith* (Boston, 1973), p. 77.

[188] W.D. Smith, *Consumption and the Making of Respectability, 1600-1800* (New York, 2002), p. 3.

[189] Morris, 'Nature of Urbanism', p. 295; B. Trinder, 'Towns and Industries: The Changing Character of Manufacturing Towns', in J. Stobart and N. Raven (eds), *Towns, Regions and Industries: Urban and Industrial Change in the Midlands, c. 1700-1840* (Manchester, 2005), p. 105.

[190] A. Kingston, *A History of Royston, Hertfordshire, with Biographical Notes of Royston Worthies* (London, 1906, reprinted Royston, 1975), p. 182; *Post Office Directory Six Home Counties, 1862*, p. 376.

[191] Morris, 'Nature of Urbanism', p. 295.

Small but Flourishing

Conclusion

It is clear, from this analysis of nineteenth-century small-town service provision, that utilising both trade directories and census returns facilitates the collection of comprehensive data regarding the individual providers. The approach also overcomes the lack of comprehensiveness of both sources owing, on the one hand, to significant numbers of service providers opting out of inclusion in a trade directory and, on the other, to the considerable number of people absent from the CEBs. Although the two sources display a confusion of terminology in their description of occupations, together they present a far broader picture of service provision than could be obtained using either in isolation. Employment figures are difficult to assess as directories contain no such information and CEBs lack consistency in their approach to this data element. One further major problem with the censuses stems from Victorian society's attitude towards working women and the concomitant attitude of the GRO and its census enumerators which, it is generally argued, led to a serious under-recording of female employment in the CEBs.

Analysis of the full range of services provided by over 4100 manufacturers, dealers and members of the professions was facilitated by nominal record linkage between the two primary data sources. Furthermore, this enabled the fact that numerous PTPSs were engaged in multiple activities to be fully explored. Baldock and Royston's business communities benefited greatly from the passing trade that stemmed from their strategic locations on the Great North Road and Old North Road respectively. The barley produced by the surrounding fertile farmlands led to malting and brewing being two major manufacturing activities across the region. Together these assets helped create increased business opportunities and demands from a 'middling society' that fuelled an increase in the number and range of local retailers, happy to exploit the benefits of these small towns' integration into developing national and international markets by utilising the growing rail network. Clearly the 'consumer revolution' had penetrated this rural corner of Hertfordshire by the middle of the nineteenth century with the appearance in these small urban settlements of many 'luxury trades' including booksellers, china and glass merchants, confectioners, music sellers, watch makers, and wine merchants.

Despite the majority view that Victorian society was prejudiced against working women, the present evidence clearly suggests it was not always the case. Here, over half the female PTPSs identified were engaged in the 'dealing' sector and a few in 'manufacturing' in addition to those working in the more traditional professional teaching roles.

Utilizing the CEBs from 1851 to 1891 enabled almost 3000 skilled and semi-skilled ATPSs to be identified. The total excludes domestic servants and probably underestimates the number of women and girls employed, especially by the clothing trade. As in the case of PTPSs this Hertfordshire data provides evidence of female ATPSs working as butchers, fishmongers, fruiterers, greengrocers, grocers and ironmongers, occupations that Victorian society generally considered too rough and heavy for women. The analysis also provides evidence that the Post Offices in these small centres were, from 1851 onwards, in the vanguard of offering employment opportunities as assistants to middle-class women. Clearly, from the present survey, there were many opportunities for boys and girls to be apprenticed in a wide range of trades, with some youngsters employed at great distances from their homes. Identifying the region's major employers proved difficult confirming, as others have noted, that employers and/or the census enumerators frequently failed to provide information on their workforce.

Analysis identified the very limited service provision available to the inhabitants of five larger (population range 800 – 1200) and eleven smaller (population range 200 – 600) villages lying within the triangle bounded by Baldock, Buntingford and Royston. The majority of goods and services available were those offered by publicans, grocers, drapers, other non-specific 'shopkeepers', bakers, blacksmiths, carpenters and wheelwrights. This evidence suggests that these villages, given the absence of any large regional urban centres, were heavily reliant on the three nearby small towns to provide more than just a channel for the sale of the surrounding countryside's farm produce.

Utilizing statistical models of Christaller's central place theory allowed the attenuated regional urban hierarchy of north-east Hertfordshire to be established. Most significantly it identified Baldock, Buntingford and Royston as high order 'central places' whose functional indexes increased between 1851 to 1890 despite population falls in the latter two cases. This evidence confirms that these small urban centres were not in decline during the latter part of the nineteenth century owing much of that success to their strategic regional location.

This research introduced the novel concept of an *extra-urban matrix* comprising the small towns, villages and hamlets interspersed between the larger towns normally recognized by urban historians as belonging to the seven ranks of Christaller's 'central place' hierarchies. Within the *extra-urban matrix* of north-east Hertfordshire the present analysis of goods and services demonstrated that, despite their modest nineteenth-century populations of less than 2500 inhabitants, Baldock, Buntingford and Royston were centres of commercial importance with surprisingly high functional indexes. Given its geographical position and significantly lower index it is suggested that Ashwell, the smallest of the four centres, while offering more than the average village was probably a satellite of neighbouring Baldock.

Evidence shows that within the regional business community of north-east Hertfordshire the majority of the providers of goods and services, principal and ancillary, had geographical origins outside of the study towns, i.e. the economy of the region was sustained and developed by inward migration. The present research has amply shown that, contrary to the views of some historians, birth-place data extracted from CEBs can provide meaningful migratory data. Despite the proximity of the four centres to London, and contrary to many migration theories, this present analysis has clearly established that a number of definable streams of migrants headed for north-east Hertfordshire rather than the capital. Indeed, the dominant flow of incoming PTPSs was northwards out of the London and Middlesex area. Distances travelled by some of these migrants suggest that these four small towns were viewed as centres of potential betterment that offered the chance of employment, business opportunities and an improved life.

Crucial to their success as centres of manufacture and dealing during the second-half of the nineteenth century was the arrival of the railway which integrated them into the wider industrial economy. While horse-drawn passenger coaching services disappeared, short-haul commercial carrier services flourished with the need to convey goods to and from the region's railheads. Integration, as exemplified by the extracts from Simpson's Letter Book, was greatly aided by business's ability to embrace other Victorian developments in communications such as the uniform postal service and the electric telegraph.

The activities of the Baldock Gas Company and similar enterprises in Buntingford and Royston gave these small towns the advantages of street and domestic lighting together with the chance for their citizens to embrace the latest in household cooking appliances. Such developments, not available during the latter part of the nineteenth century to small rural communities, help confirm the growing prosperity of these three centres.

An examination of the range of advertising found in *The Royston Crow* from 1855 onwards clearly demonstrates the entrepreneurial nature of John Warren's publishing enterprise. Many of the advertisements that appeared indicate an increasing demand for the latest in fashionable consumer goods and suggest the ability on the part of Royston's 'middling' people to engage in a degree of conspicuous consumption.

The indications of the present research obviously suggest that other clusters of successful small towns, similar in size to Baldock, Buntingford and Royston, exist elsewhere within the wider *extra-urban matrix*. While the resources needed probably preclude the present study's comprehensive dual methodology from being applied to large urban centres, it would facilitate other comparative surveys of similar regional clusters of small urban settlements. They are most likely to occur where groups of small settlements with specialist manufacturing activities are located at key foci on transport networks but well away from major urban centres. This probability presents opportunities for further avenues of research by local, economic and urban historians.

Appendix

Adapted version of Booth's classification of occupations[1]

Below are details of the sectors and sub-categories utilized in this volume for the detailed analysis of the provision of goods and services together with examples of occupations identified in the study.

Agricultural Sector

Includes agricultural machine proprietor, animal dealer (various), farmer, farm bailiff, farrier, gardener, groom, horse breeder, keeper and/or dealer, seedsman, shepherd and veterinary surgeon.

Building and Contracting Sector

Includes architect, bricklayer, builder, carpenter and joiner, civil engineer, contractor, glazier, painter, paperhanger, plasterer, plumber, sawyer, stonemason and surveyor.

Manufacturing Sector (consisting of thirteen sub-categories)

Machinery	Includes engineer and machinist.
Iron and Steel	Includes blacksmith and iron-founder.
Copper, Tin, Lead	Includes brass-founder, brazier, tinman, tinplate worker, whitesmith, wire-maker and wire-weaver.
Earthenware	Includes brick-maker, drainpipe maker, lime-burner, and tile-maker.
Flax	Rope- and twine-maker

---

[1] This is based upon a detailed breakdown of Booth's occupational groups as listed in W.A. Armstrong, 'The Use of Information about Occupations', in E.A. Wrigley (ed.), *Nineteenth-century Society: Essays in the Use of Quantitative Methods for the Study of Social Data* (Cambridge, 1972), pp. 253 - 83.

Furs and Leather Includes brush-maker, currier, fellmonger, leather cutter and tanner.

Glue, Tallow, Etc. Includes tallow chandler.

Wood Workers Includes basket-maker, cooper and sieve-maker.

Woollen Wool-stapler

Furniture Includes cabinet-maker, French polisher, upholsterer and undertaker.

Carriages and Harness Includes coach-builder, coach-maker, coach-painter, collar-maker, harness-maker, saddle-maker, saddler, and wheelwright.

Food Preparation Includes bacon smoker and corn miller.

Drink Preparation Includes maltster and brewer.

Transport and Communications Sector (latter added by Carr-Saunders, et al)

Includes cabman, flyman, coachman, carman, carrier, carter and drayman, and railway worker including engine driver, plate layer and porter.

Dealing and Distributive Trades Sector (latter added by Carr-Saunders, et al, consisting of eleven sub-categories)

Coal Includes agent, dealer, merchant and retailer.

Raw Materials Includes coprolite merchant, corn and cake merchant/chandler, flour dealer, plait dealer, sand dealer, seed dealer, stone dealer, straw dealer, timber merchant and yeast dealer.

Dress Includes Berlin wool dealer, draper (linen and/or woollen), haberdasher, hosier, mantle-maker, outfitter, stay and corset maker. Also includes boot and shoemaker, tailor, clothier, hatter and milliner, dressmaker, etc., that Booth put under manufacture.

Food	Includes butcher, cheesemonger, coffee room proprietor, dairyman, fishmonger, fruiterer, greengrocer, grocer, milkman, poulterer, provision dealer, sweetshop owner and tea dealer. Also includes baker and confectioner, etc., that Booth put under manufacture.
Wines, Spirits and	Includes beer retailer, beer seller, hotel and inn keeper
Hotels	(including commercial ones), publican, wine and spirit merchant.
Furniture	Includes furniture broker and/or dealer, and pawnbroker.
Stationery and **Publications**	Includes bill sticker, bookseller, music seller, printer, newsagent and stationer.
Household	Includes artist, domestic machine dealer, earthenware, china and/or glass dealer, fancy repository/warehouse, florist, ironmonger, jeweller, photographer, tobacconist and umbrella maker. Also clock & watch maker, instrument maker and toyshops that Booth put under manufacture.
Lodgings, etc	Lodging-house keeper
General Dealers	Includes hawker, marine store dealer, rag dealer and shopkeeper (unspecified).
Unspecified	Includes auctioneer, commercial traveller, dealer (unspecified), house agent, land dealer and land valuer.

Industrial Services Sector

Includes banking and insurance services, e.g. insurance agent, commercial clerk, debt collector, secretaries and officers of commercial companies.

Public and Professional Services Sector

Includes chemist and druggist, civil servant including tax official, dentist, general practitioner, governess, librarian, local administrator including Poor Law official, police force, magistrate, nurse, postal worker, physician and/or surgeon, solicitor, school teacher, stamp distributor and telegraphist.

Domestic Services Sector

Includes chimney-sweep, hairdresser and laundress.

Note: This scheme excludes Booth's categories of fishing, mining and quarrying which are not relevant to Hertfordshire, and general industrial labouring services that he included in the 'Industrial Service Sector' and which were excluded from this study.

Bibliography

Manuscript Sources

Hertfordshire Archives and Local Studies (HALS)

D/EFmZ1	Thomas Picking, Carpenter, Account Book, 1855 – 1869.
D/Eky/B1	Farmers' Manure Company – Ledgers, Cashbooks, Registers & Business Records, Impersonal Ledger, 1870 – 1972.
D/ESb/B59	Simpsons Brewery, Day Book of Expenditure on Barley, 1853 - 1945.
D/ESb/B90	Simpsons Brewery, Letter Book, February 1880 – June 18
D/P7/14/2	Ashwell Register Book of Parish Apprentices, 1817 - 1842.
D/P7/14/3	Ashwell: Miscellaneous Papers re Apprenticeship, 1790 - 1850.
PUG1/1/1	Baldock Gas Light & Coke Co., Minutes of Meetings of Directors, 1875 - 1888.

Census Enumerators' Books (microfilmed versions)

Ashwell

1851	H0 107 1707
1861	RG 9 812
1871	RG 10 1359
1881	RG 11 1411
1891	RG 12 1101

Baldock

1851	HO 107 1709
1861	RG 9 816
1871	RG 10 1364
1881	RG 11 1416
1891	RG 12 1105

Buntingford

1851   HO 107 1707
1861   RG 9 811
1871   RG 10 1357/58
1881   RG 11 1410
1891   RG 12 1100

Royston

1851   HO 107 1707
1861   RG 9 813/14
1871   RG 10 1359/60
1881   RG 11 1412
1891   RG 12 1102

Primary Printed Sources

Calendar of Charter Rolls, Vol. V, 15 Edward III – 5 Henry V, 1341 – 1417 (London, 1916), *41 Edward III, 1367*, p. 209.

Craven & Co's Commercial Directory of Bedfordshire & Hertfordshire, 1854 (Nottingham, 1854).

Holden's Annual London and County Directory of the United Kingdom and Wales in Three Volumes for the Year 1811, Vol. 3 (London, 1811)

Kelly, E.R. (ed.), *Post Office Directory of the Six Home Counties, Part I: Essex, Herts, Middlesex, Kent* (London, 1870).

Kelly, E.R. (ed.), *Kelly's Directory of the Six Home Counties, Part I: Essex, Herts & Middlesex* (London, 1882).

Kelly's Directory of the Six Home Counties, Part I: Essex, Herts & Middlesex (London, 1890).

Kelly's Directory of Hertfordshire with Large Map, 1895 (London, 1894).

Pigot and Co.'s Commercial Directory for 1823 – 24, Hertfordshire (London, 1824).

Pigot and Co.'s Commercial Directory for 1826 – 27, Hertfordshire (London, 1827).

Pigot and Co.'s Commercial Directory & Topography of Hertfordshire, 1833 – 34 (London, 1834).

Pigot and Co.'s Royal National and Commercial Directory and Topography of the Counties of Essex, Hertfordshire, Middlesex (London, 1839).

Pigot & Co.'s Directory for 1839, Cambridgeshire (London, 1839).

Post Office Directory of the Six Home Counties: Essex, Herts, Middlesex, Kent, Surrey & Sussex, 1851 (London, 1851)

Post Office Directory of the Six Home Counties: Essex, Herts, Middlesex, Kent, Surrey & Sussex, 1862 (London, 1862).

Robson's Directory of London & the Six Home Counties [Essex, Herts, Kent, Mdsx, Surrey, Sussex with parts of Berks & Bucks], Vol. II (London, 1838).

Newspapers and Periodicals

Herts & Cambs Reporter, November 1877 – April 1884

Herts & Cambs Reporter and The Royston Crow, May 1884 – December 1892

The Royston Crow, January 1855 – October 1877

Published Secondary Sources

Aldcroft, D.H. and M.J. Freeman (eds), *Transport in the Industrial Revolution* (Manchester, 1983).

Agar, N., 'Hertfordshire Rail Excursions in the Nineteenth Century', *Herts Past & Present (3rd Series)*, 17 (2011), pp. 28-30.

Alexander, D., *Retailing in England during the Industrial Revolution* (London, 1970).

Alexander, N. and G. Akehurst (eds), *The Emergence of Modern Retailing, 1750 – 1950* (London, 1999).

Armstrong, W.A., 'The Use of Information about Occupations', in Wrigley, *Quantitative Methods for the Study of Social Data*, pp. 191–310.

Armstrong, W.A., *Stability and Change in an English County Town: A Social Study of York, 1801 - 51* (London, 1974).

Baines, D., *Migration in a Mature Economy: Emigration and Internal Migration in England and Wales, 1861 – 1900* (Cambridge, 1985).

Balser, D., *Sisterhood & Solidarity: Feminism and Labor in Modern Times* (Boston, 1987).

Banks, J.A., 'The Social Structure of Nineteenth Century England as Seen Through the Census', in Lawton, *Census and Social Structure*, pp. 179–223.

Barker, H., ' "Smoke Cities": Northern Industrial Towns in Late Georgian England', *Urban History*, 31, 2 (2004), pp. 175-90.

Barker, H., *The Business of Women: Female Enterprise and Urban Development in Northern England, 1760 – 1830* (Oxford, 2006).

Barker, T., and D. Gerhold, *The Rise and Rise of Road Transport, 1700 – 1990* (Cambridge, 1995).

Barker, T.C. and J.R. Harris, *A Merseyside Town in the Industrial Revolution: St Helens, 1750 - 1900* (London, 1959).

Barker, T.C. and C.I. Savage, *An Economic History of Transport in Britain* (3rd edn, London, 1974).

Beavon, K.S.O., *Central Place Theory: A Reinterpretation* (London, 1977).

Beguin, H., 'Christaller's Central Place Postulates: A Commentary', *Annals of Regional Science*, 26 (1992), pp. 209-29.

Bellamy, J.M., 'Occupation Statistics in the Nineteenth Century Censuses', in Lawton, *Census and Social Structure*, pp. 165–77.

Benson, J. and G. Shaw (eds), *The Evolution of Retail Systems, c. 1800 - 1914* (Leicester, 1992).

Benson, J. and L. Ugolini (eds), *A Nation of Shopkeepers: Five Centuries of British Retailing* (London, 2003).

Berg, M., 'Women's Property and the Industrial Revolution', *J. Interdisciplinary History*, 24, 2 (1993), pp. 233-50.

Bird, J.H., 'Of Central Places, Cities and Seaports', *Geography*, 58, 2 (1973), pp. 105-18.

Blankenhorn, D., ' "Our Class of Workmen": The Cabinet-makers Revisited', in Harrison and Zeitlin, *Divisions of Labour*, pp. 19-46.

Blome, R., *Britannia, or, A Geographical Description of the Kingdoms of England, Scotland, and Ireland, with the Isles and Territories Thereto Belonging* (London, 1673).

Booth, C., 'Occupations of the People of the United Kingdom, 1801 – 81', from a paper delivered in London to The Statistical Society on 18 May 1886, reproduced in Routh, *Occupations of the People of Great Britain*, pp.1–17.

Bowen, J.P., 'The Carriers of Lancaster 1824 - 1912', *Local Historian*, 40, 3 (2010), pp. 178-90.

Boyer, G.R. and T.J. Hatton, 'Migration and Labour Market Integration in Late Nineteenth-century England and Wales', *Economic History Review*, 50, 4 (1997), pp. 697–734.

Bradley, J. and M. Dupree, 'A Shadow of Orthodoxy? An Epistemology of British Hydropathy, 1840 - 1858', *Medical History*, 47 (2003), pp. 173-94.

Brown, D., 'The Rise of Industrial Society and the End of the Self-contained Village, 1760 – 1900?', in Dyer, *The Self-contained Village?*, pp. 114-37.

Brown, J., *The English Market Town: A Social and Economic History, 1750 – 1914* (Marlborough, 1986).

Brown, J., 'Arable Farming Practices', in Mingay, *Agrarian History of England and Wales, Vol. 6*, pp. 276 – 95.

Brunt, L., 'Where there's Muck, there's Brass: The Market for Manure in the Industrial Revolution', *Economic History Review*, 60, 2 (2007), pp. 333 –72.

Burns, L.S. and R.G. Healy, 'The Metropolitan Hierarchy of Occupations: An Economic Interpretation of Central Place Theory', *Regional Science and Urban Economics*, 8, 4 (1978), pp. 381-93.

Bysouth, P.T., *Hertfordshire's Icknield Way: 19th Century Migration Frontier and Marriage Obstacle* (Cambridge, 2010).

Bythell, D., *The Sweated Trades: Outwork in Nineteenth-century Britain* (London, 1978).

Cameron, L.G., 'Hertfordshire', in Stamp, *The Land of Britain*, pp. 307-52.

Carter, H., *The Study of Urban Geography* (4th edn, London, 1995).

Carter, M. and W.K.D. Davies (eds), *Urban Essays: Studies in the Geography of Wales* (London, 1970).

Chartres, J.A., 'Country Tradesmen', in Mingay, *Victorian Countryside, Vol. 1*, pp. 300-13.

Chartres, J.A. and G.L. Turnbull, 'Country Craftsmen', in Mingay, *Victorian Countryside, Vol. 1*, pp. 314-28.

Cherry, S., *Medical Services and the Hospitals in Britain, 1860 – 1939* (Cambridge, 1996).

Christaller, W., 'Central Places in Southern Germany' ([Unpublished Doctoral Dissertation, Friedrich-Alexander University of Erlangen, Nuremerg, 1933] Trans. C.W. Baskin, New Jersey, 1966).

Church, R.A., *Economic and Social Change in a Midland Town: Victorian Nottingham, 1815 - 1900* (London, 1966).

Church, R.A., 'The Shoe and Leather Industries', in Church, *Dynamics of Victorian Business*, pp. 199–211.

Church, R.A. (ed.), *The Dynamics of Victorian Business: Problems and Perspectives to the 1870s* (London, 1980).

Church, R.A., 'Problems and Perspectives', in R. Church, *Victorian Business: Problems and Perspectives*, pp. 1–45.

Clapham, J.H., *An Economic History of Modern Britain, Vol. 1, The Early Railway Age, 1820 – 1850* (2nd edn, Cambridge, 1930).

Clapham, J.H., *An Economic History of Modern Britain, Vol. 2, Free Trade and Steel, 1850 – 1886* (Cambridge, 1932).

Clark, C., *The British Malting Industry since 1830* (London, 1998).

Clark, P. (ed.), *The Cambridge Urban History of Britain, Vol. 2, 1540 – 1840* (Cambridge, 2000).

Clark, P., 'Small Towns 1700 – 1840', in Clark, *Urban History of Britain, Vol. 2*, pp. 733-73.

Clark, P., 'Elite Networking and the Formation of an Industrial Small Town: Loughborough, 1700 - 1840', in Stobart and Raven, *Towns, Regions and Industries*, pp. 161-75.

Clark, P., 'Migration in England during the Late Seventeenth and Early Eighteenth Centuries', in Clark and Souden, *Migration and Society*, pp. 213–52.

Clark, P. and L. Murfin, *The History of Maidstone: The Making of a Modern County Town* (Stroud, 1995).

Clark, P. and D. Souden (eds), *Migration and Society in Early Modern England* (London, 1987).

Clarkson, L.A., 'The Manufacture of Leather', in 'The Agricultural Servicing and Processing Industries', in Mingay, *Agrarian History of England and Wales, Vol. 6*, pp. 466-83.

Clendinning, A., ' "Deft Fingers" and "Persuasive Eloquence": The "Lady Demons" of the English Gas Industry, 1888 - 1918, *Women's History Review*, 9, 3 (2000), pp. 501-38.

Cockman, F.G., *The Railways of Hertfordshire, Hertfordshire Local Studies, No. 1* (Hertford, 1978).

Collins, E.J.T., 'Introduction to Chapter 5, The Agricultural Servicing and Processing Industries', in Mingay, *Agrarian History of England and Wales, Vol. 6, 1750 – 1850*, pp. 384–97.

Collins, E.J.T., (ed.), *The Agrarian History of England and Wales, Vol. 7, Pt. 2, 1850 – 1914* (Cambridge, 2000).

Collinson, P., *The Birthpangs of Protestant England: Religious and Cultural Change in the Sixteenth and Seventeenth Centuries* (London, 1988).

Combs, M.B., 'Wives and Household Wealth: The Impact of the 1870 British Married Women's Property Act on Wealth-holding and Share of Household Resources', *Continuity and Change*, 19, 1 (2004), pp. 141-63.

Cook, C. and B. Keith, *British Historical Facts, 1830 – 1900* (London, 1975).

Cordery, S., *British Friendly Societies, 1750 - 1914* (Basingstoke, 2003).

Corran, H.S., *A History of Brewing* (Newton Abbot, 1975).

Cox, N., *The Complete Tradesman: A Study of Retailing, 1550 - 1820* (Aldershot, 2000).

Cox, N. and C. Walsh, ' "Their Shops are Dens, the Buyer is their Prey": Shop Design and Sale Techniques', in Cox, *Complete Tradesman*, pp. 76-115.

Crompton, C.A., 'Changes in Rural Service Occupations during the Nineteenth Century: An Evaluation of Two Sources for Hertfordshire, England', *Rural History*, 6, 2 (1995), pp. 193-203.

Crompton, C.A., 'An Exploration of the Craft and Trade Structure of Two Hertfordshire Villages, 1851 – 1891: An Application of Nominal Record Linkage to Directories and Census Enumerators' Books', *Local Historian*, 28, 3 (1998), pp. 145–58.

Crossick, G. (ed.), *The Lower Middle Class in Britain, 1870 - 1914* (London, 1997).

Curran, C., 'Private Women, Public Needs: Middle-class Widows in Victorian England', *Albion*, 25 (1993), pp. 217-36.

Curtis, G., *A Chronicle of Small Beer: The Early Victorian Diaries of a Hertfordshire Brewer* (Chichester, 1970).

Daunton, M. (ed.), *The Cambridge Urban History of Britain, Vol. 3, 1840 – 1950* (Cambridge, 2000).

Daunton, M.J., *Royal Mail: The Post Office since 1840* (London, 1985).

Davey, B.J., *Ashwell 1830 – 1914: The Decline of a Village Community. Dept English Local History, Occasional Papers, Third Series, No. 5* (Leicester, 1980).

Davidoff, L. and C. Hall, *Family Fortunes: Men and Women of the English Middle Class, 1780 – 1850* (London, 1987).

Davies, W.K.D., 'Centrality and the Central Place Hierarchy', *Urban Studies*, 4, 1 (1967), pp. 61-79.

Davies, W.K.D., J.A. Giggs and D.T. Herbert, 'Directories, Rate Books and the Commercial Structure of Towns', *Geography*, 53 (1968), pp. 41-54.

Day, C., 'Geographical Mobility in Wiltshire, 1754 - 1914', *Local Population Studies*, 88 (2012), pp. 50-75.

Dickinson, R.E., 'The Distribution and Functions of the Smaller Urban Settlements of East Anglia', *Geography*, 17 (1932), pp. 19-31.

Dodgshon, R.A. and R.A. Butlin (eds), *An Historical Geography of England and Wales* (2nd edn, London, 1990).

Drake, M. (ed.), *Time, Family and Community: Perspectives on Family and Community History* (Oxford, 1994).

Drake, M. and R. Finnegan (eds), *Studying Family and Community History: 19th and 20th Centuries, Vol. 4, Sources and Methods for Family and Community Historians: A Handbook* (2nd edn, Cambridge, 1999).

Duggan, E.P., 'Industrialization and the Development of Urban Business Communities: Research Problems, Sources and Techniques', *Local Historian*, 11, 8 (1975), pp. 457-65.

Dyer, A., 'Small Towns in England, 1600 - 1800', *Proceedings of the British Academy*, 108 (2002), pp. 53-67.

Dyer, C. (ed.), *The Self-Contained Village?: The Social History of Rural Communities, 1250 – 1900* (Hatfield, 2007).

Eastwood, D., *Government and Community in the English Provinces, 1700 - 1870* (Basingstoke, 1997).

Ellis, J., 'Regional and County Centres 1700 - 1840', in Clark, *Urban History of Britain, Vol. 2*, pp. 673-704.

Ellis, J.M., *The Georgian Town, 1680 - 1840* (Basingstoke, 2001).

Everitt, A., (ed.), *Perspectives in English Urban History* (London, 1973).

Everitt, A., 'The English Urban Inn, 1560 – 1760', in Everitt, *Perspectives in English Urban History*, pp. 91-137.

Everitt, A., 'Town and Country in Victorian Leicestershire: The Role of the Village Carrier', in Everitt, *Perspectives in English Urban History*, pp. 213–40.

Everitt, A., 'Country, County and Town: Patterns of Regional Evolution in England', *Transactions Royal Historical Society*, 5th Series, 29 (1979), pp. 79-108.

Everson, J.A. and B.P. FitzGerald, 'The Theoretical Basis of Central Place', in Everson and FitzGerald, *Settlement Patterns*, pp. 101–11.

Everson, J.A. and B.P. FitzGerald, *Concepts in Geography: 1. Settlement Patterns* (London, 1969).

Floud, R. and P. Johnson, (eds), *The Cambridge Economic History of Modern Britain, Vol. II: Economic Maturity, 1860 – 1939* (Cambridge, 2004).

Fowler, C., 'Changes in Provincial Retail Practice during the Eighteenth Century, with Particular Reference to Central-Southern England', in Alexander and Akehurst, *Modern Retailing*, pp. 37–54.

Fraser, W.H., *The Coming of the Mass Market, 1850 – 1914* (London, 1981).

Freeman, M.J., 'Introduction', in Aldcroft and Freeman, *Transport in the Industrial Revolution*, pp. 1-30.

Freeman, M.J. and D.H. Aldcroft (eds), *Transport in Victorian Britain* (Manchester, 1988).

Freeman, M.J., 'Introduction', in Freeman and Aldcroft, *Transport in Victorian Britain*, pp. 1-56.

Friedlander, D., 'London's Urban Transition, 1851 – 1951', *Urban Studies*, 11 (1974), pp. 127-141.

Friedlander, D., 'Occupational Structure, Wages, and Migration in Late Nineteenth-century England and Wales', *Economic Development and Cultural Change*, 40, 2 (1992), pp. 295–18.

Friedlander, D. and R.J. Roshier, 'A Study of Internal Migration in England and Wales: Part I', *Population Studies*, 19 (1966), pp. 239–79.

Gerhold, D., 'The Growth of the London Carrying Trade, 1681 – 1838', *Economic History Review*, 41, 3 (1988), pp. 392–410.

Gerhold, D., *Carriers and Coachmasters: Trade and Travel before the Turnpikes* (Chichester, 2005).

Getis, A. and B. Boots, *Models of Spatial Processes: An Approach to the Study of Point, Line and Area Patterns* (Cambridge, 1978).

Gleadle, K., *British Women in the Nineteenth Century* (Basingstoke, 2001).

Goose, N., 'Urban Growth and Economic Development in Early Modern Hertfordshire', in Slater and Goose, *A County of Small Towns*, pp. 96-126.

Gordon, D.I., *A Regional History of the Railways of Great Britain. Vol. 5. The Eastern Counties* (2nd edn, Newton Abbot, 1977).

Gourvish, T.R., 'Railways 1830 - 70: The Formative Years', in Freeman and Aldcroft, *Transport in Victorian Britain*, pp. 57–91.

Gourvish, T.R. and Wilson, R.G., *The British brewing industry, 1830 – 1980* (Cambridge, 1994).

Gregory, D., 'The Friction of Distance? Information Circulation and the Mails in Early Nineteenth-century England', *Journal of Historical Geography*, 13, 2 (1987), pp. 130–54.

Griffin, B., 'Class, Gender, and Liberalism in Parliament, 1868 - 1882: The Case of the Married Women's Property Acts', *Historical Journal*, 46, 1 (2003), pp. 59-87.

Grigg, D.B., 'E.G. Ravenstein and the "Laws of Migration" ', *J. Historical Geography*, 3, 1 (1977), pp. 41–54.

Grigg, D.B., 'E.G. Ravenstein and Laws of Migration', in Drake, *Time, Family and Community*, pp. 147–64.

Grigg, G.R., ' 'Nurseries of Ignorance'? Private Adventure and Dame Schools for the Working-classes in Nineteenth-century Wales', *History of Education*, 34, 3 (2005), pp. 243-62.

Haggerty, S., 'Women, Work, and the Consumer Revolution: Liverpool in the Late Eighteenth Century', in Benson and Ugolini, *Five Centuries of British Retailing*, pp. 106-26.

Hallas, C., 'The Social and Economic Impact of a Rural Railway: the Wensleydale Line', *Agricultural History Review*, 34, 1 (1986), pp. 29–44.

Hann, A., 'Industrialisation and the Service Economy', in Stobart and Raven, *Towns,Regions and Industries*, pp. 42-61.

Hardy, T., *The Life and Death of the Mayor of Casterbridge: A Story of a Man of Character* (Wordsworth Classics edn, Ware, 1994).

Harrison, R. and J. Zeitlin (eds), *Divisions of Labour: Skilled Workers and Technological Change in Nineteenth-century England* (Brighton, 1985).

Harverson, M., 'Ten Hertfordshire Parishes in 1851: A Survey of Occupations', *Herts Past & Present, 3rd Series*, 8 (2006), pp. 16-21.

Harvey, D., *Social Justice and the City* (London, 1973).

Henstock, A. (ed.), *Early Victorian Country Town: A Portrait of Ashbourne in the Mid-nineteenth Century* (Ashbourne, 1968).

Hey, D., *The Oxford Companion to Local and Family History* (Oxford, 1996).

Higgs, E., 'The Tabulation of Occupations in the Nineteenth-century Census, with Special Reference to Domestic Servants', in Mills and Schurer, *Local Communities*, pp. 27-35.

Higgs, E., *Making Sense of the Census Revisited: Census Records for England and Wales, 1801 – 1901: A Handbook for Historical Researchers* (London, 2005).

Hodson, D., ' "The Municipal Store": Adaptation and Development in the Retail Markets of Nineteenth-century Urban Lancashire', in Alexander and Akehurst, *Modern Retailing*, pp. 94–114.

Holcombe, L., *Victorian Ladies at Work: Middle-class Working Women in England and Wales, 1850 – 1914* (Connecticut, 1973).

Holderness, B.A., 'Rural Tradesmen, 1660-1850: A Regional Study in Lindsey', *Lincolnshire History and Archaeology*, 7 (1972), pp. 77-83.

Hollen Lees, L., 'Urban Networks' in Daunton, *Urban History of Britain, Vol. 3*, pp. 59-94.

Honeybone, M., *The Book of Grantham: The History of a Market and Manufacturing Town* (Buckingham, 1980).

Hopkins, E., *The Rise of the Manufacturing Town: Birmingham and the Industrial Revolution* (Stroud, 1998).

Hoppen, K.T., *The Mid-Victorian Generation, 1846 – 1886* (Oxford, 1998).

Horn, C.A. and P. Horn, 'The Social Structure of an "Industrial" Community: Ivinghoe in Buckinghamshire in 1871', *Local Population Studies*, 31 (1983), pp. 9–20.

Horrell, S., J. Humphries and H-J Voth, 'Destined for Deprivation: Human Capital Formation and Intergenerational Poverty in Nineteenth-century England', *Explorations in Economic History*, 38, 3 (2001), pp. 339-65.

Howard, P., *Take the Train from Hitchin: A Journey into our Local Railway Heritage* (Hitchin, 2006).

Hudson, P. (ed.), *Regions and Industries: A Perspective on the Industrial Revolution in Britain* (Cambridge, 1989).

Hudson, P.,'The Regional Perspective', in Hudson, *Regions and Industries*, pp. 5-38

Humphries, J., 'Female-headed Households in Early Industrial Britain: the Vanguard of the Proletariat', *Labour History Review*, 63 (1998), pp. 31-65.

Jackson, J.A. (ed.), *Migration, Sociological Studies, Vol. 2* (Cambridge, 1969).

Jaggard, E., 'Small Town Politics in Mid-Victorian Britain', *History*, 89, 1 (2004), pp. 3-29.

Jalland, P., *Death in the Victorian Family* (Oxford, 1996).

Johnson, W.B., *Hertfordshire* (5th edn, London, 1957).

Kent, D.A., 'Small Businessmen and their Credit Transactions in Early Nineteenth-century Britain', *Business History*, 36, 2 (1994), pp. 47–64.

King, C., 'The Rise and Decline of Village Reading Rooms', *Rural History*, 20, 2 (2009), pp. 163-86.

King, S., ' "We Might be Trusted": Female Poor Law Guardians and the Development of the New Poor Law: The Case of Bolton, England, 1880-1906', *International Review of Social History*, 49, 1 (2004), pp. 27-46.

Kingston, A., *A History of Royston, Hertfordshire, with Biographical Notes of Royston Worthies* (London, 1906, reprinted Royston, 1975).

Kitch, M., 'Population Movement and Migration in Pre-Industrial Rural England', in Short, *English Rural Community*, pp. 62–84.

Koditschek, T., *Class Formation and Urban-Industrial Society: Bradford, 1750 – 1850* (Cambridge, 1990).

Lancaster, B., D. Newton and N. Vall (eds), *An Agenda for Regional History* (Newcastle, 2007).

Lane, J., *Apprenticeship in England, 1600 - 1914* (London, 1996).

Langton, J., 'The Industrial Revolution and the Regional Geography of England', *Transactions of the Institute of British Geographers*, 9, 2 (1984), pp. 145-67.

Lawton, R., (ed.), *The Census and Social Structure: An Interpretative Guide to Nineteenth-century Censuses for England and Wales* (London, 1978).

Lawton, R., 'Population and Society, 1730 - 1914', in Dodgshon and Butlin, *Historical Geography*, pp. 285-321.

Lee, E.S., 'A Theory of Migration', in Jackson, *Migration*, pp. 282–97.

Levine, D., in 'The Population History of England, 1541 – 1871: A Review Symposium', *Social History*, 8, 2 (1983), pp. 139–68.

Lewis, C.R., 'The Central Place Pattern of Mid-Wales and the Middle Welsh Borderland', in Carter and Davies, *Urban Essays*, pp. 228-68.

Long, J., 'Rural-Urban Migration and Socioeconomic Mobility in Victorian Britain', *Journal of Economic History*, 65, 1 (2005), pp. 1–35.

Lord, E., *The Knights Templar in Britain* (Pbk edn, Harlow, 2004).

Marshall, J.D., 'The Lancashire Rural Labourer in the Early Nineteenth Century', *Transactions of the Lancashire and Cheshire Antiquarian Society*, 71 (1961), pp. 90–128.

Marshall, J.D., 'The rise and transformation of the Cumbrian market town, 1660 – 1900', *Northern History*, 19 (1983), pp. 128-209.

Martin, J.M., 'Village Traders and the Emergence of a Proletariat in South Warwickshire, 1750 - 1851', *The Agricultural History Review*, 32, 2 (1984), pp.179-88.

Mason, N., ' "The Sovereign People are in a Beastly State": The Beer Act of 1830 and Victorian Discourse on Working-class Drunkenness', *Victorian Literature and Culture*, 29, 1 (2001), pp. 109-27.

Matthews, D., 'Laissez-faire and the London Gas Industry in the Nineteenth Century: Another Look', *Economic History Review*, 39, 2 (1986), pp. 244–63.

McKay, I., 'Bondage in the Bakehouse? The Strange Case of the Journeymen Bakers, 1840 – 1880', in Harrison and Zeitlin, *Divisions of Labour*, pp. 47-86.

McKendrick, N., 'The Commercialization of Fashion', in McKendrick, Brewer and Plumb, *Birth of a Consumer Society*, pp. 34-99.

McKendrick, N., J. Brewer and J.H. Plumb, *The Birth of a Consumer Society: The Commercialization of Eighteenth-century England* (London, 1982).

Miles, M., 'The Money Market in the Early Industrial Revolution: The Evidence from West Riding Attorneys c. 1750 – 1800', *Business History*, 23, 2 (1981), pp. 127–46.

Miller, E., 'A Note on the Role of Distance in Migration: Costs of Mobility versus Intervening Opportunity', *Journal of Regional Science*, 12 (1972), p. 475.

Mills, D., 'Using Sources: The Census, 1801 – 1991', in Drake and Finnegan, *Family and Community History, Vol. 4, Sources and Methods*, pp. 25-35.

Mills, D.R. and K. Schurer, 'Communities in the Victorian Censuses: An Introduction', in Mills and Schurer, *Local Communities*, pp. 1-13.

Mills, D.R. and K. Schurer, 'Employment and Occupations', in Mills and Schurer, *Local Communities*, pp. 136-60.

Mills, D.R. and K. Schurer (eds), *Local Communities in the Victorian Census Enumerators' Books* (Oxford, 1996).

Mills, D.R., *Rural Community History from Trade Directories: A Local Population Studies Supplement* (Aldenham, 2001).

Millward, R. and R. Ward, 'The Costs of Public and Private Gas Enterprises in Late 19th Century Britain', *Oxford Economic Papers*, 39, 4 (1987), pp. 719–37.

Milne, G.J., 'British Business and the Telephone, 1878 - 1911', *Business History*, 49, 2 (2007), pp. 163-85.

Mingay, G.E., (ed.), *The Victorian Countryside, Vol. 1* (London, 1981).

Mingay, G.E. (ed.), *The Agrarian History of England and Wales, Vol. 6, 1750 1850* (Cambridge, 1989).

Mitchell, B.R. and P. Deane, *University of Cambridge Dept of Applied Economics Monographs, 17: Abstracts of British Historical Statistics* (Cambridge, 1962).

Morris, R.J., 'Civil Society and the Nature of Urbanism in Britain, 1750 - 1850', *Urban History*, 25, 3 (1998), pp. 289-301.

Munby, L.M., *The Hertfordshire Landscape* (The Making of the English Landscape Series, London, 1977).

Neale, R.S., *Bath: A Social History, 1680 - 1850* (London, 1981).

Nenadic, S., 'The Small Family Firm in Victorian Britain', *Business History*, 35, 4 (1993), pp. 86–114.

Noble, M., 'Growth and Development in a Regional Urban System: The Country Towns of Eastern Yorkshire, 1700 – 1850', *Urban History Yearbook* (1987), pp. 1–21.

Norton, J.E., *Guide to the National and Provincial Directories of England and Wales, Excluding London, Published Before 1856* (RHS Guides and Handbooks, No. 5, 1950).

Olsen, D.J., *The Growth of Victorian London* (London, 1976).

Owens, A., 'Property, Gender and Life Course: Inheritance and Family Welfare Provision in Early Nineteenth-century England', *Social History*, 26, 3 (2001), pp. 299-317.

Owens, A., 'Inheritance and the Life-cycle of Family Firms in the Early Industrial Revolution', *Business History*, 44, 1 (2002), pp. 21–46.

Page, D., 'Commercial Directories and Market Towns', *Local Historian*, 11, 2 (1974), pp. 85–88.

Parker, J., *'Nothing for Nothing for Nobody': A History of Hertfordshire Banks and Banking* (Stevenage, 1986).

Parrott, K., 'The Apprenticeship of Parish Children from Kirkdale Industrial Schools Liverpool 1840-70', *The Local Historian*, 39, 2 (2009), pp. 122-36.

Perren, R., 'Markets and Marketing', in Mingay, *Agrarian History of England and Wales, Vol. 6*, pp. 191–274.

Perren, R., *Agriculture in Depression, 1870 – 1940* (Cambridge, 1995).

Perry, P.J., 'Working-class Isolation and Mobility in Rural Dorset, 1837 – 1936: A Study of Marriage Distances', *Institute of British Geographers, Transactions,* No. 46 (1969), pp. 121–41.

Phillips, M., 'The Evolution of Markets and Shops in Britain', in Benson and Shaw, *Evolution of Retail Systems, Part 2, Fairs, Markets, Pedlars and Small-scale Shops*, pp. 53-75.

Phythian-Adams, C.V., *Re-thinking English Local History, Occasional Papers, Fourth Series, No. 1* (Leicester, 1987).

Phythian-Adams, C.V. (ed.), *Societies, Cultures and Kinship, 1580 – 1850: Cultural Provinces and English Local History* (London, 1993).

Phythian-Adams, C.V., 'Introduction: an Agenda for English Local History', in Phythian-Adams, *Societies, Cultures and Kinship*, pp. 1-23.

Phythian-Adams, C., ' "Small-scale Toy-towns and Trumptons"? Urbanization in Britain and the new Cambridge Urban History', *Urban History*, 28, 2 (2001), pp. 267–68.

Phythian-Adams, C., 'Differentiating Provincial Societies in English History: Spatial Contexts and Cultural Processes', in Lancaster, Newton and Vall, *Agenda for Regional History*, pp. 3-22.

Pooley, C. and J. Turnbull, *Migration and Mobility in Britain since the 18th Century* (London, 1998).

Porter, S., *Exploring Urban History: Sources for Local Historians* (London, 1990).

Potts, W., *A History of Banbury: The Study of the Development of a Country Town* (2nd edn, Banbury, 1978).

Pressnell, L.S., *Country Banking in the Industrial Revolution* (Oxford, 1956).

Preston, R.E., 'Christaller's Neglected Contribution to the Study of the Evolution of Central Places', *Progress in Human Geography*, 9, 2 (1985), pp. 177-93.

Pryce, W.T.R., 'Using Written Sources: Some Key Examples, 1, Directories', in Drake and Finnegan, *Family and Community History, Vol. 4, Sources and Methods*, pp. 57-63.

Raven, N., 'Trade Directories and Business Size: Evidence from the Small Towns of North Essex, 1851', *Local Historian*, 31, 2 (2001), pp. 83–94.

Raven, N., 'Chelmsford during the Industrial Revolution, c. 1790 – 1840', *Urban History*, 30, 1 (2003), pp. 44–62.

Raven, N. and T. Hooley, 'Industrial and Urban Change in the Midlands: A Regional Survey', in Stobart and Raven, *Towns, Regions and Industries*, pp. 23-41.

Ravenstein, E.G., 'Census of the British Isles, 1871: Birthplaces and Migration', *Geographical Magazine*, 3 (1876), pp. 173–77, 201–16, 229–33.

Ravenstein, E.G., 'The Laws of Migration', *Journal of the Statistical Society*, 48 (1885), pp. 167–227.

Ravenstein, E.G., 'The Laws of Migration', *Journal of the Statistical Society, 52* (1889), pp. 214–301.

Reader, W.J., *Life in Victorian England* (London, 1964).

Reynolds, S., *Kingdoms and Communities in Western Europe, 900 – 1300* (Oxford, 1984).

Richards, T., *The Commodity Culture of Victorian England: Advertising and Spectacle, 1851 – 1914.* The Great Exhibition of 1851 (London, 1991).

Rodger, R., *Housing in Urban Britain, 1780 - 1914* (Cambridge, 1995).

Rogers, A. (ed.), *The Making of Stamford* (Leicester, 1965).

Rogers, K.H.(ed.), *Early Trade Directories of Wiltshire* (Wiltshire Record Society, Vol. 47, Trowbridge, 1992).

Rook, T., *A History of Hertfordshire* (Chichester, 1984).

Routh, G., *Occupations of the People of Great Britain, 1801 – 1981, with a Compendium of a Paper 'Occupations of the People of the United Kingdom, 1801 – 81' by Charles Booth* (London, 1987).

Royle, S.A., 'Aspects of Nineteenth-century Small Town Society: A Comparative Study from Leicestershire', *Midland History*, 5 (1979–80), pp. 50–62.

Royle, S.A., 'The Development of Small Towns in Britain', in Daunton, *Urban History of Britain, Vol. 3*, pp. 151-184.

Schurer, K., 'Computing', in Drake and Finnegan, *Family and Community History, Vol. 4, Sources and Methods*, pp. 203-220.

Sharpe, P., 'Poor Children as Apprentices in Colyton, 1598 - 1830', *Continuity and Change*, 6, 2 (1991), pp. 253-270.

Shaw, G., 'The Content and Reliability of Nineteenth-century Trade Directories', *Local Historian*, 13, 4 (1978), pp. 205–09.

Shaw, G., 'The European Scene: Britain and Germany', in Benson and Shaw, *Evolution of Retail Systems, Part 1, The Economics and Social Context of Retail Evolution*, pp. 17-34.

Shaw, G. and Tipper, A., *British Directories: A Bibliography and Guide to Directories Published in England and Wales (1850 – 1950) and Scotland (1773 – 1950)* (Leicester, 1989).

Sheldon, C., *A History of Poster Advertising* (London, 1937).

Sheldrick, A., *A Different World: Ashwell before 1939* (Ashwell, 1992).

Shepherd, M.E., *From Hellgill to Bridge End: Aspects of Economic and Social Change in the Upper Eden Valley, 1840 – 95. University of Hertfordshire, Studies in Regional and Local History, Vol. 2* (Hatfield, 2003).

Short, B. (ed.), *The English Rural Community: Image and Analysis* (Cambridge, 1992).

Simon, B., *The Two Nations & the Educational Structure, 1780 – 1870* (Pbk edn, Southampton, 1976).

Slater, T. and N. Goose, *A County of Small Towns: The Development of Hertfordshire's Urban Landscape to 1800* (Hatfield, 2008).

Slater, T. and N. Goose, 'Panoramas and Microcosms: Hertfordshire's Towns through Both Ends of the Telescope', in Slater and Goose, *A County of Small Towns*, pp. 1-26.

Smith, C., 'Image and Reality: Two Nottinghamshire Market Towns in Late Georgian England', *Midland History*, 17 (1992), pp. 59–74.

Smith, C., 'Population Growth and Economic Change in some Nottinghamshire Market Towns, 1680 – 1840', *Local Population Studies*, 65 (2000), pp. 29–46.

Smith, C., 'Urban Improvement in the Nottinghamshire Market Town, 1770 – 1840', *Midland History*, 25 (2000), pp. 98–114.

Smith, C.T., 'The Movement of Population in England and Wales in 1851 and 1861', *Geographical J.*, 117 (1951), pp. 200 – 210.

Smith, W.D., *Consumption and the Making of Respectability, 1600 - 1800* (New York, 2002).

Stamp, L.D. (ed.), *The Land of Britain: The Report of the Land Utilisation Survey of Britain. Part 80* (London, 1941).

Stevenson, T.H.C., 'Review of the Vital Statistics of the Year, 1911', *Seventy-Fourth Annual Report of the Registrar General of Births, Deaths and Marriages in England and Wales, 1911* (HMSO, London, 1913).

Stobart, J., 'The Spatial Organization of a Regional Economy: Central Places in North-west England in the Early-eighteenth Century', *J. Historical Geography*, 22, 2 (1996), pp. 147-59.

Stobart, J., 'Regions, Localities, and Industrialisation: Evidence from the East Midlands circa 1780 - 1840', *Environment and Planning A*, 33 (2001), pp. 1305-25.

Stobart, J., 'The Economic and Social Worlds of Rural Craftsmen-retailers in Eighteenth-century Cheshire', *The Agricultural History Review*, 52, 2 (2004), pp. 141-60.

Stobart, J., *The First Industrial Region: North-west England, c. 1700 - 60* (Manchester, 2004).

Stobart, J. and N. Raven (eds), *Towns, Regions and Industries: Urban and Industrial Change in the Midlands, c. 1700 - 1840* (Manchester, 2005).

Stobart, J. and N. Raven, 'Introduction: Industrialisation and Urbanisation in a Regional Context', in Stobart and Raven, *Towns, Regions and Industries*, pp. 1-19.

Stobart, J., A. Hann and V. Morgan, *Spaces of Consumption: Leisure and Shopping in the English Town, c. 1680 - 1830* (Abingdon, 2007).

Stobart, J., *Spend, Spend, Spend! A History of Shopping* (Stroud, 2008).

Supple, B., 'Insurance in British History', in Westall, *Business of Insurance*, pp. 1–8.

Sweet, R., *The English Town, 1680 - 1840: Government, Society and Culture* (Harlow, 1999).

Sweet R. and P. Lane (eds), *Women and Urban Life in Eighteenth-century England: On the Town* (Aldershot, 2003).

Thomas, M., 'The Service Sector', in Floud and Johnson, *Cambridge Economic History*, pp. 99-132.

Thompson, F.M.L., 'Agricultural Chemical and Fertiliser Industries', in Collins, *Agrarian History of England and Wales, Vol. 7, Pt. 2*, pp. 1019–44.

Tiller, K., *English Local History: An Introduction* (Stroud, 1992).

Tilly, L.A. and J.W. Scott, *Women, Work and Family* (London, 1989).

Trebilcock, C., *Phoenix Assurance and the Development of British Insurance, Vol. 1, 1782 – 1870* (Cambridge, 1985).

Trinder, B., 'Towns and Industries: The Changing Character of Manufacturing Towns', in Stobart and Raven, *Towns, Regions and Industries*, pp. 102-18.

Trinder, B., 'Country Carriers Revisited', *Local Historian*, 42, 2 (2012), pp. 135–47.

Trollope, A., *Dr Thorne* (Everyman's Library edn, London, 1993).

Ugolini, L., 'Men, Masculinities, and Menswear Advertising, c. 1890 - 1914', in Benson and Ugolini, *Nation of Shopkeepers*, pp. 80-104.

Unwin, R.W., 'Tradition and Transition: Market Towns of the Vale of York, 1660–1830', *Northern History*, 17 (1981), pp. 72–116.

Unwin, R., *Wetherby: The History of a Yorkshire Market Town* (Leeds, 1986).

VCH Hertfordshire, Vol. II (London, 1914).

Veblen, T., *The Theory of the Leisure Class, with an Introduction by John Kenneth Galbraith* (Boston, 1973).

Vigne, T. and A. Howkins, 'The Small Shopkeeper in Industrial and Market Towns', in Crossick, *Lower Middle Class in Britain*, pp. 184–209.

Vincent, D., *Literacy and Popular Culture: England 1750 – 1914* (Pbk Edition, Cambridge, 1993).

Waller, P.J., *Town, City, and Nation: England, 1850 – 1914* (Oxford, 1983).

Walton, J.K., *The English Seaside Resort: A Social History, 1750 - 1914* (Leicester, 1983).

Walton, J.R., 'Trades and Professions in Late 18th-Century England: Assessing the Evidence of Directories', *Local Historian*, 17, 6 (1987), pp. 343–50.

Waters, C., *A Dictionary of Old Trades, Titles and Occupations* (Newbury, 1999).

Westall, O.M. (ed.), *The Historian and the Business of Insurance* (Manchester, 1984).

Whitaker, A., *Brewers in Hertfordshire: A Historical Gazetteer* (Hatfield, 2006).

Williamson, J.G., *Coping with City Growth during the British Industrial Revolution* (Cambridge, 1990).

White, P. and R. Woods (eds), *The geographical impact of migration* (London, 1980).

Wilde, P., 'The Use of Business Directories in Comparing the Industrial Structure of Towns: An Example from the South-West Pennines', *Local Historian*, 12 (1976), pp. 152–56.

Wiley – VCH Staff, *Ullmann's Agrochemicals* (Wiley – VCH, 2007).

Wilson, A.N., *The Victorians* (Pbk edn, London, 2003).

Wilson, C. and R.I. Woods, 'Fertility in England: A Long-Term Perspective', *Population Studies*, 45 (1991), pp. 399–415.

Wiskin, C., 'Urban Businesswomen in Eighteenth Century England', in Sweet and Lane, *On the Town*, pp. 87-109.

Wohl, A.S., *Endangered Lives: Public Health in Victorian Britain* (London, 1983).

Wolpert, J., 'Behavioural Aspects of the Decision to Migrate', *Papers and Proceedings, Regional Science Association*, 15 (1965), pp. 159–69.

Woollard, M., 'The Classification of Multiple Occupational Titles in the 1881 Census of England and Wales', *Local Population Studies*, 72 (2004), pp. 34–49.

Wrigley, E.A. (ed.), *Nineteenth-century Society: Essays in the Use of Quantitative Methods for the Study of Social Data* (Cambridge, 1972).

Wrigley, E.A., *People, Cities and Wealth: The Transformation of Traditional Society* (Oxford, 1987).

Wrigley, E.A., *Continuity, Chance and Change* (Cambridge, 1988).

Wrigley, E.A., 'English County Populations in the Later Eighteenth Century', *Economic History Review*, 60, 1 (2007), pp. 35-69.

Young, A., *General View of the Agriculture of Hertfordshire* (First published 1804, Facsimile edn, Newton Abbot, 1971).

Unpublished Papers and Theses

Bysouth, P.T., 'Elementary Education in North East Hertfordshire during the Late Nineteenth Century and the Effect of the 1870 Education Act on Literacy' (Advanced Certificate Dissertation, University of Cambridge, Board of Continuing Education, 1996).

Richardson, S., 'Independence and Deference: A Study of the West Riding Electorate, 1832 – 1841' (PhD thesis, University of Leeds, 1995).

Souden, D., 'Pre-industrial English Local Migration Fields' (PhD thesis, University of Cambridge, 1981).

World Wide Web Sources

Catford, N.,'Disused Stations Site Record: Buntingford', www.subbrit.org.uk/sb-sites/stations/b/ (13 February 2005, accessed 22 March 2008).

CJCLDS, *Family History Resources Files, V. 2.0, 1881 British Census* (Salt Lake City, 1999).

'Collieries of the United Kingdom at work in 1880', Coal Mining History Resource Centre, www.freepages.genealogy.rootsweb.com (Undated, accessed 11 December 2007).

Connected earth, 'how communication shapes the world', www.connected-earth.com/galleries (Undated, © BT and museum partners, accessed 21 May 2008).

'Emlyn Colliery, Penygroes', Collieries Page, www.welshcoalmines.co.uk (Undated, accessed 11 December 2007).

Encyclopaedia Britannica, www.britannica.com/eb/article-9024503/coal-gas (© 2008, accessed 3 May 2008).

Encyclopaedia Britannica, www.britannica.com/eb/article-9024703/coke (© 2008, accessed 3 May 2008).

Hubbard, M., 'English Brothers Timber Frame Specialists', www.englishbrothers.co.uk (2005, accessed 11 December 2007).

Key Dates, The British Postal Museum & Archive, www.postalheritage.org.uk/history (26 May 2008, accessed 26 May 2008).

Long, T., 'Flickering Gaslight Illuminated Pall Mall', www.wired.com/science/discoveries (28 January 2008, accessed 3 May 2008).

'MERL Archive Collections: Business Records', The Museum of English Rural Life, www.ruralhistory.org (Undated, accessed 11 December 2007).

'National Register of Archives, Cambridge Gas Light Company,

GB/NNAF/C112358', www.nationalarchives.gov.uk/nra (© 2008, accessed 12 June 2008).

'National Register of Archives, Newton, Chambers & Co Ltd, GB/NNAF/C117393', www.nationalarchives.gov.uk/nra (© 2008, accessed 19 May 2008).

Officer, L.H. and S.H. Williamson, 'Five Ways to Compute the Relative Value of a UK Pound Amount, 1830 to Present', www.measuringworth.com (© 2007, accessed 6 December 2007).

Place: Baldock Hertfordshire, Dept Geography, University of Portsmouth, www.visionofbritain.org.uk/place (17 April 2008).

Roberts, S., 'A History of the Telegraph Companies in Britain between 1838 and 1868', undated, www.distantwriting.co.uk (© 2008, accessed 1 May 2008).

'The Penny Post', The Victorian Web: Literature, History, & Culture in the Age of Victoria, www.victorianweb.org/history/pennypos.html (24 October 2006, accessed 1 May 2008).

The Times, 21 October 1895, p. 10, in The Times Digital Archive, 1785 – 1985, www.infotrac.galegroup.com/itw/infomark (2 January 2008, accessed 13 June 2008).

UK Census Collection, www.ancestry.co.uk/search/rectype/census/uk, © 2008 (April 2008).

Index

Index

Index

Index

Index

Index of individual service providers

Individual service providers

Camps, Simius:	Leather cutter	Buntingford, 1891, 130
Cane, Thomas:	Coach builder	Royston, 1871, 133
Carmichael, Thomas:	Travelling draper	Royston, 1871, 140
Cass, Grace:	Revenue officer's wife	Royston, 1871, 118
Castle, Kezia:	Butcher	Baldock, 1839, 60
Catts, Herbert:	Sewerage wks engine driver	Baldock , 1881, 143
Chamberlain, Elizabeth:	Dealer in British wines	Buntingford, 1862, 67
Charter, Charles:	Tobacconist	Baldock, 1890, 95
Christian, Benjamin:	Bank manager	Baldock, 1851, 100
Christian, William:	Bank manager	Baldock, 1862, 100
Christy, Benjamin	Farmer & brewer	Ashwell, 1851, 83
Christy, George:	Grocer & draper	Ashwell. 1871, 50
Clambert, Edward:	Fishmonger	Buntingford, 1851, 71
Clark, Robert:	Farmer	Buntingford, 1851, 96
Clayton, Joseph:	Carrier & coal dealer	Buntingford, 1862, 263
Clayton, Joseph:	Draper & fruiterer	Buntingford, 1882, 51
Clayton, Walter:	Coach painter	Buntingford, 1882, 84
Clifton, Ann:	Upholsterer	Royston, 1871, 148
Cockayne, Mary:	Solicitor's clerk's wife	Royston, 1871, 118
Cook, Charles:	Poulterer	Royston, 1851, 74
Coote, James:	Gardener & coal seller	Royston, 1851, 124
Covington, Benjamin:	Beer retailer	Ashwell, 1882, 55
Cox, George:	Carrier	Baldock, 1890, 267
Coxall, Levi:	Carrier & publican	Buntingford, 1862, 263
Craft, Emily:	Baker's shop assistant	Royston, 1881, 146
Craft, Philip:	Tailor & clothier	Royston, 1851, 139
Craft, Sarah:	Tailor's assistant	Royston, 1871, 124
Craft, Thomas:	China & glass dealer	Royston, 1859, 295
Crawley, John:	Coach maker	Baldock, 1861, 133
Croft, Mary Ann:	Workhouse matron	Buntingford, 1862, 109
Croft, William:	Master tailor	Baldock, 1881, 238
Crouch, Frederick:	Railway engine driver	Buntingford, 1881, 200
Cunningham, John:	Station Master	Baldock, 1882, 261
Dade, Sarah:	Workhouse school mistress	Royston, 1882, 109
Davies, George:	Confectioner & Postmaster	Baldock, 1862, 70
Daintry, Emma:	Post Office assistant	Royston, 1861, 149
Daintry, Thomas:	Post Master	Royston, 1851, 199
Daintry, William:	Clerk & insurance agent	Royston, 1882, 102
Dalton, Louisa:	Workhouse mistress	Buntingford, 1839, 60
Day, Agnes:	Bookkeeper	Baldock, 1861, 145
Day, Frederick:	Overseer	Baldock, 1882, 93
Day, Robert:	Butcher	Baldock, 1851, 243
Dear, James Gilbert:	Manager of Gasworks	Baldock, 1870, 282
Dear, William:	Victualler	Baldock, 1851, 43
Dodd, Jane:	Berlin wool dealer	Buntingford, 1862, 75
Dover, James:	Mineral water manufacturer	Ashwell, 1890, 83
Downes, William:	Tax official	Baldock, 1851, 91
Dyball, Lucy:	Workhouse industrial trainer	Royston, 1890, 109
Earnshaw, John:	Post Office sorter	Royston, 1891, 144
Edwards, Benjamin:	Blacksmith & publican	Ashwell, 1851, 201
Edwards, Robert:	Cheesemonger	Baldock, 1871, 74

Individual service providers

Ellis, Alice:	Corset maker's assistant	Baldock, 1891, 148
Ellis, Francis:	Corset maker's assistant	Baldock, 1891, 148
Ellis, Hope:	Stay & corset maker	Baldock, 1882, 75
Ellis, Jane:	Straw bonnet maker	Royston, 1851, 148
Emery, George:	Shoemaker	Baldock, 1851, 243
Evans, Charlotte:	Fishmonger's wife	Royston, 1871, 118
Evans, William:	Beer retailer	Ashwell, 1882, 55
Eversden, Lewis:	Engine driver, coprolites	Ashwell, 1871, 143
Farr, John:	Beer retailer	Buntingford, 1891, 70
Farr, William:	Farmer	Baldock, 1871, 96
Farrington, Sarah:	Boot & shoemaker	Buntingford, 1839, 60
Farrow, J.R.:	House decorator & plumber	Royston, 1881, 299
Fisher, William:	Carpet fitter & upholsterer	Royston, 1891, 124
Fletcher, James:	Farming apprentice	Ashwell, 1861, 124
Fordham, Edward King:	Justice of the Peace & Brewer	Ashwell, 1870, 93
Fordham, Edward Snow:	Justice of the Peace	Ashwell, 1890, 93
Fordham, Oswald:	Brewer	Ashwell, 1861, 128
Fox, Jane:	Clerk	Buntingford, 1881, 145
Freeman, Robert:	Veterinary surgeon	Buntingford, 1838, 60
Gayler, John:	Watch & clockmaker	Buntingford, 1890, 38
Gaylor, John:	Watch & clockmaker	Buntingford, 1882, 38
Geldard, Sophia:	Grocer	Buntingford, 1839, 60
Gentle, George:	Butcher	Baldock, 1851, 245
Gibbons, William:	Surveyor	Buntingford, 1861, 98
Godderd, George:	Painter	Royston, 1851, 201
Godfrey, Sarah:	Carrier	Royston, 1851, 264
Goodchild, James:	Gas-fitter & ironmonger	Baldock, 1871, 244
Goodman, T.:	Grocer	Royston, 1855, 295
Gordon, William:	Wine & spirit merchant	Royston, 1862, 49
Goslin, Benjamin:	Master tailor	Royston, 1871, 238
Gosling, B.:	Tailor	Royston, 1855, 293
Green, William:	Cabinet-maker's apprentice	Royston, 1861, 135
Hagger, Agnes:	Greengrocer's assistant	Royston, 1881, 146
Hancock, William:	Station Master	Buntingford, 1882, 261
Hankin, Emily:	Saddler	Baldock, 1870, 110
Hankin, John:	Glover & tailor	Baldock, 1851, 243
Hankin, William:	Fishmonger	Buntingford, 1851, 71
Hankin, William:	Journeyman cabinet-maker	Baldock, 1871, 134
Harrison, Lydia:	Baby linen manufacturer	Royston, 1871, 111
Harvey, Thomas:	Clock & watchmaker	Baldock, 1890, 243
Heath, Martha:	Bookkeeper	Baldock, 1861, 145
Hills, James:	Registrar	Baldock, 1862, 93
Hinkins, Frank:	Lantern slide maker	Royston, 1890, 77
Hinkins, William:	House decorator	Royston, 1871, 118
Holder, Richard:	Carrier	Royston, 1871, 245
Hood, Walter:	Master builder & undertaker	Royston, 1881, 245
Hooper, John:	Surgeon	Buntingford, 1838, 60
Hoy, Alfred:	Cabinet-maker's apprentice	Royston, 1891, 135
Hoye, Arundel:	Plumber & glazier	Baldock, 1871, 49
Humphry, Moses:	Apprentice butcher	Ashwell, 1851, 216
Humphrey, Robert:	Leather worker	Buntingford, 1891, 130

Individual service providers

Hurmmerston, William:	Policeman	Royston, 1881, 92
Hyde, Ann:	Baby linen manufacturer	Royston, 1871, 111
Hyde, Harriett:	Carpet maker	Baldock, 1891, 148
Innes, George:	Iron founder	Royston, 1891, 80
Izzard, Harry:	Dealer in domestic machines	Baldock, 1890, 77
James, Benjamin:	Policeman	Buntingford, 1881, 213
Jennings, Frederick:	Brewer & maltster	Royston, 1881, 240
Jerrard, Alfred:	Cabinet-maker's apprentice	Royston, 1891, 135
Johnson, John:	Coach painter	Buntingford, 1851, 84
Jones, Charles:	Station Master	Buntingford, 1871, 246
Jude, Mary:	Retailer of beer's wife	Royston, 1871, 118
Keen, Edward:	Plumber & glazier	Royston, 1871, 246
Kefford, Sarah:	Fruiterer & fishmonger	Royston, 1862, 112
Kitchener, Ann:	Berlin wool dealer	Baldock, 1862, 75
Lambert, Samuel:	Bank manager	Royston, 1862, 99
Latchford, Sarah:	Shirt maker	Baldock, 1871, 148
Laventhall, John:	Hawker in drapery	Royston, 1871, 140
Laver, William:	Travelling draper	Royston, 1871, 140
Lea, John:	Dairyman	Royston, 1881, 74
Lee, James:	Umbrella maker	Royston, 1882, 77
Lee, Mary:	Umbrella maker	Royston, 1890, 77
Lilley, William:	Baker	Royston, 1851, 38
Lilly, William:	Baker	Royston, 1861, 38
Little, John:	Publican	Baldock, 1851, 243
Lufman, William:	Travelling draper	Royston, 1871, 140
MacDonald, James:	Tax official	Baldock, 1871, 91
Maclin, Henry:	Inspector of Nuisances	Buntingford, 1882, 95
McKenzie, Eliza:	Waistcoat maker	Buntingford, 1871, 148
Magowan, James:	Tax official	Royston, 1891, 91
Malein, John:	Shoemaker	Baldock, 1851, 243
Manning, William:	Carrier	Baldock, 1839, 256
Mathews, Joseph:	Chemist & druggist	Royston, 1862, 296
Matthews, Ernest:	Dentist	Royston, 1890, 95
Mickley, George:	Tanner	Buntingford, 1871, 128
Middleton, Thomas:	Station Master	Royston, 1882, 259
Miles, Charles:	Hair dresser & beer retailer	Buntingford, 1890, 50
Miller, Harold:	Cabinet-maker's apprentice	Royston, 1891, 135
Miller, Joseph:	Dairyman	Royston, 1891, 74
Miller, Martha:	Confectioner & toy dealer	Royston, 1890, 70
Minchen, Louis:	Master draper	Royston, 1881, 247
Moor, Sarah:	Apprentice dressmaker	Royston, 1871, 153
Moore, Thomas:	Secretary of Gasworks	Buntingford, 1882, 282
Morton, Thomas:	Brickmaker & rail carter	Royston, 1851, 124
Mott, Elijah:	Brass founder	Buntingford, 1861, 214
Munns, Elizabeth:	Straw hat maker	Buntingford, 1839, 60
Nash, Charles:	Farmer	Royston, 1861, 96
Nash, Edward:	Architect & surveyor	Royston, 1861, 98
Nash, William T:	Sec^y, Farmers' Manure Company	Royston, 1870, 284
Neale, George:	Farrier	Baldock, 1870, 131
Newberry James:	Insurance agent	Baldock, 1862, 38
Newbury James:	Insurance agent	Baldock, 1870, 38

Individual service providers

Newby, James:	Actuary	Baldock, 1838, 60
Newman, Caroline:	Apprentice stationer	Royston, 1891, 151
Nicholls, Maria:	Post Office assistant	Buntingford, 1851, 149
Nicholls, Charles:	Cooper & brewer	Buntingford, 1851, 81
Nind, George:	Grocer	Buntingford, 1881, 200
Norman, William:	Bird stuffer	Royston, 1870, 77
Norris, James:	Innkeeper	Baldock, 1824, 252
Nunn, John:	Farmer	Royston, 1881, 124
Pack, James:	Blacksmith	Ashwell, 1851, 131
Page, Joshua:	Maltster	Baldock, 1879, 128
Page, Joshua Richmond:	Maltster	Baldock, 1871, 83
Pak, Margaret:	Sweetshop	Baldock, 1871, 74
Parker, Josiah:	Glass & china dealer	Buntingford, 1871, 246
Parrington, Thomas:	Innkeeper	Baldock, 1824, 251
Pateman, John:	Painter	Buntingford, 1891, 214
Patterson, Alfred:	Saddler & harness maker	Baldock, 1891, 50
Phillips, John:	Brewer	Royston, 1851, 128
Phillips, John:	Tailor & woollen draper	Baldock, 1881, 139
Phillips, Joseph:	Brewer	Royston, 1881, 128
Picking, Thomas:	Carpenter	Ashwell, 1855, 96
Pickering, Clara:	Librarian & bookseller	Royston, 1861, 107
Pickering, Lucy:	Librarian	Royston, 1882, 107
Pickering, Thomas:	Bookseller	Royston, 1862, 108
Pipkin, Edward:	Tanner's carman	Buntingford, 1871, 143
Porter, Isabella:	Farmer	Buntingford, 1881, 96
Porter, Martha:	Bookseller's assistant	Royston, 1881, 146
Potter, Harper:	French-polisher	Royston, 1881, 135
Price, John:	Solicitor & insurance agent	Buntingford, 1862, 101
Proctor, Sarah:	Insurance agent	Royston, 1851, 102
Pryor, John Izzard:	Brewer	Baldock, 1829, 62
Pryor, Lucy:	Confectioner's assistant	Royston, 1881, 146
Pyne, Richard:	Consulting Surgeon	Royston, 1869, 95
Quartermain, George:	Watch & clockmaker	Baldock, 1881, 246
Racher, Frederick:	Ostler	Royston, 1891, 143
Radford, Nellie:	Apprentice harness-maker	Ashwell, 1891, 151
Raven, William:	Hotelier	Baldock, 1881, 245
Rayment, William:	Maltster & brewer	Buntingford, 1881, 81
Reed, George:	Poulterer & Town Crier	Baldock, 1851, 74
Reeve, John:	Blacksmith's apprentice	Royston, 1891, 131
Reynold, Mary:	Innkeeper	Baldock, 1824, 251
Richardson, William:	Builder	Baldock, 1851, 135
Robinson, George:	Blacksmith's apprentice	Royston, 1881, 131
Routledge Henry:	Draper & grocer	Baldock, 1870, 51
Sale, John:	Farmer & brewer	Ashwell, 1851, 83
Sale, William:	Farmer	Baldock, 1881, 119
Sampson, James:	Journeyman baker	Buntingford, 1851, 214
Sanders, Edward:	Insurance agent	Royston, 1851, 246
Sanders, Martin:	Clerk	Buntingford, 1871, 245
Scott, John:	Accountant	Baldock, 1851, 101
Searle, George:	Timber carter	Buntingford, 1881, 143
Seymour, George :	Journeyman cabinet-maker	Baldock, 1871, 134

Individual service providers

Sewell, Harry:	Wallet maker	Buntingford, 1890, 77
Sharpe, George:	Surgeon	Baldock, 1851, 245
Shaw, Charles:	Photographer	Buntingford, 1880, 77
Sibley, Mrs G.:	Grove House Ladies College	Baldock, 1895, 289
Simpson, Joseph:	Brewer	Baldock, 1882, 65
Simpson, Thomas:	Brewer	Baldock, 1882, 65
Skelton, John:	Chemist & druggist	Ashwell, 1882, 49
Smith, Daniel:	Beer retailer & fruiterer	Ashwell, 1890, 41
Smith, Edward:	Innkeeper	Baldock, 1839, 252
Smith, Henry:	Assistant Overseer	Royston, 1861, 90
Smith, John:	Registrar	Baldock, 1851, 93
Smith, William:	Farmer	Baldock, 1851, 119
Sparks, William:	Commercial Innkeeper	Baldock, 1854, 288
Spicer, Thomas:	Journeyman cabinet-maker	Baldock, 1871, 134
Spinks, John:	Grocer & tea dealer	Buntingford, 1862, 74
Stamford, James:	Publican	Royston, 1871, 103
Stamford, Elizabeth:	Cab proprietress	Royston, 1882, 103
Steed, John:	Brewer & maltster	Baldock, 1851, 128
Steed, Oliver:	Brewer & maltster	Baldock, 1881, 128
Stocken, Sarah:	Post Mistress	Baldock, 1851, 102
Stocken, William:	Post Master	Baldock, 1839, 108
Stone, William:	Tailor, draper & clothier	Royston, 1861, 139
Stoten, Thomas:	Tailor	Baldock, 1851, 206
Stredder, Edward:	Upholsterer	Royston, 1851, 200
Swaine, Hannah:	Mistress blacksmith	Baldock, 1851, 110
Tailor, Robert:	Apprentice chemist	Royston, 1891, 234
Thody, William:	Butcher	Baldock, 1882, 243
Thompson, Matthew:	Tax official	Baldock, 1861, 91
Thurgood, William:	Cooper	Baldock, 1851, 243
Thurnall, Harry:	Artist	Royston, 1890, 77
Titchmarsh, Edward:	Cheesemonger	Royston, 1861, 74
Tookey, John:	Sawyer	Royston, 1861, 239
Tottman, George:	Licensed victualler	Buntingford, 1891, 238
Trolley, John:	Boot & shoemaker	Baldock, 1890, 243
Trudgett, James:	Apprentice tailor	Baldock, 1851, 216
Varty, Nathan:	Iron founder & engineer	Royston, 1870, 80
Veasey, Charles:	Solicitor	Baldock, 1870, 243
Veasey, Samuel:	Solicitor	Baldock, 1851, 243
Veasey, Thomas:	Solicitor	Baldock, 1851, 243
Volhurn, Henry	Accountant	Baldock, 1881, 101
Wale, William:	Apprentice miller	Royston, 1881, 245
Wale, William:	Umbrella maker	Royston, 1870, 77
Walker, Edward:	Medical dispenser	Royston, 1881, 245
Wall, Isabella:	Hairdresser	Royston, 1851, 103
Walman, Frederick:	Shoemaker & carrier	Baldock, 1882, 267
Walther, Helene:	School governess	Baldock, 1891, 107
Ward, George:	Ostler & groom	Royston, 1891, 143
Warner, William:	Commercial Innkeeper	Royston, 1854, 287
Warren, Herbert:	Solicitor	Baldock, 1890, 243
Warren, John:	Newspaper publisher	Royston, 1855, 262
Watson, George:	Builder's carman	Buntingford, 1891, 143